BANKS AND REMEDIES

BANKS AND REMEDIES

EDITED BY
ROSS CRANSTON
Director of the Centre for Commercial Law Studies
Queen Mary and Westfield College, University of London

PUBLISHED JOINTLY WITH
THE CENTRE FOR COMMERCIAL LAW STUDIES AND
THE CHARTERED INSTITUTE OF BANKERS

LLP

LONDON NEW YORK HAMBURG HONG KONG
LLOYD'S OF LONDON PRESS LTD.
1992

Lloyd's of London Press Ltd.
Legal Publishing and Conferences Division
One Singer Street, London EC2A 4LQ
Great Britain

USA AND CANADA
Lloyd's of London Press Inc.
Suite 308, 611 Broadway,
New York, NY 10012, USA

GERMANY
Lloyd's of London Press GmbH
59 Ehrenbergstrasse, 2000 Hamburg 50
Germany

SOUTH-EAST ASIA
Lloyd's of London Press (Far East) Ltd.
Room 1101, Hollywood Centre
233 Hollywood Road
Hong Kong

British Library Cataloguing in Publication Data

A catalogue record
for this book is available
from the British Library

ISBN 1–85044–447–1

Text set 10 on 12 pt Linotron 202 Sabon by
Promenade Graphics
Cheltenham, Glos.
Printed in Great Britain by
WBC Print Ltd., Bridgend, Mid Glamorgan

FOREWORD

A previous book in this series, *Banks—Liability and Risk*, focused on risks faced by lending banks. In an economic climate where such risks are materialising with a vengeance, *Banks and Remedies* examines the remedies available to banks when their creditor companies get too close to the edge. Banks must look at the options the law provides for them, determine policy and ensure that procedures and staff training are suited to the efficient conduct of any necessary legal action.

The whole question of what legal remedies a particular jurisdiction grants its creditors is an inherent part of that state's economic and political structure. Taking a broad view, Philip Wood (Chapter 1) classifies various states as either pro-creditor or pro-debtor. The emerging commercial legal systems of Eastern Europe are likely to be pro-creditor to encourage the provision of desperately needed financing. At the other end of the scale comes the USA which is protective of the debtor, with the UK falling midway—though maybe beginning to give increasing protection to the debtor.

Remedies available to a UK bank lender range from the informal extra-legal to the formal court regulated procedures under the Insolvency Act 1986. Richard Salter (Chapter 2) provides a thorough review of English law remedies. Before there is even a hint of trouble, it is important that a bank lay the foundations for a secure position: for example, in order to be able to take advantage of the self-help remedy of appointing a receiver without recourse to the courts it is advisable to make express contractual provision for such power when taking a charge. Further, it is vital that the bank keep full and accurate records of the debtor's account: the importance of the production of documents under the "discovery rules" cannot be over-emphasised. The giving of proper discovery, which can now involve allowing an opponent access to computer data, and obtaining optimum discovery from an opponent is often the deciding factor in litigation. Exactly which documents a bank may be required to disclose can be a difficult question but nothing is to be gained by attempting to "vet" files: rather, comprehensive and accurate filing and compliance with the discovery rules will be to a creditor bank's advantage. Chapters 3 and 4 examine discovery and related rules in England and the United States.

The issue of cross-border remedies and access to information abroad, addressed by Lawrence Collins in Chapter 5, is a very real problem especially as electronic funds transfer methods become increasingly advanced and cynicism about the use of "off-shore" companies increases. The issue is examined from the viewpoint of English law.

The informal remedy of a consensual support operation is explored by Nick Segal (Chapter 8) and Gerald Nels Olson (Chapter 9). In the UK, support operations are encouraged by the Bank of England which has produced "The London Rules" for guidance. Further encouragement in England can be found from the judiciary: in *Re M.C. Bacon* [1990] BCC 78, Mr Justice Millett held that a geniune support operation which involved the bank taking additional security in relation to past lending did not fall foul of sections 238 and 239 of the Insolvency Act 1986, which prohibit companies from transacting at an undervalue or preferring one creditor over another in disregard of the *pari passu* principle. This case is also of significance in that Mr Justice Millett gave support to the view that a bank conducting a support operation does not thereby make itself a "shadow director" of the company and therefore expose itself to the possibility of liability under section 214 of the Insolvency Act 1986. The section enables the court to order certain persons to contribute to any shortfall on insolvency in disregard of the principle of limited liability: it has caused uncertainty and worry in the banking world, but it seems that the danger may now be receding.

A support operation can be undermined if one creditor decides that enough is enough and wishes to move up the scale of remedies to something more formal. Where a bank had the foresight to take a charge wherein express provision was made for the power to appoint a receiver of the assets secured, it can institute this remedy without recourse to the courts. In the absence of such provision, it is necessary to apply for a court appointed receiver: Professor Pennington (Chapter 6) is critical of the Insolvency Act 1986 for failing to provide for an automatic power of appointment for charge holders. The creditor is entitled to a realisation of the assets in discharge of the debt and is able to block a further remedy, the appointment of an administrator of the whole company. The Act provides a code for receivers, their powers and duties and recognises a new sub-class—the administrative receiver: a receiver is an administrative receiver where he is appointed in relation to a sufficiently large proportion of the company's assets. This remedy is not available in the rest of the EC (see Hendrick Haag (Chapter 7) and Johannes Köndgen (Chapter 10)).

Moving on up the scale of remedies, we come to application to the court for the appointment of an administrator of the whole company, a concept introduced by the Insolvency Act 1986. He is given control of the company and its assets: he has extensive powers of management and the effect of his appointment is to protect the company from any legal proceedings, including creditors seeking to realise their security. An order can only be obtained on limited grounds, such as giving the company a chance to work itself out of trouble or, if that is not a realistic prospect, to achieve a more effective realisation of assets than would be effected on a winding up. As either the company, the directors or the creditors may apply for an order, the remedy is not easily classified as either pro-debtor or pro-creditor: to the extent that it operates to "freeze" the company and entitles the administrator to disregard floating charges, James Lingard in Chapter 7 makes it clear that it can be severely prejudicial to creditors: however, to the extent that it may produce a higher sum for distribution, it is to their benefit.

It is a mistake to equate US Chapter 11 proceedings with UK administration. A US Chapter 11 proceeding is less formal and is clearly pro-debtor, as the debtor himself remains in management: conflicts of interest might arise. By contrast, an administrator must be a qualified insolvency practitioner and procedures exist for court scrutiny of his actions. It is still too early to assess how useful administrations are going to be.

It is important to remember that remedies or investigations against defaulting debtors may be instigated at a public level by various regulatory bodies. Recent legislation gives public officials wide powers to investigate companies that go way beyond the usual rules on discovery: the fairness of some such powers provides a topic for debate. Ian Taylor in Chapter 11 is firmly of the view that Companies Act 1985 investigations can be oppressive and deny rights of privilege and non-disclosure granted to accused/suspected persons under the general law: further, that case law in effect precludes judicial review of such procedures. However, investigators recognise that the procedures can be open to abuse but are confident that in practice, fairness is observed. After all, a point in relation to general discovery is apposite here; surely the aim is to find out exactly what did happen and not to play some sophisticated card game where the poker face wins out.

ANNIE HOCKADAY

CONTENTS

	page
Foreword by Annie Hockaday	v
Contributors	xv
Table of Cases	xvii
Table of Legislation	xxv

CHAPTER 1. REMEDIES AND RISK: INTERNATIONAL COMPARISONS *Philip Wood*

Insolvency—a suggested scale	1
Key determinants	2
Comments on the scale	3
The French example	4
Security	5
Registration of security	7
Quasi-security	8
Set-off and cherry-picking	9
Big pocket liability	11
Conclusion	11

CHAPTER 2. REMEDIES FOR BANKS: AN OUTLINE OF ENGLISH LAW *Richard Salter*

The right to demand re-payment	13
The right to combine accounts	18
The banker's right of lien	21
The right to close the account	22
The right to enforce security	23
The right to assist in a rescue	25
The right to sue	29
Summary judgment	31
Mareva injunctions	34
Judgments and execution	35
Bankruptcy and liquidation	35
The remedy	36

CHAPTER 3. DISCOVERY IN ENGLAND *Anthony Pugh-Thomas*

What is meant by discovery? 37
Why does discovery matter? 40
How is it done? 41
Inspection 46
The use of documents produced on discovery 46
Conclusion 48
Annex 1 49
Annex 2 50

CHAPTER 4. PRE-TRIAL PROCEEDINGS IN US COURTS *Gary B. Born, Rebecca Arbogast and Marc Cohen*

Basic principles of US federalism 53
Divided legislative authority 53
Dual judicial system 54
Limited federal subject-matter jurisdiction 54
The "Erie" problem 55
Removal 56
Pre-trial pleadings under the federal rules of civil procedure 57
Complaint 57
Answer 57
Motion to dismiss 58
Counterclaims, cross-claims and third-party complaints 58
Personal jurisdiction 59
Long-arm statutes 59
Due process clause 60
General jurisdiction 61
Continuous and systematic business contacts 61
Citizenship, domicile and incorporation 62
"Tag service" 62
Specific jurisdiction 62
Purposeful availment 63
Arising from 64
Reasonableness 64
National contacts 65
Consent to jurisdiction 67
Jurisdiction based upon corporate affiliation 67
Service of process 68
Service under federal rules 68
Hague Service Convention 69
Background 69
Exclusivity of Hague Service Convention 70
Service by mail under Art. 10(a) 70
Schlunk: circumventing the Convention 71
Forum selection: venue, *forum non conveniens* and removal 71
Venue 71

Forum non conveniens 72
Raising and proving issues of foreign law 74
Pre-trial proceedings: the spectre of discovery 75
Introduction and scope of discovery 75
Discovery mechanisms 75
Interrogatories 76
Document requests 77
Depositions 77
Admissions 78
Non-party discovery 78
Resisting discovery 79
Extraterritorial discovery 80
Document discovery outside the US 81
Depositions of corporate personnel located abroad 82
Compelled discovery from third parties not subject to US jurisdiction 83
Relationship between Hague Evidence Convention and Federal Rules 84
The Aerospatiale decision 84
Post-Aerospatiale decisions 85
Impact of "blocking" and bank secrecy laws on discovery outside the US 86
Jurisdictional discovery 87
Effects of jurisdictional discovery on general discovery 88
Pre-trial conferences and scheduling orders 88

CHAPTER 5. CROSS-BORDER COURT ORDERS AND BANKS
Lawrence Collins

The context 91
Court orders and confidentiality 91
Attachment of assets 94
Attachment of English bank accounts in support of foreign proceedings 96
Recognition of judgments 97
Tracing of assets 98
Subpoenas and evidence 98

CHAPTER 6. RECEIVERSHIPS AND EXTRAJUDICIAL REMEDIES
R. R. Pennington

Introduction 101
Receiverships: origin and character 104
The conduct of a receivership 110
Purpose of a receivership 110
Powers of receivers 111
Executory contracts of the company 113
Receiver's duties in realising company's assets 114
Liabilities of lenders and debenture holders in a receivership or liquidation 115
Conclusion 117

CHAPTER 7. ADMINISTRATION AND INSOLVENCY: UNITED KINGDOM AND GERMAN APPROACHES *James Lingard and Hendrik Haag*

United Kingdom 121
Administration 121
Administration orders 122
The effect of an administration order 123
The powers of an administrator 124
The duties of an administrator 124
Voluntary arrangements 125
Conclusion 125
Germany 126
The German bankruptcy code 126
The bankruptcy reform 127
Restriction of privileges of preferred creditors 127
Reorganisation/insolvency plan 127
Protection of employees 128
Fresh start/discharge 128
Bankruptcy laws in the eastern part of Germany 128

CHAPTER 8. REHABILITATION AND APPROACHES OTHER THAN FORMAL INSOLVENCY PROCEDURES *Nick Segal*

Introduction 131
Legal issues to be addressed when considering whether formal insolvency can be avoided 134
Directors' duties 134
The first is wrongful trading 134
Secondly, there is fraudulent trading 137
Thirdly, the directors must consider their general fiduciary duties 139
Fourthly, and finally, there are the provisions relating to disqualification 140
Matters affecting lenders 141
The problem of shadow directors 141
The risk of lender liability 144
The risk of a fiduciary relationship arising 147
Practicalities of a support operation—the context and principles 147
The documentation 151
Initial standstill agreement 152
Support agreement 152
Inter-bank agreement 154
Security agreements 155
Alternatives to the classic support operation 158

CHAPTER 9. NON-JUDICIAL DEBTOR REORGANISATIONS IN THE UNITED STATES *Gerald Nels Olson*

Systemic problem of capital deterioration 163
Historical backround 164

Causes 165
The result 170
Loss of operating income 170
Increase in operating expenses 171
Delays in dealing with non-performing loans caused by 171
Impact on and reactions by financial institutions 172
Basis for action by debtors 174
Foundation for a plan 174
Components of a plan 176
Full disclosure 176
Fair treatment of each creditor and each class of creditor 177
Maximum return to creditors 177
Long-term survival of the company as a going concern 177
Going concern *v.* forced liquidation 178
Provision for federal income taxes 178
Exculpation 178
Analysis of debtor organisational structure 179
Data accumulation: document examination and legal analysis—material transactions 179
Status of debtor's liquidity—working capital loans 180
Negotiators—identity and training 181
Creditor meetings 182
Creditor committee 182
Documentation 182
Administration of plan and debt negotiation, modification and acceptance 183
Negotiation theory 183
Creditor committee meetings 183
Periodic reporting—administrative control 184
Annex A
Functional organisation charts and areas of primary risk, focus and alternative courses of action 186
Annex B
Consensual, non-judicial debtor reorganisations. Document examination and legal analysis checklist 194
Annex C
Consensual, non-judicial debtor reorganisations. Workout analysis paper—assessment of debtor position 195

CHAPTER 10. REHABILITATION AND INSOLVENCY: THE GERMAN APPROACH *Johannes Köndgen*

A law in transition 203
The "bankruptcy of bankruptcy" 203
Bankruptcy procedure: the battle of the secured creditors 203
Arrangement procedure 205
Escape routes 208
Voluntary arrangements: "reorganisation through liquidation" 208
Security pool agreements 211

A concise chronology of law reform 213
The report of the Committee for Insolvency Law 213
The Insolvency Bill of 21 November 1991 214
The legal position of bank creditors under the Insolvency Bill 215
Principles and policy considerations of the Insolvency Bill 215
The paramountcy of creditor governance 215
Facilitating rehabilitation in an integrated procedure 216
Secured creditors 217
Order of distribution 218
Some selected problems 219
Leasing, factoring 219
Security pool agreements 220
Voting rights 220
Working capital loans made to the insolvent's estate 221
Legal issues to be addressed in a voluntary support operation 221
Preferential treatment of bank creditors 221
Lender liability 222
Conflict of interest situations 222
Interfering with corporate governance 223
Lenders as shareholders 224

CHAPTER 11. OFFICIAL REMEDIES: INQUIRIES UNDER SECTION 432(2) OF THE COMPANIES ACT 1985 *Ian Taylor*

Introduction 227
The powers of inspectors and the conduct of inquiries 228
Documents 229
Questioning of witnesses 230
Submission of proposed criticism to witnesses 231
The making of the report 231
The inspectors' duty to act in accordance with the rules of natural justice 232
Privilege against self-incrimination 234
The hybrid nature of s.432(2) inquiries: balancing the powers of the investigators against the rights of the individual 237

APPENDIX 1. STRUCTURE AND PRINCIPAL TERMS OF INTER-BANK AND SUPPORT AGREEMENTS 241

APPENDIX 2. COLLATERAL POOL AGREEMENT 243

Index 289

CONTRIBUTORS

REBECCA ARBOGAST: Associate and Attorney, Wilmer, Cutler & Pickering, Washington D.C.

GARY B. BORN: Partner and Attorney, Wilmer, Cutler & Pickering, London and Washington D.C.; Adjunct Professor, Georgetown University Law Center.

MARC COHEN: Associate and Attorney, Wilmer, Cutler & Pickering, Washington D.C.

LAWRENCE COLLINS: Partner and Solicitor, Herbert Smith, London; Fellow, Wolfson College, Cambridge; Visiting Professor, Queen Mary & Westfield College, University of London.

HENDRIK HAAG: Rechtsanwalt, Hengeler Mueller Weitzel Wirtz, Frankfurt.

ANNIE HOCKADAY: Barrister, London.

JOHANNES KÖNDGEN: Professor of Law, University of St Gallen, Switzerland; formerly Judge, Court of Appeals, Hamburg, Germany.

JAMES LINGARD: Partner and Solicitor, Norton Rose, London.

GERALD NELS OLSON: Partner and Attorney, Winstead, Sechrest & Minick, Dallas.

ROBERT R. PENNINGTON: Professor of Commercial Law, University of Birmingham.

ANTHONY PUGH-THOMAS: Partner and Solicitor, Lovell White Durrant, London.

RICHARD SALTER: Barrister, London.

NICK SEGAL: Partner and Solicitor, Allen & Overy, London; Senior Visiting Fellow, Centre for Commercial Law Studies, Queen Mary & Westfield College, University of London.

IAN TAYLOR: Partner and Solicitor, Freshfields, London.

PHILIP WOOD: Partner and Solicitor, Allen & Overy, London; Visiting Professor, Centre for Commercial Law Studies, Queen Mary & Westfield College, University of London.

TABLE OF CASES

A *v.* HM Treasury [1979] 1 WLR 1056 235
AVR Aviation Ltd, *Re* (1988) 4 BCC 708 .... 28, 123
Agip (Africa) Limited *v.* Jackson [1989] 3 WLR 1367 144
Air Ecosse *v.* Civil Aviation Authority (1987) 3 BCC 492 27
Alco Standard Corp. *v.* Benalal 345 F. Supp. 14 (E D Pa. 1972) 68
Alpine Bulk Transport Co. Inc *v.* Saudi Eagle Shipping Co. (The Saudi Eagle [1986] 2 Lloyd's Rep. 221 31
AM & S European *v.* Commissioners of the European Community [1983] 3 WLR 17 45
Amusement Equipment, Inc. *v.* Mordelt 779 F. 2d 264 (5th cir. 1985) 62
Anderson *v.* Bank of British Columbia (1876) 2 Ch. D 644 43
Anlaby *v.* Praetorious (1888) 20 QBD 764 31
Anscheutz & Co, *In re* 754 F. 2d 601 (5th Cir. 1985) 82
Aries Ventures *v.* AXA Finance SA 1990 WL 37813 (SDNY 1990) 68
Asahi Metal Indus. *v.* Superior Court 480 US 102 (1987) 63–65
Aschkenasy *v.* Midland Bank Ltd (1934) 50 TLR 209; 51 TLR 34 21
Asean Resources Ltd *v.* Ka Wah International Merchant Finance Limited [1987] LRC (Comm.) 835 94
Ashtiani *v.* Kashi QB 888 (CA) 94
Astor Chemical Limited *v.* Synthetic Technology Limited [1990] BCC 97 124
Atherton, *In re* [1912] 2 KB 251 234
Atlantic Airspace Ltd *v.* Handley Page Ltd [1970] Ch. 193 114
Atlantic Computer Systems Plc, *Re* [1990] BCC 859 27
Atlas Maritime *v.* Avalon Maritime (No 3) [1991] 1 WLR 917 34
Augustus Barnett & Son Limited, *Re* [1986] BCLC 170 139
Babanaft International Co. SA *v.* Bassatne [1990] Ch. 13 .... 34, 94, 95, 97
Bache & Co. (London) Ltd *v.* Banque Vernes et Commercial de Paris SA [1973] 2 Lloyd's Rep. 437 23
Bacon, M.C., *Re* [1990] BCC 78 .... 142, 157
Bailey *v.* Finch (1871) LR 7 QB 34 19
Baird *v.* Koerner 279 F. 2d 623 (9th Cir. 1960) 185
Baker *v.* Lloyds Bank [1920] 2 KB 322 16
Ballabil Holdings Pty Ltd *v.* Hospital Products Limited [1984] 2 NSWLR 662 94
Ban Hin Lee Bank Berhad *v.* Somali Bank, *The Independent*, 28 November 1988, CA 31
Bank Mellat *v.* Nikpour [1985] FSR 87 34
Bank of Baroda *v.* Panesar [1987] Ch. 335 18
Bank of Nova Scotia 99
Bankers Trust *v.* Shapira [1980] 1 WLR 1274 .... 35, 48
Bankston *v.* Toyota Motor Corp. 889 F. 2d 172 (8th Cir. 1989) 71
Barclays Bank *v.* Illingworth CA, 10 May 1985 (unreported) 35
Barclays Bank *v.* Khaira, *The Times*, 19 December 1991 32
Barclays Bank *v.* Okenarhe [1966] 2 Lloyd's Rep. 87 20
Barclays Bank *v.* Quistclose Investments [1970] AC 567 19
Barclays Bank *v.* TOSG [1984] BCLC 1 19

Barclays Bank *v.* WJ Simms Son & Cooke (Southern) Ltd [1980] QB 677 ... 24
Barclays Bank Ltd *v.* Astley Industrial Trust Ltd [1970] 2 QB 527 ... 21
Barclays Bank Plc *v.* Bemister [1989] 1 WLR 128 ... 30
Barclays Bank Plc *v.* Rosenberg, *Financial Times*, 12 June 1985, CA ... 35
Barrow Borough Transport Ltd, *Re* [1990] Ch. 227 ... 27
BCCI *v.* Blattner 20 November 1986, unreported ... 17
Bedford Computer Corp. *v.* Israel Aircraft Indus. Ltd 1990 Bank LEXIS 964 ... 85
Benton *v.* Uddeholm Corp. 118 FRD 386 (DNJ 1987) ... 85, 86
Berker Sportscraft Ltd's Agreement, *Re*, Hartnell *v.* Berker Sportscraft Ltd (1947) 177 LT 420 ... 17
Berney *v.* Sewell (1820) 1 Jac W 648 ... 104
BGHZ 104, 44 (1988) ... 223
BGHZ 105, 168 (1988) — "Hamburger Stahlwerke" ... 224
BGHZ 55, 35; 98, 315 ... 205
Bhogal *v.* Punjab National Bank [1988] 2 All ER 296 ... 33
Blaker *v.* Herts and Essex Waterworks Co. (1889) 41 Ch. D 339 ... 107
Boehm *v.* Goodall [1911] 1 Ch. 155 ... 107
Botibil, *Re* [1947] 1 All ER 26 ... 114
Bower *v.* Foreign and Colonial Gas Co. Ltd, Metropolitan Bank, Garnishees (1874) 22 WW 740 ... 19
Bowes, *Re*, Earl of Strathmore *v.* Vane (1886) 3 Ch. D 586 ... 21
Bowman *v.* David Samuel Trust Ltd [1978] 1 All ER 616 ... 108
Boyle *v.* Bettws Llantwit Colliery Co. (1876) 2 Ch. D 726 ... 105
Brace *v.* Duke of Marlborough (1728) 2 P Wms. 491 ... 36
Bradford Old Bank *v.* Sutcliffe [1918] 2 KB 833 ... 16, 18
Brady *v.* Brady (1987) 3 BCC 535 ... 139
Brandao *v.* Barnett (1846) 12 Cl. & Fin. 787 ... 21
Bremen, The, *v.* Zapata Off-shore Co. 407 US 1 (1972) ... 67
Brightlife Ltd, *Re* [1987] Ch. 200 ... 106
Brimnes, The [1975] QB 929 ... 16
British and Commonwealth Holdings Plc ... 161
British Eagle International Air Lines *v.* Compagnie Nationale Air France [1975] 1 WLR 758 .. 18
British Guiana Bank *v.* Official Receiver (1911) 27 TLR 454 ... 18
British Waggon Co. *v.* Lea (1880) 5 QBD 149 ... 16
Brown *v.* Great Eastern Railway Co. (1877) 2 QB 406 ... 16
Brunette Machine Works *v.* Kockum Indus. Inc. 406 US 706 (1972) ... 72
Bunbury Foods Pty Ltd *v.* National Bank of Australasia Ltd (1984) 51 ALR 609 ... 18
Burnham *v.* Superior Court 110 S Ct 2105 (1990) ... 62
Burt, Bolton and Hayward *v.* Bull [1895] 1 QB 276 ... 107
Business Computers Ltd *v.* Anglo African Leasing Ltd [1977] 1 All ER 741 ... 112
Campbell, R.C. [1984] BCLC 83 ... 160
Charge Card Services, *Re* [1987] Ch. 150 ... 19
Chatsworth Investments *v.* Cussins (Contractors) Ltd [1969] 1 All ER 143 ... 113
China & South Sea Bank *v.* Tan [1990] 1 AC 536 ... 14
Church of Scientology *v.* DHSS [1979] 1 WLR 723 ... 38
Ciprari *v.* Services Aereos Cruzeiro do Sul, SA 232 F. Supp. 433 (DCNY 1964) ... 61
Clayton's Case, *see* Devaynes *v.* Noble
Cliffs-Neddrill Turnkey Int'l Organjestad *v.* M/T Rich Duke 734 F. Supp. 142 (D Del 1990) ... 73
Clough Mill Ltd *v.* Martin [1984] 3 All ER 982 ... 112
Colonial Finance, Mortgage, Investment & Guarantee Corpn Ltd, *Re* (1905) 6 SR NSW 6 ... 17
Colonial Leasing Co. *v.* Pugh Bros. Garage 735 F. 2d 380 (9th Cir. 1984) ... 67
Compagnie des Bauxites de Guinee *v.* L'Union 723 F. 2d 357 (3d Cir. 1983) ... 88
Compagnie Financiere *v.* Peruvian Guano [1882] 11 QB 55 ... 38
Company, *Re* a, (No. 001418 of 1988) [1990] BCC 526 ... 138
Company, *Re* a, (No. 005009 of 1987) *ex parte* Copp [1989] BCLC 13; (1988) 4 BCC 424 . 116, 142
Company, *Re* a [1985] BCLC 37 ... 17
Complaint of Damodar Bulk Carriers, Ltd 903 F. 2d 675 (9th Cir. 1990) ... 61

Congoleum Corp. *v.* DLW AG 729 F. 2d 1210 (9th Cir. 1984) 61
Consumer and Industrial Press Ltd, *Re* (1988) 4 BCC 68 27
Consumer and Industrial Press Ltd (No. 2), *Re* (1988) 4 BCC 72 28
Coombs & Barei Construction Pty Ltd *v.* Dynasty Pty Ltd (1986) 42 SASR 413 94
Cooper (Gerald) Chemicals Limited, *Re* [1978] Ch. 262 139
Cooper *v.* Makita 117 FRD 16 (D Me. 1987) 71
Coutts & Co. *v.* Irish Exhibition in London (1891) 7 TLR 313 18
Crompton & Co. Ltd, *Re* [1914] 1 Ch. 954 105
Cryne *v.* Barclays Bank Plc [1987] BCLC 548 .... 14, 15, 17
Cryomedics Inc. *v.* Spembly, Ltd, 387 F. Supp. 287 (D Conn. 1575) 66
Cutts *v.* Head [1984] 1 WLR 290 47
Data Disc 557 F. 2d 1280 (9th Cir. 1977) 87, 88
Davies *v.* Eli Lilly & Co. [1987] 1 All ER 801 38
Davis *v.* Bowsher (1794) 5 Term. Rep. 488 21
Dawson *v.* Isle [1906] 1 Ch. 633 21
Debtor, *Re* (No. 83 of 1988) [1990] 1 WLR 708 26
Decker Coal Co. *v.* Commonwealth Edison Co. 805 F. 2d 834 (9th Cir. 1986) 63
Decro-Wall International *v.* Practitioners in Marketing Ltd [1971] 1 WLR 361 16
Denilauler [1980] ECR 1553 97
Derby & Co. *v.* Weldon (No. 1) [1990] Ch. 48 .... 34, 95
Derby & Co. *v.* Weldon (Nos. 3 and 4) [1990] Ch. 65 .... 34, 96
Derby & Co. *v.* Weldon (No. 6) [1990] 1 WLR 1139 96
Derby & Co. *v.* Weldon (No. 9) [1991] 1 WLR 657 39
Devaynes *v.* Noble, Clayton's Case (1816) 1 Mer. 572 20
Deverges *v.* Sandeman, Clark & Co. [1902] 1 Ch. 579 17
Deyes *v.* Wood [1911] 1 KB 806 107
Diversified Industries Inc. *v.* Meredith 572 Fl. 2d 596 (8th Cir. 1977) *en banc* (1978) 185
Dobbs *v.* The National Bank of Australia Ltd (1935) 53 CLR 643 .... 23, 24
Dorothy K. Winston & Co. *v.* Town Heights Development Inc. 376 F. Supp. 1214 (DC Dist. 1974) 185
DPP *v.* Ellis [1973] 1 WLR 722 234
DST *v.* Shell International Petroleum [1990] 1 AC 295 94
Eason *v.* Linden Avionics, Inc. F. Supp. 311 (DNJ 1989) 62
Easterling *v.* Cooper Motors, Inc. 26 FRD 1 (MDNC 1960) 62
Elder-Beerman Stores Corp. *v.* Federated Dept. Stores, Inc. 45 FRD 515 (SDNY 1968) 81
EMI Records *v.* Spillane [1986] 1 WLR 967 .... 234, 235
Erba *v.* Amsterdamsche Bank NV, NJ 1957, 514 and 1959, 581 .... 7, 8
Erie R.R. Co. *v.* Thompson 304 US 64 (1938) 55
Esso Petroleum Co. Ltd *v.* Alstonbridge Properties Ltd [1975] 1 WLR 1474 17
European Asian Bank AG *v.* Punjab & Sind Bank (No. 2) [1983] 1 WLR 642 32
European Bank, *Re* (1872) LR 8 Ch. App. 41 19
Exchange Travel Agency Ltd *v.* Triton Property Trust Plc [1991] BCC 341 27
First National City Bank *v.* IRS 271 F. 2d 616 (2d Cir. 1959) 81
Firth, *Re*, *ex parte* Schofield (1879) 12 Ch. D 337 21
Fitzimmons *v.* Barton 589 F. 2d 330 (7th Cir. 1979) 66
Frummer *v.* Hilton Hotel, Int'l, Inc. 19 NY 2d 533 (1967) 67
Garcia *v.* San Antonio Metropolitan Transit Authority 469 US 528 (1985) 53
Garnett *v.* McKewan (1872) LR 6 Ex. 10 .... 18, 19
Giles *v.* Perkins (1807) 9 East 12 21
Go-Video, Inc. *v.* Akai Elec. Co. 885 F. 2d 1406 (9th Cir. 1989) 66
Goldburg, *Re* [1912] 1 KB 606 108
Goulandris Bros Ltd *v.* B Goldman & Sons [1958] QB 74 13
Government Stocks and Other Securities Investment Co. *v.* Manila Rly Co. [1897] AC 81 106
Grand Jury Subpoena Addressed to Canadian International Paper Company, *In re*, 72 F. Supp 1013 (SDNY 1947) 81
Grant *v.* South Western and Country Properties [1974] 2 All ER 465 38
Great Atlantic Insurance Co. *v.* Home Insurance Co. [1981] 2 All ER 485 45
Great Cobar Ltd, *Re* [1915] 1 Ch. 682 114

Great Lakes Dredge & Dock Co. *v.* Harnischfeger Corp. 1990 US Dist. LEXIS 12843 (ND Ill 1990) 85
Greenhalgh, WP, & Sons *v.* Union Bank of Manchester [1924] 2 KB 153 19
Greenwood Teale *v.* Williams (1894) 11 TLR 56 19
Gross, *Re* (1871) 6 Ch. App. 632 18
Guinness Peat Properties *v.* Fitzroy Robinson Partnership [1987] 2 All ER 716 44
Gulf Oil Corp. *v.* Gilbert 330 US 501 (1947) 73
Hall *v.* Helicopteros Nacionales de Colombia, SA 638 SW 2d 870 60
Handley Page Ltd *v.* Customs and Excise Commissioners [1970] 2 Lloyd's Rep. 459 112
Hanson *v.* Denkla 357 US 235 (1957) 63
Harris Simons Construction Ltd, *Re* [1989] 1 WLR 369 27
Harris *v.* Browning-Ferris Indus. Chem. Serv. 100 FRD 775 (M D La. 1984) 70
Haynes *v.* Kleinwefers 119 FRD 335 (EDNY 1988) 85
Heart of Atlanta Motel, Inc. *v.* United States 379 US 241 (1964) 53
Helicopteros Nacionales de Colombia *v.* Hall 466 US 408 (1983) 61, 63
Hemmings *v.* Stoke Poges Golf Club [1920] 1 KB 720 25
Hendy Lennox (Industrial Engines) Ltd *v.* Graham Puttick Ltd [1984] 2 All ER 152 112
Hickman *v.* Taylor 329 US 495 (1947) 185
Hines *v.* Davidowitz 312 US 52 (1941) 53
Hodson *v.* Tea Corpn Ltd (1880) 14 Ch. D 859 105
Home Office *v.* Harman [1983] 1 AC 280 46
Home Treat Ltd, *Re* [1991] BCC 165 28
Hudson *v.* Hermann Pfauter GmbH & Co. 117 FRD 33 (NDNY 1987) 85
Huxford *v.* Stoy Hayward (1989) 5 BCC 421 149
Hylwa, T.M., M.D., Inc. *v.* Palka 823 F. 2d 310 (9th Cir. 1987) 63
Instrumentation Electrical Services Ltd, *Re* (1988) 4 BCC 301 27
Insurance Company of the State of Pennsylvania *v.* Centaur 590 F. Supp. 1187 (SDNY 1984) 87
International Shoe Co. *v.* State of Washington 326 US 310 (1945) 60
Interpool Limited *v.* Galani [1988] QB 738 94
Investigation of World Arrangements, *In re* 13 FRD 280 (DDC 1952) 82
Iraqi Ministry of Defence *v.* Arcepcy Shipping (The Angel Bell) [1981] QB 65 34
Jeffreys *v.* Agra and Masterman's Bank (1866) LR 2 Eq 674 .... 19, 21
Joachimson *v.* Swiss Bank Corporation [1921] 3 KB110 22
Johnson Creative Arts, Inc. *v.* Wool Masters, Inc. 743 F. 2d 9447 (1st Cir. 1984) 66
Johnson, B, & Co. (Builders) Ltd, *Re* [1955] Ch. 634 108
K/S A/S Admiral Shipping *v.* Portlink Ferries [1984] 2 Lloyd's Rep. 166 34
Kadota *v.* Hosogai 608 P.2d 68 (Az.App. 1980) 70
Kamen *v.* American Tel. & Tel. Co. 791 F. 2d 1006 ((2d Cir) 1986) 88
Keeton *v.* Hustler Magazine, Inc. 465 US 770 (1984) 62
Keever, *Re* [1967] Ch. 182 21
Klaxon *v.* Stentor 313 US 487 (1941) 56
Koster *v.* Lumbermens Mut. Cas. Co. 330 US 524 (1947) 73
Kuwait Asia EC Bank *v.* National Mutual Life Nominees Limited [1990] BCC 567 143
Laker Airways Ltd *v.* Pan American World Airways 568 F. Supp. 811 (DDC 1983) 74, 82
Lanier *v.* American Bd. of Endodontics 843 F. 2d 901 (6th Cir. 1988) 64
Larkins *v.* NUM [1985] IR 671 98
Leese *v.* Martin (1873) LR 17 Eq 224 21
Liquidator of West Mercia Safetywear Limited *v.* Dodd (1988) 4 BCC 30 139
Liverpool City Council *v.* Irwin [1977] AC 239 15
Lloyds Bank *v.* Waterhouse [1991] Fam. Law 23 24
London and County Securities Ltd *v.* Nicholson [1980] 3 All ER 861 235
London and Globe Finance Corporation, *Re* [1902] 2 Ch. 416 21
Lonrho *v.* Shell Petroleum [1980] QB 358 40
MacKinnon *v.* Donaldson Lufkin [1986] Ch. 782 98
Maclaine Watson & Co. Ltd *v.* International Tin Council (No. 2) [1989] Ch. 286 94
Maidstone Building Provisions Limited, *Re* [1971] 3 All ER 363 138
Marc Rich [1985] 2 SCR 278 99

Marc Rich & Co., AG, *In re* 707 F. 2d 663 (2d Cir. 1983) ... 87
Mareva Compania Naviera SA *v.* International Bulkcarriers SA (The Mareva) [1980] 1 All ER 213 ... 34
Marino *v.* Hyatt Corp. 793 F. 2d 427 (1st Cir. 1986) ... 64
Max Duetwyler Corp. *v.* R. Meyer 762 F. 2d 290 (3rd Cir. 1985) ... 66
Maxwell *v.* Department of Trade and Industry and Ors [1974] QB 523 ... 232–234, 238
McLelland, Pope & Langley Limited *v.* Howard [1968] 1 All ER 569 (HL) ... 234
Meadows *v.* Dominican Republic 628 F. Supp. 599 (ND Cal. 1986) ... 66
Mees *v.* Duffas (1901) 6 Comm Cas 165 ... 16
Meesan Investments Ltd, *Re* (1988) 4 BCC 788 ... 27
Melia *v.* Le Grand Chais de France 135 FRD 28 (DRI 1991) ... 71
Mertens *v.* Haigh [1863] 3 DeGJ & Sm 528 ... 40
Metall und Rohstoff *v.* Donaldson [1989] 3 All ER 14 ... 146
Meyers 711 F. Supp. 1007 ... 65
Miller *v.* Cook (1870) LR 10 Eq. 641 ... 17
Milliken *v.* Meyer 311 US 457 (1940) ... 62
Misa *v.* Currie (1876) 1 App. Cas. 554 ... 21
Monnsen *v.* Toro Co. 108 FRD 444 (S D Iowa 1985) ... 71
Morel, EJ, (1934) Ltd, *Re* [1962] Ch. 21 ... 18
Mortimer *v.* Brown (1970) 122 CLR 493 ... 236
Moss S.S. Co. Ltd *v.* Whinney [1912] AC 254 ... 107
Mutton *v.* Peat [1900] 1 Ch. 79 ... 19
Naeem, *Re* (A Bankrupt) (No. 18 of 1988) [1990] 1 WLR 48 ... 26
National Bank of Greece *v.* Pinios Shipping (The Maira) [1990] 1 AC 637 ... 30
National Benefit Assurance Co. Ltd, *Re* [1924] 2 Ch. 339 ... 16
National Equipment Rental, Ltd *v.* Szukhent 375 US 311 (1964) ... 67
National Westminster Bank *v.* Morgan [1985] 1 AC 686 ... 147
National Westminster Bank Ltd *v.* Halesowen Presswork and Assemblies Ltd [1972] AC 785 ... 18–20, 22
Nationale Industrielle Aerospatiale *v.* US District Court 482 US 522 (1987) ... 84–86
Neste Oy *v.* Lloyds Bank [1983] 2 Lloyd's Rep. 658 ... 146
Newdigate Colliery Co. Ltd, *Re* [1912] 1 Ch. 468 ... 16, 114, 115
Newhart Developments Ltd *v.* Co-operative Commercial Bank [1978] QB 814 ... 117
Nicolene Ltd *v.* Simmonds [1953] 1 QB 543 ... 14
Nieminem *v.* Breeze-Eastern 736 F. Supp 580 (DNJ 1990) ... 73
Ninemia Maritime Corporation *v.* Trave GmbH [1983] 1 WLR 1412 ... 34
Nippon Yusen Kaisha *v.* Karageorgis [1975] 1 WLR 1093 ... 34
Norwest Holst Limited *v.* Secretary of State for Trade and Others [1978] 1 Ch. 201 ... 228
Norwich Pharmacal *v.* Customs and Excise [1974] AC 133 ... 48
Oceanica Castelana Armadora SA *v.* Mineralimportexport [1983] 1 WLR 1294 ... 21
Omni Cap. Int'l *v.* Rudolf Wolff & Co. 484 US 97 (1987) ... 66
Oppenheimer Fund. Inc. *v.* Sanders 437 US 340 (1978) ... 87
Ormandy *v.* Lynn 122 Misc.2d 954, 472 NYS.2d 274 (NYS Ct 1984) ... 71
Osbv-Pannan AB *v.* Las Verkoopmaatschappij BV NJ 1982, 443 ... 8
Owen Equipment & Erection Co. *v.* Kroger 437 US 365 (1978) ... 55
Paclantic Financing Co. Inc. *v.* Moscow Narodny Bank Ltd [1983] 1 WLR 1063 ... 33
Paget, *In re* [1927] 2 Ch. 85 (CA) ... 234
Pain *v.* United Technologies Corp. 637 F. 2d 775 (DC Cir. 1980) ... 73
Paramount Airways Ltd, *Re* Bristol Airport Plc *v.* Powdrill [1990] Ch. 744 ... 27
Parker, *Re, ex parte* Froggatt (1843) 3 Mont. D & DeG 322 ... 21
Parsons *v.* Sovereign Bank of Cananda [1913] AC 160 ... 16, 107, 112, 113
Pavelic & Leflore *v.* Marvel Entertainment Group 110 S Ct 456 (1989) ... 57
Peek *v.* Trimsaren Iron Co. (1876) 2 Ch. D. 115 ... 105
Pena 563 F. Supp. 746 ... 88
People *v.* Shapiro 308 NY 453; 126 NE 2d 559 (1955) ... 185
Pergamon Press Ltd, *Re* [1971] Ch. 388 ... 232, 233, 234, 238
Perkins *v.* Benquet Consolidated Mining Co. 342 US 437 (1952) ... 61
Permanent Houses (Holdings) Ltd, *Re* [1988] BCLC 563 ... 106

Perry *v.* Oriental Hotels Co. (1870) 5 Ch. App. 420 105
Pfeiffer Weinkellerei-Weinkauf GmbH & Co. *v.* Arbuthnot Factors Ltd [1987] 1 WLR 150 .. 112
Phoenix Beesemer Steel Co., *Re*, *ex parte* Carnforth Haematite Iron Co. (1876) 4 Ch. D 108 .. 16
Pigot *v.* Cubley (1864) 15 CBNS 701 17
Piper Aircraft & Co. *v.* Reyno 454 US 235 (1981) 73, 74
Pound, Henry, Son and Hutchin Ltd, *Re* (1889) 42 Ch. D 402 105
Practice Note [1983] 1 WLR 377 30
Prejean *v.* Sonatrack, Inc. 652 F. 2d 1260 (5th Cir. 1981) 64
Primlaks (UK) Ltd, *Re* (1989) 5 BCC 710 27
Prince *v.* Oriental Bank Corp (1878) 3 App. Cas. 325 21
Produce Marketing Consortium Limited (No. 2), *Re* [1989] BCLC 520; (1989) 5 BCC 569 . 122, 134, 135
Prosperity *v.* Lloyds Bank Limited (1923) 39 TLE 372 22
Purpoint Limited, *Re*, 8 March 1990, unreported 135
R. *v.* Director of the Serious Fraud Office, *ex parte* Ernest Saunders [1988] Crim. LR 837 237
R. *v.* Director of the Serious Fraud Office, *ex parte* Smith (Div. Ct.) [1992] 1 All ER 730 237
R. *v.* Erdheim [1896] 2 QB 260 234
R. *v.* Grantham [1984] 2 WLR 815 137
R. *v.* Harris [1970] 1 WLR 1252 235
R. *v.* Harz [1967] 1 AC 760 (HL) 234
R. *v.* Scott (1856) 169 ER 909 234
R. *v.* Seelig and Spens CA, 2 May 1991, unreported 235, 237
Radian Burners Inc. *v.* American Gas Assoc. 320 F. 2d 314; cert. denied 375 US 929 (1963) 185
Rafidain Bank *v.* Agom Universal Sugar Trading Co., *The Times*, 23 December 1986, CA 33
Republic of Haiti *v.* Duvalier [1990] 1 QB 202 .... 34, 94
Reynolds *v.* Koh 109 AD 97, 490 NYS 2d 195 (1985) 71
Rich *v.* KIS Cal., Inc. 121 FRD 254 (MDNC 1988) 85
Roberts *v.* Plant [1895] 1 QB 597 32
Robinson Printing Co. *v.* Chic Ltd [1905] 2 Ch. 123 107
Rockwell Machine Tool Co. *v.* E.P. Barrus (Concessionnaires) [1968] 1 WLR 693 41
Rolled Steel Products *v.* British Steel Corporation [1984] BCLC 466 .... 144, 145
Rosenberg *v.* International Banking Corpn (1923) 14 Ll.L.Rep. 344 22
Rother Iron Works Ltd *v.* Canterbury Precision Engineers Ltd [1974] QB 1 112
Rowbotham Baxter Ltd, *Re* [1990] BCC 113 27
Royal Trust Bank *v.* Buchler (1989) BCLC 130 124
S C L Building Services Ltd, *Re* (1989) 5 BCC 746 27
Said *v.* Butt [1920] 3 KB 497 114
San Francisco *v.* Superior Court of San Francisco 37 Cal. 2d 227; 231 P. 2d 26 (1951) 185
Sandsend Financial Consultants *v.* Wood 743 SW 2d 364 (Tex. App. Houston 1988) 85
Sante Fe 1985 ECC 187; (1984) 23 IntlM 511 91
Saunders , G.L. Ltd, *Re* [1986] 1 WLR 215 110
Scarminach *v.* Goldwell GmbH 531 NYS 2d 188 (NY Sup. Ct. 1988) 85
Scholz Research and Development, Inc. *v.* Kurzke 720 F. Supp. 710 (ND I11. 1989) 62
Scott *v.* Breeland 792 F. 2d 925 62
Sealed Case, *In re* 832 F. 2d 1268 (DC Cir. 1987) 81
Seaward *v.* Paterson [1897] 1 Ch. 545 96
SEC *v.* Banca della Svizzeria Italiana 92 FRD 11 (SDNY 1981) 87
SEC *v.* Int'l Swiss Investments Corp. 895 F. 2d 1272 (9th Cir. 1990) 68
Securities Investor Protection Corp. *v.* Vigman 764 F. 2d 1309 (9th Cir. 1985) 66
Selangor United Rubber Estates Ltd *v.* Cradock [1968] 1 All ER 567 234
Senior *v.* Holdsworth, *ex parte* ITN [1976] QB 23 38
Sevenoaks Stationers (Retail) Limited, *Re* [1990] BCC 765 141
Sewell *v.* Burdick (1884) 10 App.Cas. 74 21
Shaffer *v.* Heitner 433 US 186 (1977) 14 59
Shamrock SS Co. *v.* Storey & Co. (1899) 81 LT 413 14
Shamsji *v.* Johnson Matthey Bankers Ltd [1986] BCLC 278; [1991] BCLC 36 116
Shaw *v.* Boyd 658 F. Supp. 89 (Ed Pa. 1987) 88

Shute *v.* Carnival Cruise Lines 863 F. 2d 1437 (9th Cir. 1991); 111 S Ct 1522 (1991) 61, 63–65, 67
Silkwood *v.* Kerr-McGee Corp. 464 US 238 (1984) 53
Sinatra *v.* National Enquirer, Inc. 854 F. 2d 1191 (9th Cir. 1988) 63
Singh *v.* Atombrook [1989] 1 WLR 810 31
Siskina, The [1979] AC 210 96
Sociedade Nacional de Combustiveis de Angola UEE *v.* Lunquist [1990] 3 All ER 283 235
Societe Internationale pour Participations Industrielles et Commerciales, SA *v.* Rogers 357 US 197 87
Societe Internationale *v.* Brownell 225 F. 2d 532 (DC Cir. 1955) 82
Societe Internationale *v.* McGremery 111 F. Supp. 435 (DDC 1953) 82
Societe Internationale *v.* Rogers 357 US 197 (1958) 82
South Carolina *v.* Baker 108 S Ct 1355 53
Spencer *v.* the Queen [1985] 2 SCR 278 99
Spradlin *v.* Leursiegler Management Services Co., Inc. 926 F. 2d 865 (9th Cir. 1991) 67
St Ives Windings Limited, *Re* (1989) 3 BCC 634 125
Standard Chartered Bank Ltd *v.* Walker [1982] 2 All ER 938 .... 108, 115, 116
Standard Chartered Bank *v.* Yaacoub CA, 13 August 1990, (unreported) 33
Standard Investments Limited *v.* Canadian Imperial Bank of Commerce (1986) 22 DLR (94th) 410, 52 OR (2d) 473 147
State of Norway's Application, *Re* [1990] 1 AC 723 92
Stubbs *v.* Slater [1910] 1 Ch. 632 17
Tai Hing Cotton Mills *v.* Liu Chong Hing Bank [1986] AC 80 .... 15, 23
Tatung (UK) Ltd *v.* Galex Telesure Ltd (1988) 5 BCC 395 112
Telemetrix Plc *v.* Modern Engineers of Bristol (Holdings) Plc [1985] BCLC 213 114
Thames Ironworks, Shipbuilding and Engineering Co. Ltd, *Re* [1912] WN 66 115
Third Chandris Shipping Corporation *v.* Unimarine [1979] 1 QB 645 34
Thorpe *v.* Chief Constable of Greater Manchester Police [1989] 1 WLR 665 47
Tillett *v.* Nixon (1883) 25 Ch. D 238 105
Titford Property Co. Ltd *v.* Cannon Street Acceptances Ltd 22 May 1975, unreported 14, 15
Tournier *v.* National Provincial and Union Bank of England [1924] 1 KB 461 (CA) 91
Tse Kwong Lam *v.* Wong Chit Sen [1983] 3 All ER 54 160
Union Carbide Corporation Gas Plant Disaster at Bhopal, *In re*, 634 F.Supp. 842 (DSNY 1986) 73
United Overseas Bank *v.* Jiwani [1976] 1 WLR 964 24
United Rope Distributors, Inc, *In re*, 930 F. 2d 532 (7th Cir. 1991) 66
United Service Co. *Re*, Johnstone's Claim (1870) 6 Ch. App. 212 21
United States *v.* Bank of Nova Scotia (Bank of Nova Scotia I) 691 F. 2d 1384 (11th Cir. 1982) 87
United States *v.* Bank of Nova Scotia (Bank of Nova Scotia II) 740 F. 2d 817 (11th Cir. 1984) 87
United States *v.* First National City Bank 379 US 378 65
United States *v.* First National City Bank 396 F. 2d 897 (2d Cir. 1968) 80, 81
United States *v.* Kovel 296 F. 2d 918 (2d Cir. 1961) 185
United States *v.* Toyota Motor Corp. 561 F. Supp 351 (CD Cal. 1983) 66
United States *v.* United Mine Workers 330 US 258 (1947) 87
United States *v.* Vetco, Inc. 691 F. 2d 1281 (9th Cir. 1981) 80–82, 86, 87
Uranium Antitrust Litigation, *In re*, 480 F. Supp. 1138 (N D Ill 1979) 81, 82
Uttamchandami *v.* Central Bank of India (1989) 139 NLJ 222 19
Van Lynn Developments *v.* Pelias Construction Co. [1969] 1 QB 607 33
Volkswagenwerk AG *v.* Beech Aircraft Corporation 751 F. 2d 117 (2d Cir. 1984) 67
Volkswagenwerk AG *v.* Schlunk 486 US 694 (1988) 70, 71
Vorhees *v.* Fischer & Krecke 697 F. 2d 574 (4th Cir. 1983) 70
Wallace *v.* Universal Automatic Machines Co. Ltd [1894] 2 Ch. 547 105
Waugh *v.* British Railways Board [1980] AC 521 .... 44, 45
Wells Fargo & Co. *v.* Wells Fargo Express Co. 556 F. 2d 406 (9th Cir. 1977) 66, 67
Westpac Banking Corporation *v.* Sugden (1988) NSW Conv. R. 55–377 24
Wheeler *v.* Le Marchant (1881) 17 Ch. D 675 43

White *v.* City of London Brewery Co. (1889) 42 Ch. D 237 107
Williams *v.* Williams [1988] 1 QB 161 .... 48, 49
Williams & Glyn's Bank Ltd *v.* Barnes 26 March 1980, unreported 14, 15
Willis, Percival & Co, *Re, ex parte* Morier (1879) 12 Ch. D 491 19
Winkworth *v.* David Baron (1987) 3 BCC 4 139
Woodroffes (Musical Instruments) Ltd, *Re* [1986] Ch. 366 106
Woods *v.* Martins Bank Limited and Another [1954] 1 WLR 1018 41
World-Wide Volkswagen Corp. *v.* Woodson 444 US 286 (1980) 63, 64
Wortley *v.* Birkhead (1754) 2 Ves. Sen 571 36
Wylde *v.* Radford (1863) 33 LJ Ch. 51 21
X *v.* A Bank [1983] 2 All ER 464 99
Yandil Holdings Pty Ltd *v.* Insurance Co. of North America (1987) 7 NSWLR 571 94
Yorke (M V) Motors *v.* Edwards [1982] 1 WLR 444 33
Z Limited *v.* A.-Z. [1982] QB 558 (CA) 96

TABLE OF LEGISLATION

UNITED KINGDOM

Bankruptcy Act 1914 —
ss. 16, 17, 21 25
Bills of Exchange Act 1882 —
s. 27(3) 21
57 30
Civil Evidence Act 1968 —
s. 14(1) 234
Civil Jurisdiction and Judgments Act 1982 —
s. 25 .... 95, 97
Companies Act 1948 —
s. 223(a) 17
Companies Act 1985 —
Part XIV 235
s. 8 27
ss. 35A, 35B 146
s. 192(3) 108
221(1), (2)(a) 135
395 21
425(1) 26
ss. 425–427A 26
s. 432(2) 227, 228, 232–237, 239
(2A) 227, 232
434(2) 230, 235
(a) 229
(3), (5) 230, 235
436 229
437 227
(1), (1A) 231
(1B), (1C) 231, 235
(3)(c) 231
448(1)–(4) 229
451A 231, 235
452 .... 230, 235
(1A), (1B) 230
ss. 453, 718, 735 227
s. 741(2) 116
Sch.22 227
Companies Act 1989 —
s. 108 146
Company Directors Disqualification Act 1986 121
s. 6(3)(c) 28
7(3) 132
Sch. 1 121
Consumer Credit Act 1974 30
Part VII 16
ss. 8, 87(1) 16
s. 126 24
141 30
189 16
Consumer Credit (Enforcement, Default and Termination Notices) (Amendment) Regulations 1984 SI 1984, No 1109 16
Consumer Credit (Enforcement, Default and Termination Notices) Regulations 1983 SI 1983, No 1561 16
Conveyancing Act 1882 —
ss. 19(1), 24 106
County Court Rules 1981
0.9, rule 14 31
Country Courts Act 1984 s. 21 30
Criminal Justice Act 1987 236
s. 1 236
s. 2 .... 236, 237
(8), (14) 236
Criminal Law Act 1977
s. 6(1)(a), (b) 24
(2), (4) 24
Deeds of Arrangement Act 1914 25
Evidence (Proceedings in Other Jurisdictions) Act 1975 .... 92, 93
Fatal Accidents Act 1976 44
Financial Services Act 1986 —
s. 47 159
High Court and County Court Jurisdiction Order 1991 30
s. 2(4) 30
Insolvency Act 1985 —
s. 110 25
Insolvency Act 1986 .... 25, 27, 116, 133, 137
s. 1 .... 125, 161

Insolvency Act 1986—*cont.*
ss. 1–7 26
s. 6 161
8(3)(a) 16
9(1) 26
(3) 29, 123
(4) 29
10 29
(4) 27
11 .... 27, 123, 161
(1), (2) 27
14 .... 28, 124
(3) 28
15 .... 123, 124
(9) 28
17 28
18 124
23 125
ss. 23–26 29
s. 27 .... 28, 123–125
29(2) 108
37(1) 108, 113
40 110
42(1) 109, 111
43 109
(1) 110
44(1) 108, 109, 113
(2) 113
ss. 47, 48 109
s. 123 .... 156, 158
(1)(a) 17, 35
(e) 35
124(1) 35
165 .... 16, 111
166 111
167 16
212 124
213 137
214 .... 121, 122, 134
(1) 134
(1)–(3) 117
(4) 135
215(2) 117
ss. 230, 233, 234 28
(3), (4) 112
235–237 28
s. 238 .... 36, 156, 157
(1) 28, 29
239 .... 29, 36, 140, 156–158
245 .... 156, 158
251 .... 121, 141
ss. 252–263, 258, 260, 262 26
s. 264(1)(a) 35
267, 268 35
(1)(a) 17
314 16
323 18

Insolvency Act 1986—*cont.*
ss. 336–338, 339, 340 36
388(1), 390(2) 109
s. 423, 424(1)(a) 29
Sch.1 .... 28, 109, 111
Sch.4 111
para. 5 16
Sch.5 para. 1 16
Insolvency Rules 1986 .... 26, 161
rule 2.6 29
4.90 18
5.18 26
Insolvent Companies (Reports on Conduct of Directors) No. 2 Rules 1986 132
Judicature Act 1873 104
Law of Property Act 1925 .... 17, 162
ss. 90, 91 30
s. 101(1) 106
103 24
(i) 17
109 106
196 17
Police and Criminal Evidence Act 1984 .... 236, 237
s. 67(9) 237
Protection From Eviction Act 1977 24
Rules of the Supreme Court 1965 —
Ord.2 31
6, r.1(1)(e) 30
11 60
12, r.5 30
13, r.1 30
r.9 31
14 r. 2(1)–(3) 32
4 32
(3) 33
14A 33
24, r.2 50
r.8 37
r.14A 46
r.16(4) 41
38, r.2A 48
72(1)(2) 29
88, r.2 30
Supreme Court Act 1981 —
s. 35A 30
36(4) 49
37 34
61(1) 30
72 234
Theft Act 1968 —
s. 31 234
Unfair Contract Terms Act 1977 —
s. 3 24
(2)(b) 14

EUROPEAN AND INTERNATIONAL

Brussels Convention on Jurisdiction and the Enforcement of Judgments in Civil and Commercial Matters 1968
Art. 24 ... 95, 97
Dir.77/187/EEC ... 209
Hague Convention of the Service Abroad of Judicial and Extrajudicial Documents in Civil or Commercial Matters ... 69, 71
Arts. 1–6 ... 69
Art.10(a) ... 69–71
(b), (c) ... 69
Art.13 ... 69
Hague Convention on the Taking of Evidence Abroad in Civil or Commercial matters ... 83, 92
Arts. 1–14 ... 83
Art.9 ... 83
Art.23 ... 84
Treaty of Rome
Arts. 85, 86 ... 45

AUSTRALIA

Contracts Review Act ... 24

DENMARK

Registration Act ... 8

EIRE

Companies (Amendment) Act 1990 ... 133

FRANCE

Dailly Act 1981 ... 6
Loi de 17 Mars 1909 concernant la vente et le natissement des fonds de commerce ... 118

GERMANY

Arbeitsförderungesetz s. 141 *et seq.* ... 210
Arrangement Act 1927 (Vergleichsordnung as amended 1935) ... 206
ss. 2(1), (2), 3(1) ... 206
7(1), 13, 20(1), 27, 28, 38, 39, 40, 46–48, 57–59, 102 ... 207
Banking Code ... 126, 127
Bankruptcy Act ... 128
Bankruptcy Code 1877 (Konkursordnung) ... 214
s. 1 ... 204
4 ... 205
30 num 2 ... 222
ss. 30–32a ... 221
s. 31 num 1 ... 222
43 ... 204
47 ... 205
ss. 60, 61 ... 218
s. 64 ... 205
102 ... 216
106(1) ... 210
107(1) ... 203
127(2) ... 205
ss. 129(2), 132(1) ... 210
207, 209 ... 216
Civil Code (BGB) (Bürgerliches Gesetzbuch of 1900) —
s. 38 ... 8
138(1) ... 205
419 ... 208, 209
(1), (2) ... 118
613a ... 209
(1) ... 209
826 ... 223
Commercial Code (Handelsgesetzbuch) —
s. 25 ... 208
Insolvency Bill 1989/90 (Draft) ... 214
s. 55(2) ... 219
Insolvency Bill 1991 (Regierungsentwurf Insolvenzordnung) ... 203, 212, 215
s. 2 ... 216
8 ... 209
22 ... 216
(2) ... 216
30 ... 220
46 ... 219
(1) No 5 ... 224
ss. 54, 58 ... 218
s. 64 ... 219
83(3), 87(3) ... 220
89 ... 216
ss. 117, 121(2) ... 218
s. 145(1) ... 222
ss. 145–155 ... 221
s. 148(1) ... 222
161 ... 210
191 ... 218
(2) ... 218, 220
ss. 191–194 ... 218
s. 194(3) ... 218
195(2) ... 217
196 ... 217
197(1) ... 218

Insolvency Bill 1991 (Regierungsentwurf Insolvenzordnung)—*cont.*
ss. 253, 254, 255, 264–269 ... 216
265, 266, 281, 282, 288, 289(1), (2) . 220
s. 298 ... 216
ss. 311, 312, 315(1) ... 221
Insolvency Law (Gesamtvollstreckungsordnung) 1990 ... 214
ss. 8(2), 17(1), 18(2) ... 214
Joint Enforcement Act ... 129
Joint Enforcement Interruption Act ... 129
Unification Treaty of 31 August 1990 ... 214

UNITED STATES

Alien Venue Act 28 USC 1391 ... 71, 72
28 USC 1391(a)–(f) (1982) ... 72
Bankruptcy Act 1898 ... 4
Bankruptcy Code 1976 ... 213
Bankruptcy Code 1978 ... 3, 10
Code Civ Pro 410. 10 (1973) ... 60
Deficit Reduction Act of 1984 ... 166
Depository Institutions Deregulation and Monetary Control Act of 1980 94 Stat. 132 ... 166
para. 202 ... 165
204 ... 166
308(a)(1)(A) ... 165
paras. 501, 511 ... 166
Economic Recovery Tax Act of 1981 95 Stat. 172 ... 166
paras. 201, 212 ... 166
Federal Bankruptcy Code
Chapter 11 ... 26, 133, 176
Federal Bankruptcy Laws ... 176, 178
Federal Rules of Civil Procedure ... 55, 75
r.4 ... 66
(a), (b), (d), (i) ... 68
5(d) ... 76
8(a) ... 57
(b), (c) ... 58
rr.9(b), (c), 11 ... 57
r.12(a), (b) ... 58
(3) ... 72
(4), (5) ... 68
(h)(1) ... 68, 72
13(a) ... 59
(a)–(f) ... 58
(g) ... 58, 59
14 ... 58, 59
15(a) ... 58
16(a) ... 88, 89
(b), (c), (d), (f) ... 89
26(a) ... 75
(b)(1) ... 75, 76
(2) ... 75
(3) ... 185
Federal Rules of Civil Procedure—*cont.*
r.26(c) ... 79, 80
30(a) ... 83
(b) ... 76
(6) ... 77, 82
(d) ... 79
32 ... 78
(a)(3) ... 78
33 ... 77
(a) ... 76, 79
34(a) ... 81
(b) ... 76, 77, 79
36 ... 78
(a) ... 76, 79
37(a)(4) ... 80
(b) ... 80
(2) ... 80
44.1 ... 74
45 ... 81, 82
(b), (d) ... 79
(2) ... 78
(f) ... 80
Foreign Sovereign Immunities Act ... 58
Garn St Germain Depository Institutions Act of 1982 96 Stat. 1469 ... 167, 168
Internal Revenue Code
paras. 46, 48 ... 166
para. 163 ... 167
(d) ... 170
165 ... 170
168 ... 166, 170
465(c)(3)(D) ... 170
469 ... 170
paras. 704, 752 ... 279
para.1202 ... 170
(a) ... 167
NY Civil Practice Law 302(a) (1990) ... 60
Protection of Trading Interests Act ... 86
Restatement (Second) of Foreign Relations Law of the United States), 40 (1965) ... 86
Restatement (Third) of Foreign Relations Law of the United States), 442 (1986) ... 80, 86
Securities Act 1933
Rule 501(a) ... 261
Securities Exchange Act 1934 (15 USC 78aa 1982) ... 55
Sherman Antitrust Act 1982 (15 USC 1982) ... 55
Tax Reform Act of 1984 (100 Stat. 2085) ... 169
paras 201, 211, 251, 301, 302(a)(1), 503, 511 ... 170
para. 1001(a)(1) ... 167
Tex. Rev. Civ. Stat. Ann. —
Arts.342–606 ... 167

Texas Savings and Loan Department Rules 7 TAC 64.7(b) (1985) 168
Uniform Commercial Code
Art. 9 7
US Constitution
amend. V and XIV 60
Art. 1, 8 53
Art. VI, cl.2 53
Art. VI 70
USC 1338(a) 55
Walsh Act, 28 USC 1783 (1982) 82, 83
28 USC 1783(a) (1982) 83
11 USC (1990)
paras. 547, 548 180
12 CFR
para.7.3025 173
563. 17–1a(c) (1) 168
12 CFR—*cont.*
paras. 567.3, 563.98, 563.17 169
12 USC
para. 1464(c)(1)(B), (N), (R) 167
15 USC 15 55
18 USC 3231 55
18 USC 401–2 (1882) 80
28 USC 1330(b) (1991) 60
28 USC 1330–64 (1982), 1331 (1982), 1332 (1991), 1332(a)(2) (1991), 1334, 1335, 1337 (1982) 55
USC 1404(a) (1982) 72
USC 1441(a), (b) (1973, Supp. 1991) 56
USC 1445 (1991), 1446(b) (1991), 1447(b) (1973), 1447(d) (1973) 56
USC 1603(b)(2), 1608(d) (1982) 58

CHAPTER 1

REMEDIES AND RISK: INTERNATIONAL COMPARISONS

In financial transactions one party or the other has to bear the legal risk, and the choice is often hard to make. It is the law which decides who it is to be. This article gives some examples of the choices that legal systems have made in deciding who carries that risk in the context of banking and finance.

INSOLVENCY—A SUGGESTED SCALE

In providing a suggested scale, one is mainly concerned with showing international bankruptcy comparisons, because bankruptcy is the biggest source of trouble. On an insolvency there is not enough money to go round and so the law has to decide whether to throw the risk on to the debtor or on to creditors. The world's jurisdictions can be divided roughly into three groups:

1. pro-creditor;
2. pro-debtor;
3. not interested—these are mainly communist and fundamentalist Muslim states.

One may, somewhat impressionistically, rank the most important jurisdictions on a scale according to whether their corporate insolvency laws are pro-debtor or pro-creditor. Number 1 is extreme pro-creditor. Number 10 is extreme pro-debtor. The suggested scale is as follows:

1. Australia, Canada;
2. England, Germany;
3. Scotland;
4. Denmark, Sweden, Switzerland, The Netherlands, Japan, Korea;
5. Austria, Italy, Norway;
6. USA, Republic of Ireland;
7. South Africa;
8. Belgium, Luxembourg;
9. New Zealand;
10. France.

A pro-creditor jurisdiction allows a creditor to protect himself against an insolvency, e.g. by taking security or by a set-off. A pro-debtor jurisdiction aims to maximise the defaulter's assets so as to increase the assets available for distribution.

The pro-creditor argument is that people should be able to avoid losses resulting from a debtor default. If this is impossible, the insolvency creates risks for everybody and perhaps even risks for the system itself. The pro-debtor argument is that defaulters (and their employees) ought to be saved and that all creditors ought to contribute to this rescue.

It would be impossible to prove statistically which view results in the smallest overall economic cost. For example, one cannot say that a pro-debtor system aiming at business rescue does in fact succeed in rescuing more businesses; very often the availability of a statutory rescue procedure can push more businesses earlier into the trauma and destructiveness of a formal insolvency, whereas in the absence of a statutory procedure, major business rescues tend to be carried out by private reconstructions of bank debt which, some may say, are more efficient. There is no scientific method of measuring this.

But it does seem fair to say that a pro-creditor regime favours organised markets (by enabling participants to reduce counterparty risks, e.g. by margin, close-outs and set-off). A pro-creditor proponent would maintain that the protection of markets and the providers of finance to those markets is an absolute priority in modern commercial societies to avoid systemic risk, but a pro-debtor *aficionado* would insist that this is one rule for markets and another rule for everybody else. A pro-creditor system can also favour sophisticated capital providers. For example, the universal floating charge enables the capital-provider to be paid ahead of just about everybody else. Pro-debtor countries say that this prejudices unsecured creditors, especially trade. Those in favour of the floater would say that this security facilitates the financing of business enterprises which would not otherwise see the light of day, that the bank's position encourages it to allow the business to continue longer (so that more short-term creditors get out) and that, if the bank ultimately takes all, this is not unfair because the bank paid for all.

These are all matters for debate and many differing views have been, and no doubt will continue to be, expressed. All one can say is that the argument requires a subtle approach and that there are no easy answers. It is not the object of this chapter to express a view on which is best, but merely to present the facts.

KEY DETERMINANTS

The scale suggested above is based on key indicators used as litmus paper. The key determinants are as follows.

1. The availability of the universal floating charge (monopolistic security in favour of a single creditor and priming trade creditors).
2. The availability of a non-possessory chattel mortgage and security over receivables (invisible security creating an appearance of false wealth, but necessary for business finance). Allied to this is the upholding of finance leases, hire-purchase, retention of title and the like, without recharacterisation as mortgages.
3. Insolvency set-off (enabling the reciprocal unsecured creditor to be paid ahead of other unsecured creditors).
4. Protections to good faith creditors in relation to the recapture of preferences and the length of the suspect period (protecting the integrity of transactions at the expense of the insolvent estate).
5. Directors' personal liability on insolvency (honouring the veil of incorporation).
6. Rescission of land and equipment leases, licences and executory contracts (enabling the creditor to cancel profitable assets).

Other indicators could be used, e.g. protection of good faith post-petition creditors and the identity of priority creditors, but the above list will do.

The scale takes into account insolvency rehabilitation laws, some of which are mild, others of which have a cataclysmic effect on creditor rights. For example the US Chapter 11 is much more ferocious than the British administration which in turn is tougher than the German composition under the *Vergleichsordnung*.

COMMENTS ON THE SCALE

France is the most pro-debtor jurisdiction of all the major commercial states, followed closely by related countries like Belgium, with Luxembourg trailing along with misgivings. England has shifted a bit east as a result of the introduction of the administration procedure in 1986, leaving Australia and Canada (plus a large number of other English-based insolvency jurisdictions such as Hong Kong, Cayman, Singapore, India and others) still in the extreme pro-creditor mould.

For historical reasons, the US does not have a homogeneous legal culture and there is an acute conflict between pro-debtor and pro-creditor attitudes. This may help to explain why US case-law often seems so confusing and contrary. In 1978 the pro-debtor faction got the upper hand in the Bankruptcy Code of that year: many of the pro-debtor concepts showed great similarity with French ideas. Since then the pro-creditor faction has been fighting back and has achieved some successes. But still the US remains much more pro-debtor overall than, say, Germany and England.

Italy was pro-debtor as a result of the Napoleonic conquest. But in 1942 Hitler's lawyers persuaded Mussolini to adopt German bankruptcy ideas. Italy was thereby restored to the mercantilist tradition established by the Italian city states.

New Zealand and the Republic of Ireland were both extreme pro-debtor in the old English style, but have in the past couple of years become pro-debtor, with New Zealand (under an optional government-initiated procedure) almost as extreme as France. This volte-face appears to have been sparked off by major local insolvencies which were considered to have political ramifications. Legislation was passed (in the form of statutory managements) to protect the debtor, resulting in a cultural somersault. Some would say that these were much-needed reforms, others that they were mere political short-termism. Spain did the same in the 1920s, but Spain was already pro-debtor, along with most Latin American countries.

Germany and the Netherlands are solidly pro-creditor. Japan is less so, but is still in this camp, having taken over the German Civil Code and, somewhat reluctantly perhaps, modelled their insolvency law on the fairly pro-creditor US Act of 1898 at the request of the occupying forces after the Second World War. Korean bankruptcy laws are virtually a carbon copy of those of Japan.

Scotland's banking tradition enabled it to cut down the pro-debtor culture of medievalised Roman law which it inherited. For some reason the same did not happen in the equally Roman jurisdiction of South Africa. The Scandinavians walked a parallel path to Germany, although with less conviction—at any rate away from the Romanism which was transmuted and pastoralised by the pre-Revolution jurists and which formed the basis of the Napoleonic Code. Although Napoleon no doubt thought his code was revolutionary, in many respects it merely codified the *ancien regime*.

THE FRENCH EXAMPLE

France shows how an extreme pro-debtor culture achieves its objects. The bankruptcy laws were revised in 1967, and again in 1985, but the underlying attitudes go back for centuries—before Napoleon.

Business security in France is virtually useless. The range of security which is available is limited, notwithstanding occasional grudging carve-outs in favour of banks. What security there is is primed by prior creditors (employees, taxes etc.), so that one never knows what it is worth. It is also subject to a potential bankruptcy freeze and to the postponement of the secured debt.

Napoleonic law makes it almost impracticable to sell or charge debts and contracts, except by burdensome formalities (the *huissier* or *acte authentique*). Without these formalities, the sale of a debt is void on the debtor's bankruptcy. The rules were intended to protect debtors. By contrast, a debt in England can be sold over the telephone and the sale is effective on the seller's bankruptcy.

Notice to the debtor is not necessary for the validity of the transfer on the seller's bankruptcy, although (as in all jurisdictions) it is desirable for other purposes. A less draconian version of the French rule is followed in Korea and Japan. But Belgium and Luxembourg are faithful to the Napoleonic rigour.

French law dishonours the veil of incorporation by imposing personal liability for insolvency on directors with great ease. Although supported with some tepidity in Belgium, practically everybody else is opposed to this since they regard the protection of business enterprise as a greater good than the prevention of abuse of the corporate form. The US will sometimes adopt the half-way house of subordinating the claims of management. England has yielded some ground to the extirpators of abuse by adopting the test of wrongful trading which is a step away from the previous "light at the end of the tunnel" test (which showed great allegiance to the veil of incorporation). France disallows insolvency set-off and the insolvency administrator can cherry-pick. The French basic suspect period for preferences in 18 months whereas six months is the international norm, except for special cases such as gifts, fraud and insider deals.

A great many other examples of this pro-debtor approach could be given, e.g. the demotion of bank mortgages on ships to a long list of short-term prior creditors and a prohibition on the acceleration of loans as a result of insolvency—a surprise for bondholders. All in all, the jurisdiction takes the aggrandisement of the debtor's estate and the *pari passu* principle to its ultimate.

Legal historians must be left to debate how neighbouring countries sharing similar industrial policies could have such diametrically opposed views (which stretch far beyond insolvency). For the present, however, it is worth remarking that this division of view between the Napoleonic group and the Anglo-Germanic group of legal systems needs to be understood and confronted in the context of European harmonisation, if that process is not to end in a muddle.

SECURITY

Security is an accepted means of protection against insolvency and an exception to the *pari passu* principle.

Many non-common law states, to a greater or lesser extent, object to business security (other than over land, buildings, ships and aircraft), on the original ground that it gives an appearance of false wealth to creditors. As a result, in many jurisdictions, non-possessory chattel mortgages are difficult or impossible and security over a portfolio of receivables difficult. General floating charges are out of the question in all except the English-based countries, although they have been legislated for in a few cases, e.g. Scotland and, more hesitantly, elsewhere (Finland). Countries which share this hostility to business security include not only the Napoleonic group, but also Japan and most of Scandinavia.

In Germany, the *Sicherungsübereignung* (fiduciary transfer of title) is similar in some ways to, although short of, the English floating charge and, as in England, was sanctioned by case-law. The transfer must identify assets in the same way that identification is required for a sale of specific goods, but it can include future assets. The transfer of title need not be physical, but is effected by a custody agreement whereby the debtor agrees to hold goods on behalf of the creditor. Similar principles apply to a fiduciary assignment of receivables (*sicherungsabtretung*). The need for a degree of identification marks one of the differences with the English floater. Further, the crucial remedy of receivership (unresponsible possession without foreclosure) is not available.

In Japan, a fiduciary transfer of goods and receivables (*joto-tampo*) was judicially developed and is apparently similar to that in Germany and The Netherlands. But the contract must identify the assets and their location so the development is not nearly as advanced as in Germany. In practice banks do not rely on a general charge on goods.

In Switzerland there is also a *Sicherungszession*. But a 1986 decision of the Swiss Federal Court outlawed fiduciary assignments of all present and future receivables if unlimited in time. Banks generally take lists of identified receivables.

The Netherlands has also developed a fiduciary transfer of title. The debtor agrees to hold goods on behalf of the creditor (no physical delivery is required). The transfer can extend to a specified class of goods (perhaps even "all goods of the debtor") and can cover future additions. The security can also be applied to inventory, except that the debtor is given permission to deal in the ordinary course of business. Like the English floater, the security ranks after tax claims and certain other privileged creditors. There is a similar fiduciary assignment for receivables, except that the receivables must be identified in lists and it is not possible to assign receivables which do not spring out of existing contracts. An assignment of bank accounts covers only the credit at the time of the assignment.

In Luxembourg, it appears that a fiduciary transfer similar to German concepts is available by virtue of a Grand-Ducal Decree of 1983, if the fiduciary is a credit institution.

The Belgian *nantissement de fonds de commerce* (1919) is much more limited in scope. Assets which can be pledged include: (a) goodwill, and the name; (b) trade marks and patents; (c) supply contracts; (d) tangible assets, such as raw materials, industrial and commercial furniture and equipment, and 50 per cent of value of goods in stock; (e) securities, receivables and cash if so provided (Decision of 6 Nov. 1970, para 1971, 1200); (f) immovables, even if already subject to a prior mortgage (Decision of 26 May 1972, JT 1972, at 625). There is no right of receivership in Belgium, only public sale.

By contrast, in France there are only piecemeal exceptions in favour of business security, e.g. the Dailly Act of 1981 (*bordereau* to avoid the *huissier* problem under CC Art 2075) and a 1951 Act for machinery and equipment (very limited). Note the *nantissement de fonds de commerce* allowed under a 1909 law, but this specifically excludes stocks (inventory) and receivables.

Denmark, Norway, Spain and Portugal evidently do not contemplate anything approaching the German fiduciary transfers.

REGISTRATION OF SECURITY

The English-based jurisdictions met the "false wealth" point in the case of corporations by substituting registration so that creditors could know the extent to which the assets must be taken out of the insolvency calculation of returns. The result is that virtually unlimited corporate security is available to creditors. This is not so for individuals and a remarkable feature of English insolvency law is the difference between corporate and industrial bankruptcies: individual bankruptcy law is mildly pro-debtor, but corporate insolvency law is pro-creditor. Registration enabled companies to escape the prohibition on secret security, but nevertheless imposes its own hazards, especially for market charges and margin.

The most comprehensive registration system for security over assets other than land is to be found in the US under Article 9 of the UCC. That system in modified form is being adopted in the Canadian provinces. The more limited English corporate registration system can be found in most of the English-based countries. A crucial difference is that the US system is also a priority system, whereas the English approach was not primarily directed to ordering priorities (although this has now crept in).

A small but important group of countries get along without registration even though, as noted above, they have developed security which comes within throwing distance of the comprehensive floating charge. The most notable of these countries are Germany and The Netherlands. They seem to be unconvinced by the false wealth argument. They might point out that in any event many assets can be whipped away on insolvency, such as equipment on lease or hire-purchase, debts by set-off and land leases—without official notice to creditors of this possibility. Some German case-law seems to suggest the creditors ought to assume that the whole lot is in hock.

The Netherlands' approach to the protection of unsecured creditors is interesting. In *Erba* v. *Amsterdamsche Bank NV*[1] a bank took comprehensive security from a textile company in difficulties so that the debtor no longer had any assets available to its creditors, but kept the appearance of creditworthiness. The Hoge Raad held that the bank committed a tort if it knew or could have foreseen that on termination of the credit the *new* unpaid suppliers would be prejudiced *and* the bank had not taken care that those suppliers were paid or got their goods bank. The bank owed a duty to new suppliers who relied on

1. NJ 1957, 514 and 1959, 581.

the appearance of creditworthiness, since the bank took the profit from the resale of the goods by the debtor and also the value of goods as yet unsold which had not been paid for by the debtor. The security is not nullified, but the bank is liable to pay damages to the injured creditor to the extent their loss is increased so that in effect the bank loses the proceeds. But a supplier might be guilty of contributory negligence if he sat back and continued to supply when the debtor had defaulted in payments. Further, the test is economic viability at the time the security is taken. Another case is *Osbv-Pannan AB* v. *Las Verkoopmaatschappij BV*[2] where a Swedish parent gave substantial credit to and took extensive security from its wholly-owned Dutch subsidiary. An unpaid supplier claimed damages in tort from the Swedish parents and the Hoge Raad applied the *Erba* test.[3]

The German approach is to apply the principle of *bonos mores* enshrined in BGB, s. 38. This covers: defeating or endangering other creditors because of the excessive bargaining power of the secured creditor; unfair tying contracts which are over-restrictive of the debtor; and "over-security": this is 150 per cent in the case of receivables.

Generally banks release security to avoid the principle of fraudulently excessive security. The whole security is void, not just the excess.

In Japan there appears to be no principle of over-security as yet.

Spain has a system of registration of non-possessory chattel mortgages (Enactments of 1954 and 1955). Ditto Denmark under the Registration Act (but there are title identification requirements—the security cannot cover "all goods owned by the debtor"). The Belgian *nantissement* must be registered.

The choice then is between, on the one hand, allowing creditors to protect themselves against an insolvency without the risk of having the security set aside by some registration technicality (and without the acute international risks which domestic registrations systems can impose) and, on the other, publicity of security and augmenting the debtor's estate by failed security.

QUASI-SECURITY

There is a large group of transactions intended to avoid the inconveniences of mortgage law, commonly referred to as vendor–lessor security.

Vendor–lessor security includes hire-purchase, financial leasing, sale and repurchase (repos, stock lending), sale and lease-back, discounting (or factoring) and retention of title. These arrangements are not security in legal form, though they often have a similar, but by no means identical, effect in substance. All of them were basically developed either because security was

2. NJ 1982, 443.
3. Paul M. Storm in *Security on Movable Property and Receivables in Europe* Oxford, ESC, 1988, pp. 135–136.

not available or because security had tiresome inconveniences, including repossession obstacles, no sharing of residuals, registration and impracticable documentary formalities. Some have also been motivated in modern times by tax and accounting advantages.

The root of the problem lies in the risk that the law will recharacterise these transactions as, in substance, security which must therefore fail either because that type of security is not available or because it has not been registered.

An international comparison would reveal an extremely complicated picture. Although blurred and occasionally skewed, the bias of legal systems on this question appears to be not dissimilar from the pro-debtor/pro-creditor bias indicated above, i.e. pro-debtor states are more inclined to recharacterise. Hire-purchase and conditional sale are particularly vulnerable to being treated as void non-possessory chattel mortgages on insolvency.

SET-OFF AND CHERRY-PICKING

The international concern with netting, set-off and cherry-picking results from the colossal increase in the volume of transactions in modern societies with a consequent escalation of counterparty risk. The amounts involved on a *daily* basis are not just millions, or even billions, but trillions.

The following jurisdictions allow insolvency set-off:

England
Scotland
Jersey
Guernsey (contract in)
Isle of Man
Northern Ireland
Eire
The Netherlands
Germany
Austria
Switzerland
Italy
Denmark
Sweden
Norway
Finland
Bermuda
Cayman
Bahamas
Japan
Korea
Malaysia
Hong Kong
Singapore
Thailand
India
Pakistan
Sri Lanka
Australia
New Zealand (but not always, so this is fatal)
China
United States (subject to the automatic stay)
Canada
Panama
Israel
Nigeria

The following states do not permit insolvency set-off (except sometimes for current accounts and connexity):

France	South Africa
Belgium	Argentina
Luxembourg	Colombia
Spain	Mexico
Portugal	Venezuela
Greece	Egypt

Insolvency set-off allows the creditor to be paid as if he had security. If this is prohibited, then the creditor has to pay in, say, the deposit and prove for a dividend on the loan (thereby getting practically nothing). Pro-debtor states seek to compel this enlargement of the assets. Pro-creditor states think that creditors should be protected against the insolvency and, in particular, that the set-off is essential in markets. Both groups produce various rationalisations about the morality of the matter.

Cherry-picking is the ability of the defaulter's administrator to pick profitable contracts and to repudiate the unprofitable ones. The result is that the creditor cannot net losses and gains to reduce counterparty exposure.

The argument of the pro-debtor group is that creditors should not be able to cancel contracts so as to deprive the defaulter's estate of extra assets. The argument of the pro-creditor group is that it is unconscionable that a defaulter should be able to choose the best bits of his dealings with a particular creditor and get rid of the worst bits. This involves having the cherry without the pip, or the cream without the crust, so they say.

Generally, a state which allows insolvency set-off will also prohibit cherry-picking (so that all forms of netting are possible), but there are some important exceptions to this. Conversely, cherry-picking is usually possible in those states which prohibit insolvency set-off: the two tend to go together. Both rules insist that the creditor performs, even though the debtor refuses to perform.

Under the US Bankruptcy Code of 1978, the legislator in effect sanctioned cherry-picking, subject to limited exceptions. By contrast in England and related jurisdictions insolvency law does not allow cherry-picking and indeed the policy of insolvency set-off is so powerful that it is mandatory. Close-outs on a wide range of market contracts is also compulsory by statute in Italy, Germany, Austria and The Netherlands.

Initially, US lawyers endeavoured to avoid the unfavourable impact of the 1978 Bankruptcy Code by various artificial contractual devices, such as novations, automatic close-outs and the like. These unconvincing curiosities were quickly absorbed into financial folklore. Since then, the pro-creditor lobby in the US has prevailed upon Congress to bring US law back into line, in the case of some financial contracts, with the law in countries like England and

Germany. That leaves the Napoleonic group, plus some isolated jurisdictions such as New Zealand.

BIG POCKET LIABILITY

A big pocket regime passes the risk of loss on to those with the biggest pocket, regardless of fault. This is the approach of Robin Hood, a character whom some would regard as an attractive figure, others as a mugger.

Those who favour Robin Hood's cause think that the rich should pay the poor. Those on the side of the Sheriff of Nottingham think that life has risks and that the wretched should look for compensation only to those who directly caused their misery.

Although not necessarily bracketed with insolvency, the question in practice very often arises on insolvency, for it is then that the victim looks around for another pocket to pay.

The following are typical examples of big pocket liability: making mortgagee banks liable for environmental risk; lender liability generally; making banks liable to replace moneys lost by a delinquent customer or fixing banks with restitution claims; product liability (throwing the risk on to insurers); liability of auditors for the accounts (insurers again, if available); and liability of regulatory authorities for the collapse of a creature they supervise (throwing the risk on to the public purse).

Comparative trends in this area are complex and one may only cite some examples. In the US the big pocket theory appears to be strong. Perhaps this partly resulted from views about litigation (the contingent fee system, the inability of a winning defendant to recover costs from an unsuccessful plaintiff and the right to a jury) and perhaps also from cultural attitudes. The big pocket regime is beginning to appear in European Directives and no doubt it would be possible to ascertain which EC states are most inclined to favour this solution.

By contrast the English courts have resolutely set their face against the big pocket regime. This is particularly shown by recent case-law regarding the liability of auditors, the liability of regulatory authorities and general liability for economic loss.

CONCLUSION

Two conclusions may be drawn from this chapter. The first is that eliminating legal risk suffered by one party usually involves casting the risk on to someone else. Almost invariably, compromises, or splitting the difference, will not provide an escape. So the choice has to be made. The second is that the difference internationally between the choices made is dramatic. It follows that the advantages of a low-risk country from the point of view of creditors can be threatened by the presence of high-risk countries. No commercial jurisdiction is an island, let alone England.

PHILIP WOOD

CHAPTER 2

REMEDIES FOR BANKS: AN OUTLINE OF ENGLISH LAW

When things go wrong, banks turn to the legal means they have to recover their rights, or to obtain redress for the wrongs done to them: in other words, to their legal remedies.[1] Some are matters of self-help.[2] Others require the intervention of the courts. This chapter surveys the variety of remedies which the law of England and Wales[3] makes available, and the limits which it imposes upon the exercise of some of those remedies.

THE RIGHT TO DEMAND REPAYMENT

The most fundamental remedy possessed by a lending bank is its right to ask for its money back. In modern banking practice, most lending on overdraft is made on the terms of a facility letter containing some such phrase as "... This facility will expire on [date]. Whilst it is our present intention that this facility should remain available to you until that date and notwithstanding any other provision of this letter we nevertheless reserve the right to terminate the facility at any time by notice in writing ...,"[4] or, more commonly (if less felicitously), "... We will review this facility in six months' time, subject to normal banking terms and conditions, including the bank's right at any time to require repayment on demand ... ".

There is little reason to doubt that the first of these formulations would be

1. *Webster's English Dictionary*, cited by Pearson J in *Goulandris Bros Ltd* v. *B Goldman & Sons* [1958] QB 74 at pp. 99–100 in the course of holding that the word "remedies" in Rule D of the York-Antwerp Rules 1950 was "wide enough to cover defences as well as cross-claims, shields as well as spears, pleas as well as counts".

2. According to Professor Treitel, "The policy against self-help is strongest in French law, where the Maxim '*nul se peut se faire justice à soi-même*' (no-one is allowed to mete out justice personally) has been exceedingly influential. In that system even the process of putting a contract to an end requires, at least in theory and as a general rule, a judgment of a court. At the other extreme, in the United States of America, the Uniform Commercial Code expressly recognises 'self-help' as a 'remedy' available to an aggrieved party": *Remedies for Breach of Contract* (1988), p. 2.

3. Hereafter, simply for brevity, "English law". For similar reasons, the "English courts" means the courts of England and Wales and for "he" read "(s)he" throughout.

4. *Encyclopaedia of Forms and Precedents* (5th edn) Vol. 4 para. 138.

effective, in the absence of special circumstances, to reserve to the lender the right to ask for its money back whenever it wished.[5] However the effectiveness of the second is more open to question. The expression "subject to normal banking terms and conditions" is probably too vague to have any contractual effect at all[6]: and even an express statement that the facility is repayable on demand may not be enough to make it so, if that statement is simply part of the unconsidered "boiler plate" of the facility letter, and is repugnant to the specially agreed main provisions.

In *Titford Property Co Ltd* v. *Cannon Street Acceptances Ltd*,[7] Goff J had to consider the terms of an overdraft facility granted to property developers. The bank's facility letter stated that the overdraft was "for a period of 12 months to assist you in the purchase and development" of a specified property (over which it required a legal charge). Clause 9 of the facility letter, however, also stated that all monies, whether capital or interest, were to be repayable on demand. Goff J held that bank was not entitled to make demand before the expiry of the twelve months. The bank, in his judgment,

> . . . could not . . . with one hand grant a facility for a term for a purpose which to its knowledge clearly involves the Plaintiffs in incurring expenditure and liabilities, with a view to ultimate profit, and with the other take it away by an unqualified right to require repayment on demand at any time. . . . therefore, I must modify Clause 9, by reading it as subject to the provision as to the duration of this facility, or ignore it altogether . . .

As the *Titford* case makes clear, the issue of whether any demand is necessary to make the money lent repayable and, if so, when such a demand may be

5. In the absence of a fiduciary or other special relationship, English law imposes no obligation on a lender to exercise its right to demand repayment either "in good faith", or on any basis other than that of serving its own interests: cf. *China & South Sea Bank* v. *Tan* [1990] 1 AC 536 at p. 545D, where Lord Templeman emphatically re-stated the principle that a mortgagee "must decide in his own interest if and when he should sell" the mortgaged property. In extreme circumstances it is just possible that a challenge to the reasonableness of a provision for repayment on demand might be mounted under s. 3(2)(b) of the Unfair Contract Terms Act 1977, on the basis that by relying on it the bank was "claim[ing] to be entitled to render a contractual performance substantially different from that which was reasonably expected".

6. Compare *Nicolene Ltd* v. *Simmonds* [1953] 1 QB 543 (in which a purported sale subject to "the usual conditions of acceptance" was held too vague to be enforceable as a contract) with *Shamrock SS Co* v. *Storey & Co* (1899) 81 LT 413 (where a conduct to load coal at Grimsby "on the terms of the usual colliery guarantee" was upheld on proof of the terms usually contained in such guarantees at Grimsby). In *Williams & Glyn's Bank Ltd* v. *Barnes* (26 March 1980, unreported), Ralph Gibson J was prepared to assume, after hearing expert evidence of banking practice, that one of the usual banking conditions was that an overdraft is repayable on demand. But he went on to hold that " . . . a reference to 'the usual banking conditions' without stating what they are, and without clear language showing that such conditions are to prevail over any other terms as to duration or termination, whether express or necessarily derived from the language used, cannot negative a term which is otherwise part of the agreement . . . ": transcript, pp. 617–618. Gibson J's approach was approved by the Court of Appeal in *Cryne* v. *Barclays Bank Plc* [1987] BCLC 548, at p. 552.

7. 22 May 1975, unreported.

made, is primarily a matter of construction of the express and implied terms of the contract of loan. Having considered the *Titford* decision, Ralph Gibson J put the matter in this way in *Williams & Glyn's Bank Ltd* v. *Barnes*[8]:

> . . . in the absence of any express agreement providing for the duration of the facility, or for the date of re-payment, the Court must consider whether, according to the ordinary rules for the implication of terms into commercial contracts, any term controlling the duration of the facility or the date of repayment is to be implied. If no such term must be implied, then money lent under the facility is no more than money lent and is therefore repayable on demand . . .

Since the test for implying terms is whether the implication is *necessary*,[9] not whether it is reasonable, mere knowledge on the part of the bank that the customer intends to spend all or part of the money in a business venture that will take a long time to come to fruition cannot, by itself, give rise to an implied term requiring a period of notice for repayment calculated by reference to the probable duration of the business venture.[10] Nor will a provision referring to the expected duration of the facility always override a clause permitting immediate demand. The question of which provision is to prevail must be decided according to the normal principles of contract law.[11]

Banks will usually make loan facilities (as opposed to overdraft facilities) available on terms[12] which include "events of default", such as non-payment or insolvency, which if they occur will entitle the bank (a) to refuse further lending, and (b) to declare the outstanding balance immediately repayable. Unless these events are expressly stated, they are unlikely to be implied. So, in *Cryne* v. *Barclays Bank Plc*,[13] the Court of Appeal refused to imply into a fixed-term loan a term entitling the bank to require early repayment and/or to appoint a receiver if its security was in jeopardy.

Even where there are no express events of default, a non-payment or other breach of the loan agreement will permit the lending bank to treat the contract of loan as at an end if, but only if, the default amounts to a breach of a condition of the agreement (for example, because time of payment or other performance is of the essence) or because it amounts to a repudiation of the

8. *Supra*, transcript p. 605.

9. As Lord Wilberforce put it in *Liverpool City Council* v. *Irwin* [1977] AC 239, at p. 254: " . . . such obligation should be read into the contract as the nature of the contract itself implicitly requires, no more, no less: a test, in other words, of necessity . . . ". This stringent test was applied to the implication of terms in the contract between banker and customer in *Tai Hing Cotton Mills* v. *Liu Chong Hing Bank* [1986] AC 80 at pp. 104H–105A.

10. *Williams & Glyn's Bank* v. *Barnes* (*supra*), transcript, p. 609.

11. *Ibid*., pp. 650–652. "If the judgment of Goff J [in the *Titford* case] . . . is to be regarded as stating that in a contest for primacy between a term loan and a clause for repayment on demand, the provision for term loan must always prevail, then, with respect, I should not feel able to follow it."

12. See, for example, clause 8 of the specimen Facility Letter in the *Encyclopaedia of Forms and Precedents* (5th edn) Vol. 4 at para. 153.

13. [1987] BCLC 548.

borrower's obligations under the loan agreement. Unless time of payment is of the essence of the agreement, it may in practice be very difficult to show that persistent small delays in payment of instalments are, alone or cumulatively, sufficiently grave to amount to a repudiation.[14] The test seems to be whether the defaults in payment are such as to destroy the lender's confidence in the borrower's creditworthiness.[15] As to other events, common sense might suggest that the insolvent liquidation or personal bankruptcy of the borrower ought usually to be treated as a sufficient repudiation of a contract to repay money.[16] However, the power of a liquidator to perform *any* of the company's contracts so far as may be necessary for the beneficial winding-up of the company[17] means that the matter cannot be regarded as beyond doubt.[18] It is unlikely that the appointment of an administrator[19] or administrative receiver would be held, of itself, to amount to a repudiation of a contract of loan,[20] in the absence of special circumstances.

Service of a default notice under Part VII of the Consumer Credit Act 1974 is necessary before the creditor can become entitled, by reason of the debtor's breach of a regulated agreement[21] under that Act, to terminate the agreement, demand early repayment, treat any right conferred by the agreement on the debtor as terminated, restricted or deferred, or to enforce any security.[22]

Unless the contract of loan provides otherwise, a demand (although usual) is not a necessary element of the cause of action to recover money lent.[23] However, a demand upon the debtor will be required wherever the contract expressly so requires, and in any event in the following cases (a) where the amount of the debt is uncertain,[24] (b) where the loan is repayable by instal-

14. See, for example, *Decro-Wall International* v. *Practitioners in Marketing Ltd* [1971] 1 WLR 361; *The Brimnes* [1975] QB 929.

15. See *per* Salmon LJ in *Decro-Wall* (*supra*), at p. 369.

16. Because, in the case of a contract to repay money, the fact of insolvency demonstrates that the borrower is unable to carry the contract out: see *Re Phoenix Bessemer Steel Co, Ex Parte Carnforth Haematite Iron Co* (1876) 4 Ch. D 108 (declaration of insolvency); *Mees* v. *Duffus* (1901) 6 Com Cas 165 (declaration of insolvency); *Baker* v. *Lloyds Bank* [1920] 2 KB 322 (insolvency of indorser of bill); *Re National Benefit Assurance Co Ltd* [1924] 2 Ch. 339 (insolvency of insurer).

17. Insolvency Act 1986, ss. 165, 167, and Schedule 4 para. 5. The trustee in bankruptcy of an individual has similar powers, under section 314 and Sch. 5, para. 1.

18. The liquidation of a company is not generally a repudiation, without more, of its contractual obligations: see *British Waggon Co* v. *Lea* (1880) 5 QBD 149.

19. Who may, after all, have been appointed specifically for the purpose of achieving the survival of the company as a going concern: Insolvency Act 1986, s. 8(3)(a).

20. Cf. *Re Newdigate Colliery* [1912] 1 Ch. 468; *Parsons* v. *Sovereign Bank of Canada* [1913] AC 160.

21. Broadly, most agreements by which an individual (or partnership or other unincorporated body including at least one individual) is provided with credit not exceeding £15,000: Consumer Credit Act 1974, ss. 8 and 189: SI 1983, No. 1878.

22. Consumer Credit Act 1974, s. 87(1): Consumer Credit (Enforcement, Default and Termination Notices) Regulations 1983 SI 1983, No. 1561, as amended by SI 1984, No. 1109.

23. *Bradford Old Bank* v. *Sutcliffe* [1918] 2 KB 833.

24. *Brown* v. *Great Eastern Railway Co* (1877) 2 QBD 406.

ments and it is sought to accelerate the debtor's liability,[25] and (c) (generally) where it is sought to enforce security held for the loan.[26]

The requirements of a valid demand will depend upon the purpose for which it is made. The contract of loan may itself impose requirements as to the form and manner of any demand. Where the making of a demand is required in order to permit the enforcement of security, the security may impose further requirements. Subject to those requirements, and to any particular requirements of the general law,[27] it seems that a valid demand can be made orally. The English courts[28] have accepted as "a fair, working definition" of a valid demand the formulation proffered by Walker J in the Australian case of *Re Colonial Finance, Mortgage, Investment & Guarantee Corpn Ltd*[29]:

> . . . there must be a clear intimation that payment is required to constitute a demand; nothing more is necessary, and the word "demand" need not be used; neither is the validity of a demand lessened by its being clothed in the language of politeness; it must be of a peremptory character and unconditional, but the nature of the language is immaterial provided it has this effect . . .

Of course, banks will generally make their demands formally and in writing.

Surprisingly, there is no unanimity among writers on banking matters as to whether a demand which *substantially* mis-states the amount of the borrower's indebtedness can be effective. It is clear that a minor error in the amount due will not invalidate a demand.[30] However, James Lingard has expressed the view that if a bank demands materially more than is due to it, the borrower is justified in refuting the wrongful demand.[31] In reality it is the creditor, not the debtor, who will usually have the facilities for calculating the precise amount of compound interest due and who will, therefore, be the one who knows how much is owing. If the purpose of the demand is to give the debtor an

25. *Esso Petroleum Co Ltd* v. *Alstonbridge Properties Ltd* [1975] 1 WLR 1474. A notice of acceleration under a contractual provision must be given strictly in accordance with the contract terms: see *Re Berker Sportcraft Ltd's Agreements, Hartnell* v. *Berker Sportcraft Ltd* (1947) 177 LT 420.

26. *Miller* v. *Cook* (1870) LR 10 Eq. 641 (and cf. the Law of Property Act 1925, ss. 103(i) and 196) (power of sale under a mortgage); *Esso Petroleum Co Ltd* v. *Alstonbridge Properties Ltd* [1975] 1 WLR 1474 (guarantee); Lingard, *Bank Security Documents* (2nd edn), para. 11.4.

27. For example under the Law of Property Act 1925 (see note 26 above), the Consumer Credit Act 1974 (see note 22 above), or the Insolvency Act 1986, ss. 123(1)(a) or 268(1)(a) (see note 31 below and *Re a Debtor* (*No. 1 of 1987*) [1989] 1 WLR 271).

28. *Re a Company* [1985] BCLC 37 at p. 41; *BCCI* v. *Blattner* (CA, 20 November 1986, unreported).

29. (1905) 6 SR NSW 6, at p. 9.

30. See *Deverges* v. *Sandeman, Clark & Co* [1902] 1 Ch. 579; *Stubbs* v. *Slater* [1910] 1 Ch. 632.

31. *Bank Security Documents* (2nd ed.) para. 11.5, citing *Pigot* v. *Cubley* (1864) 15 CBNS 701 (a pledge case, distinguished in *Deverges*), *Re a Company* [1985] BCLC 37 at pp. 41–43 (a case concerning the validity of a statutory demand under s. 223(a) of the Companies Act 1948, now re-enacted in a materially amended form in s. 123(1)(a) of the Insolvency Act 1986), and *Cryne* v. *Barclays Bank Plc* [1987] BCLC 548 (where the point does not seem to have been argued). Gavin Lightman and Gabriel Moss, in *The Law of Receivers of Companies* (1986), p. 54, take the contrary view.

opportunity, albeit brief, of making payment before he is sued, or the security for the loan is enforced, he needs to be told how much he has to pay. Among the contrary arguments are these: that it is the debtor's duty to know how much he owes; that disputes over the amount due are so common that it is idle to impute to the parties an intention that a precisely correct demand should be a condition precedent to the debtor's liability; and that the calculation of the precise amount due as at the date of demand is, in most cases, an expensive waste of time, because there is no realistic prospect of the debtor paying anything. Where the debtor in fact needs to know how much to pay, he can always ask the creditor. These contrary arguments are supported by the decision of Walton J in *Bank of Baroda* v. *Panessar*[32] that a demand for "all monies due to us", without specifying the amount demanded, was a valid demand.

THE RIGHT TO COMBINE ACCOUNTS

Where the defaulting customer has two or more accounts with the same bank, one of which is in credit, English law gives the bank the right, subject to the limitations described below, to combine the two accounts and to apply the credit balance in reduction of the debt due from the customer to it.

Except in insolvency, this right of combination may be excluded by express or implied agreement,[33] and such an agreement may be inferred from the mere fact that one of the accounts is described as a current account and one as a loan account, even if both are repayable on demand.[34] English law does not permit parties to increase[35] or to diminish[36] by contract the extent of the rights of set-off conferred in bankruptcy and liquidation by statute.[37]

There can be no combination where the accounts are not held in the same right,[38] nor (it seems) where they are not held in the same name, even if the

32. [1987] Ch. 335, following the Australian case of *Bunbury Foods Pty Ltd* v. *National Bank of Australasia Ltd* (1984) 51 ALR 609.

33. See, for example, *Bradford Old Bank* v. *Sutcliffe* [1918] 2 KB 833, *Re EJ Morel (1934) Ltd* [1962] Ch. 21, and *National Westminster Bank Ltd* v. *Halesowen Presswork and Assemblies Ltd* [1972] AC 785.

34. *Ibid.* Such an agreement will normally be operative only for so long as the accounts are "alive", and will be determined by any event which terminates the relationship of banker and customer: see *British Guiana Bank* v. *Official Receiver* (1911) 27 TLR 454.

35. *British Eagle International Air Lines* v. *Compagnie Nationale Air France* [1975] 1 WLR 758.

36. *National Westminster Bank Ltd* v. *Halesowen Presswork and Assemblies Ltd* (*supra*).

37. Insolvency Act 1986, s. 323; Insolvency Rules 1986, rule 4.90.

38. *Re Gross* (1871) 6 Ch. App 632; *Garnett* v. *McKewan* (1872) LR 8 Ex. 10. However, where the customer has two accounts in his own name, one a purely private one, the other suggesting that someone else may have a proprietary interest in it, it would seem that a balance on the purely private account might be utilised to cover a debit on the other: cf. *Coutts & Co* v. *Irish Exhibition in London* (1891) 7 TLR 313.

beneficial owner is the same.[39] Similarly, a banker may not combine moneys which to his knowledge are held by the customer on trust to use them for a particular purpose.[40] Accounts whose terms, for example as to time for payment,[41] are so materially different that they could not all be terms of one account may not be combined. So, in the absence of agreement, a bank may not combine the customer's contingent, future or unmatured liabilities to it with its present debts to the customer so as to excuse payment,[42] or achieve the same result by retaining money presently payable so as to combine accounts at a future date. As Sir Page Wood VC said in *Jeffryes* v. *Agra and Masterman's Bank*[43]: " . . . you cannot retain a sum of money which is actually due against a sum of money which is only becoming due at a future time . . . "

It has not yet been judicially determined whether a bank may combine accounts maintained in different currencies.[44]

The precise theoretical analysis of this valuable right or remedy is surprisingly uncertain. One theory is that the matter is simply one of accounting, with the various accounts maintained by the bank being no more than sub-accounts of one overall account between the bank and its customer, under which only the ultimate balance either way represents an enforceable debt. An alternative analysis is that the right is properly regarded as a right of set-off, or as an analogous right, which does not produce a single balance or debt until the bank actually exercises its right to combine.

The first theory is supported by a number of dicta in the authorities, the most famous of which is probably that of James LJ in *Re European Bank*[45]: "In truth, as between banker and customer, whatever number of accounts are kept in the books, the whole is really but one account, and it is not open to the customer, in the absence of some special contract, to say that the securities he deposits are only applicable to one account",[46] and by Rory Derham, in his book on *Set-Off*[47]: " . . . an act of consolidation in fact is not required. Rather the basis of the right is that in any event there is only one liability for the

39. *Uttamchandami* v. *Central Bank of India* (1989) 139 NLJ 222.

40. *W.P. Greenhalgh & Sons* v. *Union Bank of Manchester* [1924] 2 KB 153; *Barclays Bank* v. *Quistclose Investments* [1970] AC 567.

41. Current account set-off depends upon the reciprocal claims being current. So accounts with different maturities cannot be the subject of combination: see Philip R Wood, *English and International Set-Off* (1989), at para. 3–22.

42. *Jeffryes* v. *Agra and Masterman's Bank* (1866) LR 2 Eq. 674; *Bower* v. *Foreign and Colonial Gas Co Ltd, Metropolitan Bank, Garnishees* (1874) 22 WW 740.

43. *Supra*, at p. 680.

44. See *Paget's Law of Banking* (10th edn) at p. 510 for a discussion of the competing considerations.

45. (1872) LR 8 Ch. App 41, at p. 44.

46. See also *Bailey* v. *Finch* (1871) LR 7 QB 34; *Garnett* v. *McKewan* (1872) LR 8 Ex. Cas. 10; *Re Willis, Percival & Co, Ex Parte Morier* (1879) 12 Ch. D 491, *per* James LJ, at p. 498; *Greenwood Teale* v. *Williams* (1894) 11 TLR 56; *Mutton* v. *Peat* [1900] 2 Ch. 79; *National Westminster Bank* v. *Halesowen Presswork and Assemblies* [1971] 1 QB 1, *per* Buckley LJ, at p. 46; and *Barclays Bank* v. *TOSG* [1984] BCLC 1, *per* Nourse J, at p. 22g, cited with approval by Millett J in *Re Charge Card Services* [1987] Ch. 150, at pp. 173–174.

47. (1987), at pp. 268–269.

balance. In other words, it is not so much a right to combine accounts as a right to consider that the accounts are so combined. . . . Combination of accounts is not a set-off situation . . . Rather, it is merely an accounting situation . . . "

By contrast, Philip Wood in his monumental work *English and International Set-Off*[48] rejects the "accounting" theory and prefers to regard the right as a right of current account set-off:

> . . . this idea that there is only one amount owing is no more than an expression of the fact that, in the absence of agreement to keep the accounts separate, the bank may instantly set off at any time without notice to the customer, so that at any point the bank can treat the divided accounts as being one single blended account. But two accounts are not one account and the real question is in what circumstances can the bank treat the account[s] as a single account.

and this seems to be the view of the majority of text-book writers,[49] who treat the bankers' right of combination as a species of set-off, and as a right which requires some act of exercise by the bank. It is also consistent with the approach of the judges (except Buckley LJ) at all levels in *Halesowen*,[50] and seems most nearly to reflect the commercial and legal realities of the situation.

As Wood points out, the idea that the accounts are always combined to produce a single debt is inconsistent with many of the features of distinct bank accounts prior to combination. For example, the bank will continue to charge interest on the full amount of an overdrawn bank account without netting out the credit balance. Where separate accounts are maintained, the *Clayton's Case*[51] appropriation rules are applied to the separate accounts, not to those accounts as combined. A debit balance may become statute barred and hence ineligible for set-off against a credit balance. To this list may be added three further matters: the possibility that a bank might need to give notice before exercising its right of combination[52]; the "apparent anomaly"[53] that the bank may combine accounts at different branches, but the customer may not do so without specific agreement; and the greater anomaly that the bank may not even be obliged to combine accounts at the same branch in order to honour its customer's cheques.[54] All of these matters seem *prima facie* to be inconsistent

48. (1989), para. 3–6.

49. Cresswell and Blair, *Encyclopaedia of Banking Law* para. C251; *Paget's Law of Banking*, (9th edn, by Megrah and Ryder) pp. 138–146, (10th edn, by Mark Hapgood) pp. 501–510; Holden, *The Law and Practice of Banking* (5th edn) paras. 2-55–2-72A; Ellinger, *Modern Banking Law* (1987), pp. 139–161. Goode, *Legal Problems of Credit and Security* (2nd edn), at pp. 146–147. *Contra*, Penn Shea and Arora, *The Law Relating to Domestic Banking* (1987), paras. 13.31–13.36.

50. Roskill J, Lord Denning MR and Winn LJ ([1971] 1 QB 1), Viscount Dilhorne and Lords Kilbrandon, and Cross ([1972] AC 785).

51. *Devaynes* v. *Noble* (1816) 1 Mer. 572.

52. Left open following the decision of the House of Lords in *Halesowen* (*supra*): see the discussion in Ellinger, (*op. cit.*), at pp. 154–155.

53. *Per* Mocatta J in *Barclays Bank* v. *Okenarhe* [1966] 2 Lloyd's Rep. 87, at p. 95.

54. Ellinger, (*op. cit.*), at pp. 160–161, stating that there is no authority on the point to date.

with the idea that, prior to combination, the two or more accounts constitute a single debt.[55]

THE BANKER'S RIGHT OF LIEN

English law[56] gives a banker, in addition to the right of combination of accounts, a general lien[57] over securities deposited by the customer with the bank to the extent of the customer's indebtedness to the bank. The right of lien extends to a banker acting as agent for a remitting banker,[58] and to the advising/confirming bank in a documentary credit transaction.[59]

In order to be subject to the lien, the securities must have come into the banker's hands in his capacity as banker in the course of his banking business. Curiously, although safe-custody is undoubtedly part of the modern business of banking, securities deposited merely for safe keeping are considered to be outside the scope of the banker's lien.[60]

The lien extends to "paper securities",[61] whether negotiable (such as cheques and bills of exchange[62] collected by the bank on its customer's behalf[63]) or not. So, for example, documents tendered under a letter of credit,[64] insurance policies,[65] deposit receipts,[66] orders for payment,[67] and share certificates[68] have all been held to be subject to the lien. It is unclear where it extends to documents of title to land.[69] It does not extend to goods, or

55. It may also be said that the courts treat the banker's rights of combination as requiring an act of exercise, in the context of *Mareva* injunctions. However, the case which established the usual proviso permitting the continued exercise of those rights after service of an injunction, *Oceanica Castelana Armadora SA* v. *Mineralimportexport* [1983] 1 WLR 1294, did not concern ordinary current accounts but involved debits for interest on term loans.

56. The banker's lien was recognised by the Court of King's Bench as early as 1794, in *Davis* v. *Bowsher* (1794) 5 Term. Rep. 488 and by 1846 was regarded as "undoubted" by the House of Lords in *Brandao* v. *Barnett* (1846) 12 Cl. & Fin. 787.

57. Arising by operation of law, and so not registerable as a bill of sale or under the Companies Act 1985, s. 395.

58. *Re Parker, ex parte Froggatt* (1843) 3 Mont. D & DeG 322; *Prince* v. *Oriental Bank Corp* (1878) 3 App. Cas. 325.

59. *Aschkenasy* v. *Midland Bank Ltd* (1934) 50 TLR 209; 51 TLR 34.

60. *Leese* v. *Martin* (1873) LR 17 Eq 224; *Misa* v. *Currie* (1876) 1 App. Cas. 554.

61. *Davis* v. *Bowsher* (*supra*); *Wylde* v. *Radford* (1863) 33 LJ Ch. 51.

62. *Davis* v. *Bowsher* (*supra*); *Giles* v. *Perkins* (1807) 9 East 12; *Re Firth, ex parte Schofield* (1879) 12 Ch. D 337; *Dawson* v. *Isle* [1906] 1 Ch. 633.

63. *Barclays Bank Ltd* v. *Astley Industrial Trust Ltd* [1970] 2 QB 527. Cf. the Bills of Exchange Act 1882, s. 27(3), which constitutes a collecting bank holder a holder for value to the extent of the sum for which it has a lien, and *Re Keever* [1967] Ch. 182.

64. *Sewell* v. *Burdick* (1884) 10 App. Cas. 74.

65. *Re Bowes, Earl of Strathmore* v. *Vane* (1886) 33 Ch. D 586.

66. *Jeffryes* v. *Agra and Masterman's Bank* (1866) LR 2 Eq. 674.

67. *Misa* v. *Currie* (*supra*).

68. *Re United Service Co, Johnstone's Claim* (1870) 6 Ch. App. 212.

69. As explained by Buckley J in *Re London and Globe Finance Corporation* [1902] 2 Ch. 416, at p. 420, *Wylde* v. *Radford* (*supra*) (in which it was held that the bank was not entitled to a lien on a property, where its customer had deposited a deed of conveyance of that property and another, but had executed a memorandum charging only the other) was a decision on its own

(despite earlier dicta to the contrary) to the customer's credit balance with the bank,[70] and may be displaced by contrary agreement.

A banker's lien carries the right to sell the property subject to the lien,[71] after reasonable notice to the customer.[72]

THE RIGHT TO CLOSE THE ACCOUNT

If the customer is operating his account unlawfully,[73] or commits a breach of a term which is a condition of the banker/customer contract, or commits a fundamental breach of an intermediate term of that contract, a bank may be entitled to close the account forthwith.[74] In the absence of such unlawful conduct or repudiatory breach by the customer,[75] a bank can only close a customer's credit account on reasonable notice.[76] Where a credit account is concerned, the period of notice must be long enough in the circumstances to enable the customer to make alternative banking arrangements.[77]

It is probable that there is a similar obligation upon a bank to give the customer sufficient notice to make other arrangements, even where the account is in debit, and even though no such notice would be necessary to call in the overdraft.

> . . . A banker would be very imprudent if he called in an overdraft to close an account and then, prior to the expiry of a proper period of notice, he dishonoured cheques which the customer was prepared to cover by paying in cash. It is one thing to call in an overdraft; it is quite another matter to withdraw banking facilities without giving the customer sufficient notice to enable him to make other arrangements . . .[78]

facts. Penn, Shea and Arora, *The Law Relating to Domestic Banking* (1987) expresses the view that the banker's lien does extend to title deeds (at para. 13.07). *Paget's Law of Banking* (10th edn) takes the contrary view (at pp. 495–496).

70. *National Westminster Bank Ltd* v. *Halesowen Presswork and Assemblies*, in the Court of Appeal at [1971] 1 QB 1 at pp. 32 and 46, approved by the House of Lords at [1972] AC 785, at pp. 802 and 810.

71. Always assuming that the security is capable of sale by the bank: *Brandao* v. *Barnett* (1846) 3 CB 519; *Rosenburg* v. *International Banking Corpn* (1923) 14 Ll.L.Rep. 344, at p. 347. This right is of most value where the security consists of negotiable instruments or transferable documents of title to goods.

72. Because it carries this right of sale, it is often described as an "implied pledge". Like a pledge, it depends upon possession. Unlike a pledge, however, the banker's lien is not created by agreement but arises by operation of law.

73. The law will not imply an obligation on the bank to allow its customer a reasonable time to make alternative banking arrangements, if the purpose of making those alternative arrangements is to enable him to continue his unlawful conduct: see Holden, *The Law and Practice of Banking* (5th edn) para. 3–12.

74. Since the relationship is contractual, the ordinary rules as to termination of contract apply.

75. And in any event, for prudence.

76. *Joachimson* v. *Swiss Bank Corporation* [1921] 3 KB 110, at pp. 125, 127.

77. *Prosperity* v. *Lloyds Bank Limited* (1923) 39 TLR 372.

78. Holden (*op. cit.*) at para. 3–13; see also Cresswell and Blair, *Encyclopaedia of Banking Law*, at para. C345.

THE RIGHT TO ENFORCE SECURITY

As Professor Pennington points out in Chapter 6, the range of implied self-help remedies available to a bank is limited. Bank security documents usually seek to extend the range by express provision. They will often confer express powers of sale over items of security, where none would be implied. To make those powers effective, they will often also appoint the bank, or a nominated bank official, as attorney for the owner of the security, to complete the sale in the owner's name. Provided that the necessary formalities have been observed, there is no reason in principle why provisions of this nature should not be effective.

Bank facility letters and security documents also often contain provisions entitling the bank to certify the existence of certain states of affairs, so that the bank's certificate is conclusive as between it and the borrower or giver of security. For example, a well-drawn Memorandum of Deposit by way of security will often provide that: " . . . Upon any sale of [the security] . . . which you may make . . . under the provisions . . . above, a statutory declaration made by any of your officers that the Customer has made default and that the power of sale has become exercisable shall be conclusive evidence of the fact in favour of any purchaser or other person to whom [the security] may be transferred . . ." [79]

The amount of the customer's indebtedness may also be the subject of certification by the bank. The validity of such clauses has been upheld by the High Court of Australia in *Dobbs* v. *The National Bank of Australia Ltd*,[80] and by the English Court of Appeal in *Bache & Co (London) Ltd* v. *Banque Vernes et Commercial de Paris SA*,[81] where Lord Denning MR said:

> . . . This commercial practice (of inserting conclusive evidence clauses) is only acceptable because the bankers or brokers who insert them are known to be honest and reliable men of business who are most unlikely to make mistakes. Their standing is so high that their word is to be trusted. So much so that a notice of default given by a bank or broker must be honoured. It ranks as equivalent to, if not higher than, the certificate of an arbitrator or engineer in a building contract. As we have repeatedly held, such a certificate must be honoured, leaving any cross-claims to be settled later by an arbitrator. So if a bank or broker gives a notice of default in pursuance of a conclusive evidence clause, the guarantor must honour it, leaving any cross-claims by the customer to be adjusted in separate proceedings . . .

79. *Encyclopaedia of Forms and Precedents* (5th edn) Vol. 4 paras. 236, 242, 249.

80. (1935) 53 CLR 643, which held that the clause was not void as an attempt to oust the jurisdiction of the court. It was a clause by which a party to a contract has vested a discretionary judgment in an ascertainable person. The clause was conclusive not only as to amount but also as to the legal existence of the customer's indebtedness. However, in special circumstances such as a clear case of fraud, the validity of the certificate could be challenged. It was said that the clause should not be interpreted as "covering all grounds which go to the validity of the debt".

81. [1973] 2 Lloyd's Rep. 437. The decision of the Privy Council in *Tai Hing Cotton Mill Ltd* v. *Liu Chong Hing Bank* [1986] AC 80 also provides indirect support for the validity of such clauses.

This remark is difficult to justify, either in law[82] or in fact.[83]

It is often unattractive for a bank to rely on such clauses. If given full effect, a conclusive evidence clause buried in an ordinary guarantee could have the practical consequence of making that guarantee payable on first demand, irrespective of the principal debtor's true liability, as if it were a first-demand performance guarantee. *Dobbs* suggests that it will be possible to go behind the conclusive certificate in cases of established fraud. It is also possible that the inclusion of a conclusive evidence clause in a bank guarantee or other security could be challenged under ss. 2 and/or 3 of the Unfair Contract Terms Act 1977. As there is a duty to give a correct account, a conclusive evidence clause might be said to exclude or restrict liability for breach of the duty.[84]

In addition to conferring on the bank, wherever appropriate, the right to appoint a receiver to enforce the security, well-drawn bank security documents will also often seek to remove or attenuate many of the pre-conditions for the enforcement of that security which the law would otherwise imply. It is, for example, usual to exclude the restriction which would otherwise be imposed by s. 103 of the Law of Property Act 1925 upon the bank's power of sale of mortgaged property. Some restrictions, however, cannot be excluded. Those imposed by the Consumer Credit Act 1974,[85] for example, are mandatory. It is also unusual for a bank to be able simply to take possession of mortgaged property for the purpose of exercising its power of sale. Where the tenancy is binding on the bank as mortgagee, the bank is an "owner" for the purpose of the restrictions on the eviction of a "residential occupier" without due process of law imposed by the Protection from Eviction Act 1977.[86] In any event, if violence is used to secure entry into any sort of property, the bank may be liable to prosecution under the criminal law.[87] "Violence" for these purposes

82. This high judicial trust in banks is, perhaps, the benefit they receive in return for the equally high judicial expectations of their conduct. See, for example, the comments of Woolf LJ in *Lloyds Bank* v. *Waterhouse* [1991] Fam. Law 23: " . . . the Bank's internal rules . . . now provide that an intending guarantor *must* receive independent legal advice from a solicitor before executing the relevant document. *This is what I would expect of a responsible financial institution such as Lloyds Bank* . . . ".

83. Even the banks do not consider themselves infallible. There are, after all, several cases in the law reports in which banks have sought to recover payments made by them by mistake: see, e.g., *United Overseas Bank* v. *Jiwani* [1976] 1 WLR 964; *Barclays Bank* v. *W.J. Simms Son & Cooke (Southern) Ltd* [1980] QB 677.

84. Cf. *Westpac Banking Corporation* v. *Sugden* (1988) NSW Conv. R 55–377 where, applying the Contracts Review Act, Brownlie J held that the conclusive evidence clause went far beyond what was reasonably necessary for the protection of the bank.

85. E.g., s. 126.

86. See *Bolton Building Society* v. *Cobb* [1966] 1 WLR 1.

87. Criminal Law Act 1977, s. 6(4). The offence is committed only when the accused knows that there is another person on the premises when he uses or threatens violence and knows that he is opposed to the entry: s. 6(1)(a) and (b). The fact that the person has an interest or right in the property does not constitute lawful authority to use or threaten violence to secure entry: s. 6(2). The Criminal Law Act 1977 repealed and replaced the Forcible Entry Acts.

includes violence in the manner of entry, for example by breaking open the doors of a house.[88]

THE RIGHT TO ASSIST IN A RESCUE

The unprecedented number of corporate insolvencies[89] and the rise in unemployment[90] have had dramatic effects on bank profitability. Bank provisions for bad debts were over 1.5 per cent of domestic lending in 1990–1991 and will be substantially higher in 1991–1992.[91] Banks have always realised that when a customer acknowledges his indebtedness but simply has insufficient funds, a rescue may offer the best chance not only of repayment but of future profit. The Insolvency Act 1986 contains provisions, some of which are entirely new to English law, designed to assist in such ventures.

Prior to 1985, an individual debtor who wanted to make an arrangement with his creditors to avoid the costs and other consequences of bankruptcy could seek to invoke the provisions of the Deeds of Arrangement Act 1914. But this procedure was little used.[92] The mere execution of a deed of arrangement was an act of bankruptcy, and the proposals could easily be frustrated by a dissenting creditor petitioning for bankruptcy. The Bankruptcy Act 1914 itself contained provisions for schemes of composition or arrangement, once bankruptcy proceedings were under way[93]: but, again, they were little used.

By contrast, the provisions for individual voluntary arrangements in the Insolvency Act 1986[94] have proved popular with debtors.[95] The debtor may select a licensed insolvency practitioner to act as trustee or otherwise to supervise the implementation of the proposals which he wishes to make to his creditors. A viable proposal cannot be destroyed by a selfish creditor, because the debtor can obtain a moratorium on proceedings against himself or his property

88. *Hemmings* v. *Stoke Poges Golf Club* [1920] 1 KB 720.

89. 15,051 in 1990 and 15,755 in the first three-quarters of 1991, by comparison with only 9,427 in 1988: CSO, *Financial Statistics* (January 1992), Table 8.9.

90. Rising every month from the March 1990 low of about 1.6 million to a total of over 2.5 million by the end of 1991. This is still some way below July 1986's peak figure of 3.12 million: CSO, *Social Trends* (1992), Table 4.24. Bankruptcy orders numbered 12,058 in 1990 and 15,955 in the first three-quarters of 1991, by comparison with only 6,994 in 1988: CSO, *Financial Statistics* (January 1992), Table 8.9.

91. Smith New Court's estimate, published in *The Times* for 19 February 1992, was that domestic provisions for 1991 would total 2.58 per cent of British lending, more than two-and-a-half times higher than the worst figure during the recession of the early eighties.

92. There were only 51 in 1984: Sealy and Milman, *Annotated Guide to the 1986 Insolvency Legislation* (3rd ed.), p. 294.

93. Ss. 16, 17 and 21.

94. First enacted in the Insolvency Act 1985, ss. 110 *et seq*. These provisions do not follow the specific proposals of the Cork Committee (Final Report of the Review Committee on Insolvency Law and Practice, Cmnd. 8558 (1982)).

95. There were 404 in 1987, 779 in 1988, 1,224 in 1989, 1,927 in 1990, and 2,178 in the first three-quarters of 1991: CSO, *Financial Statistics* (January 1992), Table 8.9.

by obtaining an interim order of the court.[96] While the application for an interim order is pending, the court may stay such proceedings. When it has been made, the stay is automatic. Such a procedure is, of course, open to abuse: but the debtor's attempt to use the interim order procedure to frustrate attempts to bring bankruptcy proceedings proved unsuccessful in *Re a Debtor (No. 83 of 1988)*.[97]

For a proposal to be implemented, it must be approved by a majority in excess of three-quarters in value of the creditors' voting at a creditors' meeting summoned in accordance with the Insolvency Rules 1986.[98] The approved arrangement can be challenged by application to the court if it unfairly prejudices the interests of a creditor, or if there has been some material irregularity at or in relation to the meeting.[99] Subject to that, it binds every person who had notice of and was entitled to vote at the meeting, as if he were a party to the arrangements.[100]

For companies in difficulties, there are similar provisions for voluntary arrangements,[101] although the moratorium achieved for an individual debtor by an interim order can only be achieved for a company in difficulties by the presentation of a petition for an administration order with a view to achieving approval of the voluntary arrangement. Both kinds of voluntary arrangements under the Insolvency Act 1986 have this in common: creditors have no standing to propose them.[102] The proposal must come from the individual debtor or from the directors of the debtor company. A creditor bank's only remedy, therefore, is to suggest and, if appropriate, to vote in favour of and participate in such an arrangement. In practice, however, the initiative for such arrangements may often come from the bank, either because it is the principal creditor, or because it is the debtor's most readily available source of financial advice.

By contrast, an application for an administration order[103] in relation to an insolvent company may be made by a creditor,[104] as well as by the company

96. Insolvency Act 1986, ss. 252–263.

97. [1990] 1 WLR 708.

98. Insolvency Act 1986, s. 258: Insolvency Rules 1986, rule 5.18. The provision that the majority is to be measured by the value of the debts of those actually voting, rather than of those entitled to vote, makes it much easier than formally to obtain approval for a viable proposal.

99. Insolvency Act 1986, s. 262. See *Re Naeem (A Bankrupt) (No. 18 of 1988)* [1990] 1 WLR 48.

100. Insolvency Act 1986, s. 260.

101. Companies Act 1985, ss. 425–427A: Insolvency Act 1986, ss. 1–7.

102. Contrast, for example, the position under s. 425(1) of the Companies Act 1985, where the application may be made by the company, or any creditor, member, liquidator or administrator of the company.

103. This procedure is often described as akin to the reorganisation procedure under Chapter 11 of the United States Federal Bankruptcy Code. In fact, it has closer similarities to the South African "judicial manager", and the Australian "official management" procedures. No application to the court is necessary under the Australian procedure, by which the conduct of the matter is placed entirely in the hands of the creditors. Singapore has recently introduced legislation on the UK model.

104. Including a contingent or prospective creditor Insolvency Act 1986, s. 9(1).

or the directors.[105] In that respect, therefore, a lending bank may take the initiative.

If an administration order is made, the company is given a statutory breathing-space during which it is substantially protected from its creditors. On the making of an administration order, any petition for the winding-up of the company must be dismissed, any administrative receiver must vacate office, and any receiver of part of the company's property must vacate office on being required to do so by the administrator.[106] During the period for which an administration order is in force, (a) the company cannot be wound up, (b) no administrative receiver may be appointed, (c) no other steps may be taken to enforce any security over the company's property, or to repossess goods on hire-purchase,[107] unless the administrator consents or the court gives leave, and (c) no other proceedings, execution, or distress against the company or its property may be begun or continued, again unless the administrator or the court permits.[108]

An administration order may only be made where the court is satisfied that the company is, or is likely to become, unable to pay its debts, and considers that the making of the order would be likely[109] to achieve one or more of the following purposes: (a) the survival of the company and the whole or any part of its undertaking as a going concern,[110] (b) the approval of a voluntary arrangement under the Insolvency Act 1986 or the Companies Act 1985,[111] or (c) a more advantageous realisation of the company's assets than would be effected on a winding-up.[112]

105. That is, by all the directors, or by a majority acting on the basis of a properly passed resolution: *Re Instrumentation Electrical Services Ltd* (1988) 4 BCC 301.

106. Insolvency Act 1986, ss. 11(1) and 11(2).

107. Defined to include conditional sale agreements, chattel leasing agreements and retention of title agreements: Insolvency Act 1986, s. 10(4).

108. *Ibid.*, s. 11. See *Air Ecosse* v. *Civil Aviation Authority* (1987) 3 BCC 492; *Re Meesan Investments Ltd* (1988) 4 BCC 788; *Re Barrow Borough Transport Ltd* [1990] Ch. 227; *Re Paramount Airways Ltd, Bristol Airport Plc* v. *Powdrill* [1990] Ch. 744; *Re Atlantic Computer Systems Plc* [1990] BCC 859; and *Exchange Travel Agency Ltd* v. *Triton Property Trust Plc* [1991] BCC 341, for discussions of the difficulties to which these provisions give rise in balancing the rights of the individual creditor against those of the majority.

109. After some initial uncertainty, the weight of authority now seems to favour the view of Hoffman J in *Re Harris Simons Construction Ltd* [1989] 1 WLR 368, that the requirements of this section are satisfied if the court considers that there is a "real prospect" that one or more of the statutory purposes would be satisfied. This is a more "modest threshold of probability" than the "likely, on a balance of probabilities, to be achieved" test propounded by Peter Gibson J in *Re Consumer and Industrial Press Ltd* (1988) 4 BCC 68. See *per* Vinelott J in *Re Primlaks (UK) Ltd* (1989) 5 BCC 710; *per* Peter Gibson J in *Re S C L Building Services Ltd* (1989) 5 BCC 746; and *per* Harman J in *Re Rowbotham Baxter Ltd* [1990] BCC 113.

110. Mark Homan's research paper, "A Survey of Administrations Under the Insolvency Act 1986: The Result of Administration Orders made in 1987" (noted in Goode, *Principles of Corporate Insolvency*, at p. 112) shows that in 55 per cent of the administrations surveyed, the procedure enabled all or part of the business to survive.

111. See note 101 above.

112. Insolvency Act 1986, s. 8.

The role of the administrator[113] is crucial. The debtor company retains ownership and control of its assets. However, the management of the company[114] and its affairs, business and property[115] is placed in the hands of the administrator, who is deemed to act as agent for the company. The directors are not automatically removed from office: but the administrator may remove (and replace) them. Neither the directors nor the members of the company can do anything which would interfere with the exercise by the administrator of his powers, unless the administrator consents.[116] The administrator is given the same power as an administrative receiver, liquidator or supervisor of a voluntary arrangement to obtain supplies of gas, water, electricity and telephones on payment for the present supplies, irrespective of past debts.[117] He is also given similar powers to get in the company's assets,[118] and to require co-operation and information from those concerned with the company and its dealings.[119] He may apply to the court for directions,[120] and his actions may be controlled by the court on the application of a creditor or member of the company, if his conduct of the company's affairs has been, or is, or will be, unfairly prejudicial to the interests of the creditors or members, or some part of the creditors or members.[121]

The administrator is given the unique power to override the rights of the holder of a security over the company's property,[122] and to dispose of the property in question as if the company owned it unencumbered. Unless the security is (or was when created) a floating charge, the administrator needs the leave of the court: and there are provisions designed to preserve the rights of the security holder in the proceeds of the disposal (or if the disposal is for less than full value, the full value). However, the power is a draconian one.[123]

As an office holder, an administrator is under a duty to report the conduct of the company's directors, if it appears to him that it makes them unfit to be concerned in the management of a company.[124] He may also apply to the court for orders restoring the company to the position it would have been in but for any relevant transaction with the company at an undervalue,[125] or voidable prefer-

113. Who must be a qualified insolvency practitioner: Insolvency Act 1986, s. 230.

114. The administrator's powers do not extend to acts which the company itself is not competent to perform: *Re Home Treat Ltd* [1991] BCC 165.

115. Unlike a liquidator, an administrator has no statutory power of disclaimer.

116. Insolvency Act 1986, ss. 14 and 17 and Sch. 1.

117. *Ibid.*, s. 233.

118. *Ibid.*, s. 234.

119. *Ibid.*, ss. 235–237.

120. *Ibid.*, s. 14(3).

121. *Ibid.*, s. 27.

122. Or the rights of the owners under a hire-purchase, conditional sale agreement, chattel lease agreement, or retention of title agreement: *Ibid.*, s. 15(9).

123. *Ibid.*, s. 15. See, generally, *Re Consumer and Industrial Press Ltd (No 2)* (1988) 4 BCC 72; and *Re A V R Aviation Ltd* (1988) 4 BCC 708.

124. Company Directors Disqualification Act 1986, s. 6(3)(c).

125. Insolvency Act 1986, s. 238(1).

ence of one of the company's creditors or guarantors,[126] or transaction with intent to defeat creditors.[127]

Within three months (or such longer period as may be allowed by the court), the administrator must put forward a formal statement of his proposals for achieving the statutory purpose for which he was appointed, for approval by a creditors' meeting.[128] When the administration order will serve no further useful purpose, the order may be discharged. The creditors' former enforcement rights will then revive, except to the extent that they are bound by a voluntary arrangement reached as a consequence of the administration, or are discharged by a subsequent liquidation.

A lending bank which holds a floating charge over the company's assets can prevent the making of an administration order.[129] For the interim protection given to the company simply by the making of the application for an administration order does not prevent the appointment of an administrative receiver[130]: and a petition for an administration order must be dismissed if there is an administrative receiver of the company, unless the court is satisfied that the person who appointed the receiver consents to the making of the order, or his charge is liable to be set aside.[131] Because of the effective right of veto which a floating charge gives to a bank over the appointment of an administrator (who might deal with the charged property against their wishes), banks often now insist upon taking fixed and floating charges where in the past they would have been content with a straightforward fixed charge over specific property. However, experience suggests that lending banks are often content to allow the appointment of an administrator, even where it would be open to them to appoint an administrative receiver.

THE RIGHT TO SUE

If persuasion or self-help remedies cannot achieve repayment, the lending banker may have to resort to the courts to recover his money. Although "banking" is specifically mentioned in the list of "commercial actions" in Order 72(1)(2) of the Rules of the Supreme Court 1965, most actions by banks to

126. *Ibid.*, ss. 238(1) and 239.
127. *Ibid.*, ss. 423 and 424(1)(a).
128. *Ibid.*, ss. 23–26.
129. Notice of the petition for the administration order must be given forthwith to any person who has appointed or may be entitled to appoint a receiver, and a copy of the petition and supporting affidavit and exhibits must be served on them (and on any receiver, provisional liquidator, or person petitioning for a winding-up order) not less than five clear days before the hearing: Insolvency Act 1986, s. 9(4) and Insolvency Rules 1986, rule 2.6. The period for service can be, and often is, abridged.
130. Insolvency Act 1986, s. 10.
131. *Ibid.*, s. 9(3).

recover moneys lent are not begun in the Commercial Court, but elsewhere in the Queen's Bench Division or in the County Court. Claims to enforce agreements regulated by the Consumer Credit Act 1974 and securities held for such agreements must be begun in the County Court,[132] as must actions for possession of mortgaged dwellinghouses outside Greater London,[133] Where an order for sale is required to enforce an equitable charge,[134] the County Court's jurisdiction is limited to cases where the amount owing in respect of the mortgage or charge at the commencement of the proceedings does not exceed £30,000.[135] Other mortgage actions, including actions seeking nothing more than a money judgment, if the money is secured by a mortgage, are assigned to the Chancery Division.[136] Where neither statute nor rules prescribe the division of the High Court in which an action must be begun, the plaintiff may choose the division in which to bring his claim. Once, however, he has made his choice, applications to transfer are discouraged.[137]

Most High Court actions to recover money will be begun by writ of summons. If the defendant does not give notice of intention to defend within the prescribed period,[138] the plaintiff claiming a debt may enter final judgment in default for the amount claimed and for interest, provided that the rate of interest claimed does not exceed the rate payable on judgment debts at the date of the writ.[139] If the rate of interest is higher than that, or if the writ does not set out the figures necessary to permit the exact calculation of the interest claimed[140] (e.g., because the claim is for compound interest), the plaintiff may enter final judgment for the amount claimed in the writ, and interlocutory judgment for the interest claimed, to be assessed at a subsequent hearing. Prior to judgment, interest may be payable on the amount claimed by virtue of a contract (for example, as an implied term of the contract of loan[141]), or as damages for dishonour of a bill of exchange,[142] or under the provisions of s. 35A of the Supreme Court Act 1981.

A defendant seeking to set aside a default judgment that has been entered in accordance with the rules will almost always be required (a) to explain his fail-

132. Consumer Credit Act 1974, s. 141. Where the action relates to a consumer credit agreement, any writ issued in the High Court must be endorsed with a certificate that the action is not one to which s. 141 applies: Rules of the Supreme Court 1965, O. 6, rule 1(1)(e).

133. County Courts Act 1984, s. 21, as amended by the High Court and County Court Jurisdiction Order 1991.

134. Under s. 90 or 91 of the Law of Property Act 1925.

135. High Court and County Courts Jurisdiction Order 1991, art 2(4).

136. Supreme Court Act 1981, s. 61(1); Rules of the Supreme Court 1965, O. 88, rule 2.

137. See, e.g., *Barclays Bank Plc* v. *Bemister* [1989] 1 WLR 128.

138. Fourteen days from service, unless extended or the writ has been served outside the jurisdiction (in which case a different period, of varying length depending upon the place of service, is prescribed): Rules of the Supreme Court 1965, O. 12, rule 5.

139. Rules of the Supreme Court 1965, O. 13, rule 1.

140. As prescribed by the *Practice Note* [1983] 1 WLR 377.

141. See *National Bank of Greece* v. *Pinios Shipping (The Maira)* [1990] 1 AC 637 for a banker's right to charge compound interest both before and after demand.

142. Under s. 57 of the Bills of Exchange Act 1882.

ure to give notice of intention to defend, and (b) to demonstrate that he has an arguable defence. In practice, most such applications are dealt with on the same basis as an application by the plaintiff for summary judgment.[143] However, if the judgment which has been entered is irregular, for example because it has been entered too early, the defendant has an automatic right to have the judgment set aside without consideration of the merits of his defence,[144] provided that he applies promptly upon becoming aware of the irregularity. Even so, the court has jurisdiction to allow the irregularity to be corrected, where it is the result of a slip or mistake, and it is just to do so.[145] So a judgment entered by mistake for too much can often be corrected. If the application is made before the judgment has been notified to the defendant, or if the defendant consents, it can be made *ex parte* to a Master. Otherwise, it must be made on summons.

SUMMARY JUDGMENT

Where the defendant debtor does give timely notice of intention to defend, the plaintiff bank will often wish to apply, if it can, for summary judgment under Order 14 of the Rules of the Supreme Court 1965.[146] This procedure, if successful, avoids the bank having to incur the costs and delay[147] of a full trial. Unless the case is taken on appeal to the Court of Appeal or beyond, all stages of an application for summary judgment are heard in chambers, whatever the division in which the action is proceeding. It therefore has the added merit for banks, who are understandably not anxious to publicise the loans which they have made which have gone wrong, of privacy. Finally, all evidence on such applications is given by affidavit. This is a double advantage for banks, whose evidence often comes from managers and other officials who can remember little more than is recorded in their internal records and memoranda. Those records can form the substance of the bank's evidence, without adverse comment concerning the absence of any independent recollection, and the bank's managers and officials are spared the strain of giving oral evidence.

Applications for summary judgment are made by summons, supported by

143. Rules of the Supreme Court 1965, O. 13, rule 9. There are dicta which suggest that the burden upon the defendant to establish an arguable defence on the merits may be higher under this rule than under O. 14: see, e.g., *Alpine Bulk Transport Co Inc* v. *Saudi Eagle Shipping Co (The Saudi Eagle)* [1986] 2 Lloyd's Rep. 221.

144. *Anlaby* v. *Praetorious* (1888) 20 QBD 764.

145. Rules of the Supreme Court 1965, O. 2 (power to correct mistakes) and O. 13, rule 9 (power to vary default judgments): *Ban Hin Lee Bank Berhad* v. *Sonali Bank* (*The Independent*, 28 November 1988, CA): *Singh* v. *Atombrook* [1989] 1 WLR 810.

146. Or its County Court equivalent, O. 9, rule 14 of the County Court Rules 1981.

147. Often the most material factor, where the defendant's resources are limited and the unpaid debt is increasing through the application of compound interest.

an affidavit which must verify the claim and depose to the deponent's belief that there is no defence.[148] The summons and affidavit must be served on the defendant not less than 10 clear days before the return day of the summons.[149] The affidavit can, and often does, consist of statements of information and belief concerning matters of which the deponent has no personal knowledge.[150]

The official practice form which gives a precedent for such an affidavit is formal and short, and affidavits in that form are very frequently used. However, where any substantial opposition is anticipated, many bank lawyers prefer to prepare a more lengthy initial affidavit, exhibiting those of the contemporary documents which are relevant to the "defences" which they anticipate may be raised. If this course is not followed, the first hearing of the summons may have to be adjourned. The defendant's affidavit evidence is frequently served at the door of the court immediately prior to that hearing[151]: and if the bank's first affidavit has been purely formal, it will not have put in evidence the material necessary to deal with the allegations put forward. With delays presently in excess of three months in obtaining lengthy appointments for hearings in chambers, a plaintiff bank will be anxious to avoid any unnecessary adjournments of its application.

The purpose of Order 14 is to enable a plaintiff to obtain summary judgment without trial, if he can prove his claim clearly, and if the defendant is unable to set up a bona fide defence or raise an issue against the claim which ought to be tried.[152] The wording of the rule places the onus upon the defendant to show cause why judgment should not be given against him.[153] But the reality is that a plaintiff will not obtain summary judgment unless he can satisfy the court, despite the evidence and arguments of the defendant, that the averment in his affidavit that there is no defence to the action can be made out without the need for a trial. Put at its simplest, the court will ask itself, "is there a triable issue?". If there is, or if there may be, the court will give leave to defend.

The matters relied upon by a defendant in attempting to raise a triable issue may be matters of law. For example he may assert that the bank was under a duty to him to explain its security documentation before it permitted him to sign it.[154] If so the court may, if it thinks it appropriate, decide those matters summarily.[155] This procedure may be very useful where, for example, the issue

148. Rules of the Supreme Court 1965, O. 14, rule 2(1).
149. Rules of the Supreme Court 1965, O. 14, rule 2(3).
150. Rules of the Supreme Court 1965, O. 14, rule 2(2).
151. Despite the direction to the contrary endorsed on every Order 14 summons.
152. *Roberts* v. *Plant* [1895] 1 QB 597. "The policy of Order 14 is to prevent delay in cases where there is no defence": *per* Robert Goff LJ in *European Asian Bank AG* v. *Punjab & Sind Bank (No 2)* [1983] 1 WLR 642, at p. 654.
153. Rules of the Supreme Court 1986, O. 14, rule 4.
154. See *Barclays Bank* v. *Khaira, The Times*, 19 December 1991, where T.R.A. Morison QC, sitting as a deputy judge of the Chancery Division, held that no such duty existed in law.
155. See *European Asian Bank AG* v. *Punjab & Sind Bank (No 2)* [1983] 1 WLR 642, and the new O. 14A which makes specific provision for the summary determination of issue of law.

is whether a demand under a performance bond is or is not a conforming demand.

Alternatively, the defendant may try to set up issues of fact, or mixed law and fact, such as the frequently encountered (and always mysterious) allegation that the bank manager promised that the guarantee would never be enforced, or would only be enforced once all the other securities held for the debt had been realised. A court will refuse to conduct a trial of disputed issues of fact on affidavit evidence alone, and if the defendant's evidence is credible a court will always give leave to defend where such an issue is raised. However, as Lloyd LJ recently observed, in *Standard Chartered Bank* v. *Yaacoub*[156]:

> . . . It is sometimes said that in an application under O.14 the Court is bound to accept the assertion of a Defendant on affidavit unless it is self-contradictory or inconsistent with other parts of the Defendant's own evidence, and that the Court cannot reject an assertion on the simple ground that it is incredible. The decision of Webster J in *Paclantic Financing Co Inc* v. *Moscow Narodny Bank Ltd*[157] is sometimes cited as authority for the proposition. But it is to be noticed that Webster J's formulation did not receive the imprimatur of the Court of Appeal.[158] In the subsequent case of *Bhogal* v. *Punjab National Bank*,[159] Bingham LJ put the matter more broadly. He said: " . . . the correctness of factual assertions such as these cannot be decided on an application for summary judgment unless the assertions are shown to be manifestly false, either because of their inherent implausibility or because of their inconsistency with the contemporary documents, or other compelling evidence . . . " In the present case I ask myself whether it is credible that an oral agreement was made . . . as alleged by Mr Naidoo . . . I have come to the conclusion that it is not. I reach that conclusion for three reasons. In the first place the evidence is inherently implausible, and implausible to a high degree . . . In the second place, if such an important agreement had been made, one would have expected it to have been in the forefront of Mr Naidoo's mind. Yet . . . the alleged oral agreement is referred to only as a subsidiary ground of defence . . . In the third place, the alleged oral agreement is wholly inconsistent with the subsequent correspondence between the parties.

A good affidavit, exhibiting the contemporary correspondence and entries in the bank's records, may therefore often suffice to defeat such allegations even at the stage of summary judgment. Even if the court is not sufficiently satisfied to give judgment, it may make the defendant's leave to defend the action conditional upon a substantial payment into court by way of security for the bank's claim, if satisfied that the defence put forward is "shadowy".[160]

156. CA, 3 August 1990 (unreported).
157. [1983] 1 WLR 1063.
158. At [1984] 1 WLR 930.
159. [1988] 2 All ER 296.
160. Rules of the Supreme Court 1965, O. 14, rule 4(3): *Van Lynn Developments* v. *Pelias Construction Co* [1969] 1 QB 607. However, if the court is not prepared to give judgment against the defendant, it should not impose a condition which it knows that the defendant cannot fulfil: *M V Yorke Motors* v. *Edwards* [1982] 1 WLR 444. Nor should it impose conditions where the defence is more than shadowy, even if it is less than probable: *Rafidain Bank* v. *Agom Universal Sugar Trading Co*, *The Times*, 23 December 1986, CA.

MAREVA INJUNCTIONS

A *Mareva*[161] injunction is an interlocutory order[162] of the court granted either before judgment, or in aid of execution of a judgment, which restrains the party enjoined from disposing of or dealing with his own assets.[163] It confers no priority in insolvency, and it is not the policy or purpose of the *Mareva* jurisdiction to prevent the payment by the defendant of his existing debts.[164] Rather, its purpose is to prevent a defendant from taking steps "designed to ensure" that either a subsequent judgment or order of the court, or an existing judgment or order, is rendered less effective than would be the case.[165] It may extend to assets of any kind, whether within or outside the jurisdiction of the court. But the jurisdiction to grant "worldwide" injunctions will only be exercised in special circumstances, and on terms which respect the foreign court's jurisdiction and prevent the order operating oppressively.[166]

Banks are often the recipients of such injunctions, granted against their customers (or against associates of their customers): and the problems which such orders cause for banks are well known.[167] However, in an appropriate case, they can be a valuable weapon in the bank's own armoury for recovery of monies due to it.

There are two conditions which must be satisfied before a *Mareva* injunction can be granted. First, the plaintiff must show a good arguable case that he will recover judgment against the defendant for a particular sum (or already have such a judgment). Secondly, he must show that there is a real risk that the defendant will remove or dissipate his assets, so as to make it likely that any such judgment will go unsatisfied.[168] The application is usually made *ex parte*: and, as with all *ex parte* applications, the applicant is under a duty to the court to make full and frank disclosure of all material circumstances.[169] He must also give an undertaking to pay any damages ordered by the court, if the court thereafter takes the view that the defendant has suffered any by reason of the

161. Named, with English logic and common-sense, after the *second* case in which such an order was made, *Mareva Compania Naviera SA* v. *International Bulkcarriers SA (The Mareva)* [1980] 1 All ER 213: the first case, *Nippon Yusen Kaisha* v. *Karageorgis* [1975] 1 WLR 1093, having a less readily shortenable name.

162. Made under s. 37 of the Supreme Court Act 1981.

163. Steven Gee, *Mareva Injunctions & Anton Piller Relief* (2nd edn), p. 9.

164. *Iraqi Ministry of Defence* v. *Arcepy Shipping ("The Angel Bell")* [1981] QB 65: *K/S A/S Admiral Shipping* v. *Portlink Ferries* [1984] 2 Lloyd's Rep. 166. However, the court will not allow the payment of debts, for example to associated companies, to be used as a device to evade the jurisdiction: see, e.g., *Atlas Maritime* v. *Avalon Maritime (No 3)* [1991] 1 WLR 917.

165. *Derby & Co* v. *Weldon (Nos 3 and 4)* [1990] Ch. 65.

166. *Republic of Haiti* v. *Duvalier* [1990] 1 QB 202: *Babanaft International Co SA* v. *Bassatne* [1990] Ch. 13: *Derby & Co* v. *Weldon* [1990] Ch. 48.

167. See Cresswell and Blair, *Encyclopaedia of Banking Law*, at paras. C321 to C340.22.

168. *Third Chandris Shipping Corporation* v. *Unimarine* [1979] 1 QB 645; *Ninemia Maritime Corporation* v. *Trave GmbH* [1983] 1 WLR 1412.

169. See, e.g., *Bank Mellat* v. *Nikpour* [1985] FSR 87, where Donaldson LJ stressed the need for such disclosure from those invoking "one of the law's two 'nuclear' weapons".

order which the plaintiff ought to pay. The combination of these two obligations has, in the past, sometimes proved troublesome for banks.[170]

Such an order may be combined with an order against the defendant for disclosure of his assets. In appropriate circumstances, it may also be joined with an order on the principles established in *Bankers Trust* v. *Shapira*,[171] requiring disclosure of documents by third parties through whose hands the assets sought to be traced and frozen have passed.

JUDGMENTS AND EXECUTION

Once judgment has been obtained, whether summarily or after trial, the bank may enforce its judgment by any of the available methods. It may apply to examine the defendant debtor as to his means. It may issue a writ of *Fi. Fa.* [*fieri facias*], requiring the sheriff to take the debtor's goods in execution. Where money is owed to the debtor by third parties, the bank may apply to the court for a garnishee order, requiring the debt to be paid to the bank. Where the debtor owns an interest in property, the bank may seek a charging order from the court, imposing an equitable charge on the debtor's interest to secure its claim.

Despite this wealth of remedies, banks often regard the process of obtaining a judgment simply as a clearing of the decks. The judgment sweeps away the customer's protests that he does not owe the money, and so facilitates constructive negotiations for a proper re-scheduling of the indebtedness. That, after all, is what banking is all about: and the bank's lawyers are simply a means to that end.

BANKRUPTCY AND LIQUIDATION

If all else has failed, a lending bank whose indebtedness has fallen due and not been repaid is likely to be able to rely upon its status as a creditor[172] to entitle it to petition the court for a bankruptcy or winding-up order against the debtor.

The costs of liquidation, and the principle of *pari passu* distribution of the insolvent's assets, make these formal procedures usually a last resort for the banker. At one time, it was the practice of the clearing banks never to seek a bankruptcy order against an individual debtor unless they considered that he had been guilty of sharp practice or fraud. Harder times make for harder

170. See, e.g., *Barclays Bank* v. *Illingworth*, CA, 10 May 1985 (unreported): *Barclays Bank Plc* v. *Rosenberg*, *Financial Times*, 12 June 1985, CA.

171. [1980] 1 WLR 1274. The problems caused by this case for banks on whom such orders are served make it easy to forget that the applicant plaintiff was itself a bank, seeking to trace money of which it had (it alleged) been defrauded.

172. Under the Insolvency Act 1986, ss. 123(1)(a) and (e), and 124(1) for winding-up, and under ss. 264(1)(a), 267 and 268 for bankruptcy.

attitudes: and not all banks are now so forbearing. In some cases, it may be the only way to have an effective investigation into what has become of the debtor's assets. If the debtor's assets have been diminished by transactions at an undervalue[173] or preferences,[174] there may be no option, if the case is unsuitable for an administration order. It may be the only way to obtain a proper enquiry into the directors' conduct, or to obtain possession of the bankrupt's house against his wife and children.[175] However, most bankers will feel a sense of failure if their customer ends up as one of the insolvency statistics which have been quoted earlier in this chapter.

THE REMEDY

If there were simple solutions for the problems which the banks in this country are now facing, no doubt the banks would have adopted them by now. The remedy for those problems, if there is one, lies outside the hands of mere lawyers. Even so, the range of remedies available to banks and their lawyers includes, as I have tried to show, many constructive elements. Before too long, our time may again be occupied setting transactions up, not merely doing our best to salvage planks in the shipwrecks.[176]

RICHARD SALTER

173. Insolvency Act 1986, ss. 238 and 339.
174. Insolvency Act 1986, ss. 239 and 340.
175. Insolvency Act 1986, ss. 336–338.
176. See *Brace* v. *Duchess of Marlborough* (1728) 2 P Wms. 491, where Jekyll MR ascribes to Hale CJ this graphic description of the pre-1926 seizure by a later equitable mortgagee of priority over an earlier equitable mortgagee by the acquisition of a legal mortgage with priority to both. It was said of this doctrine (as it is now said by some of the present recession) that it "could not happen in any other country but this": *Wortley* v. *Birkhead* (1754) 2 Ves. Sen. 571, at p. 574, *per* Lord Hardwicke LC.

CHAPTER 3

DISCOVERY IN ENGLAND

There are three questions which I propose to answer here:

(a) What is discovery?
(b) Why is it important?
(c) How is it done?

This chapter answers these questions from the point of view of clients and the problems which commercial entities are likely to experience. It is limited to the discovery process in the Supreme Court, and does not deal with tribunals, arbitration and the like, nor with the special position of the Crown, foreign states and other privileged litigants.

WHAT IS MEANT BY DISCOVERY?

Order 24, r. 1 of the Rules of the Supreme Court 1965 (RSC) provides that:

> After the close of pleadings in an action begun by writ there shall, subject to and in accordance with the provisions of this order, be discovery by the parties to the action of the documents which are or have been in their possession, custody or power relating to the matters in question in the action.

The very wide scope of that order can, in suitable cases, be confined with a view to protecting the interests of litigants. Order 24, r. 8, for example, provides that discovery will only be ordered if it is necessary for doing justice or saving cost and permits a party to refuse unnecessary production of documents, which he does by listing all the relevant documents but objecting to the production of particular ones on the grounds that an opponent does not need to see them. To give a general example: if production of documents relating to a very minor or tangential issue would be enormously onerous or expensive the court may refuse to order discovery.

More specifically, litigants are often concerned that documents which they are required to produce in accordance with the RSC may be misused by their opponents. They may, for example, contain sensitive financial information or trade secrets of commercial benefit to their rivals. I will look later at the restrictions imposed by the court on the use of documents, but at this stage I need say only that the court can make special orders on the application of a party: for example, in *Church of Scientology* v. *DHSS*[1] where the DHSS was concerned that the Church of Scientology might use documents disclosed on discovery for the purpose of harassing people who had complained about the activities of the church, a special order was made that documents be disclosed to the plaintiff's legal adviser only and not to the party itself. In *Davies* v. *Eli Lilly & Co.*,[2] the court had to decide whether an investigative journalist who had in the past been critical of the defendant drug manufacturers should be allowed to inspect their documents in his capacity as a general adviser to the plaintiffs and co-ordinator of their experts: the court allowed the journalist to inspect the documents, but only on terms which sought to protect their confidentiality.

To return to the rule: a party must disclose all documents "relating to the matters in question in the action". What matters are in question in the action will—or at least should—be defined by the pleadings, but please note that the test is not whether the documents are "relevant", but whether they "relate" to a matter in question which is a wider test—and it is an objective and not subjective test. It is not for the litigant to decide whether, in his view, the documents are in fact relevant: he has to assess whether the documents could be regarded as relating to a matter in issue. In the words of Lord Justice Brett in *Compagnie Financiere* v. *Peruvian Guano*,[3] a document must be disclosed if it contains information which may (not must) either directly or indirectly advance one party's case or damage the other's or may lead to a train of enquiry which may have either of these two consequences. In other words the test is wider than direct relevance to the pleaded issues.

This principle often causes consternation, particularly to foreign, but occasionally to English, litigants unfamiliar with the litigation process. I shall look later at the obligations imposed by the English law on a party to preserve documents when it expects to be involved in litigation, whether as a plaintiff or as a defendant.

What is a "document": are the obligations of discovery limited only to pieces of paper? The question of what is a document has been reviewed in a great many cases and the definition embraces, more or less—although there are some grey areas—any record of evidence or information. Photographs, film, tapes and records must be disclosed. A computer tape must be disclosed if the program it contains or the data it stores is relevant, and it does not cease to be "a document" merely because equipment is necessary to render it intelligible—*Grant* v. *South Western and Country Properties*[4] and film records taken at a festival in Windsor Great Park have been held to be a "document"—*Senior* v. *Holdsworth, ex parte ITN*[5].

Very recently the courts had to decide whether a computer database which

1. [1979] 1 WLR 723.
2. [1987] 1 All ER 801.
3. [1882] 11 QB 55, 63.
4. [1974] 2 All ER 465, 474.
5. [1976] QB 23.

might contain information capable of being retrieved and converted into reasonable form was a computer within the meaning of Order 24: Mr Justice Vinelott in *Derby & Co. and Others* v. *Weldon No. 9*[6] had to decide not only whether he could order discovery, but also whether he could direct one of the parties to transfer the database from their own computer to that of an independent expert—in his words:

> During the relevant period four systems were maintained for the money market, foreign exchange, terminal and physical trades, and they were processed each month. Back-up files at the month-end would be recorded on diskettes which were stored. Selected data was fed into the financial recording system and on to an on-line enquiry system. Month-end data files can be restored from the back-up diskettes though not all back-up diskettes can now be found and some have deteriorated to the point where restoration of the data damages the diskette reader. The restoration of this data gives rise to another problem. The IBM System 36 will only hold two months' restored back-up data in addition to current operational data, and recreating all the back-up data would accordingly take a considerable time. Moreover, often when a file has been recreated further time is needed to reprogramme the system so that current programs can access the recreated data file while continuing to access current data files.[7]

He first had to decide whether the database was a document, and concluded that it was as he found that in "most businesses" tape or disk now takes the place of the carbon copy of outgoing letters which used to be retained in files. Then he had to decide in what circumstances a party seeking discovery is entitled to inspect and take copies of the database, but he recognised that there were very considerable problems arising out of new technology. First, some means would have to be found of screening out irrelevant or privileged material when the tape was re-run. As the judge said, "the party seeking discovery cannot be allowed simply to seat himself at his opponent's computer console and be provided will all necessary access keys".

Secondly, it might be that there would be material on the computer not accessible by current programs, but which could be retrieved by reprogramming; *prima facie* in the judge's view the powers of the court would extend to requiring that the computer be reprogrammed so as to enable the relevant information to be retrieved. Thirdly, it might be necessary for the court to give directions as to when access to the computer should be granted. Acute problems will arise where a computer is in daily use.

Fourthly, safeguards would have to be embodied in order to ensure that tapes or diskettes which might have deteriorated in storage would not be damaged by use and that the use of them would not damage the computer's reader. Fifthly, provision would have to be made for the results of any analysis of the computer print-outs, any print-outs made, and so on to be available to the other party in good time so that he was not taken by surprise at trial.

It is not enough for clients merely to dump on their lawyer all the "docu-

6. [1991] 1 WLR 652; [1991] 2 All ER 901.
7. *Ibid.*, p. 657.

ments", however imaginatively defined, which are in their immediate control, as they have to produce all those in their "possession, custody or power"—and what does that mean?

First, it is clear that the owner of a document who holds it has possession, so a bank would have possession of its own documents, although an employee of the bank might have custody on his employer's behalf. Secondly, possession comprehends a litigant's documents if they are in the possession of his bailee or agents; for example, if a litigant can require his accountants or surveyors to produce documents to him he may well be obliged to do so and to disclose them in his list of documents.

Difficult questions can arise as to how far a litigant must go to obtain documents. In *Mertens* v. *Haigh*[8] Mr Mertens, a New Orleans merchant, sued Haigh & Co., Liverpool cotton brokers, for an account. The defendants sought discovery from Mr Mertens who claimed that he could not produce certain documents because they were held by his agent in New Orleans and the only way that he could obtain them would be for him to go there. Unfortunately, the American Civil War was raging at the time and Mr Mertens was a proscribed individual. The Vice-Chancellor held that was no excuse and on appeal the court ruled that it was his duty "to satisfy the court that he had taken all proper means to acquire" the documents and that he had not done.

A much more recent authority is *Lonrho* v. *Shell Petroleum*[9] where the plaintiff sought discovery of documents belonging to foreign subsidiaries of a multinational oil company for use in an arbitration between the plaintiff and the parent. The subsidiaries refused the parent's request to make their documents available. The plaintiff argued that a subsidiary's documents are always in the parent's power as the parent can, if necessary, obtain possession by winding up its subsidiary—but the House of Lords was unimpressed. Lord Diplock said that "the expression 'power' must in my view mean a presently enforceable legal right to obtain from whoever actually holds the document inspection of it without the need to obtain the consent of anyone else."[10]

And, finally, do not overlook the words "or have been".

WHY DOES DISCOVERY MATTER?

There are three main reasons: first that, despite the present tendency of the rules committees to ensure that litigants put their "cards on the table" in litigation pleadings can often be very reticent as to the true nature of the case being advanced by the parties to a legal action and discovery provides the first—and very important—opportunity of gauging the substance of one's opponents' case: they may have pleaded that on a particular day an agreement in specified terms

8. [1863] 3 De GJ & Sm 528.
9. [1980] QB 358.
10. *Ibid.*, p. 635.

was reached, when among their own documents you will find a contemporaneous note of the meeting which shows that, according to their own records, the terms of the agreement were different from those pleaded. In addition, documents may be produced by one party to litigation which will demonstrate clearly to the other party's legal advisers that the instructions he obtained from his clients were wrong—so causing him to alter, radically, the advice he has given up to that stage. It is perhaps not surprising that negotiations for a settlement often start at the stage of discovery.

Secondly, any party who does not give proper discovery is at risk: if he declines to take his solicitor's advice and refuses to disclose documents which he is advised are relevant then the solicitor must withdraw from the case.[11]

Thirdly, if the client neglects to give proper discovery, not only his solicitor but he himself will be seriously embarrassed at trial; his commercial reputation or credibility will be harmed. A classic example is to be found in the case of *Woods* v. *Martins Bank Limited and Another*[12] where, in the course of an action, certain documents which had not been disclosed in the bank's list, although they most clearly should have been, came to light. Salmon J had this to say:

> It cannot be too clearly understood that solicitors owe a duty to the court, as officers of the court, carefully to go through the documents disclosed by their clients to make sure, as far as possible, that no relevant documents have been omitted from their client's affidavit.[13]

A solicitor who fails to do so may be personally penalised as to costs as well as being reported to the Law Society, and if he fails to advise his client properly about orders for discovery may himself be committed (Order 24, r. 16(4))—powerful reasons one might think for a solicitor to take discovery seriously.

HOW IS IT DONE?

The Rules of the Supreme Court provide that discovery should, in many cases, be automatic and should be completed 14 days after close of pleading: relevant documents then have to be listed in a standard form and the list is served on the other parties to the litigation, who then have a right to inspect. I have annexed a sample list to this chapter. The time limits can be varied by consent or by order.

A prudent solicitor will, long before the time has arrived for giving discovery, have explained the process to his client so as to ensure, among other things, that the relevant papers are collected together and that any regular destruction policy is halted in respect of matters in dispute and that they are not

11. *Rockwell Machine Tool Co.* v. *E.P. Barrus (Concessionnaires)* [1968] 1 WLR 693.
12. [1954] 1 WLR 1018.
13. *Ibid.*, p. 1022.

"weeded" by a helpful client. Because of the considerations I mentioned earlier, and, in particular, the obligations imposed on a solicitor as an officer of the court which mean that he must on occasions make himself obnoxious to his client in pressing for documents, he cannot rely on an assurance that the client has collected together all relevant documents; nor, without further enquiry, can he accept that relevant documents may have been destroyed as he may have to swear, or have his client swear, an affidavit dealing with the precise circumstances in which they were destroyed.

It is the practice of my own firm to send clients a detailed note explaining the discovery process and, in the case of certain clients with whose operations we are very familiar, to include a checklist of the types of documents which we know from our experience are likely to be on their files (I have annexed a sample checklist to this chapter)—although even then, as I will illustrate shortly, the facts of a particular case may send the solicitor rambling down unfamiliar byways of a client's systems searching for rare and exotic documents.

Once the documents have been obtained then a solicitor has to group them together in a sensible fashion; that is a matter for his judgement but he will have to bear in mind, for example, that it can sometimes be significant to know precisely where in a file a document was found, what was stapled to it and so on.

The solicitor will then engage, with his client's assistance, in a treasure hunt, as almost certainly a careful reading of the documents will show that the files are incomplete—memoranda will, for example, refer to documents enclosed with them, accounts, cash-flow forecasts and the like—and they must be found or their absence explained. Letters will acknowledge other letters which are not in the file, or a document may show that a number of copies were made and distributed to different individuals: those copies will have to be found as they may have been annotated by the individuals concerned and, if so, will need to be disclosed as separate documents.

The very nature of the case may suggest further lines of enquiry—for example, in one instance when the author was acting for a bank the matter in issue was whether the bank had made a loan to an individual or to one of his companies: the bank asserted that they had loaned the money to the individual and he, perhaps not surprisingly as the company was insolvent, asserted that the company was the borrower. He attached very considerable importance to the order in which the day's transactions had been listed on the daily waste sheet and he alleged that the entries had been adjusted to support the bank's case. To rebut that allegation it was necessary to produce (a) the vouchers for the transaction, (b) the waste sheet, (c) the ledger sheets, (d) the instruction manual for staff operating the computer terminal in the branch, (e) the computer reports issued when the day's waste had been processed, (7) the balance list summary which was then on microfiche, (g) the data control file adjustment sheets on which would be recorded any fault in the computer and so on. I found exploring these byways, which I had never followed before for that client, a fascinating experience, and ultimately a very rewarding one as we were able to prove conclusively before trial that the plaintiff was wrong.

Once the documents are in order the solicitor has to decide whether any of them are privileged and need not, therefore, be produced. The fact that the document is privileged does not normally mean that it must not be disclosed—but the classic method of doing so is to describe the class of documents, for which privilege is claimed, in general terms.

The best-known head of privilege is documents prepared for the purpose of obtaining legal advice[14]: Jessel MR put the matter this way in *Wheeler* v. *Le Marchant*:

> it must not be supposed that there is any principle which says that every confidential communication which it is necessary to make in order to carry on the ordinary business of life is protected. The protection is of a very limited character, and in this country is restricted to the obtaining [of] the assistance of lawyers, as regards the conduct of litigation or the rights to property. It has never gone beyond the obtaining of legal advice and assistance, and all things reasonably necessary in the shape of communication to the legal advisers are protected from production or discovery in order that legal advice may be obtained safely and sufficiently.

Jessel MR explained the justification for that rule in *Anderson* v. *Bank of British Columbia*[15]:

> The object and meaning of the rule is this: that as, by reason of the complexity and difficulty of our law, litigation can only be properly conducted by professional men, it is absolutely necessary that a man, in order to prosecute his rights or to defend himself from any proper claim, should have recourse to the assistance of professional lawyers, and it being so absolutely necessary, it is equally necessary, to use a vulgar phrase, that he should be able to make a clean breast of it to the gentleman whom he consults with a view to the prosecution of his claim, or the substantiating [of] his defence against the claim of others; that he should be able to place unrestricted and unbounded confidence in the professional agent, and that the communications he so makes to him should be kept secret, unless with his consent (for it is his privilege, and not the privilege of the confidential agent, that he should be enabled properly to conduct his litigation).

That being so, confidential communications between the lawyer and his client which come into existence for the purpose of giving or getting legal advice are privileged at all times—although it can sometimes be a nice question as to whether a document came into existence for the purpose of obtaining legal advice or merely as part of an administrative process.

Although one might think that this basis of privilege is so clear as not to give rise to problems, it can frequently be difficult to decide whether documents which come into existence for the purpose of disseminating legal advice—and this is an acute problem within large corporate entities—are privileged. Basically a document which merely passes on legal advice within the company is privileged, but if the communication goes further there is a danger of privilege

14. (1881) 17 Ch D 675, 681.
15. (1876) 2 Ch D 644, 649.

being lost. Here is a borderline example. A company obtains legal advice on a particular problem: the company director sends a copy of the legal opinion to three or four other members of the company with a covering note. If the covering note merely tries to put into ordinary English the arcane phrases of a legal adviser, then it will probably be privileged: if the covering note suggests that the policy of the firm in respect of the particular matter on which advice was sought should not be redirected, then it may well not be privileged.

The other type of legal professional privilege arises only when litigation is in prospect or pending. And it can be much more difficult to decide whether a document, which on the face of it would not appear to be protected by legal advice privilege, is in fact protected by "litigation" privilege: there must, in the words of a leading textbook "be some definite prospect of litigation and not a mere vague anticipation of it".[16] Here is an example. A complaint is made to a bank about the conduct of one of its officers and the consequences of his alleged misconduct. That complaint will need to be investigated and traditionally that was the task of the bank's inspectors who would then prepare a report for consideration by their principals: the report expresses views on (a) the conduct of the bank's officer, and (b) the legal liability of the bank. The bank rejects the complaint: the complainant sues—is the report privileged from production? To give another example, taken from *Waugh* v. *British Railways Board*,[17] a widow claims damages under the Fatal Accidents Act 1976 alleging that the death of her husband in a collision between two trains had been caused by the Board's negligence. The widow seeks discovery of an internal inquiry report to the Railway Inspectorate incorporating statements of witnesses. The report is headed: "For the information of the Board's solicitor: this form is to be used by every person reporting an occurrence when litigation by or against the BRB is anticipated. It is to be provided by the person making it to his immediate superior officer and has finally to be sent to the solicitor for the purpose of enabling him to advise the BRB in regard thereto." The test established by *Waugh* for deciding whether documents are privileged is known as the "dominant purpose" test. In that case Lord Wilberforce held that "the report was prepared for a dual purpose: for what may be called railway operation and safety purposes and for the purpose of obtaining legal advice in anticipation of litigation, the first being more remedial than the second, that both being described as of equal rank or weight".[18] Applying that test the House of Lords concluded that the report was not privileged.

The problem was looked at most recently by the Court of Appeal in *Guinness Peat Properties* v. *Fitzroy Robinson Partnership*,[19] which concerned a letter written by architects to their professional indemnity brokers giving

16. *Bray on Discovery* (1st edn, 1885), p. 408.
17. [1980] AC 521.
18. p. 531.
19. [1987] 2 All ER 716.

insurers notice of a claim against them. The Court of Appeal held the letter to be privileged on the basis that it owed its genesis to the dominant purpose that it should be used by insurers for the purpose of obtaining legal advice on the claim and in any ensuing litigation. The court ruled that the purpose had to be ascertained by an objective view of the evidence as a whole, looking at all the circumstances surrounding the writing of the letter, rather than confining the test to a narrow subjective examination of the purpose of the writers of the letter. It was, therefore, necessary to take into account in that case the purpose of insurers in including an obligation of notification in the policy.

The mere fact that a document is stamped "confidential—for use in legal proceedings" or "this report has been prepared in contemplation of legal proceedings and to enable the company to obtain advice from its lawyers" will not, therefore, be conclusive.

Incidentally, as one Master of the Rolls, Lord Jessel, made plain in the passage quoted from *Anderson*, the privilege is that of the client, and he can, and in some cases will, be advised that it is expedient that he should waive that privilege and produce the document. Unfortunately, waiver can, on occasion, be accidental. A classic example is where parts of a document were read in court, as happened in *Great Atlantic Insurance Co.* v. *Home Insurance Co.*[20] The plaintiffs gave discovery of the first two paragraphs of a memorandum but claimed privilege from production in respect of the remainder. The first two paragraphs were read out in court at trial and the defendants claimed that amounted to a waiver of privilege in respect of the whole document. The Court of Appeal ruled that the whole memorandum was privileged and that as the plaintiffs "deliberately chose to read part of a document which dealt with one subject matter to the trial judge", they must disclose the whole. One consequence of that ruling is that solicitors, when giving discovery, need to analyse each document with great care: if part is privileged the question arises whether the document is severable.

A litigant does have the right to seal or cover up parts of documents on the grounds, for example, that they do not relate to matters in issue in the action, or contain privileged material, and he can claim that right in his list of documents or, in contested cases, can apply for an appropriate order.

Before moving on from this difficult area I should stress that the mere fact that a document may be addressed to an in-house lawyer in, say, the legal department of a bank will not of itself be sufficient to cloak it with privilege (as he may, for example, have received it in an executive and not a legal capacity as in the *Waugh* case); and even where, according to English rules, such a document would be a privileged communication, in-house lawyers enjoy no privilege before the European Commission when, for example, the Commission is investigating breaches of Articles 85 and 86 of the Treaty of Rome.[21]

20. [1981] 2 All ER 485.
21. *AM & S Europe* v. *Commissioners of the European Community* [1983] 3 WLR 17.

Inspection

After the lists have been exchanged the parties have the right to inspect each other's documents: in my view that right should always be exercised. Copy documents do not always show what is to be found on the original; for example, it may be significant to know if any passages in the original have been highlighted; if they have been annotated in any way (and sometimes a photocopier will not reproduce annotations on the back of a document); if they bear staple marks; also, and this may be very important, whether one's opponent has produced original documents, which he is obliged to do when they are in his possession, a point I will amplify when dealing with applications for further and better discovery.

The use of documents produced on discovery

The discovery process is an invasion of privacy: clients will undoubtedly be concerned that if a third party gets hold of their documents, they might be misused either to his benefit or certainly to their prejudice: details of internal structures might be leaked to the press; free and frank views of customers might be published causing embarrassment even if they did not lead to defamation actions; concerns that conduct was short of the standard which all bankers would wish to observe might attract the attention of the Sunday press. It is not, therefore, surprising that the courts offer some protection to parties who have to disclose their documentation by way of an implied undertaking or duty "not to use (the documents) for any purpose other than that of the action".[22]

However, the law has been modified as a result of the *Harman* case where Harriet Harman, then legal officer to the National Council for Civil Liberties, after the trial invited a journalist who was writing a feature for the *Guardian* to her office where she allowed him to read and take notes of the documents in the trial bundles: she was held by the House of Lords to have been in contempt but challenged that finding before the European Commission of Human Rights. Now a litigant still impliedly undertakes to the court not to use documents obtained on discovery for any purpose other than those in the proceedings in which they are disclosed, but that undertaking ceases to have effect in relation to a document "after it has been read to or by the court, or referred to, in open court", unless the court "for special reasons" orders otherwise (Order 24, r. 14A). As the sanction for breach of that undertaking is committal for contempt, care must be taken to observe it.

Clients may wonder how disputes can ever be resolved if all letters and notes debating the rights and wrongs of their conduct and that of their opponents, assessing the merits, and considering terms for settlement, may have to be produced on discovery. The law does encourage settlement by recognising that "without prejudice" negotiations can be disclosed by the parties without being

22. *Home Office* v. *Harman* [1983] 1 AC 280, 312.

disclosed to the court—but beware. Written or oral communications made for the purpose of a genuine attempt to compromise a dispute between the parties may generally not be admitted in evidence[23]: "parties should be encouraged so far as possible to settle their disputes without resort to litigation and should not be discouraged by the knowledge that anything that is said in the course of such negotiations (and that includes, of course, as much the failure to reply to an offer as an actual reply) may be used to their prejudice in the course of proceedings". But bear in mind that there does have to be (a) a dispute and (b) an attempt to settle that dispute without resort to litigation. Merely plastering "Without prejudice" on a letter will not protect it from disclosure unless those features apply. Further, once settlement has been achieved, the privilege falls away.

Finally, in this brief perambulation through the rules of discovery, a warning should be given about the application for further and better discovery. When a litigant first sees his opponent's documents there may well be gaps, for the reasons that I outlined at the beginning: the opponent too will be looking for gaps in discovery and with a view to making life uncomfortable he may well apply for an order for specific discovery of missing documents confident that if the other party then fails to produce, or if they are not available, to explain what has become of them, he will be able, in due course, to obtain a peremptory order that the claim be struck out and judgment be entered against the other party for costs.

I will illustrate the significance of applications for further and better discovery by two examples, one reported and the other from my own experience. First the reported case. It is a fashionable tactic for litigants, when they know that a bank employee has been dismissed or subjected to disciplinary proceedings, to call for production of the personal file relating to that employee's progress and to apply for a specific order that the file be produced. Over the years I have resisted such applications with some success and I can now rely on *Thorpe* v. *Chief Constable of Greater Manchester Police*,[24] which establishes very clearly that the court will not allow discovery which relates solely to credit.

An example of where a document disclosed by an opponent gave rise to a request for further and better discovery, and in due course an order, was in a case relating to the transfer of a very substantial sum of money from the plaintiff's account in a London bank to the account maintained there by his brother. The transfer had been made pursuant to a telex instruction and it was of fundamental importance to establish who had sent that telex instruction. On discovery the defendant disclosed copies of his telex bills: on those bills the total cost did not appear to be the sum of the individual items and the unit costs for calls from country A to country B did not in all cases appear to be the same, even though they were made at a time when prices had not been

23. *Cutts* v. *Head* [1984] Ch. 290, 306.
24. [1989] 1 WLR 665.

increased. The first thing was to obtain an order that the original telex bill be produced, secondly, an order that all the telexes listed on the bill be produced, thirdly, an order that the operating records of the telex machine be made available, fourthly, that the original telex bill be submitted to a forensic document examiner—and so on.

CONCLUSION

Discovery is a *continuing obligation*, and on many occasions relevant and disclosable documents may come into existence after the initial discovery process has been completed and lists of documents exchanged. The preservation of old records is a matter which should be of particular concern to banks: it will often be important to establish precisely what the bank's internal procedures were, what instructions were given by head office to branch managers and the like at the time when the incident occurred of which complaint is made in the proceedings. It is, therefore, highly desirable that the bank should try to maintain an archive of head office instructions and circulars.

Closely related to discovery are other procedures. First, there are interrogatories. However, it is unlikely that the new rules on witnesses' statements will affect the discovery process as persons seek to obtain admissions and define issues well before trial.[25] In the view of the Bar the use of witnesses' statements will not increase, since it is not difficult to evade their effect by careful pleading in reply. Secondly, there is the position of banks, who may not be a party to an action, but whose records are sought on a subpoena *duces tecum*, and the propriety of the procedural device of issuing a subpoena, having the action listed, artificially, for hearing on a specific day when the bank's records will be produced, and then adjourning the matter generally while the parties consider those records. The use of this device, first adopted by Sir John Donaldson MR in *Williams* v. *Williams*,[26] appears to circumvent the well-established rule that discovery will not be required of a stranger to an action, although that general rule has been circumscribed by such decisions as *Norwich Pharmacal* v. *Customs and Excise*[27] and *Bankers Trust Co.* v. *Shapira*[28]—both cases where third parties were required to give discovery at an interlocutory stage so as to assist in identifying the whereabouts of a plaintiff's property.

Whilst this new procedure may frequently save time (since a bank representative can attend a court at a stated time, produce the documents and then be released), bankers will understandably be concerned at the parties to the action being given an opportunity of ranging through their internal records and it will

25. Since 1986, Order 38, r. 2A empowers the court to direct any party to serve the other party with written statements of the oral evidence which it is intended to lead at trial on factual issues.
26. [1988] 1 QB 161.
27. [1974] AC 133.
28. [1981] 1 WLR 1274.

be interesting to see how the procedure develops. For example, who will be responsible for policing the production by the subpoenaed party of the documents; what documents are to be placed before the party issuing the subpoena —are only privileged documents to be excluded or will the bank be entitled to hold back or seal up documents which may relate the confidential affairs of customers other than the parties to the litigation; in what capacity does the party considering the documents hold them—as officers of the court or solicitors on the record for a particular client—and so on?

In one respect the new procedure may be of advantage to the party who is required to produce his documents. The current position with regard to subpoenas (s. 36(4) of the Supreme Court Act 1981) is that the party subpoenaed is entitled to conduct money only. The lack of realistic compensatory power appears to be encouraging the courts, when exercising the *Williams* v. *Williams* jurisdiction, to require the party seeking production of the documents to accept liability for the proper costs of the subpoenaed party, and proper costs may include the costs of legal advice on the meaning and breadth of the obligations contained in the subpoena and legal attendance at court.

I will conclude with an exhortation which is of general application to clients who find themselves involved in legal proceedings and of particular application to the process of discovery: the client who interests himself in the conduct of his own case and works closely with his solicitor, will obtain a far better result than the client who leaves everything to his lawyers—and that is particularly the case on discovery which, although it may be a time-consuming, tedious and expensive process is, as I hope I have demonstrated, extremely important.

ANTHONY PUGH-THOMAS

ANNEX 1. CHECKLIST OF DOCUMENTS HELD BY A BANK WHICH MAY BE DISCOVERABLE

1. *Documents held at the branch*

1.1 Information sheets or running summary of correspondence.
1.2 Mandate file
1.3 Advances files
1.4 Correspondence files (individual files for each customer or general files)
1.5 Other files, e.g. foreign, standing orders, ECGD, status enquiries
1.6 Signature card
1.7 Address card
1.8 Ledger sheets
1.9 Opening/closing account register
1.10 Diaries
1.11 Refer or excess book
1.12 Opening account aide memoire
1.13 Securities aide memoire

1.14 Securities register
1.15 Deeds
1.16 Paid cheques and vouchers, copies of paid cheques returned to customers
1.17 Waste sheets
1.18 Unpaid cheques register
1.19 Details of regular non-customers who use branch facilities
1.20 Advice of fate book

2. *Documents held at regional office*

2.1 Regional office correspondence file
2.2 Control sheets
2.3 Excess sheet returns
2.4 Current personnel files

3. *Other documents*

3.1 Inspection department file
3.2 Chairman's or other head office files
3.3 Other central department files
3.4 Head office standing instructions
3.5 Staff manual
3.6 Computer accounting instructions manual
3.7 Computer records
3.8 Head or regional office circulars
3.9 Stored files
3.10 Stored microfiched ledger sheets and cheques
3.11 Stock exchange and foreign services manual

4. *Other computer records*

ANNEX 2

IN THE HIGH COURT OF JUSTICE *1990 No._____*
_____DIVISION

BETWEEN:

Plaintiff

and

Defendant

PLAINTIFF'S/DEFENDANT'S LIST OF DOCUMENTS

The following is a list of the documents relating to the matters in question in this action which are or have been in the possession, custody or power of the above-named plaintiff/defendant and which is served in compliance with Order 24, r. 2 [the order dated_____].

1. The plaintiff/defendant has in his possession, custody or power the documents

relating to the matters the subject of the aforementioned order enumerated in Schedule 1 hereto.

2. The plaintiff/defendant objects to produce the documents enumerated in Part 2 of the said Schedule 1 on the ground that they are privileged as appears from their description.
3. The plaintiff/defendant has had, but has not now, in his possession, custody or power the documents relating to the matters the subject of the aforementioned order enumerated in Schedule 2 hereto.
4. It is not possible to state with accuracy when all of the documents listed in Schedule 2 were last in the plaintiff/defendant's possession, with the exception of correspondence and other documents sent by one or other of them, when it would have been on or about the date of the correspondence or covering correspondence.
5. To the best of his knowledge, neither the plaintiff/defendant nor his solicitors nor any other person on their behalf, has now, or ever had, in his possession, custody or power any document of any description whatever relating to any matter in question in this action, other than the documents enumerated in Schedules 1 and 2 hereto.

SCHEDULE 1 PART 1

Description	*Date*

SCHEDULE 1 PART 2

Description of Document	*Date*
Correspondence, memoranda, notes, minutes and reports passing between the plaintiff/defendant, his servants and agents (whether in the form of hard copy, computer record, microfilm, microfiche or howsoever) at a time when the present application was contemplated or pending the same having been prepared, sent or received for the purpose of obtaining or furnishing or discussing information and/or evidence relating to or for the purposes of the application; together with correspondence between the plaintiff/defendant and his solicitors, instructions and cases to counsel and his settled drafts and opinions, statements of witnesses and other documents which have come into existence or been made for the purpose of obtaining for or furnishing to the plaintiff's/defendant's solicitors evidence to be used in the application or information which might lead to the obtaining of such evidence or information as to the evidence which could be obtained or otherwise for the use of the plaintiff's/defendant's solicitors to enable them to conduct or advise the plaintiff/defendant whether to prosecute/defend the application or otherwise advise the plaintiff/defendant in reference thereto.	various

SCHEDULE 2

Description of Document	*Date*
Originals of copy documents listed in Schedule 1 Part 1 which were dispatched by the plaintiff/defendant to the third parties.	various

DATED THE ______ DAY OF ______ 1990.

NOTICE TO INSPECT

TAKE NOTICE that the documents in the above list, other than those listed in Part 2 of Schedule 1 and Schedule 2, may be inspected at the offices of the above-named______ plaintiff/defendant on any working day by appointment.

TO: of	SERVED the day of 1990 by
Solicitors for the plaintiff/defendant	Solicitors for the plaintiff/defendant

CHAPTER 4

PRE-TRIAL PROCEEDINGS IN US COURTS

BASIC PRINCIPLES OF US FEDERALISM

Divided legislative authority

The United States is a federal republic: legal authority is divided between a single national (or federal) government and the governments of the 50 states and the District of Columbia. Under the US Constitution, the federal government is vested with authority to make and enforce laws concerning a wide range of issues of national concern. Most significantly, the federal government is granted the power to regulate both interstate and foreign commerce[1]; this authority has been construed to extend to virtually every subject that the federal government wishes to reach, except those of the most local character.[2]

Exercising its constitutional authority, Congress has enacted a wide range of federal legislation in areas of national import. Federal law governs subjects such as banking, transportation, employment discrimination and labour relations, the environment, communications and securities. These federal statutes override, or "pre-empt", all state laws that are inconsistent with federal objectives.[3]

There are, however, a number of extremely important areas in which Congress has not chosen to exercise its legislative authority, and which are therefore governed by state law. These include basic contract law, tort law, corporation statutes, agency law and a wide range of local matters. The several states are almost entirely free to adopt whatever rules they deem advisable in areas where Congress has not acted; although all states (except Louisiana)

1. US Const. Art. I, §8.

2. G. Born and D. Westin, *International Civil Litigation in United States Courts* 5–8 (1989). See *South Carolina* v. *Baker* 108 S Ct 1355, 1360–2 (1988); *Garcia* v. *San Antonio Metropolitan Transit Authority* 469 US 528 (1985) (Tenth Amendment limits on Congress's authority to regulate states is structural not substantive); *Heart of Atlanta Motel, Inc.* v. *United States* 379 US 241 (1964) (Congress's authority to regulate interstate commerce extends to purely local activity that in the aggregate may affect interstate commerce).

3. US Const. Art. VI, cl. 2; *Hines* v. *Davidowitz* 312 US 52 (1941); *Silkwood* v. *Kerr-McGee Corp.* 464 US 238 (1984).

share the Anglo-American common law tradition, significant differences exist among the laws in different states.

Dual judicial system

Two largely parallel judicial systems exist in the US: (a) a federal court system and (b) a system of state courts. The federal court system covers the entire US and consists of trial courts (the US District Courts), appellate courts (the US Courts of Appeals), and the US Supreme Court. Each of the 50 states (plus the District of Columbia) also has an independent judicial system, typically with trial courts, intermediate appellate courts and a state supreme court.

A US federal court may only hear a case over which it has been granted both "personal jurisdiction" (discussed below at pp. 56–67) and "subject-matter jurisdiction" (discussed below at pp. 54–56). Congress has granted the federal courts subject-matter jurisdiction—or the power to decide the type of dispute in question—over only limited categories of cases. The most significant category of case decided in federal courts are those involving substantive federal law.

In contrast, state courts are generally courts of general jurisdiction that are empowered to decide any claim brought before them. In the ordinary course, each state court system deals principally with cases involving claims based on that state's law; as noted above, state law covers almost every conceivable subject matter, including commercial transactions, product liability, corporations and property rights. State courts also have subject-matter jurisdiction over all federal claims, except those relatively few that have been placed within the exclusive jurisdiction of the federal courts.

Procedural matters in all civil cases in federal district courts are generally governed by the Federal Rules of Civil Procedure.[4] Among other things, the Federal Rules govern such issues as service of process, personal jurisdiction, time for answering complaints, discovery, procedures for counterclaims and cross-claims, class actions and the procedures for pre-trial and trial dispositions of cases. "Local rules", adopted in particular federal judicial districts, elaborate on the provisions of the Federal Rules, sometimes adding significant requirements.

Limited federal subject-matter jurisdiction

Unlike state courts, the federal courts are courts of limited jurisdiction: federal courts may decide disputes only where Congress (or the Constitution in certain limited cases applicable to the Supreme Court) has granted them subject-

4. Procedural matters in state courts are governed by state procedural rules. In many states, these rules are similar to the Federal Rules. Federal and state appellate courts also have their own procedural rules. Criminal cases are governed by separate sets of rules.

matter jurisdiction.[5] Congress has established a number of significant areas of federal subject-matter jurisdiction.

First, federal courts enjoy jurisdiction over cases "arising under" federal law; this includes statutes enacted by Congress, such as antitrust and securities laws, as well as US treaties and the US Constitution.[6] Secondly, a federal court also enjoys so-called "diversity jurisdiction" over cases arising under state (or foreign) law if the amount in controversy exceeds US$50,000 and the case is between citizens of different states.[7] Thirdly, federal courts possess "alienage jurisdiction" over suits between US and non-US citizens, provided again that the dispute involves more than US$50,000.[8] Finally, federal courts also have subject-matter jurisdiction over a number of other types of specialised disputes defined by federal law.[9]

Congress has the authority to grant the federal courts exclusive jurisdiction, thereby eliminating the jurisdiction of state courts, and it has done so for a number of categories of cases, including bankruptcy proceedings,[10] cases arising under the Securities Exchange Act,[11] and federal antitrust actions.[12] Unless Congress expressly grants federal courts exclusive jurisdiction, state courts retain concurrent jurisdiction over federal causes of action.

The "Erie" problem

One of the most complex aspects of US law, for both US and foreign counsel, concerns the so-called "*Erie*" problem[13]: What law—state or federal—does a federal court apply when it decides a dispute? When a federal court decides

5. *Owen Equipment & Erection Co.* v. *Kroger* 437 US 365 (1978).

6. See 28 USC §1331 (1982). In addition to this general conferral of "federal question" jurisdiction, many federal statutes contain their own jurisdictional provisions. See e.g., 15 USC §4 (1982) (Sherman Antitrust Act); 15 USC §78aa (1982) (Securities Exchange Act of 1934); 28 USC §1337 (1982) (antitrust generally).

7. See 28 USC §1332 (1991).

8. See 28 USC §1332(a)(2) (1991).

9. This includes actions against foreign states; admiralty and maritime cases; patent, copyright, and trade mark matters; and cases in which the US government is a party. See 28 USC §§1330–1364 (1982).

10. 28 USC §1334.

11. 15 USC §78aa.

12. 15 USC §15. See also USC §1338(a) (patent and copyright cases); 28 USC §1355 (actions for the recovery or enforcement of civil fines, penalties, or forfeitures incurred under federal statute); 18 USC §3231 (crimes against the US).

13. In *Erie R.R. Co.* v. *Thompson* 304 US 64 (1938), the Supreme Court addressed the issue of what substantive law a federal court should apply when the case is not governed by the Constitution or a federal statute. The court reversed the long-standing practice by federal courts of developing their own body of case-law and applying this so-called "general federal common law" to cases brought pursuant to diversity jurisdiction. Instead, the court ruled, a federal court sitting in diversity jurisdiction should apply the state's common law as well as its statutes. Thus, under *Erie*, a federal court hearing a diversity case, must decide the case with reference to state, not federal, law. The year *Erie* was decided, the Federal Rules of Civil Procedure also went into effect; this reversed the traditional rule of federal courts applying state procedural law in diversity cases. See C. Wright and A. Miller, *Federal Practice and Procedure* §§4505–4508 (1987).

federal question cases—cases arising under substantive federal statutes like the antitrust laws—it will of course apply federal law. In doing so, the court will look both to positive federal statutes and to federal judicial interpretations thereof. When a federal court decides a diversity or alienage case, however, it ordinarily will apply the state substantive law of a state or foreign country. To determine which jurisdiction's law to apply, a court will employ the conflict of law rules of the state in which the particular federal court is located.[14] For example, when a federal district court in Virginia hears a contract dispute between diverse citizens, it will apply Virginia's conflict of law rules to determine the applicable law—in this case, the law of the jurisdiction where the contract was made.[15] On matters of state law, the federal courts must defer to state supreme courts and their interpretation of local law; in contrast, where interpretation of federal law is at issue, both state and federal lower courts may rule, with the federal Supreme Court providing the ultimate authority as to the content of federal law.

Removal

Many types of claims may be filed by a US plaintiff in either federal or state court. Thus, many federal claims can be brought in state courts, as well as in federal courts; conversely, some state law claims may be brought in federal courts under diversity or alienage jurisdiction. Although plaintiffs ordinarily have the option of choosing to file a complaint in either state or federal court, defendants may seek to alter the plaintiff's choice. Most significantly, a defendant may "remove" an action to federal court in certain cases. In particular, removal is available either (a) if the action arises under federal law, or (b) if a federal court otherwise has diversity or alienage jurisdiction and none of the defendants are citizens of the state where the action was brought.[16] A petition for removal must ordinarily be filed by the defendant within 30 days of the receipt of the pleading commencing the state court action.[17] Removal is a matter of right and cannot be refused by either the federal or state court.

If at any time before final judgment the district court determines that it lacks subject-matter jurisdiction, it may remand the case back to state court.[18] With the exception of civil rights cases, an order of a district court remanding a case improperly removed to it from a state court is not reviewable on appeal.[19]

14. *Klaxon* v. *Stentor* 313 US 487 (1941).

15. Different states have different conflict of law rules; it is entirely possible that the same case brought in federal court in different states could lead to the application of different substantive laws and conflict of law rules.

16. 28 USC §1441(a) and (b) (1973 and Supp. 1991). Limited classes of state court actions are not removable. See 28 USC §1445 (1991).

17. 28 USC §1446(b) (1991).

18. 28 USC §1447(b) (1991).

19. 28 USC §1447(d) (1991).

PRE-TRIAL PLEADINGS UNDER THE FEDERAL RULES OF CIVIL PROCEDURE

Complaint

In order to commence a lawsuit in a US court, the plaintiff files a complaint in a particular court.[20] Most US complaints provide very limited information about the plaintiff's claims. Under the Federal Rules, a complaint must provide nothing more than a "short and plain statement" concerning the court's subject matter jurisdiction, the plaintiff's entitlement to relief, and the relief sought.[21] As a practical matter, complaints usually contain only the most limited and conclusory factual allegations and legal claims. A plaintiff is not obliged to specify the amount of the damages desired, but is free to do so if it so chooses.

All pleadings, motions and other papers filed in federal district court (except for those filed by an individual appearing *pro se*) require the signature of an attorney admitted to practise in that court. Rule 11 of the Federal Rules provides that the attorney's signature certifies that the filing:

> is well grounded in fact and is warranted by existing law or a good faith argument for the extension, modification, or reversal of existing law, and that it is not interposed for any improper purpose, such as to harass or to cause unnecessary delay or needless increase in the cost of litigation.

If the court determines, upon another party's or the court's motion, that the filing does not meet the Rule 11 standards, the attorney who signed the complaint is subject to appropriate sanctions.[22] The sanctions may include payment of the opponents' expenses, including attorneys' fees, incurred in opposing the objectionable conduct, and additional monetary sanctions. Because of its broad applicability to nearly every paper filed in a case and its potential for punishing various forms of poor conduct and slipshod practices, Rule 11 motions have become a widely used, and often abused, tactic; parties have been known to file and win Rule 11 motions directed at an opposing party's Rule 11 motion.

Answer

Defendants in federal court will ordinarily respond to a complaint with either an "answer" or a "motion to dismiss" (discussed below at pp. 57–58). An answer must admit, deny, or state lack of sufficient information to respond to

20. Simultaneously, or soon thereafter, the plaintiff will cause the complaint to be "served" upon the defendant, together with a "summons" that requires the defendant to respond to the complaint. Service is discussed below at pp. 68–71.

21. Fed R Civ P 8(a). A defendant may file a motion for more definite statement of the plaintiff's claims, but such motions are disfavoured except in limited circumstances where pleading with particularity is required. See Fed R Civ P 9(b) (fraud or mistake); 9(c) (denial of performance or occurrence); 9(g) (items of special damages).

22. *Pavelic & Leflore* v. *Marvel Entertainment Group* 110 S Ct 456 (1989).

each of the factual allegations and legal claims of the complaint.[23] In addition, an answer must assert certain affirmative defences, specified in the Federal Rules, or they are waived,[24] unless the court permits the defendant to amend its answer to assert later.[25]

Under the Federal Rules, most private defendants have 20 days from the date on which process is served upon them to file an "answer" to the complaint.[26] (As a practical matter, extensions of time can usually be obtained fairly readily from the plaintiff or the trial court.) Unlike private litigants, foreign states, including their "agencies and instrumentalities", have 60 days to answer a complaint.[27]

Motion to dismiss

Rather than answering the complaint, a defendant may present certain defences by "motion". Unlike an answer, a motion does not respond directly to the complaint's basic substantive allegations, but instead asserts some legal bar to the claims. Defences that are most commonly raised by way of motion include lack of personal jurisdiction, insufficiency of service of process, improper venue, and failure to state a claim on which relief can be granted.[28]

A motion must be filed within 20 days after service of a complaint on the defendant. If the defendant's motion is subsequently denied, an answer must generally be filed within 10 days of the decision.[29]

Counterclaims, cross-claims and third-party complaints

To avoid unnecessary multiplicity of suits, defendants are permitted to assert claims against the plaintiff, co-defendants, or third parties. Under the Federal Rules, a claim by the original defendant against the plaintiff is denominated a counterclaim[30]; a defendant's claim against co-defendants (or a plaintiff's claim against a co-plaintiff) is termed a cross-claim[31]; a defendant's claim against a third party is called a third-party claim.[32] If a claim by the defendant arises out of the subject matter of the complaint, then the defendant must

23. Fed R Civ P. 8(b).
24. Fed R Civ P 8(c).
25. Fed R Civ P 15(a).
26. See Fed R Civ P 12(a).
27. See 28 USC §1608(d) (1982). Under the US Foreign Sovereign Immunities Act, a foreign state's agencies and instrumentalities are defined to include companies that are more than 50 per cent owned by the foreign state: 28 USC §1603(b)(2). See G. Born and D. Westin, *International Civil Litigation in United States Courts*, Ch. 6 (1989).
28. Fed R Civ P 12(b). A motion to dismiss for failure to state a claim asserts that, even assuming that the facts alleged by plaintiff are true, the law provides no basis for relief against the defendant.
28. Fed R Civ P 12(a).
30. Fed R Civ P 13(a)–(f).
31. Fed R Civ P 13(g).
32. Fed R Civ P 14.

assert that claim as a counterclaim or cross-claim or it will lose the chance to assert the claim elsewhere in the US.[33]

Unlike counterclaims, a cross-claim *must* arise out of the subject matter of the original suit or counterclaim, or relate to property that is the subject of the original suit. The availability of cross-claims is of particular significance to joint tortfeasors, which may cross-claim against each other for contribution in the event liability is assessed in the original suit.[34] In contrast to compulsory counterclaims, there is no fixed time within which a party must present a cross-claim; the decision whether to allow a cross-claim is within the court's discretion.

Finally, under a procedural device known as impleader, the defendant may file claims against additional parties that the defendant alleges are liable to it for all or part of the plaintiff's claims.[35] The defendant may file its claim against the third party without leave of the court if it does so within 10 days after filing the answer; otherwise it must file a motion seeking the court's permission. Unlike compulsory counterclaims, impleader is not mandatory; the defendant may choose to assert its claim in an independent action.

PERSONAL JURISDICTION

A common issue that arises in US pre-trial proceedings—particularly in international cases—is that of personal jurisdiction. A US court must have personal (or *in personam*) jurisdiction over the defendant in order to adjudicate claims against the defendant.[36] Two conditions must be satisfied before a US court may exercise personal jurisdiction: (a) there must be some statutory grant of jurisdiction; and (b) the Due Process Clause of the US Constitution must not prohibit the assertion of jurisdiction. Unless both of these requirements are satisfied, claims against the defendant may not proceed.

Long-arm statutes

All 50 states have enacted statutes (or court rules) that define the personal jurisdiction of local courts over non-resident defendants, including foreign

33. Fed R Civ P 13(a) (compulsory counterclaim).
34. Fed R Civ P 13(g).
35. Fed R Civ P 14. Plaintiffs against whom counterclaims have been raised may also implead third parties.
36. When a US court renders an *in personam* judgment, it may be satisfied out of any of the judgment debtor's assets, wherever located. The judgment is only binding, however, upon the defendant and not upon third parties: *Shaffer* v. *Heitner* 433 US 186 (1977). Alternatives to personal jurisdiction are *in rem* and *quasi in rem* jurisdiction, which can be exercised to determine the defendant's rights in property within the court's power or to adjudicate other claims that can be satisfied in whole or in part from such property, even if the court lacks personal jurisdiction over the defendant.

defendants.[37] Like Order 11 of the Rules of the Supreme Court of England, these so-called "long-arm" statutes set forth the circumstances in which personal jurisdiction may be asserted and service abroad effected.

As with other laws, state long-arm statutes vary significantly from state to state. Nonetheless, two general statutory approaches can be identified. First, a number of states have adopted detailed statutory definitions (similar to Order 11) of personal jurisdiction over non-resident defendants. For example, state long-arm statutes will often authorise local courts to adjudicate claims arising from "the transaction of any business within the state" or the "commission of a tortious act within the state".[38]

Secondly, some states have simply incorporated the Due Process Clause by asserting jurisdiction to the limits permitted by that clause. For example, California's long-arm statute provides that "[a] court of this state may exercise jurisdiction on any basis not inconsistent with the constitution of this state or of the United States".[39]

The decisions of state courts are controlling as to the reach of a state long-arm statute. State courts have often interpreted state long-arm statutes quite broadly, often reading such laws to authorise jurisdiction to the full limits of the Due Process Clause; this has occurred even as to "laundry-list" style statutes that make no reference to the Due Process Clause. When this happens, most courts have concluded that only a single jurisdictional issue remains—namely, whether a "trial court's exercise of jurisdiction . . . is consistent with the requirements of due process of law under the Constitution of the United States".[40]

Due process clause

As noted above, the Due Process Clause of the US Constitution has been interpreted as limiting the personal jurisdiction of both state and federal courts.[41] In broad outline, the Due Process Clause requires that a defendant have sufficient "minimum contacts" with the forum state so that "maintenance of the suit does not offend 'traditional notions of fair play and substantial justice' ".[42] Whether a defendant has "minimum contacts" often depends on many factual considerations, such as the ownership of property in the forum;

37. See G. Born and D. Westin, *International Civil Litigation in United States Courts* 20–22 (1989); R. Casad, *Jurisdiction in Civil Actions*, ¶4.01 (1983 and Supp.). By statute, federal courts have personal jurisdiction over a foreign state, and any agency or instrumentality of a foreign state, that is properly served with process and that is not entitled to foreign sovereign immunity. 28 USC §§1330(b) (1991).

38. See e.g. N Y Civ Prac Law §302(a) (McKinney 1990).

39. Cal Code Civ Pro §410.10 (1973).

40. *Hall* v. *Helicopteros Nacionales de Colombia, SA* 638 SW 2d 870, 871 (Tex. 1982).

41. The Due Process Clause make no express reference to jurisdictional limits: it provides simply that "No person shall . . . be deprived of life, liberty, or property, without due process of law . . . " US Const amend. V and XIV. The jurisdictional constraints that have evolved from the Clause are entirely the product of judicial common law.

42. *International Shoe Co.* v. *State of Washington* 326 US 310, 316 (1945).

representation by an agent in the forum; solicitation of business by mail or telephone in the forum; advertisements in the forum; shipment of products into the forum; or sending officers or employees into the forum. As discussed below, there is a fairly elaborate body of case-law that considers whether the "minimum contacts" requirements of the Due Process Clause is satisfied in particular circumstances.

General jurisdiction

In considering Due Process Clause limits on personal jurisdiction, it is vitally important to distinguish between "general" and "specific" jurisdiction. "General jurisdiction" is an extremely broad form of personal jurisdiction: it subjects the defendant to suit in the forum's courts on *any claim*. If general jurisdiction exists, it is irrelevant that the claims against the defendant lack any relation to or connection with the forum.[43] As the Supreme Court has explained, general jurisdiction will lie even if the cause of action is not related to the defendant's activities in the state.[44]

CONTINUOUS AND SYSTEMATIC BUSINESS CONTACTS

Because the scope of general jurisdiction is so broad, the requirements for establishing this form of jurisdiction are fairly rigorous. The most common basis for establishing general jurisdiction is the continuous and systematic engagement in business activities within the forum state.[45] This standard requires a fairly substantial, ongoing level of business activities, usually involving some physical presence, within the forum. For example, the presence of a branch office or other unincorporated facilities in the forum ordinarily provides a basis for general jurisdiction.[46]

Contacts falling short of a substantial physical presence seldom provide an adequate basis for general jurisdiction. For example, in *Complaint of Damodar Bulk Carriers, Ltd*, the Ninth Circuit held that the plaintiffs had not satisfied the "stringent standard" of general jurisdiction, even though vessels belonging to the Chilean defendants had made repeated calls to a port within the forum.[47] Although at least one lower court has been willing to assert general jurisdiction based on a non-resident's sales of products to forum resi-

43. *Helicopteros Nacionales de Colombia* v. *Hall* 466 US 408, 414 (1983).
44. *Ibid* at 414 (citing *Perkins* v. *Benguet Consolidated Mining* Co. 342 US 437 446–447 (1952)).
45. *Perkins* v. *Benguet Consol. Mining Co.* 342 US 437, 446–447 (1952); *Complaint of Damodar Bulk Carriers, Ltd* 903 F. 2d 675 (9th Cir. 1990).
46. See e.g. *Ciprari* v. *Servicos Aereos Cruzeiro do Sul, SA* 232 F. Supp. 433 (DCNY 1964).
47. *Complaint of Damodar* 903 F. 2d. 675. See also *Shute* v. *Carnival Cruise Lines* 863 F. 2d 1437, 1440 (9th Cir. 1990), *rev'd on other grounds*, 111 S Ct 1522 (1991); *Congoleum Corp.* v. *DLW AG* 729 F. 2d 1210, 1242–1243 (9th Cir. 1984).

dents,[48] sales of unrelated products generally are deemed insufficient to establish general jurisdiction.[49]

CITIZENSHIP, DOMICILE AND INCORPORATION

General jurisdiction may also be asserted over both citizens and domiciliaries of the forum. "Domicile in the state is alone sufficient to bring an absent defendant within the reach of the state's jurisdiction . . . ".[50] Thus, an individual is subject to general jurisdiction at his domicile: for example, an individual residing in New York is subject to personal jurisdiction in New York with respect to claims arising out of his business dealings in California or an automobile accident in London. Similarly, a corporation is subject to general jurisdiction in the state in which it is incorporated.[51]

"TAG SERVICE"

Some US courts will also assert general jurisdiction over non-resident defendants simply because they are served with process while physically present within the forum. Thus, in *Burnham* v. *Superior Court*, a divided Supreme Court held that the Due Process Clause was not violated when the California long-arm statute was interpreted to permit personal jurisdiction over an individual non-resident defendant *solely* because he was served with process while he was physically present within the forum.[52] Moreover, the court permitted so-called "tag" service to establish jurisdiction even as to claims having no relationship to the forum.

It is not clear that the *Burnham* case would allow so-called "tag service" over a company based upon service on its officers or directors. A number of lower courts have refused to permit general jurisdiction over a corporate defendant based on tag service upon a corporate representative.[53]

Specific jurisdiction

Even if a defendant's forum contacts do not justify general jurisdiction, the defendant may nonetheless be subject to jurisdiction with respect to claims

48. *Eason* v. *Linden Avionics, Inc.* 706 F.Supp. 311 (DNJ 1989).

49. *Keeton* v. *Hustler Magazine, Inc.* 465 US 770, 779 (1984) (in dicta suggesting sales of goods may be insufficient to support general jurisdiction); *Scott* v. *Breeland* 792 F. 2d 925 (9th Cir. 1986) (sale of record albums insufficient basis for jurisdiction over band member accused of committing tort).

50. *Milliken* v. *Meyer* 311 US 457 (1940); Restatement (Second) Conflict of Laws §29 (1971).

51. R. Casad, *Jurisdiction in Civil Actions* ¶3.02 (1983).

52. *Burnham*, 110 S Ct 2105 (1990).

53. *Amusement Equipment, Inc.* v. *Mordelt* 779 F.2d 264 (5th Cir. 1985); *Scholz Research and Development, Inc.* v. *Kurzke* 720 F. Supp. 710 (ND Ill. 1989); *Easterling* v. *Cooper Motors, Inc.* 26 FRD 1 (MDNC 1960).

that are related to or arise out of the defendant's activities in the forum. "[W]hen a State exercises personal jurisdiction over a defendant in a suit arising out of or related to the defendant's contacts with the forum, the State is exercising 'specific jurisdiction' over the defendant".[54] Due Process standards for specific jurisdiction require a showing that the non-resident defendant purposefully availed itself of the privilege of conducting activities in the forum, that the plaintiff's claim arose from that forum-related activity, and that assertion of jurisdiction is reasonable.[55]

PURPOSEFUL AVAILMENT

A non-resident defendant can satisfy the purposeful availment requirement even if it does not (and its employees do not) ever physically enter the forum. Instead, the question is whether the defendant deliberately engaged in business activities that had substantial connections with the forum: "It is essential in each case that there be some act by which the defendant purposefully avails itself of the privilege of conducting activities within the forum State, thus invoking the benefits and protections of its laws".[56]

There is considerable uncertainty over precisely what is required to satisfy the "purposeful availment" test. According to a recent Ninth Circuit decision, "[p]urposeful availment requires that the defendant engage in some form of affirmative conduct allowing or promoting the transaction of business within the forum state".[57] "[A] non-resident defendant's act of soliciting business in the forum state will generally be considered purposeful availment if that solicitation results in contract negotiations or the transaction of business".[58]

It is well settled that the mere foreseeability that a non-resident's products will make their way into the forum is insufficient to satisfy the purposeful availment test. Thus, in *World-Wide Volkswagen Corp.* v. *Woodson*, the Supreme Court declined to permit an Oklahoma court to assert jurisdiction over an East Coast automobile dealer; although it was conceded that the dealer could have foreseen that its mobile products would end up throughout the continental US, the court demanded greater evidence of a deliberate contact with the forum. "[F]oreseeability alone has never been a sufficient benchmark for personal jurisdiction under the Due Process Clause".[59]

Similarly, in *Asahi Metal Indus.* v. *Superior Court*, the court held that a Japanese manufacturer of motorcycle tyre tube assemblies was not subject to

54. *Helicopteros*, 466 US at 414, n.8.
55. See e.g. *T. M. Hylwa, M.D., Inc.* v. *Palka* 823 F.2d. 310 (9th Cir. 1987).
56. *Hanson* v. *Denckla* 357 US 235, 253 (1957).
57. *Shute*, 863 F.2d at 1441.
58. *Ibid* (citing *Decker Coal Co.* v. *Commonwealth Edison Co.* 805 F.2d 834, 840 (9th Cir. 1986) and *Sinatra* v. *National Enquirer, Inc.* 854 F.2d 1191, 1195 (9th Cir. 1988)).
59. *World-Wide Volkswagen Corp.* v. *Woodson* 444 US 286, 295 (1980).

California jurisdiction in an action arising from the alleged malfunction of such an assembly. The Japanese defendant had sold the assemblies to a Taiwanese motorcycle tyre maker, which used the assemblies in tyres, some of which were shipped to California. In a split opinion, four members of the court held that "purposeful availment" did not include merely placing a product into the "stream of commerce", even where it is foreseeable that the products will be distributed in the forum state. Rather, "purposeful availment" requires "designing the product for the market in the forum state, establishing channels for providing regular advice to customers in the forum state, advertising in the forum state, or marketing the products through a distributor who has agreed to serve as the sales agent in the forum state".[60]

ARISING FROM

Specific jurisdiction can only be exercised over claims against the defendant that "arise from" the defendant's contacts with the forum state. For example, a company that distributes only Product A in the forum cannot ordinarily be subject to specific jurisdiction there in a case involving Product B (which it distributes only elsewhere).

There is some uncertainty as to the precise scope of the "arising from" requirement. In *Carnival Cruise Lines* v. *Shute*, the Ninth Circuit expressly adopted a "but for" test for determining when a claim arises from the defendant's forum contacts: if the plaintiff's claims exist because of the defendant's forum contacts, then the claims are deemed to arise from those contacts.[61] Other Courts of Appeal have adopted more restrictive tests, especially where a tort claim is alleged to "arise from" a contract made in the forum.[62]

REASONABLENESS

Finally, any assertion of specific jurisdiction must also be "reasonable".[63] According to the Supreme Court, a number of factors bear on the reasonableness of exercising jurisdiction, including the degree of the defendant's purposeful interjection in the forum state's affairs; the burden to the defendant of defending the suit; conflict with the sovereignty of the defendant's state; the forum state's interest in adjudicating the dispute; the interstate judicial sys-

60. *Asahi* 480 US 102, 112 (1987). In *Asahi*, Justice Brennan and three other justices defined purposeful availment even less strictly and would include placing products in the "stream of commerce" with knowledge that they will reach the forum state, plus deriving economic benefit from this.

61. 863 F.2d 1437 (9th Cir. 1990), rev'd on other grounds, 111 S Ct 1522 (1991). See also *Lanier* v. *American Bd. of Endodontics* 843 F.2d 901 (6th Cir. 1988) (adopting "but for" test); *Prejean* v. *Sonatrack, Inc.* 652 F.2d 1260 (5th Cir. 1981).

62. See e.g. *Marino* v. *Hyatt Corp.* 793 F.2d 427 (1st Cir. 1986).

63. *World-Wide Volkswagen* v. *Woodson* 444 US 286 (1980).

tem's interest in obtaining the most efficient resolution of disputes; the importance of the chosen forum to the plaintiff's interest in obtaining convenient and effective relief; and the existence of an alternative forum.[64]

The Supreme Court has emphasised that, where jurisdiction over a *non-US* defendant is involved, particular caution must be exercised: "The unique burdens placed upon one who must defend oneself in a foreign legal system should have significant weight in assessing the reasonableness of stretching the long arm of personal jurisdiction over national borders".[65] Nonetheless, it is often difficult successfully to defeat jurisdiction based solely on the reasonableness test. Reasonableness is generally presumed where there are minimum contacts; the defendant must present "a compelling case to rebut it".[66]

One important recent application of the reasonableness requirement was the *Asahi Metal Indus.* case, discussed above. There, the Supreme Court also held that it was unreasonable for the California courts to assert jurisdiction over a Japanese defendant in an indemnity action by a Taiwanese plaintiff.[67] The court reasoned that California had relatively little interest in resolving a dispute between two foreign parties, and that "great care and reserve should be exercised when extending our notions of personal jurisdiction into the international field".[68]

National contacts

The preceding discussion has considered the level or quantum of contacts that a defendant must have with the forum in order to satisfy the Due Process Clause. Nearly as important is whether the forum is defined as the entire US (a "national contacts" test), or merely an individual state of the union (a "state contacts" test). This distinction can be of enormous practical significance.

To determine whether or not to apply a national contacts test, the court must first enquire whether there is statutory authority for the court to issue either nationwide or worldwide service of process. Secondly, the exercise of jurisdiction based on an aggregation of national contacts must comport with the Due Process Clause.

A number of federal statutes contain provisions explicitly authorising

64. *Ibid.*

65. *Asahi Metal Indus.* v. *Superior Court* 480 US 102, 114–115 (1987).

66. *Shute* 863 F.2d at 1445; *Meyers* 711 F. Supp. at 1007 (district court held that assertion of jurisdiction over non-US defendant in patent case was reasonable).

67. The dispute arose when a California resident was killed because of a malfunctioning tyre jointly manufactured by the Japanese and Taiwanese parties. The California plaintiff's direct claims against the foreign parties settled, leaving only the Taiwanese defendant's indemnity action.

68. 480 US at 115 (quoting *United States* v. *First National City Bank* 379 US 378, 404 (Harlan J., dissenting)). See Born, *Reflections on Judicial Jurisdiction in International Cases*, 17 GaJInt'l & Comp L 1, 24–25 (1987).

worldwide or nationwide service of process.[69] In cases presenting claims arising under federal laws, where nationwide or worldwide service of process is authorised, most courts have asserted personal jurisdiction over foreign corporate defendants based upon an aggregation of their national contacts. Thus, virtually all Courts of Appeal have held that where a federal statute permits nationwide service of process on defendants, the question becomes whether the party has sufficient contacts with the United States, not any particular state.[70]

A few courts have gone further and held that a state long-arm statute may supply the necessary statutory authority for applying the national contacts test. For example, in *Cryomedics Inc.* v. *Spembly, Ltd.*, the district court applied a national contacts test in a federal patent case after borrowing an expansive state long-arm statute.[71] Other courts, however, have refused to rely upon a state long-arm statute to aggregate the foreign defendant's contacts with the entire US for the purpose of asserting personal jurisdiction, even in cases based upon substantive federal law.[72] It appears that no court has sought to use a national contacts test where both a state's substantive law and its long-arm statute are involved.[73]

Virtually all lower courts have held that the Due Process Clause permits the use of a national contacts test in cases where a federal long-arm statute specifically authorises a federal court to aggregate the defendant's contacts.[74] Indeed, most lower courts have concluded that the Due Process Clause is not offended when a federal court relies upon an expansive state long-arm statute in apply-

69. See 2 J. Moore, J. Lucas, H. Fink and C. Thompson, *Moore's Federal Practice* ¶4.42 [2.–1], at 4–386 to 4–391 (1987) (listing over 15 statutes).

The Supreme Court has rejected the argument that Rule 4 of the Federal Rules of Civil Procedure, should be interpreted as establishing a general federal long-arm standard in federal question cases. In *Omni Cap. Int'l* v. *Rudolf Wolff & Co.* 484 US 97 (1987), British defendants moved to dismiss the claims against them for lack of personal jurisdiction. The plaintiff conceded that the state long-arm statute did not encompass defendants' contacts with the state, and the court construed the relevant federal statute as neither explicitly nor implicitly providing for nationwide service of process. The court declined to fill in the interstices of federal statutory law by creating a rule to authorise service on an alien in a federal question case where the alien is not amenable to service under the applicable state long-arm statute. Although the court recognised that such a narrowly tailored service of process provision might serve statutory purposes, it concluded that it is for Congress or those who propose the Federal Rules of Civil Procedure, rather than the federal courts, to create such a rule. *Ibid.* at 97.

70. G. Born and D. Westin, *International Civil Litigation in United States Courts* 69–90 (1989). See *Securities Investor Protection Corp.* v. *Vigman*, 764 F.2d 1309, 1315 (9th Cir. 1985) (aggregating nationwide contacts in Securities Exchange Act suit) (citation omitted); *Fitzsimmons* v. *Barton* 589 F.2d 330, 333 (7th Cir. 1979) (same); *Go-Video, Inc.* v. *Akai Elec. Co.* 885 F.2d 1406 (9th Cir. 1989) (antitrust laws); *Meadows* v. *Dominican Republic* 628 F.Supp. 599 (ND Cal. 1986) (Federal Sovereign Immunities Act suit); *United States* v. *Toyota Motor Corp.* 561 F.Supp. 351 (CD Cal. 1983) (federal tax statute).

71. 387 F.Supp. 287 (D Conn. 1575). See also *In re United Rope Distributors, Inc.* 930 F.2d 532 (7th Cir. 1991) (dicta).

72. *Johnson Creative Arts, Inc.* v. *Wool Masters, Inc.* 743 F.2d 947, 950 (1st Cir. 1984); *Max Duetwyler Corp.* v. *R. Meyer* 762 F.2d 290, 295–297 (3d Cir. 1985).

73. *Wells Fargo & Co.* v. *Wells Fargo Express Co.* 556 F.2d 406, 416–419 (9th Cir. 1977).

74. *Securities Investor Protection Corp., supra.*

ing a national contacts test.[75] It is doubtful, however, whether a state court could constitutionally apply a national contacts test.

Consent to jurisdiction

US courts will also accept personal jurisdiction based upon a defendant's consent to litigate in the forum.[76] In *National Equipment Rental, Ltd.* v. *Szukhent*, the Supreme Court held that the Due Process Clause does not prevent a party from knowingly consenting to suit in a specified forum.[77] Some lower courts will strain, particularly in consumer contracts, to overturn consent-to-jurisdiction clauses on grounds of unconscionability, lack of notice and the like.[78] But where sophisticated commercial entities are involved, such results are unlikely.

Jurisdiction based upon corporate affiliation

In limited circumstances, a US court may also assert personal jurisdiction over a non-US parent corporation based solely upon the fact that the defendant owns a US subsidiary. Courts have held that a non-US parent is not subject to jurisdiction solely on the basis of the local activities of a US subsidiary—even a 100 per cent owned subsidiary—if the subsidiary is carrying on its own business and has a measure of independence from the parent. On the other hand, if the local subsidiary is a "mere department" or "alter ego" of its foreign parent —determined with respect to common ownership and personnel, financial and operational control, and disregard for corporate formalities—a court will exercise jurisdiction over the parent.[79]

Particularly in antitrust cases, the trend in the US has been in the direction of greater jurisdictional reach. Any significant showing that the subsidiary's business is closely integrated with the parent's may well result in a finding that the parent is doing business in the US.[80] In the absence of an alter ego relationship, some courts will exercise jurisdiction over a foreign parent on an agency theory if the local subsidiary conducts all of the business in the forum that the parent would conduct if it were present.[81]

75. *Wells Fargo, supra.*
76. However, a litigant generally may not consent to subject-matter jurisdiction.
77. 375 US 311 (1964). *Accord Carnival Cruise Lines, Inc.* v. *Shute* 111 S Ct 1437 (1991); *The Bremen* v. *Zapata Off-Shore Co.* 407 US 1 (1972).
78. *Colonial Leasing Co.* v. *Pugh Bros. Garage* 735 F.2d 380 (9th Cir. 1984). But see *Carnival Cruise Lines* 111 S Ct 1437 (1991), and *Spradlin* v. *Leursiegler Management Services Co., Inc.* 926 F.2d 865 (9th Cir. 1991).
79. *Volkswagenwerk AG* v. *Beech Aircraft Corporation* 751 F.2d 117, 120–122 (2d Cir. 1984).
80. G. Born and D. Westin, *International Civil Litigation in United States Courts* 104–117 (1989).
81. *Frummer* v. *Hilton Hotel, Int'l, Inc.* 19 NY, 2d 533 (1967). See *Wells Fargo* 556 F.2d at 422–424.

SERVICE OF PROCESS

Service under federal rules

Service of process is another common area of pre-trial dispute, especially in international cases. In the federal courts, original "process" is a summons identifying the court and the parties, and specifying the time within which the defendant must respond and the consequences of failing to do so.[82] Service of process itself does not confer personal jurisdiction (except arguably in the case of tag jurisdiction), subject-matter jurisdiction or proper venue. Conversely, even when jurisdiction exists and venue is proper, a plaintiff's failure to comply with applicable service of process rules will lead to dismissal of the complaint.[83] An objection to improper service of process will be waived unless asserted in a defendant's answer or motion to dismiss.[84]

In federal court, service must be made in the manner prescribed by the Federal Rules. Service may be made on most individual or corporate defendants by personal delivery, registered mail, or in any manner prescribed by the law of the state in which the court sits.[85] For service outside the US, service under the Federal Rules ordinarily may be made (a) in the manner prescribed in the laws of the country where service is to be made; (b) by letter rogatory; (c) by personal service; (d) by mail, return receipt requested; or (e) "as directed by order of the court".[86]

Provided that no treaty is implicated (see pp. 69–71, below), US law generally accords little weight to the fact that service abroad pursuant to the Federal Rules violates the laws of the nation where service is effected. A typical case is *Alco Standard Corp.* v. *Benalal*, where a Spanish defendant challenged the validity of service upon it in Spain on the grounds that the service had violated Spanish law.[87] The court flatly rejected the argument, declaring that "the only relevant question for this court concerns the sufficiency of the service of process under laws of the United States".[88] Most other US decisions are to the same effect.[89] (Of course, if enforcement of any resulting US judgment is required abroad, the violations of foreign law may well become significant.)

82. Fed R Civ P 4(a) and (b). When service is made pursuant to state rules, process may consist of a summons, notice, or order in lieu of summons. See Fed R Civ P 4(b).

83. See Fed R Civ P 12(b) (4) and (5). Dismissal will ordinarily be "without prejudice" to plaintiff's right to file the suit again and to seek to effect proper service. But if the plaintiff is unable to serve the defendant in the manner prescribed, or if the limitation period for the action has expired in the mean time, dismissal can mean the end of the action.

84. See Fed R Civ P 12(h)(1).

85. Fed R Civ P 4(d).

86. Fed R Civ P 4(i).

87. 345 F Supp 14 (ED Pa. 1972).

88. *Ibid.* at 26.

89. e.g. *SEC* v. *Int'l Swiss Investments Corp.* 895 F.2d 1272 (9th Cir. 1990). But see *Aries Ventures* v. *AXA Finance SA* 1990 WL 37814 (SDNY 30 March 1990).

Hague Service Convention

Background

Service of process in international matters is often affected by the Hague Convention on the Service Abroad of Judicial and Extrajudicial Documents in Civil or Commercial Matters ("Hague Service Convention").[90] The Hague Service Convention came into force for the US in 1979. The UK and most other EC Member States are signatories to the Convention. The Convention applies only to "civil or commercial matters" and to "judicial or extrajudicial documents".[91]

The Hague Service Convention establishes a mechanism for service of US civil process on persons within the territory of other signatories to the Convention. Under the Convention, service usually begins with a written request by the plaintiff's attorney, who is a "judicial officer" within the meaning of the Convention.[92] The letter of request is prepared in the form prescribed by the Convention and attaches the US summons and complaint; these documents must be submitted to the "central authority" of the nation in which service is to be made. The central authority is required to review the letter of request for compliance with the Convention and promptly inform the applicant of any defect.[93] If the letter of request is in proper form, the foreign central authority will either effect service itself or through the appropriate local court[94] and will transmit a certificate of service to the plaintiff's attorney.[95]

A foreign central authority may refuse a request for service if it fails to meet the formal requirements of the Convention[96] or if "compliance would infringe [the requested state's] sovereignty or security".[97] Service will be refused if the letter of request and underlying documents are not in the appropriate language or accompanied by an accurate translation as required by the foreign state. Service may also be refused if the letter of request concerns matters that are not "civil or commercial" or seeks service of documents that are not "judicial or extrajudicial" within the Convention's meaning.

The Hague Service Convention provides several alternatives to the use of the central authority to effect service. Provided that a signatory state does not object, Art. 10(a) permits service "by postal channels", and Art. 10(b) and 10(c) permits "judicial officers, officials or other competent persons of the

90. 20 UST 361, TIAS No. 6638.

91. Hague Service Convention, Art. 1. There is some debate in the US over the precise scope of the Convention. It is clear that criminal proceedings are not civil or commercial matters within the meaning of the Convention. It also seems clear that the Convention applies principally to service of documents that initiate (e.g. complaints) or terminate (e.g. judgments) a lawsuit. Other documents are commonly served on the US lawyers representing the party in the case.

92. Hague Service Convention, Art. 3.

93. *Ibid.*, Art. 4.

94. *Ibid.*, Art. 5.

95. *Ibid.*, Art. 6.

96. *Ibid.*, Art. 4.

97. *Ibid.*, Art. 13.

foreign state to effect service". Article 8 permits diplomatic and consular agents to make service abroad on their own nationals, and, if a signatory state does not object, to others located in that state.

Exclusivity of Hague Service Convention

US courts generally have held that service of process within the territory of a signatory of the Hague Service Convention must comply with the procedures of the Convention, unless the other country has agreed to permit service by other means. The US Supreme Court has expressly held that the Hague Service Convention is the exclusive mechanism for serving process *into* nations that are party to the Convention.[98] Because the Convention is a treaty of the US, it is the "supreme law of the land", US Const. Art. VI, and therefore pre-empts—or overrides—inconsistent state and federal service rules. In the words of the Supreme Court, "By virtue of the Supremacy Clause, US Const. Art. VI, the Convention pre-empts inconsistent methods of service prescribed by state law in all cases to which it applies".[99] Thus, a foreign defendant may only be served in a signatory state in a manner that is consistent with the Hague Service Convention; service that is inconsistent with the Convention is invalid as a matter of US law, even if it was effected pursuant to a rule of local US law.

Service by mail under Art. 10(a)

An issue involving service in countries that are parties to the Hague Convention is whether service by mail is permitted. A number of lower courts have held that the Hague Service Convention permits service of process by registered mail. These courts have relied on Art. 10(a) of the Convention, that reads in relevant part as follows:

> Provided that the state of destination does not object, the present Convention shall not interfere with—
> (a) the freedom to *send judicial documents*, by postal channels, directly to persons abroad . . .
>
> (emphasis supplied)

A number of signatories to the Convention have not objected to Art. 10(a)'s provisions concerning "the freedom to send judicial documents by postal channels".

There is a significant division of authority among the lower US courts concerning Art. 10(a). A number of courts have held that, where no objection by the receiving state exists, service by mail is effective under Art. 10(a). These

98. *Volkswagenwerk AG* v. *Schlunk* 486 US 694 (1988).

99. *Ibid.* at 2108. See *Vorhees* v. *Fischer & Krecke* 697 F.2d 574 (4th Cir. 1983); *Harris* v. *Browning-Ferris Indus. Chem. Serv.* 100 FRD 775 (MD La. 1984); *Kadota* v. *Hosogai* 608 P.2d 68 (Az. App. 1980).

decisions have generally reasoned that a nation's failure to object to the provisions of Art. 10(a) indicates a willingness to permit service by mail.

On the other hand, a number of other courts have held that Art. 10(a) is not a service of process provision. These courts have emphasised that the language of Art. 10(a) does not authorise "service" of process, as several other sections of the Convention do, but instead refers only to the "sending" of other judicial documents. The lower courts that adopt this position also have emphasised that the service mechanisms of the Hague Service Convention are straightforward and expeditious, and that when the central authority mechanisms are followed, US courts respect the sovereignty of foreign nations.[100]

Schlunk: circumventing the Convention

In *Volkswagenwerk AG* v. *Schlunk*, the Supreme Court held that the Hague Service Convention did not apply to service effected within the US upon a foreign defendant.[101] Moreover, the court held that local law defined when service was fully effected within the US. The court affirmed a lower court decision permitting service upon Volkswagen AG (a German company) by means of serving Volkswagen AG's US subsidiary, reasoning that local Illinois law permits substituted service upon a foreign parent by means of serving its US subsidiary, when the subsidiary is shown to be merely the "alter ego" of the parent. The court held that, because service could be effected entirely within the US, there was no need for service "abroad"—and thus that the Hague Service Convention was simply not implicated. One lower court has extended *Schlunk* to permit substituted service within the US on a foreign company by means of service on a local secretary of state.[102]

FORUM SELECTION: VENUE, *FORUM NON CONVENIENS* AND REMOVAL

Venue

Under US law, venue refers to the place where an action may properly be brought. Venue rules are designed to ensure that litigation will generally proceed in the most convenient forum, particularly for defendants. Because of its federal system, US venue rules are often complex. Nonetheless, the Alien Venue Act (discussed below) usually prevents venue from being a significant issue in international litigation.

100. *Bankston* v. *Toyota Motor Corp.* 889 F.2d 172 (8th Cir. 1989); *Mommsen* v. *Toro Co.* 108 FRD 444, 446 (SD Iowa 1985); *Reynolds* v. *Koh* 109 AD 2d 97, 490 NYS 2d 295 (1985); *Ormandy* v. *Lynn* 122 Misc.2d 954, 472 NYS 2d 274 (NYS Ct 1984); *Cooper* v. *Makita* 117 FRD 16 (D Me. 1987).
101. 486 US 694.
102. *Melia* v. *Le Grand Chais de France* 135 FRD 28 (DRI 1991).

In the federal courts, a federal question case may be brought only where all the defendants reside, where the claim arose, or as otherwise provided by law.[103] A diversity case may be brought where all the plaintiffs or all the defendants reside or where the claim arose[104]; in addition a corporation may be sued where it is incorporated, licensed to do business or doing business.[105] These restrictions can create significant obstacles and complexities in domestic US litigation.

Under the Alien Venue Act, however, a non-US citizen ("an alien") may be sued in any district.[106] The Supreme Court has held that this venue provision overrides more restrictive venue rules contained in specific statutes like the patent laws.[107] As a consequence, venue is typically not a significant issue in cases against non-US defendants.

A federal court may dismiss an action if venue is improper in the plaintiff's chosen forum. More commonly, however, the court will transfer the case to a proper federal forum. Even if venue is proper, a federal court may transfer the case to another more convenient federal forum.[108] Federal trial judges have very broad discretion in granting or denying such transfers. As with personal jurisdiction, improper venue will be waived if no objection is included in the defendant's answer to the complaint or filed before an answer in the defendant's motion to dismiss.[109]

Forum non conveniens

A foreign defendant sued in a US forum may sometimes be able to dismiss the complaint on grounds of "*forum non conveniens*". The common law doctrine of *forum non conveniens* gives the trial court discretion to evaluate the practical inconveniences posed to the litigants of litigating in one forum rather than another.[110] The court seeks to determine not only the inconvenience to the defendant of plaintiff's forum choice, but the relative advantages and disadvantages to all parties of each available forum. In making its determination, the court will consider factors relating both to the private interests of the litigants and to the public interest. These factors include the residence and nationality of the parties; the convenience to the parties and witnesses of litigating in one forum or another; the location of the evidence; the benefits of local deter-

103. 28 USC §1391(b) (1982).
104. 28 USC §1391(a) (1982).
105. 28 USC §1391(c) (1982).
106. 28 USC §1391(d) (1982). Special provisions govern venue over a foreign state or any agency or instrumentality of a foreign state. See 28 USC §1391(f) (1982).
107. *Brunette Machine Works* v. *Kockum Indus. Inc.* 406 US 706 (1972).
108. A federal statute specifically authorises federal courts to transfer cases to other federal courts in the interest of justice and convenience: 28 USC §1404(a) (1982).
109. See Fed R Civ P 12(b)(3), 12(h)(1).
110. The discussion in this section deals with *forum non conveniens* in federal court. Most, but not all, states have *forum non conveniens* doctrines, but they may differ somewhat from the federal doctrine.

mination of localised controversies; and the potential for avoiding unnecessary problems in interpreting and applying foreign law.[111]

The classic *forum non conveniens* case is *Piper Aircraft & Co.* v. *Reyno*,[112] where the Supreme Court upheld a *forum non conveniens* dismissal of an action arising from an aeroplane crash in Scotland. The plaintiffs—the survivors of several Scottish citizens and residents killed in the crash—filed suit in US federal court against the US manufacturers of the aircraft. The trial court dismissed the case because of the close connections between the action and Scotland: the decedents' heirs were Scottish; the crash occurred in Scotland; the pilot was Scottish; and a large portion of the relevant evidence was located in the UK. The Supreme Court agreed, concluding that the US nationality of the aircraft manufacturers was insufficient to justify permitting a case with such extensive connections with the UK to proceed in the US, the forum preferred by the plaintiffs because of its more favourable law.[113]

The *forum non conveniens* doctrine rests largely on the discretion of the trial judge. "The *forum non conveniens* determination is committed to the sound discretion of the trial court. It may be reversed only where there has been a clear abuse of discretion."[114] There are, however, a number of important guidelines that govern *forum non conveniens* analysis.

First, a defendant has a much better chance of obtaining *forum non conveniens* dismissal if the plaintiff is not a US citizen or company. A US plaintiff's choice of forum is ordinarily entitled to considerable deference: "a plaintiff's choice of forum should rarely be disturbed . . . [Only] when trial in the chosen forum would establish . . . oppressiveness and vexation to a defendant . . . out of all proportion to plaintiff's convenience" is dismissal appropriate.[115] In contrast, however, no deference is afforded to the plaintiff's choice of forum if the plaintiff is not an American.[116] (A few courts have suggested that a foreign plaintiff can "win" a measure of deference if it shows that its choice of a US forum was motivated solely by reasons of convenience.[117])

Secondly, *forum non conveniens* analysis devotes virtually no attention to the substantive laws applicable in different fora. In *Piper*, for example, the

111. See *Gulf Oil Corp.* v. *Gilbert* 330 US 501, 508–509 (1947). The *forum non conveniens* doctrine does not permit the defendant entirely to escape the burden of litigating, since a prerequisite to dismissal is the existence of an adequate alternative forum. Rather, the doctrine compels the plaintiff to pursue its action in a forum that may be more favourable to the defendant.

112. 454 US 235 (1981).

113. *Ibid.* at 260–261. Similarly, in *Pain* v. *United Technologies Corp.* 637 F.2d 775 (DC Cir. 1980), the court upheld dismissal on *forum non conveniens* grounds of a suit by French, Norwegian, British, American and Canadian plaintiffs arising out of a crash in the North Sea of a helicopter manufactured in the US, but owned and operated in Norway. See also *In re Union Carbide Corporation Gas Plant Disaster at Bhopal* 634 F.Supp. 842 (SDNY 1986).

114. *Piper Aircraft* Co. v. *Reyno* 454 US 235, 256, 257 (1981).

115. *Ibid.* at 241 (quoting *Koster* v. *Lumbermens Mut. Cas. Co.* 330 US at 524 (1947).

116. See, *ibid.* at 251–252; *Pain* v. *United Technologies Corp* 637 F.2d 775, 795–796 (DC Cir. 1980).

117. *Nieminen* v. *Breeze-Eastern* 736 F.Supp. 580 (DNJ 1990); *Cliffs-Neddrill Turnkey Int'l Organjestad* v. *M/T Rich Duke* 734 F.Supp. 142 (D Del. 1990).

court granted a *forum non conveniens* dismissal, notwithstanding the fact that Scottish law was far less favourable to the plaintiffs than the applicable US law. "The possibility of a change in substantive law should ordinarily not be given conclusive or even substantial weight in the *forum non conveniens* inquiry."[118] Only if the alternative foreign forum provides "no remedy at all", are changes in substantive law relevant.[119]

Thirdly, even if the balance of convenience weighs in favour of dismissal, a trial court cannot dismiss a case on *forum non conveniens* grounds, unless the plaintiff can obtain relief in another forum. As noted above, the alternative forum requirement will only bar dismissal if the plaintiff will be effectively deprived of any remedy. For example, if the alternative forum will not permit the plaintiff's claim to be raised or the remedy available is so inadequate as to amount to no remedy at all, then the alternative forum requirement will not be satisfied.[120] But a reduced likelihood of recovery or less favourable measure of damages will not prevent dismissal.

Raising and proving issues of foreign law

Rule 44.1 governs the procedure for raising the applicability of, and the method of proving, foreign law. Rule 44.1 requires that a party that contends, by virtue of applicable conflict of law rules, that a cause of action be determined by foreign law must "give notice by pleadings or other reasonable written notice" to this effect. This notice requirement will be satisfied by a simple statement that foreign law is applicable. That statement may be included in the complaint, a responsive pleading (the matter often will be raised as one of the public interest factors in a *forum non conveniens* motion) or, to leave no doubt of the adequacy of the form of notice, in a separate document filed with the court and served on the other parties.[121]

Although there is no hard and fast rule concerning the timeliness of a Rule 44.1 notice, it is advisable for a litigant to file one fairly early in the case—as soon as it has decided on its theory of the case and what substantive law it wants the court to apply. A litigant that waits to raise an issue of foreign law, especially to the eve of trial, runs the risk that the court will find the notice untimely and refuse to apply foreign law.

Questions of foreign law are considered to be issues of law, to be decided by the court and reviewable *de novo* on appeal. Rule 44.1 authorises the judge to

118. *Piper Aircraft* 454 US at 247.

119. *Ibid.* at 254–255.

120. *Ibid.* at 254. In the *Laker* antitrust suit, the US trial court took the view that the doctrine of *forum non conveniens* was inapplicable because the British courts have no power to adjudicate a claim under the US antitrust laws. See *Laker Airways Ltd.* v. *Pan American World Airways* 568 F.Supp. 811 (DDC 1983).

121. C. Wright and A. Miller, *Federal Practice and Procedure*, §2443 at pp. 402–403 (1971). Other, more informal methods of notice often are also acceptable. *Ibid.*

ascertain the content of foreign law in any way he or she determines is appropriate, including affidavits, live expert testimony, and independent research.

PRE-TRIAL PROCEEDINGS: THE SPECTRE OF DISCOVERY

Introduction and scope of discovery

US procedural rules permit a litigant to obtain "discovery" both from its adversary and from third-party witnesses (i.e. persons that are not plaintiffs or defendants in the lawsuit). As is well known, discovery under the Federal Rules is extremely broad. Indeed, the breadth of US discovery accounts in significant part for the deep concern with which most foreign parties view US litigation.

The Federal Rules entitle a party to discover any "non-privileged" information that is relevant to the subject matter of the lawsuit.[122] Discovery may relate to any claim or defence of the party seeking discovery (or any other party), or may be designed merely to ascertain the existence or location of relevant documents or "persons having knowledge of any discoverable matter". The Federal Rules of Civil Procedure expressly provide that "[i]t is not ground for objection that the information sought will be inadmissible at trial if the information sought appears reasonably calculated to lead to the discovery of admissible evidence".[123] Even the trial preparation materials of a party or his or her lawyer may be discovered, but only on a showing of special need. State discovery procedures are generally similar.

Discovery mechanisms

The principal discovery methods available under US procedure are written interrogatories, requests for production of documents, requests for admission and depositions upon oral examination.[124] All of these procedures are available to obtain discovery from parties; third parties can only be required to produce documents and submit to depositions. A party ordinarily initiates discovery by seeking answers to interrogatories and document production,

122. "Parties may obtain discovery regarding any matter, not, privileged, which is relevant to the subject matter involved in the pending action . . . It is not ground for objection that the information sought will be inadmissible at trial if the information sought appears reasonably calculated to lead to the discovery of admissible evidence" Fed R Civ P 26(b)(1). The most frequently asserted privilege is the attorney–client privilege, which shields from discovery certain communications between lawyers and their clients. Other privileges recognised in many US jurisdictions protect confidential communications between physicians and their patients, between spouses, and between accountants and their clients.

123. Fed R Civ P 26(b)(2).

124. Fed R Civ 26(a). Other available discovery methods are requests for permission to enter on land or other property; requests for physical or mental examination of a party; and depositions on written questions.

then takes depositions, and concludes with requests for admission. The procedures can be used, however, in any sequence the party chooses. Unless the court orders otherwise, the number of discovery requests made by a party is unlimited.[125]

Federal discovery rules provide only limited time for responding to discovery requests. Unless the court otherwise orders, the time for responding to interrogatories, document requests, and requests for admission is only 30 days or, in the case of defendants, 45 days after service of the complaint, whichever is longer[126]; depositions may be scheduled on any "reasonable" notice.[127] As a practical matter, however, courts routinely grant extensions of time to respond to discovery requests. Although parties should not necessarily count on receiving more than one 30-day extension, 60 or even 90-day extensions are not uncommon. Courts usually can also be persuaded to defer all discovery (or all discovery except that relating to specified issues) pending determination of jurisdictional and other threshold dispositive motions.[128]

Access to discovery provided in US litigation ordinarily is not restricted to the parties and court personnel. Absent a confidentiality agreement among the parties or entry of a "protective order" by the court, any member of the public (including representatives of government agencies, competitors or newspaper reports) can inspect and obtain copies of responses to discovery from court files or from any party, witness or lawyer for a party or witness who is willing to provide it. Ordinarily documents produced in discovery will not be filed with the court, unless used to support a motion or offered into evidence at trial. In addition, courts will sometimes dispense with filing of responses to discovery and deposition transcripts to save filing space. (See Fed R Civ P 5(d).) But again, absent a protective order, parties, witnesses and their lawyers are free to make information obtained in discovery publicly available.

Interrogatories

The discovery mechanisms that litigants typically utilise first is interrogatories. Indeed, a plaintiff will often serve interrogatories together with the complaint. Interrogatories are written questions to which a party must respond in writing under oath. Interrogatories often seek identification of documents and witnesses. When the answer to an interrogatory can be obtained from business records of a party, and the burden of obtaining an answer from the records is substantially the same for either party, it is a sufficient answer for a party to make the relevant records available for inspection and copying. Answers to interrogatories are ordinarily admissible in evidence against the responding

125. Fed R Civ P 26(b)(1).
126. Fed R Civ P 33(a), 34(b), 36(a).
127. Fed R Civ P 30(b).
128. C. Wright and A. Miller, *Federal Practice and Procedure* at §§2009 n.35, 2040 n.86.

party at trial as admissions.[129] Accordingly, as a practical matter, answers, although responsive, are usually brief and as noncommittal as possible.

Document requests

Perhaps the single most important discovery mechanism under US procedural rules is the document request. Under the Federal Rules, a litigant can require either parties or non-parties to produce for inspection and copying all non-privileged documents relating to the litigation.

Requests for production of documents are often, but not invariably, served together with interrogatories. Although the rules require that a request for production describe "each item and category" of documents requested "with reasonable particularity", US courts routinely approve far broader requests than those permitted, for example, under English procedure. A request for "all documents relating to the special audit of X date" would be unobjectionable so long as the subject matter of the audit is relevant to the lawsuit. When accompanying interrogatories, document requests often simply demand production of "all documents identified in, used in the preparation of, or relating to" the interrogatory answers. Documents must be produced either in the form kept in the ordinary course of business or organised and labelled to correspond to the request.[130]

Depositions

The Federal Rules permit litigants in civil suits to take depositions of any party or non-party witness. A deposition is the oral questioning of an individual (the "deponent") by the lawyers for the other parties. The deponent is sworn to tell the truth and the deposition generally is transcribed verbatim by a stenographer or is videotaped. If it is otherwise admissible under general evidentiary rules, a deposition transcript may be used at trial.

A deposition typically is initiated by a notice from one party to all other parties setting forth the name and address of the witness and the time and place of the examination.[131] A deposition can be scheduled on any "reasonable" notice and at any place specified by the requesting party. In practice, time and place are usually negotiated between the parties before or shortly after the notice is served.

The deposition of a party, an officer, director, managing agent or designee

129. Fed R Civ P 33.
130. Fed R Civ P 34(b).
131. If a party does not know the identity of the employees of a corporation or other entity with knowledge of a particular subject, it may in the notice or subpoena, name the corporation or entity as the deponent. The corporation or entity must then designate one or more witnesses who consent to testify on its behalf concerning the subject in question: Fed R Civ P 30(b)(6).

of a party, or any witness not available to testify in person[132] may be used at trial or at an interlocutory hearing against parties with reasonable notice of the deposition. Statements made in a deposition can be used to contradict or impeach the deponent's testimony as a witness (or in any other manner permitted by the rules of evidence). Objections to using a deposition as evidence at trial may be made on any ground that would permit excluding evidence given by a trial witness.[133]

Admissions

Under the Federal Rules, a party may serve other parties with written requests for the admission of any relevant matters. Each matter whose admission is requested is deemed admitted, unless the requested party answers or objects. An answer must either deny the matter or detail the reasons why the answering party cannot truthfully admit or deny it. Any matter admitted is deemed conclusively established for purposes of the pending action (but not for any other purpose).[134]

Non-party discovery

Much pre-trial discovery is directed at, and obtained from, other litigants in the lawsuit in question. Nonetheless, under the Federal Rules, a party may also take discovery from non-party witnesses—that is, persons not named as parties to the action. The principal mechanism for accomplishing this is by "subpoena", which is served on the person or company from whom discovery is sought. A subpoena may require the witness to appear at a deposition and testify, produce documents, or both. Failure to comply with a subpoena, without seeking relief from the court, is punishable as contempt of court.

Although subpoenas are technically issued under the seal of the court, they are usually issued in blank by the court, and are completed and served by litigants without judicial approval. Unlike discovery requests directed against parties, a subpoena must be served by hand or mail on the witness himself. In the federal courts, a subpoena may only be issued by the court in the district where the deposition is to be taken. Absent a special court order, a subpoena may only require the witness to attend a deposition within 100 miles of the place where the witness resides, is employed or transacts business, or is served.[135]

Although a subpoena will direct a witness to appear at a particular place

132. In addition to unavailability by reason of death, injury, illness or imprisonment, a witness is considered unavailable if he or she is more than 100 miles from the place of trial or hearing or is outside the US, and if the absence was not procured by the party offering the deposition: Fed R Civ P 32(a)(3).

133. Fed R Civ P 32.

134. Fed R Civ P 36. A party may seek the leave of court to withdraw or amend an admission.

135. Fed R Civ P 45(d)(2).

and time, the actual place and time of the appearance of the witness is often negotiated in advance of issuance of the subpoena between counsel for the party issuing the subpoena and the witness. Unlike parties, third-party witnesses cannot be required to answer written interrogatories or respond to requests for admission.

RESISTING DISCOVERY

Pre-trial discovery is often highly contentious. Parties seeking discovery typically make the broadest requests conceivable, and persons from whom discovery is sought often resist nearly all the adverse parties' demands. These disagreements are usually settled by negotiations between the parties' counsel, but on occasion the trial judge (or a magistrate) will become involved.

A party can refuse to respond to interrogatories, document requests or requests for admission by delivering a statement of objections to the requesting party.[136] Objections can be based on relevance, burdensomeness or privilege, as well as on several grounds of particular interest to foreign litigants, as discussed below. However, a party cannot properly avoid appearing to testify without filing a motion requesting such relief with the court.[137]

A non-party witness (as opposed to a party) may resist compliance with a subpoena by serving objections within 10 days of service.[138] Alternatively, in the case of a subpoena *duces tecum*, a witness may file a motion to "quash" or modify the subpoena on the grounds that it is unreasonable or oppressive.[139] Ordinarily, the recipient of a subpoena will proceed via the objection route, which forces the adverse party to seek a court order compelling compliance.

As noted above, a number of grounds are available for resisting discovery. A person from whom discovery is sought may seek a protective order against "annoyance, embarrassment, oppression, or undue burden or expense".[140] The application of these terms is left largely to the trial court's discretion; it is safe to say, however, that many discovery demands that foreign litigants regard as "annoying" or "oppressive" will routinely be approved by US judges. For "good cause shown", the court may order that discovery not take place or that discovery take place only on specified terms and conditions, including a designation of the time, place, form or scope. A protective order may also require that discovery take place with no one present, except persons designated by the court, that a deposition be sealed, or that a trade secret or

136. Fed R Civ P 33(a) (interrogatories), 34(b) (document requests), 36(a) (requests for admission).

137. See Fed R Civ P 26(c), 30(d). The same requirement applies to a deponent who wishes to limit or terminate questioning at a deposition.

138. Fed R Civ P 45(d).

139. Fed R Civ P 45(b).

140. Fed R Civ P 26(c).

other confidential information must not be disclosed, or be disclosed only in a designated way.[141]

If a person fails to provide requested discovery, the requesting party may move for an order compelling discovery.[142] If a party then fails to comply with an order compelling discovery, the court may "make such orders in regard to the failure as are just".[143] The trial court has broad discretion in rendering such orders. Among other things, a court may order that particular facts be deemed established in favour of the party seeking discovery; that the disobedient party not be permitted to support or oppose designated claims or defences or to introduce designated matters in evidence; that certain pleadings or parts of pleadings be stricken; that further proceedings be stayed until the order is obeyed; that the action (or defence) be dismissed; that a default judgment be entered; that the failure to comply be treated as contempt of court (and punished by monetary fine); or that the disobedient party or its attorney pay the reasonable expenses, including attorneys' fees, incurred as a result of the failure to comply.[144]

A third-party witness who fails "without adequate excuse" to obey a subpoena may be held in contempt of court.[145] The penalty for contempt is imprisonment, fine or both.[146]

EXTRATERRITORIAL DISCOVERY

In principle, the Federal Rules authorise the discovery of materials located outside US territory, just as they authorise discovery within the US. As one Court of Appeal has observed, "[i]t is no longer open to doubt that a federal court has the power to require the production of documents located in foreign countries if the court has *in personam* jurisdiction of the person in possession or control of the material".[147] Countless lower US courts have used this authority to order extraterritorial discovery from foreign companies.[148]

Two requirements must be satisfied before a US court will order direct

141. Fed R Civ P 26(c).

142. Under the Federal Rules, the district court can require the party or witness who loses the motion, as well as the advising lawyer, to pay the reasonable expenses incurred in connection with the motion, including attorneys' fees, unless the court finds that the making of or opposition to the motion "was substantially justified or that other circumstances make an award of expenses unjust" Fed R Civ P 37(a)(4).

143. Fed R Civ P 37(b)(2).

144. Fed R Civ P 37(b).

145. Fed R Civ P 45(f).

146. 18 USC §§401–402 (1982).

147. *United States* v. *First National City Bank* 396 F.2d 897, 900–901 (2d Cir. 1968). See Restatement (Third) Foreign Relations Law of the United States §442(1)(a) (1987) ("A court . . . in the United States, when authorised by statute or rule of court, may order a person subject to its jurisdiction to produce documents, objects, or other information relevant to an action . . . even if the information or the person in possession of the information is outside of the United States.").

148. *United States* v. *Vetco, Inc.* 691 F.2d 1281 (9th Cir. 1981); see G. Born and D. Westin, *International Civil Litigation in United States Courts* pp. 266–278 (1988) (citing cases).

extraterritorial discovery from a foreign party under the Federal Rules of Civil Procedure. First, the party from whom discovery is sought must be subject to the personal jurisdiction of the forum court. Secondly, if the discovery of documents is requested, the foreign party must "control" those documents,[149] while if depositions are sought, then the deponents must be "officers, directors or managing agents" of the foreign corporate party.[150] Similar, but more rigorous, requirements apply to non-party witnesses.

Document discovery outside the US

With one important exception, discovery may not be compelled from either a party or a non-party witness, unless that person is subject to the personal jurisdiction of the forum court.[151] The standards of jurisdiction applicable to parties are those set forth above (pp. 59–64), while those applicable to non-parties are solely those set forth in case-law interpreting and applying the Due Process Clause.

The Federal Rules permit broad discovery of documents located outside the US from both parties[152] and non-party witnesses[153] subject to US jurisdiction. A party that is subject to the court's jurisdiction must provide discovery of documents that are within its "possession, custody or control".[154] A corporation is presumed to control all corporate documents and records, whether they are located inside or outside the US.[155] Corporations with unincorporated offices or branches both within and outside the US will ordinarily be required to produce documents located in both their US and non-US offices.[156]

149. *United States* v. *Vetco, Inc.* 691 F.2d 1281 (9th Cir. 1981); see G. Born and D. Westin, *International Civil Litigation in US Courts* p. 270 (1988).

150. See C. Wright and A. Miller, *Federal Practice and Procedure*, at §2103. Lower-level employees are treated as non-party witnesses, whose depositions can be compelled only if they are independently subject to the jurisdiction and subpoena service of the District Court. *Ibid*. Nonetheless, as a practical matter, it is often difficult to avoid "voluntary" production of important fact witnesses even if they are lower-level employees.

151. *In re Sealed Case* 832 F.2d 1268 (DC Cir. 1987); *United States* v. *First National City Bank* 396 F.2d 898 (2d Cir. 1968); *In re Uranium Antitrust Litigation* 480 F.Supp. 1138 (ND Ill. 1979). This requirement that personal jurisdiction exists does not apply to jurisdictional discovery is discussed below.

152. Fed R Civ P 34(a).

153. Fed R Civ P 45; C. Wright and A. Miller, *Federal Practice and Procedure*, §2454, at p. 425 (1971).

154. Fed R Civ P 34(a).

155. *In re Grand Jury Subpoena Addressed to Canadian International Paper Company*, 72 F.Supp. 1013 (SDNY 1947) ("The fact that a corporation's records and documents are physically located beyond the confines of the United States does not excuse it from producing them if they are in its possession and the court has jurisdiction of the corporation."); *United States* v. *First National City Bank* 396 F.2d 897 (2d Cir. 1968); *First National City Bank* v. *IRS* 271 F.2D 616, 618 (2d Cir. 1959); *Elder-Beerman Stores Corp.* v. *Federated Dept. Stores, Inc.* 45 FRD 515 (SDNY 1968).

156. See C. Wright and A. Miller, *Federal Practice and Procedure*, §2210, at p. 624 (1983). Cf. *In re Grand Jury 81–2*, 550 F.Supp. 24 (WD Mich. 1982) (Deutsche Bank ordered to comply with subpoena served on New York branch requesting production of documents from Frankfurt offices).

United States corporations can be compelled to produce documents held by their subsidiaries, including both US and foreign subsidiaries. The rationale is that a corporation controls its subsidiaries, and hence their documents.[157] In contrast, foreign corporations with no links to the US generally may not be required to produce documents held abroad solely because a US subsidiary of the parent is subject to the US court's personal jurisdiction. Nonetheless, discovery probably can be obtained from a foreign parent if the US subsidiary and foreign parent have substantially overlapping officers or directors, and the documents relate to the activities of the subsidiary as well as the parent.[158]

Non-party witnesses can also be required to produce documents that are within their possession, custody and control. In order to obtain document discovery from non-party witnesses, however, those persons must be subject both to the personal jurisdiction and the subpoena power of the court. For foreign entities, the latter requirement generally means that service must be effected within the judicial district where the district court is located.[159] Even where service can be effected, US courts are sometimes reluctant to order non-party discovery of evidence located in foreign offices of a foreign company, even if the company also has offices or branches in the US.[160]

Depositions of corporate personnel located abroad

Under the Federal Rules, a corporate party can be required to produce for deposition any "officer, director, or managing agent" with knowledge of the dispute.[161] This obligation extends to persons outside, as well as within, the US.[162] In contrast, as noted above, a corporation cannot be compelled to produce lower-level employees for deposition; corporate employees are treated as non-party witnesses and a party desiring to depose an employee must proceed by way of subpoena.[163]

157. *United States* v. *Vetco* 644 F.2d 1324 (9th Cir. 1981); *In re Investigation of World Arrangements* 13 FRD 280, 285 (DDC 1952).

158. *In re Uranium Antitrust Litigation* 480 F.Supp. 1138, 1144 (ND Ill. 1979). See also *Societe Internationale* v. *McGremery* 111 F.Supp. 435, 440–442 (DDC 1953) (requiring production because of "interlocked web of corporate organisation, management and finance"), aff'd, *Societe Internationale* v. *Brownell* 225 F.2d 532, 536 (DC Cir. 1955), rev'd on other grounds, *Societe Internationale* v. *Rogers* 357 US 197, 204 (1958).

159. Fed R Civ P 45. For US citizens, the so-called Walsh Act permits service of a subpoena outside of the territorial jurisdiction of the district court, and indeed, outside of the US, in specified circumstances: 28 USC §1783.

160. See e.g. *Laker Airways Ltd* v. *Pan American World Airways* 607 F.Supp. 324 (SDNY 1985). In *Laker*, the District Court quashed subpoenas *duces tecum* served on the New York offices of Midland Bank and Samuel Montague & Co. The subpoenas demanded production of documents located in the British offices of both companies. The District Court held that it would be "inappropriate" to order discovery of the documents because they were regularly maintained in Britain and because the US offices of the two companies had no involvement in the subject matter of the litigation.

161. Fed R Civ P 30(b)(6).

162. See *In re Anschuetz & Co.* 754 F.2d 602, 617 (5th Cir. 1985) (US district court has power to order depositions within the US of persons located outside the US).

163. C. Wright and A. Miller, *Federal Practice and Procedure*, §2103, at p. 374.

The attendance of a non-party witness at a deposition requires service of a subpoena on the witness.[164] If the witness is a corporation subject to the court's jurisdiction and to service, it can be required to produce its officers, directors, and managing agents for deposition—even if they are located overseas. Failure to produce corporate officers, directors or managing agents (but not employees) for deposition will result in sanctions against the corporation.

Finally, the so-called Walsh Act authorises US courts to issue subpoenas to US nationals or "resident[s] of the United States who are in a foreign country".[165] In civil cases, a subpoena may issue only if "necessary in the interest of justice" and if there is no other way to obtain the documents or testimony.[166] The Walsh Act ordinarily will not permit discovery from foreign companies or their personnel, if discovery is not otherwise available under the Federal Rules.

Compelled discovery from third parties not subject to US jurisdiction

The Federal Rules only permit a federal court to compel discovery from non-party witnesses when they are subject to the federal court's jurisdiction and to subpoena service. In all other cases, the Hague Evidence Convention or customary letters rogatory provide the only mechanism for obtaining compelled discovery abroad.

The Hague Convention on the Taking of Evidence Abroad in Civil or Commercial Matters ("Hague Evidence Convention"),[167] came into force for the US in 1979. The Convention was intended to provide an internationally acceptable framework for litigants to obtain evidence abroad in civil or commercial litigation. The UK and most other European nations are also party to the Convention.

The Convention's basic mechanism for evidence-taking is the "Letter of Request" procedure of Arts. 1–14. Under these provisions, Convention signatories are obliged to establish "central authorities"—governmental departments responsible for receiving incoming letters of request from foreign nations and arranging for them to be executed. A litigant may request the domestic court in which its suit is pending to send a letter of request—seeking production of specified materials or other evidence—to the central authority in the country where the sought-after evidence is located. The foreign central authority is then obliged to forward the letter of request to the foreign court where the witness is located; that court then conducts an evidentiary proceeding and returns the completed letter of request to the requesting court. In executing a letter of request, the receiving court will ordinarily follow its own rules of procedure and practice.[168]

164. Fed R Civ P 30(a).
165. 28 USC §1783 (1982).
166. 28 USC §1783(a) (1982).
167. 23 UST 2555, TIAS No. 744.
168. Article 9.

In general, the Convention *requires* signatory states to fulfil all properly completed letters of request. The Convention establishes only limited exceptions to this obligation. First, a signatory country may refuse to execute letters of request in the very limited circumstances in which its "sovereignty or security are threatened".[169] Secondly, and more importantly for litigants in US courts, a signatory country may declare under Art. 23 that it "will not execute letters of request issued for the purpose of obtaining pre-trial discovery of documents as known in common law countries".[170] Most signatories to the Convention have issued some sort of declaration under Art. 23.

Relationship between Hague Evidence Convention and Federal Rules

The Aerospatiale decision

Until 1987, US courts were sharply divided over the effect of the Hague Evidence Convention on the discovery methods of the Federal Rules that are available where the court possesses personal jurisdiction over the witness. In *Societe Nationale Industrielle Aerospatiale* v *US District Court*,[171] the Supreme Court ended this disagreement. First, the court rejected the suggestion that the Convention is wholly inapplicable to discovery from abroad where the recipient of the discovery request is subject to US personal jurisdiction and could be required under the Federal Rules to produce materials in the US; the court specifically held that the Convention was available for both party and non-party discovery. Secondly, the court held that the Convention was *not* the exclusive means of discovering evidence located in the territory of a foreign signatory nation and "did not deprive the District Court of the jurisdiction it otherwise possessed" under the Federal Rules.[172] The court emphasised that the Convention provided merely "optional procedures" and did not "require any contracting state to use" those procedures. Finally, the court concluded that the Convention *must* be used in certain circumstances, which are defined by the doctrine of international comity.[173]

The court divided over what comity requires. A five-justice majority concluded that comity calls for a case-by-case weighing of foreign and US "interests", and certain other factors, to ascertain when first-use of the Convention is mandated. This comity analysis required lower courts to consider a variety of factors to determine whether extraterritorial discovery pursuant to the Convention should be required, including: (a) the sovereign interests of the US;

169. Article 12.
170. Article 23.
171. 482 US 522 (1987).
172. *Ibid.* at 540.
173. 482 US at 543–546.

(b) the sovereign interests of the concerned foreign nation; (c) the scope and intrusiveness of the requested discovery; (d) the likelihood that resort to the Convention's procedures would be effective in a given case; and (e) the difficulties that a foreign party would encounter if forced to comply with US-style discovery.[174] The court specifically refused to provide guidance for the application of these factors in specific cases: "We do not articulate specific rules to guide this delicate task of adjudication."[175]

Post-Aerospatiale decisions

Recent lower-court decisions applying *Aerospatiale* have provided a measure of additional guidance as to when the Convention, rather than the Federal Rules, must be used to obtain extraterritorial discovery.[176] A number of lower courts have held that the party that urges first-use of the Convention bears the burden of demonstrating that comity requires this. At least one lower court has reached the opposite conclusion.[177]

The majority of post-*Aerospatiale* decisions have *not* required first-use of the Convention.[178] These decisions have relied on the perception that discovery under the Federal Rules is quicker and more effective than Convention discovery.[179] Lower courts have also tended to place a relatively low value upon foreign sovereign interests.[180]

Despite this, foreign litigants have obtained some benefits from raising the Convention as a defence to US-style direct discovery. Thus, lower US courts have usually ordered direct discovery under the Federal Rules *only after* requiring a narrowing of the breadth, intrusiveness and burdensomeness of the relevant discovery requests.[181] As one lower court has declared, "expansive discovery without concomitant relevance is not what the court envisioned when it handed down the *Aerospatiale* decision . . . I believe that a number of

174. *Ibid.* at 545–546.

175. *Ibid.* at 546.

176. See Born and Hoing, "Comity and the Lower Courts: Post-Aerospatiale Applications of the Hague Evidence Convention", 24 Int'l Law. 393 (1990).

177. *Hudson* v. *Hermann Pfauter GmbH & Co.* 117 FRD 33 (NDNY 1987).

178. *Bedford Computer Corp.* v. *Israel Aircraft Indus., Ltd* 1990 Bank LEXIS 964 (US Bankr. NH 15 Feb 1990) (documents from Israel); *Great Lakes Dredge & Dock Co.* v. *Harnischfeger Corp.* 1990 US Dist. LEXIS 12843 (ND Ill. 1990) (depositions from Germany); *Haynes* v. *Kleinwefers* 119 FRD 335 (EDNY 1988) (interrogatories and document requests from Germany); *Rich* v. *KIS Cal., Inc.* 121 FRD 254 (MDNC 1988) (interrogatories from France); *Benton* v. *Uddeholm Corp.* 118 FRD 386 (DNJ 1987) (interrogatories and document requests from Sweden); *Scarminach* v. *Goldwell GmbH* 531 NYS 2d 188 (NY Sup. Ct 1988) (interrogatories and document requests from Germany); *Sandsend Financial Consultants* v. *Wood* 743 SW 2d 364 (Tex. App. Houston 1988) (deposition and document request from Channel Islands). But see *Hudson* v. *Hermann Pfauter GmbH & Co.* 127 FRD 33 (NDNY 1987).

179. *Benton* 118 FRD at 391.

180. *Rich* 121 FRD at 258; *Benton* 118 FRD at 391.

181. *Benton* 118 FRD at 390; *Rich* 121 FRD at 260; *Scarminach* 531 NY 2d at 191; *Bedford Computer Corp.* 1990 Bankr. LEXIS 964.

the requests are not 'simple' [as required by *Aerospatiale*] and may require streamlining if we are to proceed under the federal rules".[182]

Impact of "blocking" and bank secrecy laws on discovery outside the US

A number of countries have enacted so-called "blocking" statutes to forbid US courts access to evidence on foreign soil. In general, these statutes make it a crime to disclose certain information or documents to third parties, including foreign government authorities or litigants. Some such statutes are self-executing, while others (like the Protection of Trading Interests Act) apply only if a foreign government enters specific orders concerning particular discovery disputes. Many countries also have bank secrecy laws which forbid banks or bank officials from disclosing client records or information without their customer's consent.

It goes without saying that the target of a US discovery request that conflicts with another country's blocking statute is in a difficult situation. Violation of the blocking statute may result in serious penalties, while non-compliance with a US discovery order may result in equally harsh sanctions, including fines or imprisonment for contempt, dismissal of the complaint or entry of a default judgment.

United States courts are not entirely insensitive to the harshness that results from conflicting legal obligations. In determining whether to order discovery or impose sanctions for non-compliance with a discovery request, courts usually will consider constraints imposed by blocking statutes.[183] A representative lower-court decision is *United States* v. *Vetco Inc.*,[184] a case involving enforcement of an IRS subpoena seeking documents in Switzerland. In *Vetco*, the court held that it "must balance competing interests" in deciding whether to order extraterritorial discovery in violation of foreign law. The factors balanced by the court included the "vital national interests" of the US and Switzerland, the "extent of hardship" suffered by the defendant, the "location" of the documents, the defendant's nationality, the "importance of the documents" and the "availability of alternative means of compliance". Weighing these various factors, the court ordered discovery. It emphasised that any IRS summons reflects a strong governmental interest, that the Swiss defendants were owned by a US company and that Switzerland had expressed no particular interest in the case.

Courts enjoy broad discretion to impose sanctions, notwithstanding a blocking statute. As a practical matter, trial judges show no sympathy for litigants that fail to make every reasonable effort to comply with discovery orders. At a minimum, a litigant seeking to avoid sanctions must produce all

182. *Benton* 118 FRD at 390.

183. See Restatement (Second) of Foreign Relations Law of the United States, §40 (1965); Restatement (Third) of Foreign Relations Law of the United States, §442 (1986).

184. 691 F.2d 1281, 1286–1291 (9th Cir. 1981).

relevant information and documents consistent with the blocking statute's restrictions and must make reasonable efforts to obtain a waiver of blocking restrictions.[185] A litigant that solicits imposition of a blocking order or that removes documents to a jurisdiction with blocking restrictions will likely face severe sanctions.[186]

Jurisdictional discovery

There is one important exception to the general rule that a person must be subject to the forum's personal jurisdiction before the court may order discovery. This exception relates to so-called jurisdictional discovery, which is directed solely at obtaining facts needed to determine whether a defendant is subject to the court's jurisdiction.

Disputes over personal jurisdiction are often decided solely on the basis of the parties' pleadings and written affidavits concerning jurisdictional facts. Nonetheless, district courts possess broad discretion to order discovery into facts relevant to personal jurisdiction over the defendant.[187] After allowing such discovery, the district judge may permit additional written submissions or conduct an evidentiary hearing on jurisdiction.

The decision whether or not to allow jurisdictional discovery generally lies within the discretion of the trial court. Plaintiffs ordinarily are entitled to conduct discovery on the issue of personal jurisdiction, provided that they have alleged a plausible basis for jurisdiction over the defendant, and there are disputed issues of fact. One Court of Appeal has held that, "[d]iscovery may appropriately be granted where pertinent facts bearing on the question of jurisdiction are controverted or where a more satisfactory showing of the facts is necessary".[188] Courts typically will grant leave to conduct jurisdictional discovery if a *prima facie* showing of jurisdiction has been made—that is, if the plaintiff alleges facts that would support a colourable basis for jurisdiction.[189]

Jurisdictional discovery will be denied if the plaintiff has failed to allege a

185. See *Societe Internationale pour Participations Industrielles et Commerciales, SA* v. *Rogers* 357 US 197 (1958) (upholding order for production of documents but rejecting sanction of dismissal against plaintiff who attempted in good faith to obtain waiver of Swiss bank secrecy law).

186. *In re Marc Rich & Co., AG* 707 F.2d 663 (2d Cir. 1983); see also *United States* v. *Bank of Nova Scotia ("Bank of Nova Scotia II")* 740 F.2d 817 (11th Cir. 1984); *United States* v. *Bank of Nova Scotia ("Bank of Nova Scotia I")* 691 F.2d 1384 (11th Cir. 1982); *United States* v. *Vetco* 644 F.2d 1324 (9th Cir. 1981); *SEC* v. *Banca della Svizzeria Italiana* 92 FRD 111 (SDNY 1981).

187. For example, in *Oppenheimer Fund, Inc.* v. *Sanders* 437 US 340, 351 n.13 (1978), the Supreme Court observed that "where issues arise as to jurisdiction or venue, discovery is available to ascertain the facts bearing on such issues". See also *United States* v. *United Mine Workers* 330 US 258, 292 n.57 (1947); C. Wright and A. Miller, *Federal Practice and Procedure*, §2009 n.34 (1970).

188. *Data Disc* 557 F.2d 1280, 1285 n.1. (9th Cir. 1977).

189. *In re Marc Rich & Co.* 707 F.2d 663, 670 (2d Cir. 1983) (party seeking jurisdictional discovery must demonstrate "a reasonable probability that ultimately it will succeed in establishing the facts necessary for the exercise of jurisdiction"); *Insurance Company of the State of Pennsylvania* v. *Centaur* 590 F.Supp. 1187, 1189 (SDNY 1984).

credible basis for jurisdiction, or if there is no reason to believe the plaintiff will succeed in establishing jurisdiction.[190] Additional criteria relevant to the availability of jurisdictional discovery are the complexity of the facts, the extent to which facts are within the defendant's control, the extent to which the plaintiff has availed itself of opportunities to establish jurisdictional facts, and the degree to which the defendant has submitted evidence of no US contacts.[191]

Finally, although the plaintiff ordinarily must show affirmatively that the defendant is subject to personal jurisdiction,[192] the precise weight of this burden depends upon the plaintiff's opportunity to conduct jurisdictional discovery. If jurisdictional discovery has been conducted, then the plaintiff must generally show by a preponderance of the evidence that the defendant is subject to personal jurisdiction; if no such discovery is made available, then only a *prima facie* showing of jurisdictional facts is required.[193]

Effects of jurisdictional discovery on general discovery

The presence of an unresolved, dispositive jurisdictional issue does not necessarily bar general discovery on other issues, but trial courts have discretion to stay discovery on the merits until the jurisdictional question is resolved.[194] In the words of one leading commentator, "the court has discretion to stay discovery on other issues until [a] critical issue [that is in dispute] has been decided. In accordance with this principle . . . a court may decide that in a particular case it would be wise to stay discovery on the merits until challenges to jurisdiction have been resolved."[195]

PRE-TRIAL CONFERENCES AND SCHEDULING ORDERS

During the pre-trial phase of a case, the judge will ordinarily convene one or more pre-trial conferences. The purposes of pre-trial conferences are to expedite disposition of the case, establish early and continuing control of the case by the judge, discourage wasteful pre-trial activities, improve the quality of trial and facilitate settlement.[196] Within 120 days after filing of the complaint, the court will consult with counsel for the parties and enter a scheduling order setting time limits for joining additional parties, amending pleadings,

190. See, e.g. *Compagnie des Bauxites de Guinée* v. *L'Union* 723 F.2d 357, 362 (3d Cir. 1983); *Shaw* v. *Boyd* 658 F.Supp. 89 (ED Pa. 1987).

191. See *Kamen* v. *American Tel. & Tel. Co.* 791 F.2d 1006 (2d Cir. 1986) (error to deny plaintiff jurisdictional discovery based upon conclusory and hearsay statements offered by defendant); "Use of Discovery to Obtain Jurisdictional Facts" 59 Va L Rev 533 (1973).

192. *Data Disc* 557 F.2d at 1285; *Pena* 563 F.Supp. at 746.

193. *Data Disc* 557 F.2d at 1285.

194. C. Wright and A. Miller, *Federal Practice and Procedure*, at §§2009 n.35, 2040 n.86.

195. Wright and Miller, at §2040.

196. Fed R Civ P 16(a).

filing motions and completing discovery.[197] Thereafter, one or more pre-trial conferences may be held to formulate and simplify the issues in the case; to avoid unnecessary proof (such as proof of the authenticity of documents); to rule in advance on the admissibility of evidence; to explore settlement possibilities; to schedule exchange of any pre-trial briefs; and to deal with other matters that may expedite disposition of the action.[198] A final pre-trial conference will be held close to the time of trial to devise a plan for the trial and a programme for facilitating the admission of evidence.[199]

After any pre-trial conference, a pre-trial order will be entered reciting the actions taken and governing the subsequent proceedings.[200] Failure to comply with a pre-trial order will subject a party or its lawyer to the same sanctions as failure to comply with a discovery order.[201] The final pre-trial order will sometimes include a recitation of stipulated facts, issues in dispute, and witnesses and documents to be presented at trial. Efforts to dispute stipulated facts, raise new issues, or present additional witnesses or documents at trial will be rejected, absent a showing of extraordinary circumstances.

GARY B. BORN
REBECCA ARBOGAST
MARC COHEN

197. Fed R Civ P 16(b).
198. Fed R Civ P 16(c).
199. Fed R Civ P 16(d).
200. Fed R Civ P 16(a).
201. Fed R Civ P 16(f).

CHAPTER 5

CROSS-BORDER COURT ORDERS AND BANKS[1]

THE CONTEXT

There can be no doubt that today the need for cross-border co-operation between courts and enforcement agencies is greater than ever. Modern systems of communication, social mobility, the decline in business ethics and the revolution in electronic methods of settlement of international bank payments have all played their part in the increase of conduct which, both in its civil and criminal aspects, requires international remedies. If the traditional banking confidentiality rules applied as they have been understood since the decision in *Tournier*,[2] then the guilty, as well as the innocent, would be able to take advantage of banking secrecy in circumstances such as (and these are only examples) infringement of securities or revenue legislation; drug trafficking; fraud and breach of trust; the avoidance of execution of judgment debts. The freezing of foreign assets and the obtaining of evidence abroad have become ever more important. The US Securities and Exchange Commission has been in the forefront of efforts to obtain international co-operation in securities frauds, and has been successful in obtaining evidence abroad.

COURT ORDERS AND CONFIDENTIALITY

In the *Santa Fe* case,[3] the US Securities and Exchange Commission brought civil proceedings in New York alleging that insider trading had taken place

1. This paper draws on the following previously published papers: Collins, "Banking Secrecy and the Enforcement of Securities Legislation", in *Conflicts of Interest in the Changing Financial World*, ed. Goode 1986, pp. 81–90; "Problems of Enforcement in the Multinational Securities Market: A United Kingdom Perspective" (1987) 9 Univ. Penn. J. Int. Bus. L. 487; "The Territorial Reach of Mareva Injunctions" (1989) 105 L.Q.R. 262; "Fraudulent Conduct in International Law" [1989] Curr. L. Prob. 255.
2. *Tournier* v. *National Provincial and Union Bank of England* [1924] 1 KB 461 (CA).
3. 1985 ECC 187; (1984) 23 Int LM 511.

prior to the announcement of a takeover of Santa Fe by Kuwait Petroleum Corporation. For the purposes of the New York proceedings, the Securities and Exchange Commission required evidence which was situated in England, documents and testimony from employees of a Luxembourg bank with a branch in England. Under the Hague Convention for the Taking of Evidence Abroad, to which both the UK and the US are parties, a judge in the US may request the English court to arrange for the evidence to be collected or taken in England, and pursuant to this procedure the English court made an order requiring examination of witnesses who had been employed in London by a Luxembourg bank, International Resources and Finance Bank SA, through whose London branch purchases of stock and options in Santa Fe had taken place. The employees sought to set aside the order requiring their examination on the ground, *inter alia*, that they were forbidden by Luxembourg law from revealing the identity of clients of the bank. In that case the relevant information related mainly to the operation of the London branch, and there was considerable doubt as to whether Luxembourg law did in fact forbid the disclosure of the information, but whether or not it did forbid it, it was held that there was no real or substantial risk of the applicants being charged with any criminal offence in Luxembourg. But Drake J accepted that there might be circumstances in which it would be against the public interest to order disclosure of confidential information, since there was:

> A public interest in maintaining the confidential relationship between banker and client, so that wherever a banker seeks to be excused from answering a question which would involve the breach of that confidentiality, it is proper . . . for the court to consider such request and to judge it in the context of the circumstances in which it is made. There is . . . also clearly a public interest, and a very strong one, in not permitting the confidential relationship between banker and client to be used as a cloak to conceal improper or fraudulent activities, evidence of which would otherwise be available to be used in legal proceedings, whether here or abroad.

In international securities fraud cases the recent decision of the House of Lords in *Re State of Norway's Application*[4] has opened the door to more effective gathering of evidence in England (and other common law jurisdictions) in aid of foreign civil proceedings. The Hague Evidence Convention of 1970 provides for mutual assistance between countries for the purpose of evidence gathering in "civil or commercial" matters. The normal use of the Convention is for the execution of letters rogatory (or letters of request) issued by a court in one country for the taking of evidence in another country, usually under the supervision of the courts of the latter country. The Hague Evidence Convention of 1970 is given effect in the UK by the Evidence (Proceedings in Other Jurisdictions) Act 1975.

The decision in *Re State of Norway's Application* concerned the question (*inter alia*) whether a letter of request from a Norwegian court to the English

4. [1990] 1 AC 723.

court to take evidence for the purposes of a tax claim pending in Norway was a "civil or commercial" matter. The evidence was sought from (*inter alios*) the taxpayer's English bankers, Lazards. The doubt arose because in civil law countries (although not in Norway) a tax claim is regarded as part of public law and hence not part of civil or commercial law, whereas in England in general the expression "civil law" merely excludes criminal law, and tax proceedings which are not criminal in character would be regarded as civil. The question for decision was how to approach the classification of the expression "civil or commercial" in the 1975 Act. Two differently constituted divisions of the Court of Appeal in separate phases of the litigation had expressed different views. In the first decision[5] the Court of Appeal was unanimous in concluding that the appropriate approach was to classify the claim under the law of the requesting court, and accept this classification, provided that it was not in conflict with any fundamental principle recognised under English law; but Kerr LJ would have preferred to apply an internationally acceptable definition if there had been material before the court to supply the definition. In the second case[6] May and Balcombe LJJ held that the expression "civil or commercial" should be given a generally acceptable international interpretation based on that used in civil law countries, which would exclude fiscal matters. Woolf LJ thought there was no such internationally acceptable interpretation, but reached the same result by deciding that whatever the ambit of civil or commercial matters, fiscal matters did not fall within it.

But the House of Lords held that an application for assistance came within the scope of the 1975 Act if the foreign proceedings were "civil or commercial" by the law of the requesting state, and also if they were civil (i.e. not criminal) by English law. Accordingly, in the present case the application was within the 1975 Act because the proceedings were not criminal, and they were civil under Norwegian law.

So far as banking confidentiality was concerned, it was accepted by the parties that the question of confidentiality could only be answered by the court undertaking a balancing exercise, weighing on the one hand the public interest in preserving the confidentiality owed by the witnesses as bankers to their customers, and on the other hand the public interest in the English court assisting the Norwegian court in obtaining evidence in England. The judge had found that the crucial question was who was the settlor of a trust administered by the bank. The judge resolved the question by ordering the witnesses to reveal the identity of the settlor only if one of the witnesses said in evidence that the ultimate settlor was the taxpayer under investigation. This resolved the question of what might have happened if the true owner of the account was someone unconnected with the case (such as the queen of England), whose confidentiality would thus be destroyed for no good reason. The Court of Appeal and the

5. [1987] QB 433.
6. [1988] 3 WLR 603.

House of Lords refused to interfere with the exercise of this discretion by the judge.

ATTACHMENT OF ASSETS

It is not necessary to say much about the nature of *Mareva* injunctions. A *Mareva* injunction is, of course, an injunction restraining the disposal of assets pending trial, or pending execution of a judgment—although perhaps, as the Master of the Rolls observed in the *DST* case,[7] injunctions granted after judgment perhaps should not be treated as if they were *Mareva* injunctions.

Until 1988, it was generally thought that *Mareva* injunctions were limited to assets in England, and could not be granted in relation to assets abroad. In *Ashtiani* v. *Kashi*[8] the Court of Appeal held that the basis of the *Mareva* jurisdiction was "clearly limited to assets within the jurisdiction"[9] and the Court of Appeal refused to order disclosure (ancillary to the *Mareva* injunction) in relation to assets outside the jurisdiction. In Australia and Hong Kong, however, it was held that the *Mareva* jurisdiction did apply to foreign assets[10] and the English Court of Appeal held that disclosure orders relating to foreign assets could be made after judgment had been given against the defendant.[11]

In the first of the cases, *Babanaft International Co. SA* v. *Bassatne*,[12] judgment had been given in a civil fraud action against the judgment debtors in the sum of US $15 million. The judgment debtors were foreign nationals; one lived mainly in Switzerland and the other mainly in Greece, and they owned property in various countries through a network of companies which were incorporated in jurisdictions (Panama, Liberia and the Dutch Antilles) in which it was difficult for outsiders to obtain information about their ownership, control and assets. It was held that an injunction could be granted to restrain a person properly before the court from the disposal of assets abroad, and that the decision in *Ashtiani* v. *Kashi* was merely a decision on the practice in relation to the exercise of the discretion as it then was, and not a decision on the limits of the jurisdiction of the court. In *Republic of Haiti* v. *Duvalier*,[13] the defendants were "Baby Doc" Duvalier, who was President of Haiti from 1971 to 1986, and various members of his family. The Republic of Haiti alleged in

7. *DST* v. *Shell International Petroleum* [1990] 1 AC 295, revd on other grounds *ibid.*, p. 329.
8. [1987] QB 888 (CA).
9. At p. 899, *per* Dillon LJ.
10. See *Ballabil Holdings Pty Ltd* v. *Hospital Products Limited* [1984] 2 NSWLR 662, affd (1985) 1 NSWLR 155; *Coombs & Barei Construction Pty Ltd* v. *Dynasty Pty Ltd* (1986) 42 SASR 413; *Yandil Holdings Pty Ltd* v. *Insurance Co. of North America* (1987) 7 NSWLR 571; *Asean Resources Ltd* v. *Ka Wah International Merchant Finance Limited* [1987] LRC (Comm.) 835.
11. *Interpool Limited* v. *Galani* [1988] QB 738; *Maclaine Watson & Co. Ltd* v. *International Tin Council (No. 2)* [1989] Ch. 286.
12. [1990] Ch. 13.
13. [1990] 1 QB 202.

proceedings in France that the Duvalier family had embezzled very large sums of money from the Republic of Haiti. The restraint was sought on the basis of the combined effect of s. 25 of the Civil Jurisdiction and Judgments Act 1982 and Art. 24 of the Brussels Convention on Jurisdiction and the Enforcement of Judgments in Civil and Commercial Matters of 1968, i.e. an ancillary proceeding in aid of proceedings which were pending in a foreign country on the substance. The Court of Appeal applied *Babanaft* by granting a pre-judgment injunction, the effect of which was to restrain English solicitors who had acted for the Duvalier family from dealing with assets which they held on its behalf abroad. In *Derby & Co. Ltd.* v. *Weldon (No. 1)*,[14] the plaintiffs claimed that the defendants, through dishonest conduct, had been responsible for the insolvency of a group of companies which had caused huge losses to the plaintiffs. The Court of Appeal found, as a matter of fact, that there were grounds for supposing that the defendants had acted dishonestly and that they had the ability to lock away assets in inaccessible overseas companies, and that there was a very real risk that assets in England and abroad would remain hidden or be spirited away so as to render any future judgment useless. In those circumstances, the Court of Appeal applied the *Babanaft* principle to the ordinary pre-judgment case where the substantive proceedings were pending in England and granted a worldwide *Mareva* injunction. In the words of Kerr LJ in *Babanaft* "some situations, which are nowadays by no means uncommon, cry out—as a matter of justice to plaintiffs—for disclosure orders and Mareva-type injunctions, covering foreign assets of defendants."[15]

In each of these cases, however, the Court of Appeal had to grapple with a very serious question which arises in relation to injunctions covering foreign assets, namely the effect of such injunctions on third parties, particularly third parties who are abroad. A *Mareva* injunction in the normal case has a direct effect on third parties who are notified of it and who hold assets comprised in the order. This is because of the principle that a person who, knowing of an injunction, aids and abets the party enjoined in committing a breach of it, is guilty of a contempt of court tending to obstruct the course of justice.[16] The effect on third parties is crucial for the effectiveness of the *Mareva* jurisdiction. For a defendant (especially a foreign defendant) may not respect the terms of the injunction, and because a bank which allows the defendant to remove or dissipate assets in breach of a *Mareva* injunction is guilty of contempt, that is usually sufficient in the domestic context to freeze the money held by the bank. But in each of these cases relating to foreign assets the Court of Appeal limited the effect of the injunction as regards thirds parties, because it would be wrong for the English court to subject acts abroad to the principle that those who aid and abet a breach of an English injunction are guilty of contempt of court. The broad effect of the decisions was to exempt third parties in respect of acts

14. [1990] Ch. 48.
15. [1990] Ch. 13, 33.
16. See *Seaward* v. *Paterson* [1897] 1 Ch 545; *Z Limited* v. *A–Z* [1982] QB 558 (CA).

abroad from compliance with the order unless and until the order had been rendered enforceable by the courts of the place where the assets were. In *Derby & Co. Ltd* v. *Weldon (Nos 3 and 4)*,[17] the Court of Appeal gave the order extraterritorial effect as regards third parties who were subject to the jurisdiction of the court and who had been given written notice of the order at their residence or place of business within the jurisdiction and who were "able to prevent acts or omissions outside the jurisdiction of this court which assist in the breach of the terms of the order".

In practice it is likely to be disclosure orders relating to foreign assets, which lead to the discovery of those assets, and subsequent attachment proceedings in the foreign countries, that are likely to be more effective than *Mareva* injunctions relating to assets abroad. It is only when the identity and location of the assets is known that the plaintiff is in a position to secure an effective order which binds third parties. In many foreign countries an attachment operates not only *in personam*, but also *in rem*, in the sense that if, for example, a bank account is involved it operates like a garnishee order, so that the bank repays the defendant at its peril, since it may be compelled to pay the plaintiffs again. In those circumstances a *Mareva* injunction would, in the words of Nicholls LJ in *Babanaft*, be a holding injunction, to give the plaintiff time to apply to the relevant foreign court for appropriate orders of attachment.[18]

ATTACHMENT OF ENGLISH BANK ACCOUNTS IN SUPPORT OF FOREIGN PROCEEDINGS

Here the question is whether a plaintiff in proceedings abroad can freeze English accounts. In England, prior to 1982, it was not normally possible for a plaintiff in a foreign proceeding, who was pursuing his case abroad, to obtain the freezing of a foreign defendant's assets in England. The leading case was unfortunate decision of the House of Lords in *The Siskina*.[19] The *Siskina* was carrying marble slabs originating in Italy and destined for Saudi Arabia. The *Siskina* was owned by a one-ship Panamanian company, but managed by Greeks in Piraeus. The ship owners, when the ship was near the entrance to the Suez Canal, alleged that the charterers had not paid the full freight due under the charterparty and ordered the master to turn back and go to Cyprus and unload the cargo, where the ship owners issued a writ *in rem* against the cargo. After discharge of the cargo, the vessel left Cyprus and sank on the way to Greece. The ship owners made a claim on London underwriters and were likely to receive US$750,000. The cargo owners were anxious about these moneys, since the ship owners had no other assets, and in particular the cargo owners were anxious that the money should not be paid to the ship owners

17. [1989] 2 WLR 412. See also *Derby* v. *Weldon (No. 6)* [1990] 1 WLR 1139.
18. See [1990] Ch. 13, 43.
19. [1979] AC 210.

because they would then be beyond reach of their claim for compensation for the storage charges etc., which had been caused by the wrongful arrest of the cargo in Cyprus. The cargo owners sought to have the insurance money of US$750,000 retained in England until their claim for damages was settled. The bills of lading contained a clause giving exclusive jurisdiction to the courts of Genoa. The only connection of the case with England was the location of the insurance money. The House of Lords held that it was not possible to obtain an injunction to hold money in the jurisdiction if there was no other cause of action over which the English court had jurisdiction.

Article 24, however, of the Brussels Convention of 1968 (to which the UK and most of the other members of the EEC are now parties) provides that application may be made to the courts of a contracting state for such provisional measures, including protective measures, as may be available under the law of that state, even if, under the Convention, the courts of another contracting state have jurisdiction as to the substance of the matter. English law has been altered by s. 25 of the Civil Jurisdiction and Judgments Act 1982, the effect of which is that where proceedings are pending in another part of the UK or in another contracting state, the English court may freeze a bank account here in support of the foreign proceedings. But although there is power to extend this provision to cases in which proceedings are pending in other countries, that power has not yet been exercised.

RECOGNITION OF JUDGMENTS

In the *Babanaft* case Kerr LJ showed that, under the 1968 Convention, there might be circumstances in which a foreign attachment of an English bank account might have to be recognised in this country. In the *Denilauler* case,[20] a case before the European Court arising out of a reference by a German court, a French plaintiff had sued a German company in France, and in the course of the French proceedings the court made an order authorising the freezing of the German company's bank assets in the Frankfurt branch of a French banker's security. The order was made *ex parte* and the plaintiff sought to have it enforced in Germany. The basic thrust of the questions referred by the German court concerned the applicability of the various provisions in the Convention, which envisaged the giving of notice of proceedings to the judgment debtor before judgment is given against him by the original court or notice of the judgment itself prior to enforcement. The court concluded that although Art. 24 did not preclude provisional or protective measures ordered in the state of origin from being the subject of recognition, this did not apply where the provisional or protective measures were ordered *ex parte* and were intended to be enforced without prior service.

20. [1980] ECR 1553.

TRACING OF ASSETS

In *Larkins* v. *NUM*[21] sequestrators were appointed by the English court over the property of the National Union of Mineworkers (NUM), following its failure to obey the orders of the English court in connection with the miners' strike in 1984. The order of sequestration authorised the sequestrators to prosecute proceedings in the Republic of Ireland to recover funds of the NUM on deposit with a bank. Subsequently, the English court appointed a receiver over the NUM's assets with authority to institute proceedings in any jurisdiction to recover assets belonging to the NUM. It was held that the claim by the sequestrators in the Republic of Ireland was not maintainable because the sequestration process was penal in effect, being a process of establishing the authority of the court against a recalcitrant litigant and punishing it for contempt. But the claim by the receiver was maintainable because there were independent grounds for his appointment, and the receivership was not an indirect method of enforcing the sequestration and thereby enforcing the penal law or process of a foreign state.

SUBPOENAS AND EVIDENCE

This chapter has already mentioned evidence from banks in England in relation to proceedings pending abroad. It is only possible to touch upon some of the very difficult questions relating to subpoenas and evidence in connection with bank accounts held abroad.

In a sense *MacKinnon* v. *Donaldson Lufkin*,[22] was a comparatively simple case. It was a civil fraud action pending in England in which the plaintiff sought documents from the defendant's New York bank, Citibank. The plaintiff obtained a subpoena requiring Citibank, which had a London branch, to produce by an officer evidence of the trial of the action, including all relevant documents relating to the defendant's account. The subpoena was directed to, and served on, the bank at its London branch. Hoffmann J held that even though Citibank had a branch in London and was present there:

> it does not follow from the fact that a person is within the jurisdiction and liable to be served with process that there is no territorial limit to the matters on which the court may properly apply its own rules or the things which it can order such a person to do . . . . The content of the subpoena and order is to require the production by a non-party of documents outside the jurisdiction concerning business which it has transacted outside the jurisdiction. In principle and on authority it seems to me that the court should not, save in exceptional circumstances, impose such a requirement on a foreigner and, in particular, a foreign bank. The principle is that the state should refrain from demanding obedience to its sovereign authority by foreigners in respect of their conduct outside the jurisdiction . . . It seems to me that the subpoena and order in this

21. [1985] IR 671.
22. [1986] Ch. 782.

case, taking effect in New York, are an infringement of the sovereignty of the United States. The need to exercise the court's jurisdiction with due regard to the sovereignty of others is particularly important in the case of banks. Banks are in a special position because their documents are concerned not only with their own business but with that of their customers. They will owe their customers a duty of confidence regulated by the law of the country where the account is kept . . . If every country where a bank happened to carry on business asserted a right to require that bank to produce documents relating to accounts kept in any other such country, banks would be in the unhappy position of being forced to submit to whichever sovereign was able to apply the greatest pressure.

Therefore, the solution in that case was to require the evidence to be obtained in New York. In some cases US courts have required branches of foreign banks in the US to produce details of accounts in foreign countries, even though they were forbidden by the criminal law of the relevant foreign country from producing the information. Thus, in the famous *Bank of Nova Scotia* case the Miami branch of the Bank of Nova Scotia (of course, a Canadian bank) was ordered to produce information relating to its Cayman Islands branch, and when it refused because of the criminal sanctions which would be imposed in the Cayman Islands, the US court imposed substantial daily fines on it.

If the witness is within the jurisdiction and is not legitimately subject to a foreign secrecy law, then the court may compel the evidence. Thus, in *Spencer* v. *The Queen*,[23] the Supreme Court of Canada held that the Ontario court could subpoena a resident and citizen of Canada concerning information which he had acquired while being the manager of a Bahamas branch of the Royal Bank of Canada. The Supreme Court decided that foreign law could not exempt a witness, otherwise competent, compellable and present, from giving evidence within his knowledge in the Canadian courts. The judgment of the majority held that to allow the witness "to refuse to give evidence in the circumstances of the case would permit a foreign country to frustrate the administration of justice in Canada in respect of a Canadian citizen in relation to what is essentially a domestic situation". Such an approach could have serious repercussions on the operation of Canadian law generally.

In the *Marc Rich* case in England,[24] Mr Justice Leggatt was prepared to grant an injunction in favour of Citibank's Swiss customer, restraining Citibank from disclosing in New York confidential information held by it as banker in England for its Swiss customer. It will be recalled that the *Marc Rich* case involved an investigation into the crude oil trading of a US company which was the wholly-owned subsidiary of a Swiss company. In proceedings brought in the US by the Department of Justice, subpoenas were served on the Swiss company and its US subsidiary, and subsequently on Citibank in New York. The documents covered by the subpoena served on Citibank in the US were in fact kept at its London branch in its capacity as bankers to the Swiss

23. [1985] 2 SCR 278.
24. *X* v. *A Bank* [1983] 2 All ER 464.

company. The Swiss company brought proceedings in England against the London branch of Citibank to restrain it from disclosing confidential information held by it in its capacity as banker. Perhaps it is too cynical to suggest that the interests of both the bank and the customer were served by the English injunction, since the customer was preventing disclosure of its documents and the bank was obtaining the benefit of a potential "foreign governmental compulsion" defence. The case may be regarded as a somewhat artificial device both to prevent production of the material in the US and to relieve the bank from sanctions in the US. The artificiality of the device in that case is underlined by the fact that it would be inconceivable for a customer of a bank in England to obtain an injunction restraining production by the bank of documents which are the subject matter of a subpoena in English proceedings. It is by no means easy to see why, in the US proceedings, it should make a great deal of difference whether the bank is under a duty of confidentiality in general (without an express court order in the foreign jurisdiction) and subject to an injunction (breach of which is punishable) brought in a suit by a customer to enforce that very same duty. It should also be noted that the operation of UK companies legislation relating to disclosure is not affected by the fact that the person under a duty to disclose is a bank subject to banking secrecy in a foreign jurisdiction.

LAWRENCE COLLINS

CHAPTER 6

RECEIVERSHIPS AND EXTRAJUDICIAL REMEDIES

INTRODUCTION

The exercise by creditors and other claimants for money payments of self-help remedies to recover what they claim without first obtaining judgment in a competent court has never stood high in judicial favour, and the history of the self-help remedies which were conceded by the early common law has been one of continual diminution by judicial attrition. The one outstanding exception to this has been the realisation of mortgages and charges over any kinds of property by the exercise of powers of sale and powers to appoint receivers conferred by, or under, the mortgage or charge.

The self-help remedies conferred by law which remain and which immediately spring to mind are distress or distraint on the goods of the debtor or alleged debtor, the recaption or retaking of goods of the claimant which have been wrongfully taken by another, the exercise of a common law lien or right of retention over goods of a debtor of the claimant and the set-off of a debt owed by a creditor of the claimant against a debt which the claimant owes to him, coupled with the tender of the balance of the amount which the claimant owes, if it is greater than the debt which is owed to him. All of these remedies and the few other self-help remedies which still exist have been subjected by successive judicial decisions to qualifications and conditions, the most important of which is that no forcible entry on the land of another person must occur in the exercise of a self-help remedy. The remedy of distress, for example, may only be exercised by a landlord against his tenant to recover arrears of rent, or by certain tax authorities authorised by statute to distrain for taxes payable to them, but if there is a likelihood that entry on the land where the goods to be distrained upon are located will be forcibly resisted, the person levying the distress may not proceed without a court order empowering him to do so, and if the distress is for unpaid rent in respect of most kinds of residential accommodation, a court order is essential in any event. Again, the remedy of recaption cannot be exercised without the claimant first obtaining judgment against the wrongful detainer of the goods if a forcible entry on the detainer's land is likely to occur, or if the retaking of the claimant's goods involves a trespass on the land of a person other than the detainor.

In fact, the only self-help remedies conferred by law which are not inhibited by the need to avoid forcible entries or trespasses on land are those where the subject matter of the remedy is already in the possession or under the control of the claimant who exercises the remedy. A creditor who has a lien over goods of his debtor in those restricted situations where a lien attaches to the goods by law (for example, the lien of a repairer of goods or equipment for the cost of the repair, or of a warehousekeeper for the cost of storing goods, or the lien of a bank over negotiable instruments held by it for a customer who is indebted to the bank), can realise the subject matter of the lien by selling or disposing of it and paying himself out of the proceeds, or if the subject matter is money, by simply paying himself out of it. Similarly, but for different reasons, the exercise of a right of set-off cannot give rise to the possibility of a forcible entry or trespass, and so no court order is required before a right of set-off is asserted. In such cases the limiting factor on the availability of the self-help remedy is that imposed by the restrictions on the persons who, and the circumstances in which, the remedy can be exercised. Liens can only be claimed by certain categories of creditors to recover amounts payable to them for their services, and rights of set-off may be exercised only by claimants for liquidated amounts which are immediately payable, and the set-off can be effected only against debts for liquidated sums which are immediately payable by the creditors to the person against whom the set-off is asserted.

The restrictions which judicial decisions have imposed on the availability and the exercise of the few self-help remedies which the law still concedes make it tempting for claimants to seek to reserve self-help remedies to themselves by contractual provisions. Express contractual provision or, at least, mercantile usage was the foundation for the lien and power of resale now generally enjoyed by an unpaid seller of goods who is still in possession of them, and was likewise the foundation of the right of a pledgee who advances money on the security of a deposit of goods to sell them if the borrower does not repay the debt secured according to its terms. These rights are now implied in every contract of sale or pledge, unless the contract otherwise provides, and they may therefore now be treated as extensions of the self-help remedies conferred by law. Implied contractual rights of self-help are not numerous, however, even though they may be important to a particular category of creditors, for example, the implied pledge or lien which a bank has over shipping documents delivered to it under a letter of credit, and over the goods to which the documents relate, when the customer of the bank who procured the issue of the letter of credit has not put it in funds to pay the amount which it is obliged to pay to the beneficiary of the letter of credit.

Because of the limited availability of contractually implied self-help remedies, a claimant can usefully extend the remedies available to him by law only by stipulating for them in the contract with his debtor. Examples of such extensions are: (a) the contractual liens and powers of sale which are often reserved to suppliers of goods to a customer on a regular basis where the powers are expressed to extend to all goods which the supplier agrees to deliver, but which have not actually been delivered, whether the amounts unpaid by the purchaser relate to those goods or to other goods which have already been delivered; and (b) the power often contractually reserved to a seller of goods who retains the ownership of them until they are paid for, to retake the goods if the purchaser defaults in payment and to resell them in order to satisfy the unpaid price. This latter remedy again is one which can be exercised without a court order only if there is no likelihood of a breach of the peace resulting, and if no trespass on a third person's premises will occur in effecting the retaking.

The self-help remedies which are of particular concern to banks are the lien which a bank has at common law over securities or investments belonging to its customer, the documents relating to which have been deposited with the bank by him (whether the securities are negotiable or not) and the power of a bank to realise such securities which are negotiable; the right of a bank to set off debit and credit balances on separate accounts held with it by the same customer in the same right or, in other words, to consolidate the accounts held by such a customer; and the implied pledges of the kind already referred to where the bank finances and acquisition of goods, securities or investments by its customer and the shipping or other documents relating to them are received by the bank from its customer or from the seller to him. In this connection a bank is assisted by the fact that certain transferable documents of title to goods (particularly bills of lading and warehouse warrants issued by warehouses in certain ports governed by local Acts of Parliament) are treated as the equivalent of the goods to which they relate, with the consequence that the depositary bank which has financed the acquisition may reimburse itself, not only by selling the documents of title received by it, but also by selling the goods which they represent.

One particular form of self-help remedy which a bank or any other lender may exercise by virtue of a contractual provision is probably, from a bank's point of view, the most extensive and useful remedy which it may employ to recover a loan made by a bank to a company. It is the contractual remedy of appointing a receiver (or a receiver and manager) of a company's business undertaking, or of part of that undertaking or of assets comprised in it, in order to realise a charge or mortgage created by the company in favour of the bank, whether the loan or advance secured by the charge is made by the bank to the company or to any other company or individual (e.g. a loan to a parent company of a group secured by charges over the assets of its subsidiaries). If the appropriate contractual provisions are included in the loan agreement, debentures or a trust deed creating the mortgage or charge, a receiver may be appointed with the widest powers to realise the assets comprised in it, or to manage the whole or part of the company's undertaking with a view to recovering the amount owing out of receipts, or by eventually selling the undertaking or assets at an enhanced price. The remainder of this chapter will be concerned with such receiverships.

RECEIVERSHIPS: ORIGIN AND CHARACTER

Receiverships, for the purpose of recovering loans or advances made to companies, are closely associated in practitioners' minds with the enforcement of floating charges created by companies, but they are by no means confined to such charges. Receiverships may be initiated to enforce any kind of mortgage or charge, whether fixed or floating, and whatever kind of assets the charge encumbers.

The jurisdiction of the Chancery Court to appoint receivers with power to collect the income of the property on which a debt is secured, or to effect the sale of such property under an order of the court, goes back to the 18th century, and the only limit on the Chancery jurisdiction was the self-imposed one that the court would not intervene if the secured creditor had an adequate remedy at common law, for example, if he held a legal mortgage of land and was entitled after the contractual date for redemption to take possession of the land himself in order to collect the income from it.[1] Since the Judicature Act 1873 came into force in 1875, however, all divisions of the High Court have had jurisdiction to appoint receivers in appropriate circumstances. The court now appoints them at the request of both legal and equitable mortgagees and at the instance of persons who have only charges over property or assets, which must, except in the case of a charge by deed over land which is expressed to be created by way of a legal mortgage, inevitably be equitable in character.[2]

For a short period following the decision by the Court of Appeal in Chancery in 1870 that a floating charge created by a company over the whole or part of its assets and undertaking was valid in equity, and would be enforced as a fixed charge attaching to assets of the class charged which were owned by the company at the time when it went into liquidation, the holders of such floating charges who wished to enforce them on the company's default, or on their security becoming at risk of being lost or rendered inadequate although the company had not gone into liquidation, resorted to the Chancery Court to appoint a receiver with power to realise the assets charged. The court appointed such a receiver in a number of cases.[3] By the mid 1870s, however, lenders to companies sought to avoid the delay entailed in applying to the court to appoint a receiver of the assets and undertaking of a company which had been charged in their favour by inserting in the loan agreement or deben-

1. *Berney* v. *Sewell* (1820) 1 Jac W 648.
2. *Tillett* v. *Nixon* (1883) 25 Ch D 238; *Re Crompton & Co. Ltd* [1914] 1 Ch 954.
3. See, for example, *Perry* v. *Oriental Hotels Co.* (1870) 5 Ch App 420; *Peek* v. *Trimsaren Iron Co.* (1876) 2 Ch D 115; *Boyle* v. *Bettws Llantwit Colliery Co.* (1876) 2 Ch D 726).

tures powers for them to appoint a receiver out of court, who was authorised by the loan agreement or debentures to realise the company's assets and to carry on its business undertaking with a view to an eventual realisation.[4] The circumstances in which a receiver might be appointed without an application being made to the court were listed exhaustively in the loan agreement or debentures under which the loan was made, or in the debenture trust deed which was now coming into use when a large-scale issue of debentures was made. During the last 20 years of the 19th century practitioners elaborated the list of circumstances in which a receiver might be appointed, so that they included not only the company's failure to pay the principal and interest on the loan on the due dates and any breach by the company of its covenants or obligations, but also a long list of adverse events the occurrence of any of which might make it difficult for the company to fulfil its financial or other obligations, or would indicate that the company was heading for a situation where it might become difficult for it to meet its obligations, or if the company went into liquidation under an order of the court or voluntarily.[5]

During the 1890s and the early years of the 20th century the courts worked out in a succession of cases the adverse events affecting a company which had created a floating charge over its assets, that would induce the court to appoint a receiver of those assets on the application of a lender or debenture holder on the ground that there was a serious risk that the assets subject to the charge would be lost or would prove inadequate (in other words, that the security would be in jeopardy). The court was largely helped in cataloguing such events by the contemporary specification of them in loan agreements, debentures or debenture trust deeds as entitling the lender or debenture holders to appoint a receiver without the aid of the court. The fact that such a receiver could be appointed, however, was held to be no reason for the court to refuse to appoint a receiver itself.[6] Nevertheless, because a receivership initiated without an application to the court was usually cheaper and more expeditious than one resulting from an appointment by the court, it was in practice only when an appointment out of court could be made only with the consent of the holders of a certain minimum fraction of debentures issued in a series that applications were made to the court by minority debenture holders, who could not elicit the support of sufficient of their fellow debenture holders to effect an appointment out of court.

One significant feature of the appointment of a receiver by the court or out of court as a consequence of a jeopardising event occurring, however, is that it is not the occurrence of that event which causes the floating charge to crystallise and attach specifically to the assets of the company (even if the event is the

4. See *Re Henry Pound, Son and Hutchin Ltd* (1889) 42 Ch D 402.
5. See *Hodson* v. *Tea Corpn Ltd* (1880) 14 Ch D 859; *Wallace* v. *Universal Automatic Machines Co. Ltd* [1894] 2 Ch 547.
6. *Re Henry Pound, Sons and Hutchins Ltd, supra.*

cessation of the company's business activities); crystallisation occurs only on the appointment of the receiver because of the occurrence of that event.[7] This is not so, of course, if a floating charge crystallises by the company going into liquidation; crystallisation then occurs on the relevant winding-up order being made or a winding-up resolution being passed, and the fact that a receiver is only later appointed does not postpone the date of crystallisation.

The fact that a floating charge does not crystallise when an event occurs which justifies the appointment of a receiver by the court or out of court, but only when a receiver is actually appointed in consequence of that event, is one of the reasons why loan agreements, debentures and trust deeds which create floating charges nowadays often provide that the charge shall crystallise immediately on the occurrence of any of the designated events, or on notice being given to the company by the lender or lenders in consequence of one of those events (a provision for automatic crystallisation). Such a provision has been held by the courts to be valid, and its effect is to invalidate as against the lender or debenture holders purported dispositions of the company's assets by its directors after the occurrence of the relevant event or the giving of notice to the company of its occurrence, unless the lender, debenture holders or receiver consent.[8] As a matter of nomenclature, clauses in loan agreements, debentures or covering trust deeds creating floating charges which list the events which will entitle the lender, debenture holder or trustee of the trust deed to appoint a receiver, or which will cause the immediate crystallisation of the floating charge on their occurrence or on notice being given to the company thereafter, are often misleadingly called default clauses, even though not all the events specified in them involve breaches of obligations by the company. A better name for such clauses would be "enforceability" or "crystallisation" clauses, corresponding to the acceleration clause inserted in documents relating to unsecured loans or unsecured loan stock, in order to make the loan immediately repayable on the occurrence of specified adverse events.

Although there are many points of similarity between the appointment of receivers by the court and out of court with power to realise assets of a company (such as freehold and leasehold land and premises owned by the company at any time before its secured indebtedness is discharged, or book debts owing to it at any such time), there are also material differences between them. Power to appoint a receiver out of court must be conferred explicitly by the instrument creating a floating charge or to enable a receiver appointed under a charge over specific assets to realise them by sale or otherwise. The statutory power of a mortgagee or chargee by deed of any property to appoint a receiver under the Law of Property Act 1925, ss. 101(1) and 109 (re-enacting the Conveyancing Act 1882, ss. 19(1) and 24)) enables him to appoint a receiver only

7. *Government Stocks and Other Securities Investment Co.* v. *Manila Rly Co.* [1897] AC 81.

8. *Re Woodroffes (Musical Instruments) Ltd* [1986] Ch 366; *Re Brightlife Ltd* [1987] Ch 200; *Re Permanent Houses (Holdings) Ltd* [1988] BCLC 563.

for the purpose of collecting the income of the property charged and applying it in paying the secured debt. Such a receiver cannot realise the property, and even the statutory power to appoint a receiver to collect income cannot be exercised by a lender secured only by a floating charge.[9]

The explicit power in a loan agreement, debenture or trust deed to appoint a receiver out of court to realise assets comprised in a charge must, of course, specify exhaustively the events in which the appointment may be made, and an appointment may not be made in any other circumstances, even though the security is at risk of loss or the company has failed to fulfil its contractual obligations. On the other hand, the court's jurisdiction to appoint a receiver with power to realise the assets charged by a specific or floating charge or, in the case of a floating charge over a company's assets and undertaking, to carry on the company's business with a view to eventual sale (in which case the receiver will also be appointed by the court to be a manager), is not limited to the occurrence of the events of default or enforceability listed in the instrument creating the charge. The court can make the appointment whenever the company has failed to pay any part of the principal of the loan or interest on it in accordance with its contractual undertaking to do so, or when the security for the loan is exposed to a serious risk of loss.

Furthermore, the characters and capacities of receivers appointed by the court or out of court under the instrument creating the charge are different. A receiver appointed by the court is an officer of it, and not an agent of the secured lender or of the debenture holder who applied for his appointment or the debenture holders generally, nor is he an agent of the company.[10] Consequently, such a receiver is personally liable upon contracts which he enters into in the course of his receivership (with a right to be indemnified out of the assets in respect of which he was appointed if the contracts were proper ones for carrying out his functions), and the receiver is also personally liable to the company and third persons, if he or persons employed by him commit acts which are wrongful as regards them in the course of the receivership.[11] In contrast, a receiver appointed out of court under a power conferred by an instrument creating a mortgage or charge is deemed to be the agent of the person who appoints him, who is consequently responsible as his principal for the fulfilment of contracts entered into by him and for all wrongs committed by him or by persons employed by him in the course of the receivership (including his failure to realise the company's assets at the best price reasonably obtainable).[12] At common law the appointor of the receiver alone was liable as the receiver's principal upon contracts made by him for the purpose of the

9. *Blaker* v. *Herts and Essex Waterworks Co.* (1889) 41 Ch D 339.

10. *Moss S.S. Co. Ltd* v. *Whinney* [1912] AC 254; *Parsons* v. *Sovereign Bank of Canada* [1913] AC 160).

11. *Burt, Bolton and Hayward* v. *Bull* [1895] 1 QB 276; *Boehm* v. *Goodall* [1911] 1 Ch 155.

12. *White* v. *City of London Brewery Co.* (1889) 42 Ch D 237; *Robinson Printing* Co v. *Chic Ltd* [1905] 2 Ch 123; *Deyes* v. *Wood* [1911] 1 KB 806.

receivership, but by the Insolvency Act 1986, s. 37(1) and s. 44(1) (re-enacting Companies Act 1985, s. 192(3)), a receiver or manager of the whole or any part of the property of a company who is appointed by an instrument and not by the court, is made personally liable upon all contracts entered into by him in carrying out his functions. A receiver appointed out of court remains personally liable for wrongs committed by him or persons employed by him against third persons, in addition to the vicarious liability of the person who appointed him to those third persons.[13]

Because of the liabilities which lenders, or debenture holders or trustees for them would normally incur for breaches of contracts made by receivers appointed by them out of court and for wrongs committed by such receivers, it has been the practice since the last decade of the 19th century for loan agreements, debentures and trust deeds to provide that, for all purposes, a receiver appointed under a power conferred by the instrument shall be deemed to be agent of the company, which shall alone be responsible for and bear the consequences of his acts and defaults. Such a provision exempts the lender or debenture holders from liability in respect of contracts entered into by the receiver, including those entered into by the receiver after his deemed agency has come to an end on the company going into liquidation, and it also exempts the lender or debenture holders from liability for wrongs committed by the receiver otherwise than on the express instructions of the lender or debenture holders.[14] By the Insolvency Act 1986, ss. 37(1) and 44(1), however, the fact that a receiver or manager is deemed by the loan agreement, debentures or debenture trust deed under which he is appointed to be an agent of the company does not affect his personal liability upon contracts made by him for the purpose of the receivership. The fact that a receiver who is deemed to be and acts as an agent of the company ceases to be such an agent on the company going into liquidation, does not terminate his powers of realisation and management, and he exercises them thereafter as a principal, and not as an agent of the person who appointed him or of the company.[15]

Before concluding a consideration of the nature of receivership, reference must be made to the creation of a new sub-species of receiver appointed out of court under a power conferred by a loan agreement, or by debentures or a debenture trust deed. This sub-species was established by the Insolvency Act 1986, and comprises, in practice, most of the receivers of companies' property and assets who are appointed out of court. It is that of administrative receivers, who are defined by the Insolvency Act 1986, s. 29(2), as receivers or managers "of the whole (or substantially the whole) of a company's property appointed by or on behalf of the holders of any debentures of the company secured by a

13. *Re Goldburg* [1912] 1 KB 606.

14. *Re B. Johnson and Co. (Builders) Ltd* [1955] Ch 634; *Standard Chartered Bank Ltd* v. *Walker* [1982] 3 All ER 938.

15. *Bowman* v. *David Samuel Trust Ltd* [1978] 1 All ER 616.

charge which as created, was a floating charge, or by such a charge and one or more other securities, or a person who would be such a receiver or manager but for the appointment of some other person as the receiver of part of the company's property". An administrative receiver, therefore, is one appointed under a floating charge which extends to the whole or substantially the whole of a company's assets and undertaking (other than those comprised in a fixed charge), and his appointment, too, must extend to the same wide range of assets, but the fact that the floating charge has already crystallised before his appointment, or that another person has already appointed a receiver of part (but not the whole or substantially the whole) of the company's property under a mortgage or charge which has priority to the floating charge, does not affect the status of the appointee as an administrative receiver.

An administrative receiver is deemed by law to be the agent of the company whose assets are the subject of the receivership, but his agency continues only until the commencement of its liquidation, and like any other receiver appointed out of court, he is personally liable upon all contracts made by him in carrying out his functions, both before and after the company goes into liquidation, with the consequence that the lender or debenture holders for whose benefit he is appointed are not so liable (Insolvency Act 1986, s. 44(1)). The reason for the creation of the new category of administrative receivers is that they (unlike other receivers) are required to be qualified insolvency practitioners (Insolvency Act 1986, ss. 388(1) and 390(2)), and that on their appointment the directors of the company and certain other persons are required to submit to them a statement of the company's affairs on which they are required to report to the company's creditors (ss. 47 and 48). Additionally, an administrative receiver is given certain statutory powers for the purpose of his receivership (unless the loan agreement, debentures or debenture trust deed under which he is appointed otherwise provide) (s. 42(1) and Sch. 1); and with leave of the court an administrative receiver may dispose of property of the company in respect of which he was appointed free from any security to which that property is subject (such as a prior-ranking specific mortgage or charge, or a prior-ranking floating charge whose holder has not appointed a receiver), if the court considers that this would promote a more advantageous realisation of the company's assets (s. 43(1)).

It should be observed, however, that although an administrative receiver is defined, and his powers and functions are prescribed by the Insolvency Act 1986, the Act confers on a lender or debenture holders, who is or are entitled to a general floating charge over the whole or substantially the whole of a company's assets, no statutory power to appoint an administrative receiver. However, if by the loan agreement, debentures or debenture trust deed an express power is conferred on them to appoint a receiver of the whole or part of the assets charged, a receiver who they appoint to realise or manage the whole, or substantially the whole, of those assets will automatically be an administrative receiver, whether he is so described in his instrument of appointment or not.

THE CONDUCT OF A RECEIVERSHIP

Purpose of a receivership

The purpose of a receivership is that the receiver shall realise sufficient of the assets of the company comprised in the charge under which he is appointed to pay the total outstanding amount of the loan or debt secured on those assets, plus the cost of the receivership and, if the charge is or includes a floating charge, any preferential debts and liabilities of the company which the receiver is compelled by the Insolvency Act 1986, s. 40 to discharge out of the company's assets in priority to the amount secured by the floating charge. If the receiver is empowered by the court or the instrument under which he is appointed to manage the company's business undertaking and does so, his receipts from the continued carrying on the company's business, less his expenses properly incurred in doing so, will be added to the proceeds of eventually realising the company's assets, whether piecemeal or by the sale of the company's business as a going concern, and the proceeds of carrying on the business will be applied in the same way as the proceeds of sale of those assets. If the proceeds of realisation and the net receipts from the receiver carrying on the company's business suffice to meet all the amounts payable out of them by the receiver, any cash balance left in his hands and any unrealised assets of the company in his possession must be returned to the company, and must not be applied by the receiver paying secured or unsecured liabilities of the company, which rank for payment only after the secured debt in respect of which the receiver was appointed.[16]

If a receiver sells or disposes of assets of the company which are subject to mortgages or charges, or to securities arising by operation of law (such as liens or the security obtained by judgment creditors who have attached assets of the company in execution), the receiver may either sell the assets subject to those charges or securities, so that they continue to affect the assets in the hands of the purchasers, or (and this is more likely) the receiver may discharge those charges or securities out of the proceeds of realisation of the assets and transfer an unencumbered title to the purchasers. This is so, of course, only if the amounts of those charges or securities rank for payment out of the assets in question in priority to payment of the debt secured by the loan agreement or debentures under which the receiver is appointed. In this connection, it should be observed that if an administrative receiver is authorised by the court under the Insolvency Act 1986, s. 43(1) to dispose of assets which are subject to a security ranking in priority to the floating charge under which the receiver was appointed, the receiver must apply the proceeds of realisation primarily in discharging that prior-ranking security, and if the proceeds are less than the net amount which, in the court's opinion, would be realised on a sale in the open market (presumably on a sale by a willing seller to a willing buyer), the receiver

16. *Re G.L. Saunders Ltd* [1986] 1 WLR 215.

must make good the difference out of the company's other assets subject to the floating charge or, if necessary, personally, in order to discharge the amount of the security (s. 43(3)).

Powers of receivers

The purpose of receiverships initiated by creditors to enforce mortgages or charges over a company's assets is always the same, namely, the realisation of their security. However, the law does not, with one exception, confer a list of powers on a receiver appointed out of court to achieve that purpose, in the way that the Insolvency Act 1986, ss. 165 and 166 and Sch. 4 confers a catalogue of powers on liquidators in the winding-up of companies. The one exception is the administrative receiver, who is deemed to have the powers listed in the Insolvency Act 1986, Sch. 1, unless the loan agreement, debentures or trust deed under which he is appointed provide otherwise (Insolvency Act 1986, s. 42(1)). The statutory powers of an administrative receiver are as wide as those of a liquidator, and in some respects are more extensive. For example, an administrative receiver has power to carry on the business of the company generally (and not merely for the purpose of winding up the company's affairs, as a liquidator may do); he also has power to establish subsidiaries of the company and to transfer to any of the company's subsidiaries the whole or part of the business and property of the company; and, in general, he has power to do all such things (including the carrying out of work) as may be necessary for the realisation of the property of the company. The powers of an administrative receiver can be added to or diminished by the provisions of the loan agreement, debentures or trust deed under which he is appointed, and unless that instrument requires the consent of the lender, debenture holders or the trustees of a debenture trust deed, or any other person, to the exercise of an administrative receiver's statutory or other powers, he may act on his own initiative without obtaining anyone's consent. The powers of a receiver appointed out of court, who is not an administrative receiver, must be defined exhaustively by the loan agreement, debentures or trust deed under which he is appointed, since no powers are conferred on him by statute, and no doubt, in practice, the powers of administrative receivers will continue to be set out exhaustively in the same way, despite the statutory provisions conferring powers on them.

A receiver of any description of a company's assets takes them in the condition they are in when the receiver is appointed, and cannot claim legal or equitable rights in respect of them which the company itself could not enforce against third persons. For example, if a receiver is appointed under a charge which includes present and future book debts owing to the company in connection with its business, the company's customers who owe it such book debts may set off against the receiver's claims the amounts of debts or cross-claims which they could set off in actions brought by the company itself at the date when the charge crystallised, or if the charge is a specific or fixed charge over book debts, at the date when the charge was notified to them.[17] The amounts to be set off against the receiver's claims must either be liquidated amounts which are due and payable by the company at whichever of those two dates is appropriate, however, or they must be accrued liquidated or unliquidated claims against the company arising under the same contract or transaction with it as that under which the receiver claims, or a closely related contract or transaction.[18]

Another example of the principle that the receiver takes the company's assets and rights as they exist at the time of his appointment is provided by the practice in recent years of suppliers of goods to companies retaining the title to the goods by express provision in the supply contract, until the price of the goods or the total outstanding indebtedness of the company to the supplier has been fully paid. If, at the time of the receiver's appointment, the title to such goods has not vested in the company or in a person to whom the company has resold them and any period of credit allowed by the supplier to the company has expired, the supplier may reclaim the goods if they are still identifiable and the receiver does not pay the amount owed to the supplier, and if in those circumstances the receiver refuses to return them to the supplier or disposes of them to a third party the receiver will be liable to the supplier in damages for the tort of conversion.[19] If, on the other hand, the supplier of the goods to the company has by the supply contract reserved to himself the right of the price or the hire rental at which the company has resold or hired out the goods or any products made with them to third persons, so as to entitle the supplier to payment of the amount owed to him by the company out of the resale price or the hire rental, the reservation will now, in almost all situations, amount to an equitable charge on the resale price or hire rental, and the suppliers' claim to it will be ineffective against the receiver, unless it has been registered against the company at the Companies Registry as a charge on its book debts owing from its own customers.[20]

An administrative receiver (like a liquidator or an administrator acting under an administration order) is protected against the absolute liability which would be imposed on him at common law for taking or disposing of any property which he believes belongs to the company (such as goods in its possession under a contract by which the seller retains the title until the price is paid) by provisions in the Insolvency Act 1986, s. 234(3) and (4), under which he escapes liability to the owner or other person entitled to the property if he acts in good faith and reasonably believes that he is entitled to take or dispose of

17. *Parsons* v. *Sovereign Bank of Canada* [1913] AC 160; *Rother Iron Works Ltd* v. *Canterbury Precision Engineers Ltd* [1974] QB 1.

18. *Handley Page Ltd* v. *Customs and Excise Commissioners* [1970] 2 Lloyd's Rep 459; *Business Computers Ltd* v. *Anglo African Leasing Ltd* [1977] 2 All ER 741).

19. *Clough Mill Ltd* v. *Martin* [1984] 3 All ER 982; *Hendy Lennox (Industrial Engines) Ltd* v. *Graham Puttick Ltd* [1984] 2 All ER 152.

20. *E. Pfeiffer Weinkellerei-Weinkauf GmbH & Co.* v. *Arbuthnot Factors Ltd* [1987] 1 WLR 150; *Tatung (UK) Ltd* v *Galex Telesure Ltd* (1988) 5 BCC 395.

the property, and he has a lien or prior charge on it enforceable against the owner for expenses incurred by him in taking or disposing of it. This provision extends to all kinds of property, such as land, investments, book debts and industrial property rights, as well as goods, but it does not, of course, confer a title to the property on the receiver or any person to whom he disposes of it. Nor will the provision protect a receiver who is aware of an adverse claim to the property (e.g. that of an unpaid seller who has retained the title to goods delivered to the company).

Executory contracts of the company

A receiver or manager is not bound personally by contracts entered into by the company before he is appointed, even though he carries out part of the company's obligations under such contracts, for example, by delivering goods which the company has contracted to sell.[21] The only way in which a receiver or manager can become bound by such a contract is by a novation, under which he agrees with the other contracting party to perform the company's obligations under the original contract in consideration of that party releasing the company from those obligations. It is unusual for a receiver or manager to agree to such a novation in practice, but it would be possible to imply a novation from conduct by the receiver which clearly indicates to the other party that he may perform his obligations safely under the contract in reliance on the receiver performing the company's obligations (for example, delivering goods in reliance on the receiver stating that they will be paid for).[22]

Furthermore, a receiver appointed out of court (including an administrative receiver) becomes personally responsible for the performance of the company's future obligations under contracts of employment entered into by it with its employees if he adopts such contracts in carrying out his functions, but nothing done or omitted by the receiver within 14 days after his appointment is taken to amount to an adoption by him of such a contract (Insolvency Act 1986, s. 37(1) and (2) and s. 44(1) and (2)). This provision will apparently apply only if the receiver continues to accept the services of the company's employees for the purpose of the receivership, for example, where he continues to carry on the company's business after 14 days from his appointment. Contracts of employment are not defined for the purpose of the provision, but presumably they are confined to contracts of service, and do not include contracts for the supply of services by independent contractors.

It has been suggested by the court in a case where the point was not essential for the decision, that a receiver who does not fulfil a contract made by the company before his appointment may be liable personally to the other contracting party for the wrong or tort of procuring a breach of contract by the company, if

21. *Parsons* v. *Sovereign Bank of Canada* [1913] AC 160.
22. *Chatsworth Investments Ltd* v. *Cussins (Contractors) Ltd* [1969] 1 All ER 143.

by his deliberate act he causes the company's obligations not to be fulfilled.[23] It is doubtful whether this is correct, at least when the receiver has good reason for not carrying out the company's obligations under the contract in order to protect the interests of the lender or debenture holders who appointed him. Furthermore, if the receiver is deemed to act as the agent of the company by the terms of the loan agreement, debentures or trust deed, it would seem that, like any other agent, he will not be personally liable for causing the breach of contracts which his principal, the company, has entered into, and that the other party will merely have an unsecured claim for damages against the company itself if its obligations are breached.[24] The other contracting party may not obtain an injunction against the receiver to prevent him from causing the company to break a contract into which it has entered, nor may he obtain an order requiring the receiver to perform the contract specifically; if an injunction or order of specific performance is obtained by the other party against the company in a situation where the contract can be enforced by injunction or can be specifically enforced, the court's order is not binding on the receiver or the lender or debenture holders for whose benefit he was appointed, and they are not guilty of contempt of court by not conforming to the order.[25] On the other hand, if contracts entered into by the company create or result in the creation of proprietary interests in favour of third persons, such as an option to purchase land or shares in a company, the receiver will be personally liable to the persons entitled to such interests if he infringes them, and he may be restrained by injunction from doing so.[26] He may, however, rely on the statutory defence that he honestly and reasonably believed that the property belonged to the company in this situation.

Receiver's duties in realising company's assets

Although a receiver may not be personally liable to fulfil the company's obligations under a contract entered into by it, he should not cause damage to its goodwill by failing to fulfil those obligations if the goodwill has a saleable value; this is so even if the cost of performing the contract exceeds the benefits which the company will obtain under it, and that excess is less than the loss of goodwill which will be caused to the company if the contract is not carried out.[27] But a receiver is liable for causing harm to the company's goodwill by not fulfilling its outstanding contracts only if he can perform them by utilising the company's assets and resources already available; he is not required to incur personal liability by himself entering into further contracts so as to

23. *Re Botibol* [1947] 1 All ER 26.
24. *Said* v. *Butt* [1920] 3 KB 497.
25. *Atlantic Airspace Ltd* v. *Handley Page Ltd* [1970] Ch 193.
26. *Telemetrix plc* v. *Modern Engineers of Bristol (Holdings) plc* [1985] BCLC 213.
27. *Re Newdigate Colliery Co. Ltd* [1912] 1 Ch 468; *Re Great Cobar Ltd* [1915] 1 Ch 682.

enable him to fulfil the company's existing contracts, for example, by borrowing.[28]

The liability (if any) which a receiver incurs by failing to fulfil existing contractual obligations of the company, is not incurred to the other contracting party, but only to the lender, debenture holders or trustees for them who appointed the receiver, and the liability is limited to making good the value of the company's goodwill which is lost in consequence of the contract not being fulfilled.[29] Liability is also incurred by the receiver to the company itself to the extent that if the value of the lost goodwill, when added to the company's other assets, would more than suffice to discharge the loan secured by the charge under which the receiver was appointed and also the costs of the receivership, the surplus can be claimed by the company from the receiver.[30] Side by side with the receiver's equitable obligation to account for any diminution of the company's assets caused by his default, a receiver is liable in damages to the company if he causes it loss by the negligent conduct of the receivership, for example, by realising its assets at a price less than that obtainable by the exercise of proper care.[31] Such a liability is also incurred by the receiver to guarantors of the indebtedness secured by the charge under which the receiver was appointed, and they can recover from him as damages the amount by which the contributions exacted from the guarantors under their guarantee has been increased by the receiver's negligence in failing to realise the company's assets or to collect debts payable to it with proper care.[32]

Liabilities of lenders and debenture holders in a receivership or liquidation

A lender, debenture holders or trustees for them who appoint a receiver do not generally incur any liability in consequence of the improper or negligent conduct of the receiver; this is because he is expressed in the relevant loan agreement, debentures or trust deed to be an agent of the company, and it bears the loss caused by his defaults. However, if the appointor of the receiver or the lender or debenture holders on whose behalf he is appointed instruct him to pursue a course of conduct, or to do or abstain from doing an act, which involves a breach of duty on his part, or which is likely to cause a loss to the company not justified by the need to protect the interests of the lender or debenture holders, the person or persons giving the instruction or advice will be liable to the company for the loss it suffers (for example, the too-rapid realisation of its assets at depressed prices), and it will be irrelevant that by the loan agreement, debentures or trust deed the receiver is deemed to be the agent

28. *Re Thames Ironworks, Shipbuilding and Engineering Co. Ltd* [1912] WN 66.
29. *Re Newdigate Colliery Co. Ltd, supra.*
30. *Re Newdigate Colliery Co. Ltd, supra.*
31. *Standard Chartered Bank Ltd* v. *Walker* [1982] All ER 938.
32. *Standard Chartered Bank Ltd* v. *Walker, supra.*

of the receiver.[33] Although a lender, or debenture holders or their trustee may be under a duty to the company to exercise their powers or influence over a receiver appointed by them with proper regard to the company's interests, however, they are not under any duty towards the company to exercise their powers only if they can reasonably foresee that the company will suffer no loss or detriment in consequence, and they are at liberty to act so as to protect their own interests, even if the company will inevitably suffer harm by them doing so. Consequently, a lender or debenture holders may insist on prompt payment of what the company owes under the loan agreement or debentures, and may refuse to allow it a reasonable additional time to raise money from another source in order to discharge that amount before appointing a receiver to enforce their security. The company then has no claim against the lender or debenture holders for doing this even if, given a reasonable opportunity, the company might have raised the money elsewhere.[34]

It is possible for a lender, or debenture holders or their trustees to become shadow directors of a company to which they have made advances for the purposes of the Companies Acts 1985 to 1989, and the Insolvency Act 1986, if the board of directors of the company is accustomed to act in accordance with their directions and instructions (Companies Act 1985, s. 741(2)). If lenders or debenture holders habitually give instructions or directions to the board of a company to which they have made advances or from which they have taken security for indebtedness and the board has habitually conformed to the instructions, the lender or debenture holders may be shadow directors of the company, even though the primary purpose of the lender or debenture holders in giving the instructions or directions is to protect their loan or security, or to ensure that the company continues to fulfil its contractual obligations to them or to maintain their security at a level which will suffice to satisfy the amount owed to them, if they eventually realise the security.[35] The instructions or directions accepted by the board must, of course, relate to the management of the company's affairs for the lenders or debenture holders to become shadow directors, and it would seem that they must be so comprehensive that all, or the most important, management decisions are taken out of the hands of the board.

The practical significance of lenders or debenture holders being shadow directors of the company is that if the company goes into an insolvent liquidation, they may be ordered by the court to make contributions to its assets which will be available to meet all its debts and liabilities (including its unsecured debts), but such contributions may be ordered only if at some time before the onset of the company's insolvency, the lenders or debenture holders should have realised that it could not avoid an insolvent liquidation, and they

33. *Standard Chartered Bank Ltd* v. *Walker, supra*; *Re Potters Oils Ltd (No. 2)* [1986] 1 All ER 890.

34. *Shamji* v. *Johnson Matthey Bankers Ltd* [1986] BCLC 278; [1991] BCLC 36.

35. *Re a Company (No. 005009 of 1987), ex parte Copp* [1989] BCLC 13.

did not thereafter take "every step with a view to minimising the potential loss to the company's creditors as . . . [they] ought to have taken" (Insolvency Act 1986, s. 214(1) to (3)). The danger in the lenders or debenture holders "policing" their loan or security too actively, therefore, is that they may find in the company's liquidation that the effectiveness and priority of their claims as secured creditors, and their powers to realise their security, are diminished by the contribution to the company's assets which they are ordered to make for the benefit of the general creditors of the company. Bearing in mind that the court may charge the contribution ordered from them on the amount which the company owes them and on any security which they hold for that amount (s. 215(2)), the lender and debenture holders may find that instead of being creditors with priority for payment out of the security in the liquidation, they are made to rank only equally with the company's general creditors and that the total fund in which they share will have been partly constituted by themselves.

Lenders and debenture holders of a company may become shadow directors only if they habitually give instructions or directions to its board of directors and the board habitually conforms to them. This may be avoided by the lenders or debenture holders giving their instructions to a receiver or manager appointed by them under an enforcement or default clause in the loan agreement or debentures which is sufficiently widely drawn to enable the appointment to be made when they consider that their loan or the security for it is at risk. The receiver or manager then takes over all the powers of the directors which are necessary for the receivership (including managing the company's business as a going concern), and the directors cannot interfere with the receiver's exercise of those powers, or exercise them themselves.[36] If it is the receiver who acts on the lenders' or debenture holders' instructions, they may be liable to the company at common law for negligence in the way indicated above, but they will not be shadow directors of the company, and so cannot be ordered by the court to contribute to its assets in a liquidation.

CONCLUSION

This chapter has been mostly concerned with receiverships of companies under loan agreements and debentures as a means of recovery available to lenders (especially banks) by way of self-help. Receiverships provide a remedy which is unique to the common law jurisdictions, that is the Commonwealth countries and the US. In the civil law countries it is not possible for a creditor to enforce a security for his debt without obtaining an order of the court, unless he is in possession of the security of the subject matter under a pledge. Although the court may appoint a suitable person to manage those of the assets of a business

36. *Newhart Developments Ltd* v. *Co-operative Commercial Bank Ltd* [1978] QB 814.

undertaking which are comprised in a security, acting as an officer of the court with a view to an ultimate sale, this remedy is not much used in practice. The order of the court which is usually sought is for the sale of the assets comprised in the security under the court's directions.

The limited range of remedies for the recovery of secured loans under civil law systems results largely from the fact that a floating charge over the whole assets and undertaking of a company is not recognised as a valid security by them. Under German law it is possible for a company to make a global transfer of its present and future book debts, and it can make such a transfer by way of security (*Sicherungsvorausabtretung oder Globalzession*), but such a global security transfer of book debts can only be enforced by proceedings in court. Similar global transfers cannot be made in respect of present and future interests in land, or any other classes of assets of a company other than book debts. Moreover, an attempt to make such a global transfer of assets is highly dangerous, because by the German Civil Code, §419(1) and (2) if a person (including a creditor) takes a transfer of the whole of the assets of another person (including a company), whether the transfer is of the beneficial interest in those assets or by way of security, the transferee automatically becomes liable for all the debts of the transferor at the date of the transfer to the extent of the value of the assets transferred. French legislation of 1909 (*Loi de 17 mars 1909 concernant la vente et le nantissement des fonds de commerce*) permits companies to charge their business undertakings (*fonds de commerce*) as security for their indebtedness, but the assets comprised in the charge are confined to the company's goodwill, business name, fixed assets and equipment, trade marks and insignia (logos), patents and the lease of the company's business premises (if any), and the charge cannot, even by express mention, extend to the company's current assets (that is, its raw materials, consumables, manufactured and semi-manufactured goods, stock in trade or inventory and book debts). Moreover, a charge over a company's business undertaking can be enforced only under an order of the court for the sale of the charged assets comprised in it.

The limitation in civil law systems that any security (other than a pledge of goods or negotiable paper in the lender's possession) may be enforced only by a judicial sale or other judicial process, is symptomatic of the reluctance of those systems to permit self-help remedies, because being based on Roman law, they regard the pursuit of legal remedies as necessarily involving litigation. Consequently, the number of occasions when self-help remedies are available under civil law systems to enforce rights of any kind are extremely limited. There is nothing in civil law equivalent to the common law remedy of a landlord to distrain for unpaid rent, although he is regarded as having a charge on the property comprised in a lease for unpaid rent and the charge can be enforced by judicial proceedings. The remedies of an unpaid seller of goods who has given no credit for the price are confined to retaining possession of the goods until they are paid for without himself being in breach of contract, although in French law the seller has the little-used right to retake the goods if the price is not paid for seven days after delivery. In practice, unpaid sellers who wish to have some security over the goods do so by contractual provisions reserving the title to the goods to themselves until the goods are paid for, but if the goods have been delivered to the seller, they can be recovered *in specie* only by judicial proceedings. English law and that of the other common law jurisdictions are more liberal in permitting self-help remedies, provided that no forcible entry on land is involved, but even so, the occasions when such remedies may be employed are relatively few. Whether the availability of self-help remedies by law is desirable or not is a matter on which opinions unavoidably differ, but there can be no doubt that the availability of receiverships under English law to enable the secured creditors of companies to recover the amounts owed to them without having to resort to a court to appoint the receiver or to order the realisation of the assets comprised in the security, provides a valuable practical benefit for secured creditors, especially when the companies concerned are declining rapidly.

R. R. PENNINGTON

CHAPTER 7

ADMINISTRATION AND INSOLVENCY: UNITED KINGDOM AND GERMAN APPROACHES

UNITED KINGDOM

Administration

Perhaps the most important practical distinction between the UK and US approaches to ailing companies is that under the UK system, the court will only appoint a licensed insolvency practitioner to be administrator or to be supervisor under a voluntary arrangement. The concept of debtor in possession plays no part in English or Scottish law.[1]

This has the adverse effect that directors are reluctant to relinquish control by applying for an administration order until they are forced to do so by the twin sanctions of the Company Directors Disqualification Act 1986 and potential liability for wrongful trading.[2] Under s. 6 of the former Act, the court shall disqualify a director or shadow director[3] of a company which becomes insolvent from being a company director and from being engaged in the promotion, formation or management of a company for two to 15 years, if his conduct as a director makes him unfit to be concerned in the management of a company. The factors to be taken into account are set out in Sch. 1 to the Act and include any breach of duty to the company.

Wrongful trading arises if, at some time before insolvent liquidation, directors knew or ought to have concluded that there was no reasonable prospect that the company would avoid insolvent liquidation.[4] It is a defence if the person concerned took every step with a view to minimising the potential loss to the company's creditors as he ought to have taken. The general view is that resignation is not in itself a sufficient defence; the director should ensure that the company stops trading. Moreover, companies are obliged by the

1. Contrast the Examiner procedure under Irish law.
2. Concepts not known in the US.
3. "Shadow director" is defined by the Insolvency Act 1986, s. 251 to mean "a person in accordance with whose directions or instructions the directors of the company are accustomed to act", but it does not apply to a person if the directors act on advice given by that person in a professional capacity. Rescuing banks must be careful to limit their activities to monitoring—through lawyers and accountants—and not issue directions or instructions to the board.
4. Insolvency Act 1986, s. 214.

Companies Acts to prepare annual accounts and the directors will be assumed for the purpose of s. 214 to know the financial position of the company if they ought to have prepared accounts which would have disclosed it.[5]

Wrongful trading (and potential disqualification) forces directors to seek insolvency advice much earlier than they would otherwise. If properly advised, rescue by syndicates of banks is often a viable possibility. Unfortunately, there are instances where directors are advised by lawyers without appropriate insolvency experience and sometimes apply for administration orders on such advice when a corporate rescue would have been more beneficial to all concerned.

Judges have said that the court would sometimes welcome a discretion to appoint an officer of the company to be its administrator, but that is not legally possible in the UK. The general view is that management which has caused or failed to prevent the crisis are the last people who should have control.

Administration orders

Because an administration order seriously prejudices the rights of creditors, it will only be made if the court is satisfied that the company is *likely to become insolvent* and that the making of the order is likely to achieve one or more of the following purposes:

1. the survival of the company and part of its undertaking as a going concern;
2. the approval of a voluntary arrangement (or a Companies Act scheme of arrangement); or
3. a more advantageous realisation of assets than would be effected on a winding-up.

The survival of the company is only achievable in those rare situations where the problem is only a cash-flow difficulty. However, a more advantageous realisation than would be effected on a winding-up is a test relatively easily fulfilled. Winding-up for this purpose probably means compulsory liquidation because voluntary winding-up can only be achieved if the shareholders pass the necessary resolution and shareholders of an insolvent company have little incentive to co-operate. Compulsory liquidation involves a hiatus period between petition and winding-up order and a period during which the official receiver controls the company pending the creditors meeting to elect a liquidator. It will, therefore, usually be more advantageous to have an administration order. A number of administration orders are also made with a view to a voluntary arrangement (see below).

There must be a "real prospect" that one or more of the above purposes will

5. *Re Produce Marketing Consortium Limited* (No. 2) [1989] BCLC 520.

be achieved.[6] In practice, the court is influenced by a report from an insolvency practitioner about the financial position and prospects of the company.

Section 9(3) of the Insolvency Act requires the court to dismiss a petition for an administration order if an administrative receiver has been appointed prior to the hearing, unless the debenture holder consents or the security is liable to be discharged. This has led to banks taking, in addition to fixed charges, floating charges over the whole or substantially the whole of the assets of the company—a practice which has assisted the preservation of businesses and jobs because the receiver has the power to sell the business as a whole.

The advantages of an administration order over a receivership are that it is more likely to be recognised in foreign jurisdictions; that creditors are precluded from repossessing goods except with the consent of the administrator or the leave of the court; that security ranking in priority to the debenture cannot be enforced without the consent of the administrator or the leave of the court and that long-standing contracts may not be capable of termination on an administration order, as this is a relatively new process.

The effect of an administration order

On the making of an administration order, any petition for winding-up shall be dismissed and any administrative receiver or other receiver shall vacate office.[7] While the order is in force, no resolution may be passed to wind up the company—though in practice resolutions are passed to wind up the company conditional on the court approving the resolution and discharging the administration order. This has the problem that preferential creditors at the commencement of the administration may lose their status, unless special arrangements are made to see them paid. This needs to be done if the ensuing liquidation is voluntary rather than compulsory.

Other effects are that no steps may be taken to appoint an administrative receiver or otherwise enforce security (widely defined) or repossess goods, and no proceedings may be taken or execution or distress levied against the company or its assets, except with the consent of the administrator or the leave of the court.[8]

Secured creditors who are unfairly prejudiced by the administration order can apply to the court for relief under s. 27 of the Insolvency Act 1986. The approach adopted by the court in exercising its discretion will probably follow that adopted in relation to s. 15 in the case of *Re ARV Aviation*.[9] There, the court held that it would look at all the circumstances of the case and balance the prejudice felt by the secured creditor against the prejudice felt by unsecured creditors who would potentially benefit from the purpose for which the

6. *Re Harris Simons Construction Ltd* (1989) BCLC 202.
7. Insolvency Act 1986, s. 11.
8. *Ibid.*
9. *Re ARV Aviation* (1989) BCLC 664.

administration order was made. It is not necessary to show misconduct by the administrators.[10] The courts are unwilling to fetter their discretion by laying down precise tests, but have said they will weigh up the interests of the parties involved in each case.

As an alternative to applying for relief under s. 27, creditors may apply to the court for leave to enforce their security or to bring proceedings (as was done in *Royal Trust Bank* v. *Buchler*), or may bring proceedings against the administrator for negligence or misfeasance under s. 212 of the Insolvency Act 1986.

The powers of an administrator

By s. 14 of the Insolvency Act 1986, the administrator may do all things necessary for the management of the affairs, business and property of the company, and he also has power to remove and replace directors and to call meetings of members and creditors. However, in exercising his powers he is deemed to act as agent of the company and it has been held that he can be injuncted from repudiating a contract binding on the company.[11]

By s. 15, the administrator can exercise his powers in relation to assets subject to a floating charge as if they were not subject to the security. As regards fixed-charge assets, he may apply to the court to authorise him to dispose of the property as if it were not subject to the security, provided the net proceeds or, if greater, the open market value are applied towards discharging the sum secured. The administrator can, therefore, not only prevent security being realised, but also force its sale subject to supervision by the court.

If administrators are authorised by the court under s. 15 to override fixed charges, problems may well arise about how to apportion the price obtained for the business as a whole. The purchaser will primarily be influenced by tax considerations; the administrator by a need to obtain creditors' approval to his proposals. The fixed chargee will need to have his security valued and be prepared to apply to the court under s. 27 for relief.

The duties of an administrator

It is the duty of the administrator to take control of all the assets of the company, and to manage its business and affairs until his proposals have been approved by the creditors in accordance with any directions given by the court. After his proposals have been approved, he is to manage the company in accordance with those proposals.

It is also the duty of the administrator under s. 18 to apply to the court for the administration order to be discharged or varied, if it appears to him that the purposes specified in the order have been achieved or are incapable of

10. See *Royal Trust Bank* v. *Buchler* (1989) BCLC 130.
11. *Astor Chemical Limited* v. *Synthetic Technology Limited* [1990] BCC 97.

achievement. The court then has a wide discretion to make such order as it thinks fit.

Under s. 23, the administrator is to make proposals for achieving the purposes of the order within three months of the administration order or such longer period as the court may allow. The administrator must summon a meeting of creditors to decide whether or not to approve the proposals. However, the meeting can only modify those proposals if the administrator consents to each modification. Any creditor or member of the company who considers that he has been unfairly prejudiced by the proposals may apply to the court under s. 27, but any such application must be made within 28 days after the approval of the proposals.

Voluntary arrangements

Although, in theory, it is possible for directors to propose a voluntary arrangement under s. 1 of the Insolvency Act 1986, such an arrangement has to be supervised by a licensed insolvency practitioner. In practice, a voluntary arrangement will only succeed if dissenting creditors can be kept at bay and this usually entails applying for an administration order. Voluntary arrangements of companies are rarely successful without this protection, unless the number of creditors involved is small. However, voluntary arrangements coupled with administration orders are useful because an administrator in his capacity as such has no power to make a distribution binding on all creditors.[12]

As in administration, the proposals must be put to creditors' meetings. The requisite majority in a voluntary arrangement is three-quarters in value. In addition, where no administration order has been made, there must also be members' meetings. The proposals under a voluntary arrangement cannot affect the right of a secured creditor to enforce his security and shall not prejudice a preferential creditor without his agreement.

As in the case of proposals by an administrator, any creditor or member who is unfairly prejudiced by the proposals may apply to the court for relief, provided the application is made within 28 days of the reports of the meetings being made to the court.

In practice, voluntary arrangements under the Insolvency Act 1986 are likely to be rare, unless made by an administrator or a liquidator.

Conclusion

Historically, insolvency procedures were designed to collect the assets of the debtor and distribute them to the creditors entitled. Now, there is a realisation of the need to rehabilitate business and save jobs; a process assisted by calling in expert help at an early stage. Rehabilitation usually requires an injection of

12. *Re St Ives Windings Limited* (1989) 3 BCC 634.

new capital and a strengthening of management, and may, therefore, entail selling the business. The next development (already evident in the US) may well be a perceived need to protect the environment.

The UK concept of debentures charging all the assets of a company to the banks has done much to protect the UK banking system, but at the expense of trade and other creditors. It is arguable that the law should be amended so that floating charges only validly secure new moneys as opposed to old debt; just as retention of title could usefully be restricted to the price for the particular goods retained.

JAMES LINGARD

GERMANY

The German bankruptcy code

Describing the German legal principles on the administration of an insolvent company can be done rather quickly: they do not exist. The German Bankruptcy Code (Konkursordnung—KO) dates back to the year 1877 when the term "liquidation" was still understood in its literal sense: to make the assets liquid, that is to sell them and pay out a cash dividend to the creditors.

While this principle continues to dominate bankruptcy proceedings in Germany, practice during the last 150 years or so has brought about major changes in the way it is applied. Most importantly, the ever-increasing demand of creditors for collateralisation of their claims has led to the situation that, upon the occurrence of bankruptcy, all important assets of a company have been charged, encumbered or transferred by way of security to preferred creditors and are not available to unsecured creditors. It is fair to say that in about 80 per cent of all insolvencies formal bankruptcy proceedings are not initiated because the insolvents' assets will not even be sufficient to warrant the payment of the trustee in bankruptcy (Konkursverwalter) and court fees. This embarrassing result has been called "the bankruptcy of bankruptcy proceedings".

The lack of a registration system in which security rights on chattels can be recorded and would be open to inspection by other creditors makes the situation even worse. What appears to be a prosperous company may suddenly turn out to be deprived of all after secured creditors have ascertained their rights. The average bankruptcy dividend for the unsecured creditor is as low as 2 per cent of its claim. The annual overall economic loss has been estimated at about DM50 billion.

But also in the circumstances of large companies' bankruptcies, the principle of liquidation has proved unsatisfactory. Obviously, the proceeds received from a liquidation of assets are significantly less than the price that could be achieved if the viable part of the business could be sold as a going concern. Furthermore, by destroying the business all employees have to be laid off, although it may have been possible to rescue a significant number of jobs in connection with the continuation of a smaller core business which has been relieved from its liabilities.

In many cases trustees in bankruptcy have therefore decided to set up a so-called rescue company (Auffanggesellschaft) that purchases the core business of the bankrupt company as a going concern and continues the operation. This procedure has not been contemplated by the bankruptcy code and constitutes, if not a violation, at least a circumvention of the law.

The bankruptcy reform

These developments have caused the legislator to prepare a radical reform of the German bankruptcy laws. A draft of a new bankruptcy code has been developed and is under discussion.[13] It is unlikely, however, that the reform would actually become law before a couple of years.

The major issues of the insolvency law reform are as follows.

Restriction of privileges of preferred creditors

It had been expected that the reform must place a strong emphasis on the reinforcement of the principle of equal treatment for all creditors. This aim could only be accomplished if the preferred status of security rights were abolished or at least significantly restricted. Yet, the reform is half-hearted in this respect. Secured claims are to retain their value. However, under the new concept secured creditors will take part in the insolvency proceedings. Unlike under the present Bankruptcy Code they will not be allowed to claim possession of their security immediately upon the institution of the proceedings. Rather, they will have to leave the charged chattle for use by the bankruptcy trustee and will only be entitled to the proceeds once the trustee has decided to sell the security. Nevertheless, the influence of the secured creditors in the realisation of the security remains significant; they enjoy a pre-emptive right with respect to a sale and, under certain circumstances, may take the initiative to accelerate the realisation of the security. While the collateral is used by the trustee in bankruptcy, the owners of the security will receive a usage fee.

Reorganisation/insolvency plan

There will be no separate procedures for reorganisation and liquidation. The insolvency plan serves as the universal instrument for the realisation of the assets. The plan may provide for a reorganisation of the debtor, including by transfer of the debtor's business to a new company, or for its liquidation. The

13. See Bundesministerium der Justiz, *Gesetz zur Reform des Insolvenzrechts: Diskussionsentwurf*, Köln, 1988.

plan will be negotiated among all creditors—whether secured or unsecured—and the shareholders of the failed company. If the creditors agree, the debtor may retain possession of the assets under supervision of a trustee.

A so-called "reorganisation by transfer" will be introduced as another way for a successful reorganisation of the debtor company. The transfer can be accomplished by a sale of the business as a going concern, which will require the consent of the creditors, or may be provided by the insolvency plan. All concerned parties have the right to obtain independent price quotes to make certain that the value of the assets is realised at market terms.

Protection of employees

The rights of employees will generally not be abridged by the new insolvency procedure. The remaining assets are liable for redundancy payments. However, the amount payable under a severance scheme (Sozialplan) will be limited.

Fresh start/discharge (Restschuldbefreiung)

Under the present law, an individual's liability continues for 30 years without discharge. Apparently, this results in a situation where the debtor has no incentive to pay anything at all, but will live at the expense of his relatives for the rest of his life. The reform contemplates releasing the debtor from his almost life-long financial burden. Even without the consent of the majority of the creditors, a debtor will be conceded a fresh start if his insolvency was not caused by negligence and he has taken part in the insolvency procedure in a constructive manner. Yet, after completion of the procedure, the debtor has to surrender that part of his income which is subject to attachment by his creditors for a period of seven years. Thereafter, the release from the residual liability will become effective *vis-à-vis* all creditors, including those not having asserted their claims in the proceedings.

Primarily, the proposal for a discharge has been driven by social and not economic reasons, and reflects the high value of an individual's right to a self-responsible life.

Bankruptcy laws in the eastern part of Germany

Finally, I would like to make some short remarks regarding the bankruptcy law effective in the new states (*neue Länder*) which have acceded to the Federal Republic in the process of German reunification. The pertinent law is the Joint Enforcement Act (Gesamtvollstreckungsverordnung). Like the Bankruptcy Act of the old Federal Republic, the purpose of the Joint Enforcement Act is equal satisfaction of all creditors. However, the Joint Enforcement Act shows several features of a more modern approach towards an efficient solution of the problem. The Act provides for the possibility of setting up a moratorium, a postponement of payments. Furthermore, after completion of the collective execution the creditors can only pursue their claims if the debtor has acquired new assets which exceed his basic needs. This also means a limited discharge for debtors acting in good faith.

The legal remedies given to creditors under the Joint Enforcement Act may prevent a reorganisation of East German businesses, which is an important concern in connection with the recovery of the East German economy. The Joint Enforcement Interruption Act (Gesetz über die Unterbrechung von Gesamtvollstreckungsverfahren) has been introduced in order to pave the way for an effective reorganisation. A third party, who, for example, may be interested in purchasing the insolvent company, may apply for an interruption of enforcement for a period of up to three months. The period may be extended for another three months if a plan for reorganisation has been submitted.

In order to protect the rights of the creditors, the party applying for interruption has to guarantee all liabilities which the insolvent company will incur during the interruption. Applicant, and guarantor, can be any natural or judicial person, or the Treuhandanstalt. It is still an open question whether the Joint Enforcement Interruption Act is an efficient tool for providing a successful reorganisation procedure instead of liquidation.

HENDRIK HAAG

CHAPTER 8

REHABILITATION AND APPROACHES OTHER THAN FORMAL INSOLVENCY PROCEDURES

INTRODUCTION

It is a truism that a business is more valuable as a going concern than when subject to a forced sale. It is also well recognised that the commencement of formal insolvency procedures in relation to a company almost invariably has an adverse effect on the value of its business. Leaving aside the niceties of the distinctions between the administration order procedure, liquidation and receivership, any insolvency procedure, to a greater or lesser extent signals a fire sale to the outside world (an administration solely for the purpose of the company's survival is the exception). Such procedures usually focus on a more or less rapid realisation of a company's assets and the disposal of its business in order to discharge the claims of creditors so that it is more difficult to obtain the full and proper value of the company's business. Accordingly, when a company is facing financial difficulties, serious consideration must be given to whether the company can be rehabilitated without resort to formal insolvency procedures.

Recourse to a process of support or intensive care for a company in financial difficulty involves banks recognising that the simple enforcement of their strict legal rights does not necessarily achieve instant repayment and that a careful, informed review of all available options (while reserving the bank's rights) may produce a better return. The uncertainties of dividends payable in a formal insolvency also often justify a close look at alternatives to receivership (if the banks have security), administration and liquidation. Of course, the merits of any proposed support operation have to be tested by reference to what would otherwise be available if resort was had to such a formal procedure.

Formal insolvency, therefore, is almost always to be viewed as a last resort. This is true from the perspective of both the banks and management. From the banks' point of view, when a customer is in difficulty there is an incentive to develop a method of dealing with the company's problems which enables the company to carry on trading with minimum disruption with continued support from the bank creditors on suitable terms. There are now, after some 20 years' experience, well-established principles for managing this type of problem and for constructing a support or rescue operation by banks for their customers. Not every customer in difficulty is amenable to this type of solution—it presupposes a viable business, or part of a business, which is capable of being rehabilitated by steps taken to reschedule the company's indebtedness (by, for example deferring and revising payment obligations) or to reorganise its assets and affairs (by for example, major disposals being made or a refinancing). A yet further truism in this area is that a company to be rescued must have had a successful past. Nobody bothers to rescue companies which have always been failures. If a company's difficulties are too severe, administration or receivership may be unavoidable. This is particularly the case where creditors are pressing so heavily that they threaten to pull the customer's business apart and recourse is necessary to the automatic stay provisions (which freeze the enforcement of creditors claims against the company) which arise in an administration. Identifying whether a customer is capable of being rescued is therefore the first crucial question (and one of the most pressing matters) to be resolved by bankers dealing with the problem loan. The rescue, apart from offering the prospect of repayment in full if ultimately completely successful, can offer more immediate gains to the banks. For example, new or enhanced security may be available or there may be the chance of the fresh injection of funds from other sources, such as the shareholders or other banks.

There is also an incentive from management's perspective in seeing their company remain outside formal insolvency. In the first place, management and proprietors obviously face the loss of their livelihood and investments if their company fails and becomes insolvent. Apart from the obvious financial implications of formal insolvency, insolvency procedures still bring with them the stigma of (usually culpable) failure. We have not yet reached the stage in the UK, as perhaps has happened in the US, of regarding the reorganisation of companies in difficulty through the use of court procedures as being an acceptable, even standard, tool of business management. The administration order procedure may, in time, be perceived in this way. For the present, in terms of perception, it remains bad news for management to be associated with a company which has had to have recourse to formal insolvency procedures. Moreover, it is not only problems of perception which mean that management is keen to avoid the commencement of formal insolvency procedures. Once formal insolvency procedures start the activities and position of directors comes under considerable formal scrutiny. In the first place, once an administrative receiver has been appointed, an administration order has been made or the company has gone into liquidation, the relevant insolvency practitioner is under a duty to submit to the secretary of state a report on the conduct of the directors of the company. (See s. 7(3) of the Company Directors Disqualification Act 1986 and the Insolvent Companies (Reports on Conduct of Directors) No. 2 Rules 1986.) This could lead to action being taken for the disqualification of those directors. Secondly, once a formal insolvency procedure has commenced, control of the company is taken away from management and handed over to a qualified insolvency practitioner. In the UK there is no equivalent to the "debtor in possession" approach adopted in Chapter 11 cases under the US Bankruptcy Code (although Eire now has an insolvency procedure which does leave management in control, namely the provisions relating to the appointment of an examiner under the Companies (Amendment) Act 1990). Directors trying to grapple with the financial difficulties of their company are, not surprisingly, reluctant to hand over control to an insolvency practitioner. Accordingly, subject to the constraints imposed on directors by their insolvency-related duties, there is also an incentive for management to try to work out a company's financial problems without resort to formal insolvency.

Therefore, the interests of both management and bank creditors can favour a rescue outside formal insolvency. There are other practical advantages too. Rescue operations can also be put into place without the full glare of publicity which follows the commencement of a formal insolvency procedure. The avoidance of adverse publicity can have a significant impact on the ability of a company in difficulty to survive, and upon the realisable value of its assets.

These interests and considerations establish the dynamics for a negotiation between the borrower and its bankers on the terms of a support operation. Both sides to such a negotiation are able to retain the threat of resort to formal insolvency if satisfactory arrangements cannot be hammered out. Of course, these negotiations involve more than two sides—the negotiations between the banks are as intensive as, and often more difficult than, negotiations with the borrower. If the support operation is to have the approval of all the banks there must be benefits for all concerned. There will usually be a multiplicity of interests, and even different rights and obligations within the bank group which need to be ironed out. Some banks may start out as secured, while others start out as unsecured. It is necessary to develop a plan which will enable the banks to see the merits in moving forward together—the unsecured banks probably being allowed to share in the security (on terms as to sharing of recoveries) while the secured creditors will look to ensure a return which is more advantageous than an immediate failure of the borrower.

This highlights, of course, a central problem in the support operation approach—it is entirely consensual and contractual, requiring the agreement of all concerned or the payment in full of dissenters (and those not party to the arrangements). If dissenters are to be forced to vary their rights, a voluntary arrangement under the Insolvency Act 1986 is required (see p. 161, below). This is why it is important that (a) experienced bankers (aware of what can and can not be achieved in such situations) take charge of the management of a support operation to ensure that the bank (and major creditor) group is made to feel that they are being fairly treated, and to avoid, where possible, banks trying to negotiate for inappropriate, unsustainable advantages, (b) a common consensus is developed among the banking community to establish widely recognised methods and principles to deal with these types of problems to facilitate a "rational decision" (the words of the Governor of the Bank of England) on how to proceed and (c) there is encouragement from regulators, and others with influence, for the use and development of sensible procedures for support operations. Hence the recent pronouncements from the Bank of England (of which, more below)—which of course, recognise that ultimately it is a decision for creditors whether to go along with a rescue—but offer support and assistance to banks in moving forward, where possible.

LEGAL ISSUES TO BE ADDRESSED WHEN CONSIDERING WHETHER FORMAL INSOLVENCY CAN BE AVOIDED

Before going on to consider the details of how support arrangements work, it is worth looking at the legal context in which these arrangements have to be put in place to see the risks to and pressures on directors of the borrower (and on the banks) which shape the arrangements and their implementation.

Directors' duties

As soon as a company runs into financial problems, its directors must consider their position and the duties imposed on them in that context. Any support operation for a company in difficulty has to enable directors to be satisfied that they are acting consistently with their duties and bankers involved in structuring the support operation must be aware of these matters. There are four main areas of concern for directors.

The first is wrongful trading

Section 214 of the Insolvency Act 1986 (the "Act") requires directors to monitor the financial position of their company and once the directors conclude, or should conclude, that there is no reasonable prospect of their company avoiding an insolvent liquidation, a duty is imposed on them to take every step which a reasonably diligent person would take to minimise potential loss to the company's creditors. If, after the company has gone into insolvent liquidation, it appears to the court that a director has failed to comply with this duty, then the court may require the director to make such contribution to the company's assets as it thinks proper. It has been held, in *Re Produce Marketing Consortium Limited*,[1] that the jurisdiction under s. 214 is primarily compensatory rather than penal.

> *Prima facie* the appropriate amount that a director is declared to be liable to contribute is the amount by which the company's assets can be discerned to have been depleted by the director's conduct which caused the discretion under section 214(1) to arise . . . the

1. (1989) 5 BCC 569.

fact that there was no fraudulent intent is not of itself a reason for fixing the amount at a nominal or low figure.

This approach has recently been supported in *Re Purpoint Limited.*[2] What is of considerable significance here is that the conduct of directors is to be assessed not only by reference to what they actually knew or concluded, but also by reference to what they should have known or concluded. Section 214(4) of the Act states that:

the facts which a director of a company ought to know or ascertain, the conclusions which he ought to reach and the steps which he ought to take are those which would be known or ascertained, or reached or taken, by a reasonably diligent person having both—

(a) the general knowledge, skill and experience that may reasonably be expected of a person carrying out the same functions as are carried out by that director in relation to the company, and
(b) the general knowledge, skill and experience that that director has.

Accordingly, it is appropriate in cases where the company's own financial records are incomplete and inadequately kept, to treat directors as being aware of financial and other information which they would have been aware of had the company's books and records been properly kept. "Certain minimum standards are to be assumed to be attained. Notably there is an obligation laid on companies to cause accounting records to be kept which are such as to disclose with reasonable accuracy at any time the financial position of the company at that time" (Companies Act 1985, s. 221(1) and (2)(a), *per* Knox J in *Re Produce Marketing Consortium Limited*).

Therefore, in the context of a support operation directors have to assess, in the light of all the circumstances and assuming full information, whether there is a reasonable prospect of their company avoiding insolvent liquidation. If the directors cannot say that there is a reasonable prospect of avoiding an insolvent liquidation, or are unsure of the position, then they are in the wrongful trading zone and the duty to take steps to minimise potential loss to creditors which then arises could require them to cause the borrower to cease trading and commence a suitable insolvency procedure. Of course, this duty could require other action to be taken; however, when liquidation is a realistic possibility, it is usually prudent for the board to allow control to be handed over to an insolvency practitioner rather than risk an inquiry after the failure of the directors' efforts into whether the steps ultimately taken by the directors were adequate.

In a support operation, there will be a number of stages (although the directors have to keep matters under constant review). At the outset, the directors will wish to see that the bank creditors are engaged in serious discussions and that those discussions could lead, if ultimately successful, to arrangements which will (perhaps with other arrangements) secure the future of the company. In these early stages, the directors will need to satisfy themselves that the

2. 8 March 1990, unreported.

company's financial predicament still leaves room for a genuine and realistic prospect that insolvent liquidation can be avoided. They will also wish to be satisfied that the banks, at least initially, have not rejected the possibility of a rescue. This can involve the directors in a difficult assessment in the early days when the precise extent of the borrower's problems and its ability to resolve them are unclear. However, the theoretical possibility that the company's bankers will be amenable to offer support to the company is not sufficient. The wrongful trading duties require directors to approach the company's bankers at an early stage and to take steps to move the discussion forward as quickly as possible. Once there has been a reasonable opportunity to consult with the company's principal bank creditors, then the directors are required to consider whether what the banks are prepared to accept is sufficient to provide a reasonable prospect of avoiding liquidation. A successful support package, from the directors' perspective, would usually include a new moneys facility to ensure that the company is able to pay its debts as they fall due, with a rescheduling of outstanding facilities to ensure that the company's commitment to make payment to the banks is matched by the detailed, verified, projections for income arising out of cash flow, asset disposals and other receipts. Once the terms of the support arrangement have been put in place and documented, the directors then need to review the position if circumstances change (particularly cash-flow forecasts) in such a way so as to indicate that there has to be a reassessment of whether there is a reasonable prospect of avoiding insolvent liquidation.

Directors of companies in financial difficulty often look to the prospect of some kind of refinancing, or a disposal programme involving significant sections of the company's assets and business, to solve their problems. Provided that the company's financial predicament is, as a practical matter, capable of being resolved by a refinancing or asset disposal programme (or similar arrangement), then the knowledge that the company's financial advisers are seeking to find third parties interested in participating in such a refinancing or restructuring is usually sufficient to enable the directors to conclude that they are not in the wrongful trading zone; that is there is a reasonable prospect of avoiding an insolvent liquidation. However, a prudent board of directors will wish to ensure that the response in the market place is sufficiently favourable to indicate the potential for ultimate success and that the board's view is supported by experienced advisers. Over-optimism in this context may not necessarily mean that directors run the risk of wrongful trading liability in the very short term, but such an approach will involve serious risks if adopted for very long. Unfortunately, one of the difficulties bankers and their advisers often face in rescue operations is the over-optimism of management who are finding it difficult to come to terms with their company's difficulties.

Despite the concerns which were initially expressed when the wrongful trading provisions were first enacted, that the wrongful trading duties would make support operations extremely difficult, advisers to boards of companies in difficultly generally adopt a sensible, albeit cautious, approach in practice. Directors are not required to cause their company to cease trading immediately a problem is identified but are, instead, required to obtain full information about their company's affairs, and its immediate prospects, and to keep under constant review the prospect of insolvent liquidation. Provided that they proceed on the basis of full professional advice, and on the basis of a realistic assessment of the company's position and prospects, then wrongful trading liability ought to be avoided. Directors of well-managed companies who adopt sensible commercial strategies based on full information have little to be concerned about, provided they know when to stop. Having said this, it has to be recognised that the wrongful trading provisions do impose onerous duties on directors, particularly in difficult situations where there may be genuine doubts about the ability of a company to avoid liquidation, and therefore will, in some circumstances, make a support operation very difficult, if not impossible. This may mean that resort to formal insolvency procedures is inevitable. Perhaps the leading "company doctor" of the current recession, David James (of Eagle Trust and now Danair fame) has found the wrongful trading provisions "to be wholly regrettable and negative", particularly when taken in conjunction with the fact that the wrongful trading duties are extended to shadow directors, an issue discussed further below.

Secondly, there is fraudulent trading

Section 213 of the Act stipulates that if in the course of the winding-up of a company, it appears that any business of the company has been carried on with intent to defraud creditors of the company or creditors of any other person, or for any fraudulent purpose, the court may declare any persons who are knowingly parties to the carrying on of the company's business in this way to be liable to make sure contributions to the company's assets as the court thinks proper. Breach of these provisions will also constitute a criminal offence. These provisions deal primarily with liability for incurring further credit without good reason for believing that the debt will be repaid.

These are the fraudulent trading provisions which were in force prior to the enactment of the Insolvency Act 1986. The provisions were generally regarded as inadequate since proceedings in relation to fraudulent trading were rarely successful because of the need to establish "dishonesty" according to the burden of proof required by the criminal law. It was because of these inadequacies that wrongful trading was introduced to cover conduct which would not be subject to the fraudulent trading provisions. Essentially, fraudulent trading will be established where the borrower *obtains credit* when the directors know that there is no good reason for thinking that funds will become available to pay the debt when it becomes payable or shortly thereafter.[3]

3. See *R.* v. *Grantham* [1984] 2 WLR 815.

There will be some circumstances in which the fraudulent trading provisions are wider than the wrongful trading provisions (for example, because the fraudulent trading provisions apply to those who have been a party to fraudulent trading rather than simply to directors and shadow directors). However, the wrongful trading provisions are likely to be of more practical significance in the context of a support operation than fraudulent trading. Fraudulent trading requires the establishment of real moral blame according to current notions of fair trading and (it is to be hoped!) that this will be rare in relation to support operations, certainly of major companies. However, it is worth bearing in mind that the civil law fraudulent trading remedy is not dead. For example, in *Re A Company No. 001418 of 1988*[4] a company's managing director (and majority shareholder) was held to be liable for fraudulent trading since he was held to have had no reason for thinking that the company could pay its debts as they fell due or shortly thereafter, taking into account the following matters: the company owed Customs and Excise for VAT something in excess of £10,000; the Inland Revenue was owed in excess of £46,000 in relation to PAYE and National Insurance; there had been a serious deterioration as to the deficiency of net assets; the company's bankers (who were continually consulted), were continuing to show concern; extended credit was being taken from the major supplier; there was no basis on which the director could believe that the company was trading profitably, i.e. he knew that the position was continuing to deteriorate; large directors' remuneration continued and the company continued to pay for certain private expenditure of the director. In this case, not only was the director held to be liable to contribute the trading loss during the period of fraudulent trading, but also was required to pay over £25,000 as a "punitive element".

The good news from the perspective of bank creditors is that, in this case, there was no suggestion that the bank was also liable. It has been held that a person is not a party to carrying on a company's business with intent to defraud its creditors unless he actively participates in its management. If he merely fails to warn its directors that it is insolvent and that no further debts should be incurred on its behalf, he cannot be made liable under the statutory provision, even though he is guilty of negligence in failing to give that advice and could be sued by the company for breach of duty as an officer of the company or for breach of a contract to advise properly.[5] To impose liability on a bank or other third party it must be shown that the bank actually took part in making management decisions which were intended to defraud creditors, or were known to be likely to cause them loss. This is inherently unlikely in the case of a bank, except in the most exceptional cases. While banks are, accordingly, most unlikely to be liable themselves for fraudulent trading, care does have to be taken since a creditor of a company who accepts payment of his

4. [1990] BCC 526.
5. See *Re Maidstone Building Provisions Limited* [1971] 3 All ER 363.

debt out of money which he knows its directors have obtained by fraud, may be compelled personally to restore the money so applied by means of a fraudulent trading order.[6] Furthermore, and finally in this context, it is worth noting that before the bank or other third party can be held to be liable as being a party to fraudulent trading, it is necessary to establish that the board of the company/borrower had themselves carried on the company's business with intent to defraud creditors. That is, the conduct of the third party, such as a bank, is only relevant where there is a prior establishment of a liability on the part of the company's directors.[7]

Thirdly, the directors must consider their general fiduciary duties

Directors must act bona fide in the interests of the company. This is a long-established principle. This duty, owed to the company, generally requires consideration of the interests of shareholders. There is, however, an increasing body of case-law which indicates that when a company is in financial difficulty the content of the directors' duty to act in the interests of the company becomes a duty to consider the best interests of creditors.

For example, in the Court of Appeal in *Brady* v. *Brady*,[8] Nourse LJ noted as follows:

> The interests of the company, an artificial person, cannot be distinguished from the interests of the persons who are interested in it. Who are those persons? Where a company is both going and solvent, first and foremost come the shareholders present and no doubt future as well. How material are the interests of creditors in such a case? Admittedly, existing creditors are interested in the assets of the company as the only source for the satisfaction of their debt. But in a case where the assets are enormous and the debts minimal it is reasonable to suppose that the interests of the creditors ought not to count for very much. Conversely, where the company is insolvent, or *even doubtfully solvent* the interests of the company are in reality the interests of existing creditors alone.
>
> (Emphasis added)

This approach was also taken in the Court of Appeal decision in the *Liquidator of West Mercia Safetywear Limited* v. *Dodd*,[9] where the approach in recent Australian decisions confirming that the interests of creditors intrude where a company is insolvent, was approved. Despite the views of Lord Templeman (in *Winkworth* v. *Edward Baron*[10] where it was said that a company owes a duty to its creditors to keep its property inviolate and available for the repayment of its debts), the better view appears to be that this is a duty owed to the company and not direct to creditors.

Accordingly, when directors are being asked to consider the terms of a possible support arrangement in circumstances where the company is in difficulty

6. See *Re Gerald Cooper Chemicals Limited* [1978] Ch 262.
7. See *Re Augustus Barnett & Son Limited* [1986] BCLC 170.
8. (1987) 3 BCC 535 at 552.
9. (1988) 4 BCC 30.
10. (1987) 3 BCC 4.

they will be forced to give general consideration to the interests of the company's creditors as a whole. In most cases this should not produce a practical problem since, if the support operation is designed to rehabilitate the company and turn it round, this is almost inevitably in the interests of all creditors. However, of course, some support operations focus closely (and properly) on the position of the bank creditors and it must not be forgotten that all creditors' interests need to be considered. This issue often arises when banks request security in a support operation. There is much debate as to whether the provision of such security might be said to be a preference within s. 239 of the Act (discussed in detail below)—the giving of a preference can also make the directors liable for misfeasance. But even where concerns regarding a possible preference can be dealt with, the directors need to consider their common law fiduciary duties. Of course, in a negotiation with the company's bankers, the more reasons the directors can give for avoiding having to provide security the better it is from their point of view. In most cases the directors will be made aware by the banks and their advisers at an early stage that if they wish to have the opportunity at all to consider a support operation, and therefore be able generally to look after the interests of creditors, security has to be given as a precondition to the banks' support. I have come across some cases recently though, in which directors have refused to give security.

Fourthly, and finally, there are the provisions relating to disqualification

Directors of insolvent companies may be disqualified for between two and 15 years, from being a director of the company or in any way whether directly or indirectly, being concerned or taking part in the promotion, formation or management of the company. The court must make a disqualification order against a particular person where (a) it is satisfied that he is or was a director or shadow director of the company which has become insolvent during or after the time he was a director or shadow director and (b) it is satisfied that the person's conduct as a director is such that the person is unfit to be concerned in the management of the company. For these purposes, a company becomes insolvent if it goes into insolvent liquidation, or goes into administration or an administrative receiver is appointed to it.

In deciding whether a person is unfit to be concerned in the management of a company, the court considers the full range of the director's conduct, including the extent of the director's responsibility for the causes of the company becoming insolvent. The court will also, for example, consider the extent of the director's responsibility for the company entering into transactions at an undervalue or preferences.

It is not unusual, in cases of companies facing cash-flow problems, for directors to refrain from paying creditors, except when those creditors press for payment strenuously. This is often a difficulty in cases where the principal bank creditor to the company is refusing to increase overdraft limits and a company is desperately trying to carry on trading within its existing limit, which it keeps bumping up against. While directors may take the view (and in practice often do) that it is acceptable to keep the company alive by holding at bay as many of the company's creditors as possible, perhaps for a short period while alternative arrangements are made, nevertheless directors who so act do run a risk. For example, in *Re Sevenoaks Stationers (Retail) Limited*,[11] Dillon LJ said:

> Mr Cruddas made a deliberate decision to pay any of those creditors who pressed for payment. The obvious result was that the two companies traded, when in fact insolvent and known to be in difficulties, at the expense of those creditors who, like the Crown happened not to be pressing for payment. Such conduct on the part of a director can well, in my judgement, be relied on as a ground for saying that he is unfit to be concerned in the management of the company. But what is relevant in the Crown's position is not that the debt is a debt which arose from a compulsory deduction from employees' wages or a compulsory payment of VAT, but that the Crown was not pressing for payment and the director was taking unfair advantage of that forbearance on the part of the Crown and, instead of providing adequate working capital was trading at the Crown's expense while the companies were in jeopardy. It would be equally unfair to trade in that way and in such circumstances at the expense of creditors other than the Crown.

Matters affecting lenders

The problem of shadow directors

As is now well known, potential liability for wrongful trading covers not only directors but also shadow directors and there has been extensive debate, and the odd dictum, on the question of whether a bank creditor can become a shadow director, and liable for wrongful trading by intervening too closely in the management of the company during a support operation.

Section 251 of the Act defines "shadow director" as "a person in accordance with whose directions or instructions the directors of the company are accustomed to act (but so that a person is not deemed a shadow director by reason only that the directors act on advice given by him in a professional capacity)". This provision was introduced to ensure that the true managers of a company's affairs could not avoid being bound by the duties imposed on directors simply by avoiding a formal appointment as a director while standing back pulling the strings of the (puppet) board. For the provisions to apply, the board needs effectively to have abdicated its management responsibility in favour or a third party, whose decisions it passively implements over a period of time. Accordingly, the bank creditor is far from the paradigm envisaged by the draftsman of the Act and in most cases where a bank creditor indicates that any action which the company/borrower is asked to take is a requirement of the bank's continued support and the continued availability of facilities which the

11. [1990] BCC 765 at p. 799.

borrower's board is free to accept or decline as it sees fit, then there should be little difficulty. There is a significant difference (albeit a narrow line) between the bank saying "you can draw cheques whenever you wish, but I tell you now that I am only prepared to make funds available to £Xm" (where that figure is the estimate of the borrower's working capital requirements and payments to suppliers) *and* "you will make cheques payable for your trade supplies and the bank will honour these but you are not to pay any other creditors". Banks who become involved in a support operation will do well to make the position clear at the outset of any discussions concerning a support operation (in many cases this is well worth documenting in a formal letter at the outset) and should insist on the company receiving advice from experienced solicitors (and insolvency practitioners) wherever possible.

In these circumstances, it was hardly surprising to find Knox J in *Re A Company No. 005009 of 1987*[12] taking the view that the claim that a bank might be a shadow director was not "obviously unsustainable". There can be little doubt that in extreme cases, where a bank chooses to intervene in management decisions relating to a borrower and to act other than as a creditor and where the company's directors become accustomed to do what they are told by the bank, then the bank could well end up being held to be shadow director. This approach is consistent with the principles underlying similar rules in other jurisdictions.[13] However, it is equally clear that in most cases this will not happen—as became apparent when the facts applying in the *Re A Company* case were fully aired. When the matter came before Millett J at the full trial, the shadow director allegations were, according to Millett J, "rightly abandoned by the applicant after 6 days of oral evidence".[14] The *M.C. Bacon* case involved the standard situation of a bank trying to deal with the position of a troubled customer. Following the loss of the company's major customer in December 1986, arrangements were made to hand over management of the company to the son of one of its proprietors but, unfortunately, the company was in a difficult financial position and its overdraft started to rise strongly in March 1987. The company's clearing bank was approached in April 1987 and, in accordance with standard practice in this sort of case, asked for full financial information, including cash-flow forecasts and a debenture. The figures prepared by the company at this time indicated that it was only marginally solvent, on a balance sheet test, if at all and the bank insisted on the company operating within its overdraft limit. In May 1987 officials of the bank were reporting to regional head office that the company appeared to be insolvent, although there were reasonable grounds for thinking that the company could recover. Despite attempts by the company in the period from May until August

12. (1988) 4 BCC 424.
13. See, for example "Creditor Liabilities Resulting From Improper Interference With the Management of A Financially Troubled Debtor" (1975) *The Business Lawyer* vol. 31, p. 343.
14. See *Re M.C. Bacon Limited* [1990] BCC 78 at p. 79.

to try to sell its business, the company eventually went into liquidation on 24 August 1987. The judge was satisfied that the relationship between the directors and the bank was "an arm's-length one" and it is clear that he thought there was no evidence that the bank had done anything other than protect its own position as a creditor.

Another recent example of the reluctance of the courts to impose a liability on banks in these circumstances is provided by the decision of the Privy Council in *Kuwait Asia EC Bank* v. *National Mutual Life Nominees Limited.*[15] In this case, the Kuwait Asia Bank had a 49.9 per cent shareholding in a New Zealand company. This New Zealand company had a subsidiary which subsequently went into liquidation. A number of the bank's employees were on the board of this subsidiary. Through its indirect shareholding, and the appointment of its employees to the board of the subsidiary, the bank was closely associated with the management of the sub-subsidiary. However, on the evidence, the Privy Council was not prepared to accept that the bank was liable to creditors of the sub-subsidiary (a) by reason of its position as a shareholder who controlled the appointment of a director to the company's board since, in the absence of fraud or bad faith, such a shareholder owed no duty to take care that directors so appointed discharged their duties as directors properly; (b) the bank was not responsible for the breach of the duties owed by directors of the sub-subsidiary to creditors since they were agents of the sub-subsidiary and acted as directors of that company and not as agents or employees of the bank and (c) the bank was not a shadow director. It had been alleged that the bank was a shadow director because it nominated two out of five directors to the board. However, the bank was clearly unable to control the majority of the board, even assuming that its two appointees acted as the bank required. Furthermore, "there is no allegation *and it is also inherently unlikely* that the directors in these circumstances were accustomed to act on the direction or instruction of the bank" (emphasis added).

It is true that the *Kuwait Asia Bank* case does not involve a support operation directly, but it does indicate that the courts will require clear and direct evidence that a customer's board of directors has become accustomed to act on the directions or instructions of the bank. This means that bank officials must avoid the temptation of telling the customer which liabilities to discharge and which liabilities need not be paid. The intensive care units in all major institutions are now familiar with the shadow director problem and, provided that care is taken in structuring a support operation, and in the manner in which the requirements of the bank *qua* creditor are communicated to the company, then there should be few problems. The *Kuwait Asia* case also indicates that additional problems do not automatically flow from the fact that the bank may also have, or take, a shareholding in a troubled customer. Having said that, as the remarks of David James quoted above indicate, the concern about banks

15. [1990] BCC 567.

being held to be shadow directors remains real and vigilance is required to avoid a problem developing.

The risk of lender liability

For a number of years, banks in the US have had to concern themselves with the risk of what is generally labelled "lender liability" when seeking to exercise certain rights and remedies against a customer. Lender liability has been imposed in workout situations as a result of a lender's improper interference with and control of a customer, as well as in circumstances where a bank seeks to enforce its security and accelerate its loan after default where enforcement was to be construed as unduly burdensome and harsh. This is not the appropriate place in which to review, in detail, whether there are any grounds on which it can be said that an English court would be inclined to follow any of the US lender liability cases. However, a few brief comments on some of the potential risks faced by banks who are dealing with customers in difficulty are perhaps worth while.

There is a potential problem faced by a bank which is asked to make further advances in circumstances where its customer is, or in the bank's view, may be continuing to trade improperly. Alternatively, the bank may receive repayments of its indebtedness during the period of a support operation, when it may have doubts as to whether the directors are trading improperly. Is this likely to cause any difficulty?

We have already seen that where directors cause the company to trade improperly (for example, because they fail to take into account the interests of creditors during a period when the company is of doubtful solvency), then the directors may be acting in breach of their fiduciary duties. As Slade LJ noted in *Rolled Steel Products* v. *British Steel Corporation*[16]:

> The *Belmont* principle thus provides a legal route by which a company may recover its assets in a case where the directors have abused their fiduciary duties and a person receiving such assets is on notice that they have been misapplied. The principle is not linked in any way to the capacity of the company; it is capable of applying whether or not the company had the capacity to do the acts in question.

Accordingly, as is well known, a breach of duty by directors may affect third parties, including banks where such third parties are on notice of the breach of duty. A considerable body of case-law, and legal literature, has developed on the precise circumstances in which a third party can be liable for inter meddling in a trust. The crucial point is the degree of knowledge of the breach of trust which the third party must have in order to impose liability on it. In the most recent decision on the topic, *Agip (Africa) Limited* v. *Jackson*,[17] Millett J distinguished between three forms of liability for inter meddling in a trust.

16. [1984] BCCLC 466 at p. 510.
17. [1989] 3 WLR 1367.

First, there is liability for knowing receipt where a person received for his own benefit property transferred in breach of trust. In this case the recipient is liable if he "received it with notice, actual or constructive, that it was trust property and that the transfer to him was a breach of trust; or if he received it without notice but subsequently discovered the facts". Secondly, an agent who received trust property lawfully and not for his own benefit would be liable if he misappropriated the property or dealt with it in a manner he knew to be inconsistent with the trust. Thirdly, a stranger to the trust would be liable if he knowingly assisted in the furtherance of a fraudulent and dishonest design. Millett J held that in these circumstances constructive notice is not sufficient for liability. It has to be noted that the precise basis of liability in these cases is still in doubt. There are now a large number of cases incorporating dicta seeking to analyse the precise degree of knowledge of wrong doing by the relevant third party which will establish a liability to account.[18]

This is obviously not the appropriate forum in which to debate the details of these rules. Instead, it is simply worth recording that it is possible that banks might become embroiled in difficulties in a support operation where it turns out that directors have been trading improperly because of the application of the principles governing constructive trusts. This will particularly be a problem where the bank has full knowledge of what the borrower is doing and thinking, as it would usually expect to do during a properly managed rescue (where investigating accountants are almost invariably used to go through all the company's books and records and where the bank would also usually expect to receive details of board decisions). It is somewhat troubling that constructive notice, without want of probity or dishonesty, may be sufficient in these circumstances to ground liability, particularly in relation to the knowing receipt cases. Indeed, in *Rolled Steel Products* itself, there is some suggestion that constructive notice is sufficient to ground liability as a recipient of the funds of the company which had been misapplied, whilst Peter Birks argues that liability should start out as being strict (however, with a range of defences, including one arising from the defence of a bona fide purchaser without notice).

Furthermore, the chances of liability seem to be greater where the bank actually receives a benefit from the transaction and payment under review. As Tony Shea notes (in his article in the *Butterworths Banking and Financial Law Review 1987*, referred to at note 18), "A good many cases have referred to a special situation which applies when a bank receives a benefit from the transaction and it is certainly possible to argue that constructive knowledge (in

18. For a useful summary of some of the main developments see Tony Shea's article "Constructive Trusts and Banks: Recent Developments" in *Butterworths Banking and Financial Law Review 1987* and, more recently, Anu Arora's article "The Bank's Liability as a Constructive Trustee" [1990] JBL 217. In addition, there is much debate among commentators as to the juridical basis for liablility here. For example, see "Misdirected Funds: Restitution from the Recipient" by Peter Birks [1989] LMCLQ 296 and "Misdirected Funds Again" [1989] LQR 528 and Charles Harpum's note at [1990] CLJ 217 where he dissents from some of the views of Peter Birks.

the sense of gross negligence in failing to enquire) is sufficient if the bank itself benefits from the transaction". He cites, as a benefit case, *Neste Oy* v. *Lloyds Bank*,[19] in which a bank learned that its customer had decided to cease trading and that a receiver was to be appointed. Before the appointment of the receiver, the bank received a payment which it credited to the customer's bank account and which it wished to combine against other debts of that customer. The bank knew no more than the fact of the receivership and cessation of trading and that some of the payments from the plaintiff were in advance of expenditure incurred by the customer. It would have been allowed to combine accounts had there been no reason to make enquiry, but it was held that it should have enquired as to the circumstances of the receivership. This would have revealed that the funds concerned were the subject of a trust. This set of circumstances is obviously not on all fours with the case of a bank receiving payments in reduction of indebtedness during a support operation when there may be issues about whether the directors are properly allowing the company to continue to trade. However, the case is instructive.

In most cases in a support operation it is unlikely that a bank would have the requisite degree of knowledge of a breach of duty by the directors to make it accountable on these principles. Risks are undeniably run in a lengthy support operation, where the bank has all the requisite information to form a view as to the reasons behind the actions of directors and in some circumstances banks may properly be said to be put on inquiry. However, where banks insist on the borrower being advised by experienced solicitors and other advisers of standing and in the absence of unusual circumstances it is to be hoped that there would be no practical problem.

It is also to be hoped that the position may be improved with the coming into force of s. 108 of the Companies Act 1989. This provision incorporates new provisions (s. 35A and 35B) into the Companies Act 1985. The new s. 35A stipulates that "in favour of a person dealing with a company in good faith, the power of the board of directors to bind the company, or authorise others to do so, should be deemed to be free of any limitation under the company's constitution". However, it is not clear that this provision would assist where directors are acting in breach of their general fiduciary duties.

As a final comment it is worth noting that on occasions it has been suggested that a bank might be liable in tort if it procures the directors to act in breach of their duties. However, the Court of Appeal has made it clear that it does not consider that there is the need for an independent tort of procuring a breach of trust. The principles relating to constructive trusts as discussed above are, the Court of Appeal thought, adequate to deal with those persons who incite a breach of trust or wrongfully meddle with trust assets or interfere with the relationship of trustee and beneficiary.[20]

19. [1983] 2 Lloyd's Rep 658.
20. See *Metall und Rohstoff* v. *Donaldson* [1989] 3 All ER 14 at pp. 58–59.

The risk of a fiduciary relationship arising

Another risk to be managed in structuring a support operation is the possibility that the relationship between the bank, or the agent bank with responsibility for organising and negotiating the rescue, will go beyond what is usual and turn into one in which the borrower starts relying on the bank to give advice to sort the problem out. Once again, as with most the of issues identified in this area, few practical problems result when the rescue is managed by experienced bank officials. Where a major corporate borrower is independently advised it is hard to see how a situation could develop realistically where the bank leading the rescue could be said to be in a fiduciary relationship with that customer. However, it is as well to be aware of the relevant principles, once again, to deal primarily with the lengthy and difficult rescue. There are clear authorities indicating that, in exceptional circumstances, a bank will be held to owe fiduciary duties to its customer.[21]

Practicalities of a support operation—the context and principles

The practical background to the start of a support operation is succinctly summarised by the Governor of the Bank of England in a speech he made at the annual dinner of the Equipment Leasing Association on 25 October 1990.[22] He said:

> At the best of times a company's liquidity requires active and careful management. But the task becomes many times more complex when trading difficulties arise and this is further compounded when a large number of banking relationships are involved. The key question for creditors is simple enough to express. It is whether to put the company into administration or liquidation as quickly as possible—or alternatively, to attempt to bring the company's liquidity situation back under control. But how is this vital judgement to be made?
>
> Understanding this problem is, I think, helped by reminding oneself of the usual pattern of events. The alarm bells generally ring first on a realisation, which can often be sudden, that a company cannot raise the cash to pay its immediate bills. Sometimes it is the company which blows the whistle; sometimes one of its bankers. This could be a small bank which is seeking to reduce its loan book and so tries to pull a line, or it could be the company's main bankers who see that its overdraft is creeping uncomfortably upwards and is exceeding agreed limits. Typically, a meeting will be called to which easily identifiable creditors are invited. Three things often become evident at this stage. The first is that no one, including the company, has a sufficiently complete and robust picture of the company's financial position to make a soundly based decision on its future. Secondly, the amount of debt including off balance sheet items, and the number of creditors are usually larger than anybody supposed. And thirdly, it is far from uncommon that the creditors find they have varying interests.

21. In England, see *National Westminster Bank* v. *Morgan* [1985] 1 AC 686 and in Canada see *Standard Investments Limited* v. *Canadian Imperial Bank of Commerce* (1986) 22 DLR (4th) 410, 52 OR (2d)473. For an excellent treatment of banks and fiduciary duties see "Banks, Fiduciary Obligations and Unconscionable Transactions" by Donovan Waters [1986] *Canadian Bar Review* 37.

22. Published in the Bank of England quarterly bulletin for November 1990, vol: 30, No. 4, p. 511.

Once the banks have been alerted to the borrower's immediate difficulties (and this information can come from a variety of sources ranging from information provided to the clearing bank through regular reporting channels to a sudden meeting with the borrower as a result of a particular crisis), there is then a fairly standard sequence of events which moves as follows.

1. There is an urgent attempt to identify very quickly the nature of the borrower's immediate problems and what is required to preserve the status quo. It is crucial to identify what needs to be done to give the borrower a breathing space in order to enable its affairs to be thoroughly examined so that an informed decision can be taken as to how to proceed.
2. Where, as is now extremely common, the borrower has a large number of lending bankers, it is necessary to bring those bankers together to inform them of the position and co-ordinate action. Ensuring that all lending banks are fully informed of the position at a very early stage is important. The banks will in most cases then nominate who they wish to lead the discussions with the borrower and will usually form a steering committee of banks who will be given a mandate to liaise and assist the lead bank. If the available information indicates that it is appropriate, the banks at this stage will agree to a lending standstill for a short period while the process of reviewing the borrower's affairs is put in place. This standstill entails the maintenance of existing credit lines and, where necessary, the provision of extra funds. Such a standstill is usually documented at an early stage, but may well not initially be legally binding.
3. The process of reviewing the borrower's affairs then commences. The borrower will at this point have involved its own team of advisers, as will the lead bank. Of crucial importance is the role of investigating accountants who will usually be nominated by the lead bank to undertake an investigation of the affairs of the borrower and its principal subsidiaries. The aim of this investigation is to obtain a clear picture of the borrower's assets and liabilities, evidence of its recent trading performance and other activities (including the role of management), together with its immediate and medium-term financial prospects. The underlying objective of this first stage is to identify the problem areas affecting the borrower's activities and the precise impact of those problems on its financial position. This will establish what steps are required to enable the borrower to survive.

   It is important to get the instruction to investigating accountants right. There is a choice between having these instructions from the borrower, coupled with an authority for all information to be disclosed to the banks and having the instructions from the lead bank, coupled with the borrower's undertaking to reimburse the banks for the costs of the exercise. The latter approach is preferable. The investigating accountants are advisers to the banks and their duties should be made clearly to them. Problems which arise from failing to be clear on these issues can be seen in *Huxford* v. *Stoy Hayward*.[23]

This leaves open the precise method by which the necessary rearrangement of the financial structure of the borrower is to be effected. In practice, the investigating accountants will usually be part of the process of generating possible solutions to the difficulties. However, the initial stage is for them to complete their review of the affairs of the borrower to enable the banks to decide how they wish to proceed.

4. In some ways overlapping with the role of the investigating accountants, the borrower will be invited to prepare a business plan putting forward its proposals for dealing with its difficulties. It is important that such proposals are those of the borrower since it must retain the management of its affairs. The banks will not, in general, be closely involved in preparing the business plan, although the investigating accountants will have a significant role.
5. Assuming that the result of the foregoing steps suggests that a rescue appears to be workable, then a basis for proceeding must be established. There are two elements to this. First, the position as between the banks and the borrower. Secondly, the position as between the various banks. As regards the position between the banks and the borrower, the principal concern is to establish the terms on which facilities will be made available during the support period (including, whether the facilities are to be put on an "on demand" or "term" basis, in which latter event they will be subject to wide events of default; covenants; fees and the like) and whether new, or further, security is to be granted to the banks. As regards the position between the banks, the principal objective is to ensure the fair treatment of all banks, reflecting current advantages and disadvantages and equality in going forward. This will involve agreement on the sharing and utilisation of recoveries, the equalisation of interest rates and loss and recovery sharing.

This approach to providing financial support for companies which have liquidity problems and other difficulties has recently been reviewed and reiterated by the Bank of England. In view of the current economic climate, the Bank of England earlier this year undertook discussions with various banking associations in London to consider the most effective methods of dealing with workouts. They received substantial support for the system of multi-bank support which has evolved in London since the late 1970s (now dubbed "the London Rules"). The Bank of England was keen to ensure that banks in London were fully familiar with the principles underlying, and the spirit guiding this multi-

23. (1989) 5 BCC 421.

bank approach to supporting companies in difficulty. Accordingly, the Bank prepared a draft note which, subject to the approval of banking associations in London, was intended to form the basis of a circular to members of the relevant association. The following principal points emerge from the views expressed by the Bank of England (in addition to the points mentioned above).

1. The immediate standstill put in place in the early days of a support operation should embrace both conventional loans and other types of commitment, such as performance bonds, guarantees, irrevocable credits and forward exchange contracts, which are necessary for a business to continue to trade.
2. Where new funds are required, they should be provided *pro rata* to existing exposure at the time when the company's difficulties first come to the attention of the company's creditors. (The bank does not specifically deal with the problem of the precise date which is to be treated as the benchmark for the standstill—this can often cause some argument.) New moneys always enjoy priority security to reflect the additional risk accruing to lenders.
3. Consideration needs to be given to widening discussions to the borrower's shareholders (who can often play an extremely important role in a rescue) and other major creditors such as bond holders, trade suppliers and customers.
4. The bank to be chosen to lead the group of bankers must have the resources, in terms of staff and experience, to enable it properly to fulfil its role. There are, of course, highly experienced and expert teams in the intensive care units of each of the main clearing banks, as well as in other major financial institutions. The Bank of England has, properly, emphasised the crucial importance of ensuring the quick and comprehensive dissemination of important information to banks so as to ensure that no lender is left feeling disadvantaged in terms of information.
5. The Bank of England also comments upon its own role, which is discrete and usually helpful in making dissentient banks articulate and justify their positions, and in assisting in the search for a solution to a borrower's difficulties. The Bank describes its role as that of "a constructive neutral chairman and intermediary". There have been many cases recently where bank syndicates have been led round to the Bank of England for further discussions on matters which the syndicate has been unable to resolve among its members. This is an undeniably useful, if not always successful, process.
6. The Bank of England also highlighted a number of recurring practical problems which crop up regularly in support operations. The Bank highlights the difficulties in integrating holders of commercial paper and other marketable debt. Many holders of such commercial paper

will not be banks and may be quite small companies who will not regard themselves as lenders at all and will want their money back on the due date. They are, not surprisingly, therefore disinclined to become embroiled in a lengthy support operation. Furthermore, there are problems in identifying who the holders of commercial paper actually are: these are bearer instruments and it is not always possible to work out who is holding them.

The Bank of England also has referred to the difficulties with MOFs—that is, multi-option facilities. The difficulty here has been competition between the committed and uncommitted banks at the time that the borrower's difficulties arise. Those banks holding short-term uncommitted lines will expect to be repaid in the ordinary course by the partly drawn committed banks. The committed banks can only avoid paying out the drawn uncommitted lines if they can establish that an event of default has occurred. However, what do you do where there is an argument as to whether there is, in fact, such an event of default? This is precisely what happened in the now very public and much celebrated inter-bank discussions relating to the Laura Ashley Company.

Quite rightly, reference has also been made by the Bank of England to the need to avoid making different arrangements for different forms of lending. Clearly, in a support operation there are some material differences of interest which have to be given proper recognition. For example, if any of the banks have existing cross-guarantees supported from asset-rich subsidiaries, then there should be recognition given to the strength of their position. However, the range of bank and other creditors in a support operation for a major public company is usually immensely diverse, including overdraft and term lenders, publicly quoted debenture holders of loan stock; subordinated guarantors of loan notes issued by the company; Swiss bond holders who have subscribed to a bond issue (and there may be a very large number of these), as well as others. Trying to balance the interests of all of these lenders can be immensely difficult. Unless lenders are prepared to focus exclusively on points of substance, the whole support operation can quickly collapse and, as the Bank of England has said "the principle of joint bank support could quickly be undermined".

THE DOCUMENTATION

The fundamental commercial document will be the report prepared by the investigating accountants incorporating their advice and recommendations to the banks. The factual part of the report will have been discussed in detail with the borrower's management while the advice and recommendations will be generally kept private to the banks.

The legal documentation recording the support operation will usually comprise the following.

Initial standstill agreement

The purpose of this agreement is to ensure that the banks do not break away and act independently during the important initial period of information gathering and appraisal. The central idea is to ensure that facilities are maintained in the very short term during the information-gathering process. The standstill agreement will usually select a standstill date (usually the date on which all the banks first get together to discuss the borrower's difficulties) and will set out the facilities made available by the main lending banks, together with their exposure at the standstill date. The banks will then generally agree for a short period that they will not seek to accelerate the borrower's repayment obligations in this initial standstill period. These very short-term arrangements are often expressed to be non-binding, although banks will tend to treat their moral commitment as being of some significance and will therefore not enter into the arrangements lightly. Some parts of the initial standstill agreement will be expressed to be binding, however, for example the provisions which indicate that the banks are not waiving any of their rights, together with some commitments by the borrower.

The standstill agreement will then, if it is to be anything other than a few pages long, set out the basis for proceeding and will indicate that, for example, security is to be granted and that an inter-creditor agreement will be entered into.

The length and form of this document depends very much on the circumstances of the case. It is helpful to have a document setting out the ground rules which form the basis for taking the support operation further. However, it is crucial that the banks do not become bogged down in discussing the detail of an overly long standstill agreement and therefore deflected from the important practical questions of keeping the borrower alive and moving on to finding solutions to its difficulties.

Support agreement

The support agreement is effectively a facility letter between the banks and the borrower which sets the terms on which facilities will continue to be made available during the period of the support operation.

Most support agreements establish a "support period" by reference to a termination or review date and will make clear that the arrangements set out in the agreement are only operative during that period. A termination date will usually be selected and the support period will end on that date (which can be varied by agreement between the agent bank appointed pursuant to the inter-creditor agreement, as to which see below), or the date on which an event of default is declared, whichever is the earlier. Facilities can be left as being repayable on demand to provide the banks with maximum flexibility, although in larger, more formal support operations facilities will only become repayable on the termination date, or prior acceleration upon the occurrence of an event of default.

The support agreement will incorporate all the usual provisions which can be expected to be found in facility agreements. The terms of any new facilities to be made available will be recorded, and extensive covenants on the part of the borrower will sometimes be required. These are the provisions by which the banks can monitor the performance of the borrower and ensure "control" of its activities—in the sense that the borrower will be committed not to undertake certain activities (e.g. in relation to disposals and transfers, the granting of security and guarantees, the level of borrowings, the level of capital expenditure and dividends) or to undertake such activities only within limits if it wants the support arrangements to continue. Breach of any of these covenants will enable the agent bank to declare a default and bring the support period to an end. The covenants are therefore obviously important in any lengthy support operation and must ensure that the banks are able to monitor, on the basis of very full information, the progress of the borrower in fulfilling its survival and rescue plan.

The borrower's plans may well include a wide-ranging disposal programme and the support agreement will address this both in terms of covenants and by provisions which indicate what is to happen to sale proceeds. Such sale proceeds are often paid into an account under the control of the agent (or possibly a third party to avoid charge card problems when security is taken over the account). The support agreement will indicate how the proceeds are to be dealt with. Since such sale proceeds are usually required by the borrower for its cash-flow purposes and to meet working capital requirements, arrangements are often built in which require the agent to release to the borrower moneys from the sale proceeds account and the balance in the account can then be paid to the banks in permanent reduction of their facilities. Care has to be taken here in establishing the basis on which the borrower is entitled to withdraw sums from the account operated by the agent. It is important that the agent does not become embroiled in the details of which liabilities can and cannot be paid—otherwise the shadow director risk, referred to above, raises its ugly head. It is also important to ensure that a floating charge is not created inadvertently.

If the facilities made available by the banks are effectively converted into term loans during the support period, then the events of default provisions must be wide ranging and give the banks the maximum flexibility to bring the support period to an end if the borrower's affairs deteriorate, if the commercial underpinning for the support operation alters fundamentally or if third parties take action against the borrower.

The support agreement will also seek to deal with all facilities made available to the borrower and bring them into line wherever possible, for example by providing a common interest rate.

Inter-bank agreement

This agreement sets out the arrangements between the banks and will deal with the following main matters: it will establish the agent bank as the agent for all banks, setting out the powers and terms of the agent's authority; it will establish the decision-making process by which decisions on major matters affecting the support operation can be taken; it will establish the basis on which recoveries are to be shared and dealt with under security granted to the banks or otherwise; and it will incorporate what are loosely called loss-sharing arrangements.

The terms on which the agency is established will enable the agent to hold any security as trustee for all the banks, to exercise the rights granted to the agent under the support agreement and any other security, and to receive the proceeds of any disposal programme by the borrower. Important decisions will be subject to control by the other banks. It is possible that there can be four separate types of decision—those requiring unanimous consent of the banks; those requiring a majority of banks to agree; those requiring agreement by the steering committee; and those delegated to the agent. For example, the decision whether or not to accelerate the repayment obligation and make demand prior to the termination date under the support operation will usually require majority consent while most minor and administrative decisions (for example the approval of small disposals) will be left to the steering committee. The submission of participating banks to the collective decision-making process established by the inter-creditor agreement is an essential part of the structure established for such a rescue.

The provisions dealing with the appointment of the agent bank will also include the usual immunities and protections for the agent, together with provisions concerning the reimbursement of the agent for its cost and expenses in carrying out its functions.

The arrangements relating to the sharing of security realisations and other payments are infinitely variable, according to the particular circumstances of the case. There is likely to be a distinction drawn between the period prior to acceleration of the indebtedness owed to the banks or the enforcement of security granted to the banks and the period thereafter. In the period prior to acceleration or enforcement the proceeds of disposals effected by the borrower will usually be shared rateably by the banks in proportion to their exposures at the start of the support period. As repayments are made to the banks there would usually be a permanent reduction in the facilities made available to the borrower. After enforcement, and subject to the loss-sharing arrangements discussed below, all recoveries (including those by way of set-off and, perhaps, pursuant to guarantees, and preferential claims under Sch. 6 of the Insolvency Act 1986) are pooled and then distributed to pay sums owing, first, under any security interests existing prior to the support arrangement; then in discharge of any new moneys advanced during the support period; then to discharge principal and interest owing at the date of enforcement and finally towards the discharge of interest accruing after the enforcement date. Separate arrangements have to be made to deal with contingencies which have not fallen in on or prior to the enforcement date.

There are two major additional aspects to what is usually described as "loss sharing". First, are the provisions relating to the equalisation of exposure at the enforcement date to iron out any arbitrary differences in the amounts drawn under various facilities between the start of the support period and the enforcement date. It may just happen that certain facilities are more heavily drawn upon than others on the date on which enforcement actually takes place. In order to ensure that there is no unfair prejudice during the support period, arrangements are made to put the banks back into the position they were in at the start of the support period. This is done by ensuring that banks' exposures on the enforcement date remain in the same proportion that they were in at the start of the support period. Accordingly, for example, if a bank was originally committed to advance 10 per cent of the aggregate of facilities committed by all the banks at the start of the support period, then its outstanding indebtedness in respect of its facilities should be 10 per cent of the aggregate indebtedness (made available by all banks) at the enforcement date. To achieve this, each bank is required to make a payment (through the agent bank) to the other banks to bring the advances made by the bank up to its relevant percentage. Decisions will have to be taken about what type of indebtedness actually counts for the purposes of these equalisation payments.

Secondly, the inter-creditor agreement will include provisions requiring banks to bring into account all recoveries made by them, on whatever basis. Accordingly, a bank which happens to have the benefit of a credit balance on one account in the name of the customer must treat the balance, and the consequent recovery by way of set-off, as a recovery to be shared between all the banks on the basis of the inter-creditor agreement.

Security agreements

There is nothing special about the terms of the security agreements granted by the borrower during a rescue. The simple principle to be applied is that the banks will wish to get security immediately (so as to start running the period during which the new security may be vulnerable) and have as much security as is possible. In the case of major public companies which run into difficulties, there is quite often a good deal of further security available, since such companies, prior to their difficulties, will usually have been able to borrow on an unsecured basis. The new security will require a consideration of whether consents are necessary from other creditors in respect of negative pledges held by them and all the usual checks in relation to the granting of security will need to be undertaken.

Matters are complicated where there is existing security. It is not unusual to find lenders who have advanced moneys for the acquisition of specific properties, for example, holding security over those properties which they will wish to preserve. Security for the banks in the support operation is usually achieved through a composite guarantee and debenture in the usual form providing fixed security over real property, debts, goodwill, shares and subsidiaries, and intellectual property rights. There will also, obviously, be a floating charge (particularly important now to ensure that the secured creditor can veto the making of an administration order). Where there is existing security, arrangements will be made for second charges to be granted to the banks in the support operation and for priority arrangements to be dealt with in the inter-bank agreement (some holders of fixed charges resist the taking of second charges since they are concerned at losing control in the enforcement process, however, their concerns can usually be dealt with in the inter-creditor agreements).

New security, in order to survive, has to overcome the problems arising from the provisions relating to transactions at an undervalue (s. 238 of the Act), preferences (s. 239 of the Act) and floating charges for other than new money (s. 245 of the Act). I do not propose to examine each of these provisions in detail, since their terms and the difficulties surrounding their operation are well known. However, the following are some brief comments on the important issues as they affect rescues.

First, s. 238 of the Act enables a liquidator or administrator to apply to the court to have a transaction (which is widely defined and will include the giving of security) set aside if it was entered into at an undervalue at any time within two years prior to his appointment. A transaction is given at an undervalue where there is a gift or the consideration received by the company is significantly less than the consideration which it gives (there is no clear indication of what "significantly less" actually means).

There are effectively two ways of avoiding liability under s. 238. First, the section is only triggered and becomes operative if the borrower, at the time or in consequence of the transaction in question, is insolvent (within the meaning of s. 123 of the Act). Insolvent for these purposes includes, among other things, being unable to pay debts as they fall due and an excess of liabilities over assets. Accordingly, if it turns out that the borrower was solvent on this basis at the time that fresh security was granted then there can be no question of a transaction at an undervalue having been given.

In addition, it is a defence for the borrower to show that it entered into the transaction in good faith, for the purpose of carrying on its business and that there were reasonable grounds for believing that the transaction would benefit the borrower. The problem with this defence is that it focuses primarily on the attitude of the borrower and requires objectively reasonable grounds to be established supporting any purported benefit to the company. This makes it very difficult for any outsider, such as a bank, to be absolutely clear that the defence is available. Certainly, properly prepared board minutes and confirmation of the company's financial position from its auditors will assist. However, inevitably, there will be doubts about the solvency of the borrower once it has got into a support operation!

According to Millett J in *Re M.C. Bacon Limited*,[24] s. 238 of the Act cannot be used to attack new security granted in respect of old and existing indebtedness. According to the judge:

> The mere creation of a security over a company's assets does not deplete them and does not come within [s. 238]. By charging its assets the company appropriates them to meet the liabilities due to the secured creditor and adversely affects the rights of other creditors in the events of insolvency. But it does not deplete its assets or diminish their value. It retains the right to redeem and the right to sell or remortgage the charged assets. All it loses is the ability to apply the proceeds otherwise than in satisfaction of a secured debt. That is not something capable of valuation in monetary terms and is not customarily disposed of for value ... by granting the debenture the company parted with nothing of value and the value of the consideration which it received in return was incapable of being measured in money or money's worth.

It remains to be seen whether this rather literal analysis is correct. As a matter of first impression, it is difficult to see how the granting of security cannot be said to involve the assignment of valuable rights (of property) to the mortgagee amounting to consideration which can be valued in money or in money's worth (by reference to the assets subject to the security interest). It also seems unclear why the consideration provided by the bank cannot also be valued in money or money's worth. It is true that the equity of redemption is a complicating factor and also needs to be valued. In any event, the thrust of Millett J's analysis is that in cases where a borrower is already indebted to the banks, any challenge to new security should be by reference to the preference provisions rather than s. 238 (*quaere* any challenge on the basis of a breach of fiduciary duties where the undervalue is obvious and clearly significant).

As regards s. 239 and the preference provisions, these stipulate that the court may make an order restoring the position, on an application by a liquidator or administrator, if a company within six months prior to liquidation or administration permits anything to be done which puts a creditor (or guarantor or surety) in a better position than he would have been in in an insolvent liquidation, and the company was influenced by a desire to produce that result.

It is important to note that the six months period is increased to two years if the preferred person is connected with the company.

Once again, as with s. 239, there is no possibility of a preference if the company is solvent at the time that the preference is given. There is also, as noted

24. [1990] BCC 78.

above, no preference if it can be shown that the company did not improve the position of the bank creditor pursuant to the relevant desire. Millett J also had to consider the meaning of being influenced by a desire to prefer in the *M.C. Bacon* case. He made it plain that in order to establish the requisite desire it was not sufficient simply to establish a desire on the part of the company to make the payment or grant the security which it sought to avoid.

There must have been a desire to produce the effect mentioned in [s. 239 of the Act], that is to say, to improve the creditor's position in the event of an insolvent liquidation. A man is not to be taken as desiring all the necessary consequences of his actions. Some consequences may be of advantage to him and be desired by him; others may not affect him and be matters of indifference to him; while still others may be positively disadvantageous to him and not be desired by him, but be regarded by him as the unavoidable price of obtaining the desired advantages. It will still be possible to provide assistance to a company in financial difficulties provided that the company is actuated only by proper commercial considerations. Under the new regime a transaction will not be set aside as a voidable preference unless the company positively wished to improve the creditor's position in the event of its own insolvent liquidation.

He took the view that these requirements were not satisfied in the case before him which, as has been noted above, involved the common situation of a bank insisting on security as a precondition to continued support (by maintaining overdraft lines) at a time when it became aware of its borrower's difficulties. Accordingly, in most support operations where the security is being given pursuant to the general arrangements connected with the rescue and attempt at rehabilitating the borrower, there should be no problem in taking security. The position has to be watched where there are personal guarantees granted by the directors or where the security is granted at a time when there is no realistic prospect of the borrower surviving.

Section 245 of the Act renders invalid a floating charge if it is created within 12 months of the onset of a liquidation or administration. Once again, the period is extended to two years if the floating chargee is connected to the borrower. There is no problem unless the borrower is insolvent at the time that the floating charge is granted, or in consequence of it (within the meaning of s. 123 of the Act) and the security will be held to be valid to the extent of money paid by the bank or the value of goods or services supplied by the bank (*quaere* does this cover the granting of a guarantee or performance bond to parties dealing with the borrower?) or the reduction of any debt (including a debt owed to the bank being granted the floating charge?) occurring at the same time or after the creation of the floating charge.

ALTERNATIVES TO THE CLASSIC SUPPORT OPERATION

Of course, it is not always appropriate when a company is in financial difficulties for a full-blown support operation to be implemented and, indeed, the standard remedies of receivership, administration or liquidation may also be inappropriate. There are alternative methods of proceeding, or variations on the standard support operation, which may be appropriate, some of which are briefly considered below.

The discussion above of support operations does not deal directly with exit routes. The usual support operation is designed initially to deal with immediate urgent problems and the precise commercial solutions obviously depend on the financial position of the borrower. Sometimes the borrower is simply facing a short-term (but serious) liquidity problem and once it has been nursed through its short-term difficulties, perhaps caused by unfavourable trading conditions, it can return to more normal banking arrangements without the close supervision of investigating accountants, an agent bank and a steering committee (sometimes, of course, the borrower just runs out of cash again). Sometimes, the borrower's difficulties will require more dramatic action, for example, involving a significant and rapid reduction in indebtedness through an extensive asset disposal programme. The borrower may have unencumbered assets or assets otherwise surplus to its immediate requirements, which can be sold to reduce its debt burden. Alternatively, the borrower may be forced to dispose of more than simply surplus assets by identifying its core, profitable businesses and reducing its activities to focus on these. Other parts of its business can then be sold off. Once again, the period of support and monitoring can come to an end if the asset disposal programme goes according to plan and is successful so as to place the borrower in a position where its revised cash flows and assets enable it to service its debt on a timely and proper basis.

In more severe cases, it may be necessary to support the borrower in order to enable it to realise assets as quickly as possible and find refinancing. This can be done through, for example, rights issues or perhaps through a sale of a controlling interest in the borrower's shares—whether the borrower is a private or listed company. Obviously, where the borrower is listed on the stock exchange a further set of considerations, primarily for the directors, arise. Apart from the problems of the renegotiation of bank debt under the glare of publicity arising from continued dealing on the stock exchange in the company's shares, careful attention must be paid to the *Yellow Book* obligations, as well as to statutory provisions such as s. 47 of the Financial Services Act 1986. Great care has to be paid to formulating announcements and to considering a suspension of the listing of the company's shares. It is certainly not unusual to find that banks and their advisers are negotiating with a borrower in difficulties at the same time as the borrower's financial advisers are having to consider the terms of a formal takeover bid. Terms of offers to acquire the borrower's shares are often made conditional upon matters relating to the financing of the borrower.

A change of control will usually facilitate injections of funds into the borrower. This will usually be used in part for working capital purposes and, in part, to reduce bank debt. Refinancing may also involve some form of restructuring of the assets and business of the borrower. Where the predicament of the borrower is particularly severe, the banks may be requested to convert debt into equity. Difficulties arise in the case of public companies because shareholder approval is needed. Various devices have been used to get round this problem, for example by the insertion of a new parent company into which the bank creditors inject funds in return for shares (usually preference shares) or, through the use of a new vehicle company (which is a subsidiary of the parent company in the borrowing group) into which the banks subscribe for preference shares to enable the company to acquire a reasonably attractive part of the group's business (with the proceeds of the preference share issue finding their way back to the banks who have to release their security over the assets transferred to the new company). The variety of arrangements that can be created here is very large. Banks are often keen to buy in the assets of a borrower in difficulty, to enable them to have a free reign in managing those assets to best advantage. This is particularly so where the assets subject to the bank's security have (perhaps temporarily) fallen significantly in value and are therefore not saleable in the short term. This can be done if very carefully structured. The Privy Council decision in *Tse Kwong Lam* v. *Wong Chit Sen*[25] has made it plain that subject to onerous rules relating to value and method of sale, a mortgagee can sell to a company in which he has a material interest (as major shareholder for example). However, this is probably not possible where the purchasing company is a wholly-owned subsidiary of the bank mortgagee, certainly without a court order.

A further alternative, which has been used occasionally recently, is the use of the company doctor. It had been thought that the introduction of wrongful trading might well deter experienced business persons from taking on the role of the company doctor because the risks of personal liability were perceived to be material. A company doctor (as to which see *R.C. Campbell*[26]) faces the wrongful trading duty like any other director—indeed, it is arguable that his particular knowledge, skill and experience may mean that he is under a more onerous duty than an ordinary director. Nevertheless, there are some courageous individuals (notably David James) who are prepared to take on the task of being a company doctor, for suitable remuneration, and they will orchestrate significant changes to the management of the borrower, as well as to its business strategy and policies, in order to see the company through difficult times. It is an oft-repeated remark in the context of companies in difficulties that management is frequently the principal cause of the borrower's difficulties and so such changes can be crucial.

There are, of course, formal procedures available for implementing arrangements with creditors. Prior to the Act coming into force, the only statutory

25. [1983] 3 All ER 54.
26. [1984] BCLC 83.

assistance for the rehabilitation of troubled companies was to be found in the provisions of the Companies Act 1985 relating to schemes of arrangement (s. 425). It was well recognised for some time that these provisions should be supplemented or replaced by a new procedure, since in practice they had proved to be both cumbersome and unnecessarily complicated (in particular because of the need to identify separate classes of creditors and to have separate class meetings for each) and therefore unsuitable in the context of an attempt to rationalise the affairs of the company which is nearly or actually insolvent. The scheme of arrangement is still occasionally used (and was mooted in the case of British & Commonwealth Holdings plc in the period when there was an attempt to construct a rescue prior to administration). However, the Act introduced the voluntary arrangement procedure which provides a formal structure for the formulation and discussion of proposals to the borrower and its creditors for a composition in satisfaction of its debts or a scheme of arrangement of its affairs (s. 1 of the Act). This procedure is often used in conjunction with an administration order. However, it is also available outside administration or any other insolvency procedure. That is, the borrower does not need to be technically insolvent. The procedure allows the borrower's creditors and members (pursuant to resolutions passed by the requisite majorities at meetings convened to consider proposals for the voluntary arrangement) to alter the quantum and status of creditors' claims against the company so as to allow the company to continue in operation with a revised (and often much reduced) burden of debt. Crucially, the proposals or plans for the voluntary arrangement, once approved as laid down by the Act and the Insolvency Rules 1986, take on the status of a contract binding all the company's creditors and members who were entitled to vote on whether to approve or reject them, irrespective of whether a particular creditor or member actually voted or attended the meetings called to consider the proposals. This "cram-down" effect marks out the voluntary arrangement (and the scheme of arrangement) from the standard consensual and contractual arrangements put in place in a standard support operation. In the standard support operation the consent of all parties who are not to be paid in full immediately needs to be negotiated and bargained for. The voluntary arrangement can, in appropriate circumstances, enable a borrower to be rehabilitated and rescued, despite the wishes of a dissentient minority. Creditors who disagree do have the opportunity to challenge the voluntary arrangement as approved on the ground that it unfairly prejudices their interests or because there has been some material irregularity at or in relation to meetings convened to consider the proposals (s. 6 of the Act).

Voluntary arrangements outside administration, particularly where there is disagreement between creditors, face the real difficulty of the absence of the automatic stay on the enforcement of claims of creditors which arise on the commencement of an administration pursuant to s. 11 of the Act. In addition, there are problems with voluntary arrangements since the cram-down provisions do not necessarily enable all creditors to be dealt with within the proposal.[27]

It is also worth remembering, when considering alternatives to ordinary insolvency procedures that there may be circumstances in which it is appropriate for secured creditors to take possession of their security as mortgagees in order to control the realisation of the borrower's assets. Banks have, for a considerable time, been put off acting as mortgagees in possession because of a proper concern about the onerous duties which are imposed on a secured creditor when taking possession of his security. However, a closer examination of the true position indicates that the concerns are not insuperable.

Historically, a mortgagee in possession has always been obliged to account for rents received as part of the process of accounting to the mortgagor. This duty to account was founded on the principle that, notwithstanding the provisions of the Law of Property Act 1925, a mortgagee in possession is in a position analogous to that of a trustee of a mortgaged property. Over the years, it became standard practice in redemption actions for the courts to make automatic orders that an account should be taken of all moneys due to the mortgagee from the mortgagor under the mortgage, and that an account should be taken of the rents and profits of the mortgaged assets received by the mortgagee or which without the wilful default of the mortgagee might have been so received. In the taking of these accounts, the mortgagee needs to show not only what he has in fact received from the mortgaged property during the period for which he was in possession, but also that he would not but for his own default have received more. However, the underlying principle is that the mortgagee is only required to do what a prudent property owner would sensibly do so that, for example, if the property in question is not lettable the mortgagee does not have to bring into account an occupational rent merely because he is in possession of the mortgaged property. Furthermore, most standard security documents give the mortgagee wide powers to deal with the management and realisation of the mortgaged property. Frequently, it is easiest and simplest for the bank to appoint receivers to deal with the mortgaged property. However, banks are sometimes looking to take control themselves in more complex cases where the management and realisation of the security may take many years and involve the specialist skills of, for example, other financial institutions or project managers.

NICK SEGAL

27. See, in relation to the difficulties arising in relation to company voluntary arrangements, the article entitled "Company Voluntary Arrangements" by Steve Hill [1990] *Insol L&P* 47. As regards voluntary arrangements in general, see Segal in *Gore-Browne on Companies* (paragraphs 31.24–31.36).

CHAPTER 9

NON-JUDICIAL DEBTOR REORGANISATIONS IN THE UNITED STATES

The purpose of this chapter is to provide (a) a brief summary of the factors leading to what has become a national crisis of capital adequacy in the US which has inexorably eroded the capital base of the nation's businesses and then its financial institutions, (b) an overview of the issues presented in connection with a consensual, non-judicial debtor reorganisation in response to the systemic pressures caused by this capital erosion and (c) a framework for an understanding of the scope of work involved in a consensual debtor reorganisation.

SYSTEMIC PROBLEM OF CAPITAL DETERIORATION

Debtors and creditors in the US are in the grip of a systemic cycle of capital deterioration of unprecedented proportion. Public and governmental opinion suggests that the current problem of capital deterioration is driven by collapsing real property values first in the South-west and now in New England, the Mid-Atlantic states and the South-east, but that the problem does not extend to other parts of the country. The problem of collapsing real property values, however, *is pervasive* throughout the US. The effects of collapsing real property values, when combined with other problems with national implications (including increasing rates of default of LBOs, junk bonds and other highly leveraged transactions) and regional economic problems, such as the oil and gas problems in the South-west and sagging performance by the so-called "high tech" industry in the North-east, are precipitating broad-based credit real property business failures at an alarming rate and the erosion of the nation's financial institutions' capital footings. The "deleveraging" of American business is the buzzword of the 1990s.

Experience in the South-west and current experience in other areas of the country indicate recurring patterns of reaction to this crisis by both debtors and creditors. These reactions are marked by early and persistent denial of the problem, accompanied by protestation that "this problem can't happen to us"; "it's happening to someone else"; and "the problem isn't as deep and will not last as long as you think". Experience has shown that when regulatory examiners of our federally-regulated financial institutions force recognition of the problem, both debtor and creditor management are thrown into an intractable reactionary mode. Debtors face abrupt and precipitous termination of long-standing historical credit relationships. Creditors often are unable to stand against the pressure of constantly increasing and restrictive regulatory action, the effect of regulators' actions on their operations, the turmoil of resulting constant crisis management, the distortion on the institution's balance sheet caused by a dramatic shift from earning to non-earning assets, including increased levels of "other real estate owned" ("OREO") and other repossessed collateral, and the wave of litigation and bankruptcies which the repossession and foreclosure process invites as the debtor's ticket to survival.

The cycle of industry-wide insubstance foreclosure and actual foreclosure or repossession of collateral, marking to market of value mandated by accounting and regulatory policy, increasing costs to carry and manage assets and to administer problems which the creditors are inadequately prepared to manage and resolve, and the dramatic effect of negative leverage on both debtors and creditors resulting in recurring capital losses is unavoidable *unless* a proactive approach is taken by debtor and creditor management in both instances early in the cycle. The mission of management must be to minimise capital loss, to stabilise the downward spiral of negative leverage and to deflect as much carnage as possible to hapless unprepared competitors. Failure to act quickly, decisively and proactively, pursuant to a clear plan and established priorities, will result, in short shrift, in the dissipation of both the debtor and the creditor's capital and the elimination of their remaining flexibility.

This chapter examines historical bases for this national crisis of capital adequacy, describes in more detail the indicia of the problem and prescribes a proactive general programme to minimise the effect of this crisis on a given debtor by early problem recognition, prompt detailed and anticipatory response, accurate asset valuation, early loss allocation and consensual balance sheet restructuring. The debtor's goal should be to recognise the problem early, deal with it in at least as favourable a manner as the debtor's creditors and the bankruptcy courts ultimately would require the debtor to deal with it and take painful but acceptable losses necessary to enable the debtor to survive and live to fight again another day.

HISTORICAL BACKGROUND

The roots of the current crisis in capital adequacy are found in the late 1970s. This period was characterised by the following factors: high inflation in all goods and services; an abrupt run up in interest rates, with prime exceeding 20 per cent; an oil crisis that made marginal production profitable; resultant heavy investment in real property and energy as inflation hedges; and severe problems experienced by financial institutions, particularly thrifts, arising from:

(a) significant under-capitalisation and over-leverage. While the early 1970s had been a period of growth, the Federal Home Loan Bank Board ("FHLBB") during these relatively "good times" consistently *reduced* capital requirements, rather than holding the line in requiring a relatively high ratio of capital to liabilities. This retreat was made during a time the thrifts had sufficient earnings to develop an adequate capital base;

(b) limitations imposed by law with respect to the rates banks and thrifts could pay for small deposits. Unregulated financial institutions were not so limited. Disintermediation was the logical result as small depositors sought to minimise the ravages of high inflation by taking advantage of the rates offered by money market funds and cash management accounts;

(c) banks and thrifts being forced to replace the small depositors with large certificates of deposit at competitive rates. This had a particularly devastating effect on thrifts whose assets consisted primarily of lower fixed-rate residential mortgages. The resulting negative spread caused thrifts to lose capital at an alarming rate.

CAUSES

These factors led to a series of reactionary events in the early 1980s which resulted in a "finance/tax push" on real property values. First, in 1980, Congress passed the Depositary Institutions Deregulation and Monetary Control Act ("DIDIMCA"),[1] under which three major actions were taken.

1. Federal Deposit Insurance Corporation ("FDIC") and Federal Savings and Loan Insurance Corporation ("FSLIC") deposit insurance was increased to US $100,000 from US $40,000.[2] This was done with no analysis and as an afterthought.
2. The liability side of the balance sheet for banks and savings and loans

1. Depository Institutions Deregulation and Monetary Control Act of 1980, Pub L No. 96–221, 94 Stat. 132. §202 indicates that the Act was promulgated as an attempt at an orderly phase-out and ultimately an elimination of limitations on the maximum rates of interest and dividends which could be paid on deposits and accounts by depository institutions. Congress determined that all depositors were entitled to receive a market rate of return on their savings as soon as it was economically feasible for depository institutions to pay such a rate.

2. *Ibid.* at §308(a)(1)(A).

was deregulated. Banks and savings and loans could now pay competitive rates for deposits without restriction.[3]

3. Federal laws were adopted pursuant to which state usury laws were pre-empted to provide for:
   (a) unlimited interest rates on first lien loans on residential property (houses, condominiums, apartments, townhouses)[4]; and
   (b) Interest rates (on business and agricultural loans of US $25,000 or more) that could equal 5 per cent above the discount rate at the Fed window.[5]

(Remember, at this time, rates were still at an historical high and the Fed discount rate was exceeding 14 to 15 per cent.) These provisions (a) allowed deposits to be brokered in fully insured US $100,000 increments,[6] (b) allowed rates on deposits at whatever level was needed to attract the deposit,[7] and (c) allowed investment of deposits at rates exceeding state usury laws.[8] DIDIMCA superficially may have alleviated the disintermediation problem, but it did not stop the haemorrhaging of the thrifts which were still carrying lower fixed-rate assets.

In the mean time, inflation in real property prices continued, even as the general inflation rate abated. Real property inflation was fuelled by the tax shelter business, which received a large push from the Economic Recovery Tax Act of 1981 ("ERTA").[9] ERTA improved tax shelter opportunities in real property principally by reducing the depreciable life of improvements to 15 years from 35 years.[10] In addition to this new incentive, investors already could deduct investment interest paid or accrued and could take advantage of

3. *Ibid.* at §204. Authority to control the rates paid on deposits by depository institutions under Public Law 89–597 was provided for a term of six years from the date of enactment of the legislation in order to give thrift institutions time to incorporate the new powers granted to them so they may increase their earnings and be in a position to attract deposits by paying market interest rates. The Federal Reserve Board, the FDIC and the FHLBB, however, were permitted to regulate depository institutions' advertising of interest rates.

4. *Ibid.* at §501. States were permitted to override the federal pre-emption of state usury limits on home mortgage loans within the period after 1 April 1980, and prior to 1 April 1983. The override could consist of the adoption of a law or a vote by voters in favour of any provision, constitutional or otherwise, which stated explicitly that the state did not want the federal pre-emption to apply to loans made in that state.

5. *Ibid.* at §511.

6. Depository Institutions Deregulation and Monetary Control Act, *supra*, note 2.

7. Depository Institutions Deregulation and Monetary Control Act, *supra*, note 3.

8. Depository Institutions Deregulation and Monetary Control Act, *supra*, notes 4 and 5.

9. Economic Recovery Tax Act of 1981, Pub L No. 97–34, 95 Stat. 172. §212 of the Economic Recovery Tax Act amended §§46 and 48 of the Internal Revenue Code and increased the investment tax credit for rehabilitation expenditures to 15 per cent for non-residential 30-year-old buildings, 20 per cent for non-residential 40-year-old buildings; 25 per cent credit for residential and non-residential certified historic structures; and repealed the accelerated cost recovery and demolition disincentives for certified historic structures.

10. *Ibid.* at §201; IRC §168 (the recovery period was subsequently extended to 18 years by the Deficit Reduction Act of 1984 and then to 19 years in 1985). The taxpayer was given the option to elect to use the straight-line depreciation method over 15 years, 35 years or 45 years for 15-year public utility property.

non-recourse mortgage financing for purposes of deducting losses.[11] And, if the property were held for longer than one year, it was entitled to the 60 per cent long-term capital gains exclusion,[12] thus ensuring a maximum tax of 20 per cent on disposition (in 1984, the holding period was shortened to six months[13]). Before long, limited partnerships or syndications became an attractive way to invest in real property because they generated tax savings and profits that passed through to investors. Broader participation in the apparently highly profitable real property business was seen as a panacea for the thrifts.

In 1982, Congress passed the Garn St Germain Depository Institutions Act ("Garn St Germain").[14] Garn St Germain allowed thrifts to:

(a) expand their lending powers by allowing commercial and non-residential real property lending[15] (so-called acquisition, development and construction loans, as well as commercial loans[16]);
(b) make direct investments in real property[17] (state-chartered institutions in some jurisdictions already enjoyed broad investment authority);
(c) participate in ownership of real property through joint ventures, partnerships and similar vehicles[18];
(d) eliminate loan-to-value ratios for residential mortgages[19];
(e) in some instances, utilise loan-to-value ratios up to 100 per cent.[20]

The result was that the savings and loan charter was more flexible than a bank charter.

Entrepreneurs were encouraged to acquire savings and loans and operate them as *giant real property companies*. State laws were amended allowing state savings and loans expanded powers. California, Florida and Texas were examples. California allowed 100 per cent of a California thrift's assets to be contributed to a subsidiary service corporation for investment activities. Texas allowed leverage of 20-to-1 on capital in service corporations.[21] Capital requirements of savings and loans were dropped to 3 per cent of liabilities on a

11. IRC §163.
12. IRC §1202(a).
13. Tax Reform Act of 1984, Pub L No. 98–369, §1001(a)(1).
14. Garn St Germain Depository Institutions Act of 1982, Pub L No. 97–320, 96 Stat. 1469. Federal savings associations were granted expanded lending and investment authority by this Act, as an attempt to provide them with the flexibility necessary to maintain their role of providing credit for housing.
15. 12 USC §1464(c)(1)(B).
16. 12 USC §1464(c)(1)(R).
17. 12 USC §1464(c)(1)(B).
18. 12 USC §1464(c)(1)(N).
19. 12 USC §1464(c)(1)(B).
20. *Ibid.*
21. Tex. Rev. Civ. Stat. Ann. Art. 342–606 (Vernon 1981).

long-term averaging basis, as opposed to 5 per cent.[22] Banks' capital requirements remained at $5\frac{1}{2}$ per cent primary and 6 per cent secondary. Leverage in the savings and loan industry was $33\frac{1}{3}$ times capital raised, and in the banking industry, 15 times capital raised.

Regulatory and examination forces of state and federal regulatory bodies were not expanded to handle effectively the regulation of the broadened powers arising from DIDIMCA and Garn St Germain. In addition to new powers, there was a quantifiable risk increase as the amount of deposit insurance rose $2\frac{1}{2}$ times from US $40,000 per account to US $100,000. Incredibly, the FDIC system had 10 times more personnel than the FSLIC system. And in the midst of all this change, the Federal Home Loan Bank ("FHLB") of Little Rock, Arkansas, was moved to Dallas, Texas, causing significant loss of experienced personnel. Then several events occurred: oil and gas prices dropped; Empire Savings of Texas failed; Continental Illinois Bank failed; Penn Square Bank of Oklahoma failed; certain instances of fraud, deceit and abuse appeared; and reactive re-regulation commenced.

These events precipitated the current crisis which emerged first in the thrift industry and in Texas banking and now threatens the capital base of the nation's businesses and its financial institutions. Re-regulation of the financial institutions and the elimination of tax incentives for real property removed the finance/tax push on real property values and have caused values to shrink and capital to "evaporate" from our financial system. The crisis began slowly, but quickly gathered momentum.

Beginning in 1984 and 1985, re-regulation of the thrifts commenced in earnest. FHLBB Chairman Edwin Gray probably overreacted to stinging criticism from Congress. Personnel in the FHLB of Dallas were shaken up, with tough regulators appointed to key positions. New appraisal standards were adopted,[23] resulting in lower values and lower comparables, and often were applied on a retroactive basis. New capital regulations were adopted requiring more capital,[24] when the name of the game should have been to preserve exist-

22. Rules of the Texas Savings and Loan Department, 7 TAC §64.7(b) (1985).

23. 12 CFR §563.17–1a(c)(1). The rule sets forth three appraisal standards that, at a minimum, must be included in the appraisal policies of every insured institution and service corporation. First, the appraisal must be based upon the definition of market value as set forth in the regulation. This definition contemplates the consummation of a sale as of a specified date and the passing of title from buyer to seller under open and competitive market conditions requisite to a fair sale. Secondly, the appraisal must be presented in a narrative format. The appraisal report must be sufficiently descriptive to enable a reviewer to readily ascertain the estimated value reported and the rationale for that estimate. The analysis is required to be as detailed and in depth as the complexity of the real property requires. Thirdly, an appraisal must contain a sales history of the real property appraised. Generally, sales within the three previous years must be disclosed.

24. 12 CFR §567.3. This section provided that increased individual capital requirements could be established upon a determination that a savings association's capital had or could have become inadequate in view of its circumstances. Higher capital levels could have been appropriate for savings associations receiving special supervisory attention, savings associations that had or were expected to have losses resulting in capital inadequacy, savings associations with poor liquidity or cash flow, savings associations growing either internally or through acquisitions, to list just a few

ing capital. New growth restriction regulations were adopted.[25] Classification of asset regulations were adopted.[26]

All of these measures treated the emerging thrift crisis as one that could be cured by simply tightening the rules. These measures failed to take into account their effect on the dynamics of the real property industry and its interrelation with the value of assets held by thrifts and banks. The upshot of the sudden change in the rules was that property values depreciated quickly and insidiously in a downward spiral that continues today. The FHLBB's overreaction led to precipitous decline in available financing by thrifts. Revised appraisal standards and nervous appraisers caused lower appraised values that, by way of comparables, caused still further lowering of values. Existing capital evaporated from this loss of real property value. There was incipient negative leverage. For each dollar of capital loss, thrifts were required to shrink assets US 33\frac{1}{3}$ and banks US $15. Yet shrinkage was difficult since the depreciating values meant that there were no buyers or new financing available. When shrinkage did occur, it was usually from sale of earning assets, and the loss of income from those earning assets further reduced capital, requiring still more asset shrinkage. The consequence of this downward spiral is obvious. Moreover, the loan portfolios of many of the financial institutions began to consist primarily of term loans which were due to be paid in full at maturity. Needless to say, the majority of these loans were not paid at maturity. As a result, the institutions were deprived of a major source of asset shrinkage.

New tax legislation then took tax incentives out of property ownership, causing further loss of real property value and hence financial institution capital. For example the Tax Reform Act of 1986 ("TRA")[27] virtually eliminated tax as a consideration in the purchase of real property. The easy write-offs that once made otherwise marginal real property development profitable were gone. The year 1986 was the last in which developers could take advantage of the faster depreciation allowed under the old law. Under the TRA, the depreci-

of the considerations in determining whether a higher capital requirement was warranted. The standards for determining what the appropriate capital requirement would be was based on the conditions or circumstances leading to a determination that a higher minimum capital requirement was necessary, the exigency of those circumstances, the overall strength of the savings association and its related entities, the savings association's liquidity and the savings association's policies and practices.

25. 12 CFR §563.98. This section established new restrictions for equity risk investments by savings associations. The limits for investments were based on tangible capital in relation to total liabilities. In addition, permissible investments were described and diversification was required.

26. Memorandum R41c of 11 September 1986, amending 12 CFR §563.17.

27. Tax Reform Act of 1986, Pub L No. 99–514, 100 Stat. 2085. The 60 per cent deduction for long-term capital gains was repealed; residential real property was to be depreciated over 27$\frac{1}{2}$ years under the straight-line method, non-residential real property was to be depreciated over 31$\frac{1}{2}$ years under the straight-line method; the investment tax credit was repealed; the rehabilitation tax credit was substantially reduced; "at risk" rules now applied to real property; and losses from "passive activities" could only be off-set income from other passive activities.

able life for real property improvements went from 19 years to $31\frac{1}{2}$ years.[28] The "at risk" rules changed, limiting tax write-offs to the amount actually invested.[29] The deductibility of interest used to finance investment property was limited to the amount of net investment income.[30] Moreover, new "passive loss" rules required that losses from an activity in which an individual did not materially participate could be deducted only from income derived from (a passive) activity.[31] Formerly, an investor could deduct these losses from *any* income, including salary.[32] The capital gains tax exclusion was repealed,[33] resulting in a maximum rate of 28 per cent instead of 20 per cent.[34] Finally, the investment tax credit was eliminated[35] and the rehabilitation credit substantially reduced.[36]

THE RESULT

As a result of the initial finance/tax push in real property values and the subsequent removal of that finance/tax push, a spiralling depression in values has occurred with losses in value as high as 50 per cent, rivalling the October 1987 stock market débâcle. There has not been a *shift* of wealth; there has been a *loss* of wealth. Operating losses have become monumental. For banks and thrifts, these are caused by the following.

Loss of operating income

(a) No new loans being made since no growth is allowed (i.e. there is no capital to support any growth; to the contrary, shrinkage is required);
(b) borrowers not paying interest, much less principal; and
(c) income not being realised from collateral by reason of legal issues and

28. *Ibid.* at §201. This section of the Tax Reform Act amended §168 of the Internal Revenue Code.
29. *Ibid.* at §503. This section repealed §465(c)(3)(D) of the Internal Revenue Code, which excluded the holding of real property from the application of the "at risk" rules.
30. *Ibid.* at §511. This section amended §163(d) of the Internal Revenue Code. Investment interest expense was only to be deducted against net investment income after this Act was passed.
31. IRC §469 (1986).
32. IRC §165.
33. Tax Reform Act of 1986, *supra* at §301. This section amended §1202 of the Internal Revenue Code.
34. *Ibid.* at §302(a)(1).
35. *Ibid.* at §211.
36. *Ibid.* at §251. The rehabilitation tax credit for certified historic structures was reduced from 25 per cent to 20 per cent, a credit of 10 per cent was provided for substantial rehabilitation of buildings placed in-service before 1936, there was to be no credit for any buildings placed in-service after 1935, that was not certified historic, and the credit was subject to the limitations on passive losses and credits.

lending liability considerations (one of the smaller bank holding companies currently is a defendant in more than 350 lender liability lawsuits handled by 49 different law firms).

Increase in operating expenses

(a) Increase in cost of funds in spite of FDIC insurance (the so-called Texas premium);
(b) legal fees running up to US $500,000 per month at many thrifts;
(c) consultant fees equal to that same amount being incurred per month;
(d) property operating and management costs increasing with respect to OREO in non-performing assets; and
(e) hidden costs arising from constant regulator involvement, required independent reappraisals and additional accounting and personal expense.

Delays in dealing with non-performing loans caused by

(a) Borrowers' lender liability lawsuits (sometimes successful), often brought to buy time to deal with the adverse tax consequences of foreclosure;
(b) injunctions and restraining orders limiting enforcement of rights against security;
(c) regulatory delays—most thrifts and many banks are under some type of regulatory control or scrutiny; and
(d) inter-creditor disagreements on participated loans.

The rush to real property investment incentised by previously favourable tax legislation and fuelled by the massive availability of capital for real property investment provided by banks and thrifts created an enormous constituency of owners who, in the face of the loss of tax benefits due to changes in the tax laws, now face significant adverse tax consequences on asset disposition. The problem of adverse tax consequences is exacerbated by collapsing values and the resulting lack of resources from asset sales proceeds to pay the tax bill. Now, no other similar tax advantaged purchaser exists, and financing available for acquisition has been severely restricted. The market for buying and selling real property has stopped. Owners generally cannot sell for a price which would pay the tax bill for the phantom gains from the disposition of property upon which the outstanding debt is in excess of the owner's adjusted basis in the property as reduced by depreciation deductions, much less provide for recovery of equity or the making of a profit. Just as importantly, the debtors who own the real property cannot permit foreclosure on the collateral by the creditors, since that would trigger the same tax problems for the debtor as a sale to a third party. Financial institutions, which are under pressure to shrink, seek to force foreclosure against the collateral, but generally pay no attention to the underlying systemic tax and value problems which face the debtor. This then results in costly and time-consuming litigation and bankruptcies initiated as protective action by debtors and designed, in most cases, to delay and to afford to the debtor some way to shift the *unrecognised losses already in the system*, including both tax losses and real losses of equity, to others.

In the late 1980s, in a continuation of the quest for higher returns and fee income and, based in part on the commercial acceptability of borrowing on the basis of expected cash flow and anticipated asset dispositions and the introduction and market acceptance of non-investment grade corporate high yield debt, as an alternative to real property financing and equity investments, investors began to concentrate heavily in these highly leveraged transactions ("HLTs") such as leveraged buy-outs. These HLTs afforded significant tax incentives by allowing interest on corporate debt to be deducted, as distinguished from non-deductible dividends on equity. The rise in HLTs has corresponded to the general tendency of American business to leverage themselves to unprecedented levels. Debt service requires ever larger portions of debtor companies' cash flow. Current concern with the level and social responsibility of massive HLT investment is well known. The decline of business revenues due to regional economic woes and increases in interest rates erode the liquidity margin between success and default. Debtor companies with substantial amounts of floating rate debt, zero-coupon debt or short or medium-term debt that must be refinanced, when faced with the reduced flexibility of federally-insured financial institutions which can no longer freely refinance these HLTs and when faced with a contracting market where the debtor cannot readily spin-off assets at acceptable prices, find that there is no practical alternative to a reorganisation. The real question in any reorganisation will be how the cost of that deleveraging and loss recognition will be shared and how it will be effected.[37]

IMPACT ON AND REACTIONS BY FINANCIAL INSTITUTIONS

While the grim scenario described above has been suffered primarily by thrifts and banks in Texas and in New England, it is inevitable that it will spread in varying degrees to financial institutions in other regions. On 19 December 1989, the Office of the Comptroller of the Currency ("OCC") issued a Fact

37. The author acknowledges reference to materials contained in and recommends Cieri, *An Introduction to Legal and Practical Considerations in Restructuring of Troubled Leveraged Buyouts*, 45 *Bus Law* 333 (Nov. 1989) with respect to restructuring of HLTs.

Sheet[38] in which it clearly sets out its intention to identify those banks which may be vulnerable to softening real property markets and to review those banks with potential problems. Those banks most likely to be subject to an OCC target exam are those that: (a) have a large real property loan portfolio; *or* (b) are in a market that the OCC macroeconomical model indicates as approaching an over-built condition. The Fact Sheet states that: "If banks are not recognizing problem real estate loans, examiners will ensure that they do so in the future".[39]

The intermediate-term effect on these institutions will be unpleasant, at best. Federal banking regulations require that OREO be marked to market no less frequently than annually.[40] Actual practice of the OCC in a pervasively declining regional market has been to require that banks *anticipate future* value declines by establishing "OREO valuation reserves", also a direct charge to capital, unlike the loan loss reserve. As the real property market in a region dries up, comparable sales become so infrequent that they are deemed meaningless by bank regulators. The Texas and New England experience has shown that the value of a bank's OREO portfolio then is determined by the judgement of regulators using discounted cash-flow computer models and the regulators' assumptions, even when those regulators are based in other parts of the nation and may have no personal knowledge of the regional market. This discounted cash technique also is used to value land, an appraisal method not sanctioned by any professional appraisal body. The effect of OREO write-downs and valuation reserves on a bank's earnings and capital can be devastating. These same write-down and valuation practices will be applied to other assets, including HLTs. The impact of these events on the marketplace includes general credit tightening and restrictive requirements for additional collateral and equity support for businesses generally.

All of these developments receive high-profile attention as they affect the nation's financial institutions. The ragged edge of this massive deleveraging and resulting loss of wealth, however, is visited first upon the capital of the nation's entrepreneurs: its investors, the capitalist heartland of America. The deterioration of capital and the intransigence of the nation's financial institutions in their battle for survival places a premium on the peaceful and non-destructive allocation of loss and the preservation of the base of the nation's business, in the most efficient manner possible. The goal of a non-judicial

38. Under the heading *Current and Future Actions*, the Fact Sheet states that the OCC is using its experts in real property lending problems to assist in reviewing targeted banks. The Fact Sheet states that the purpose of this review is to help assess banks' vulnerability to softening real property markets and review real property loan portfolios in banks with potential problems. The Real Estate Valuation Model was to be used to identify those banks with potential problems or weaknesses in targeted markets. The OCC stated that this model would be refined to fit the characteristics of individual markets.

39. The Fact Sheet also stated that the OCC would require the targeted banks to take whatever corrective action was necessary with respect to real property lending practices and loan portfolios.

40. 12 CFR §7.3025.

debtor's reorganisation is to provide for such an efficient and equitable loss allocation with respect to that debtor short of bankruptcy and to preserve its business as a valuable going concern.

BASIS FOR ACTION BY DEBTORS

In a declining and adverse economy, debtor companies tend to recognise and attack problem assets or financing on an individual basis. This tendency is exacerbated when one or more of the debtor's creditors, caught in the downward spiral of the systemic capital adequacy crisis, behave in a reactionary mode and focus only on its problems with the debtor and do not take cognisance of the debtor's other credit relationships and problems. At some point, the company may come to the realisation that it is unable to maintain many separate negotiations for the resolution of its problems simultaneously on a coherent basis. The debtor company will recognise that many of its problems are interrelated and that some of its lenders or investors are more aggressive in seeking collection and pursuing default remedies than others. The company will have been prone to resolve its problems with its most troublesome creditors on a preferential basis and to defer the resolution of problems or potential problems with its more patient creditors, to their mutual detriment.

Each creditor considers its loan transaction and prospects for collection from a narrowed perspective. As the debtor's financial condition deteriorates, each creditor seeks to spread its grip over the debtor's resources to maximise its prospects for collection. When the debtor seeks to respond to each creditor on an individual basis and where each creditor adopts its hegemony over the debtor's financial resources through cross-collateralisation, requirements of completion deposits, establishment of performance hurdles or deadlines which limit flexibility and distort decision-making, additional collateralisation and the like, the debtor may find that in the process of bartering his beads to the Indians, he runs out of beads before he runs out of Indians. What is required is a comprehensive action plan for the consensual, non-judicial reorganisation of the debtor company.

FOUNDATION FOR A PLAN

The process of formulation of a plan of action for a debtor company in this environment of the systemic capital adequacy crisis and the responses generated by its financial institution creditors requires a change of focus or frame of reference by the debtor, as well as its creditors, and a comprehensive understanding of the debtor and its creditors' legal and financial positions. This process requires close interaction between the debtor's senior management, independent certified public accountants, who must present the debtor's financial condition in a coherent and credible fashion, legal counsel and other professionals, all of whom together can create an overall strategy for the resolution of the debtor's legal and financial problems. The process also requires someone who can supervise the delegation of specific tasks to specialists. Unless the debtor's efforts are co-ordinated properly and the work handled efficiently, the debtor's efforts will become paralysed and the expense undertaken in the preparation of a plan of consensual non-judicial reorganisation (a "Plan") will be wasted. Consensual non-judicial debtor reorganisation is a dynamic process which requires the application of a variety of business and legal disciplines, including real property, tax, banking, business entities, securities, financial institution regulatory practice, bankruptcy and litigation. Depending upon the composition of the debtor's asset base, the process may require the application of other, more specialised business and legal practice areas. Charts illustrating the participants in this process, their respective roles and objectives, and their general areas of focus are collectively attached as Annex A. This chapter does not address these specific legal disciplines, but rather, the context of, basis for and the creative, but very practical, process of equitable allocation of loss occasioned by the systemic problem of capital deterioration, on the most efficient basis.

No consensual Plan for the reorganisation of a debtor can be accomplished without successful individual renegotiation of the affected loan or credit transactions. Conversely, the only way in which the debtor company can achieve a successful non-judicial consensual reorganisation is by placing these individual successful renegotiations in the context of an overall Plan which is designed to maximise return to all of the creditors on a fair and equitable basis and to motivate the debtor to follow through with the Plan and avoid, ultimately, judicial reorganisation or liquidation. The Plan must accommodate the financial and legal positions inherent in each individual negotiation situation, and each individual negotiation situation must be placed in the context of the overall Plan.

Generally, the overall Plan in its initial stages is a reflection of a coherent communication of the debtor's financial condition. The effect of this broad-based communication into the creditors of the debtor will have the effect of repositioning many of the debtor/creditor relationships from their status prior to presentation of the Plan. This process of repositioning generally will go through several stages in which the overall nature of the Plan may shift, based upon shifting individual negotiations, and individual negotiations will vary in light of the economic implication of the Plan upon the specific transaction and based upon the legal implications of the relationship and of the Plan itself. Constant appreciation by the debtor and its counsel and accountants with respect to the shifting debtor and creditor dynamics is essential to the successful implementation of the Plan.

Although the company may have considered its alternatives under the

Federal Bankruptcy Laws, either with respect to particular assets, groups of assets or the individual principals of the company, and in fact may have caused certain affiliated entities to seek protection under the Federal Bankruptcy Laws, it generally is the debtor company's objective to avoid taking the entire company and its principals into bankruptcy. The objective of a consensual reorganisation for a debtor company is to obtain the essential benefits of protection afforded under the Federal Bankruptcy Laws without the attendant costs, stigma and potential loss of control. The basic equitable principles which underlie a successful consensual reorganisation are the same basic equitable principles that underlie the completion of a successful reorganisation under Chapter 11 of the Federal Bankruptcy Laws.[41] A consensual reorganisation, however, is *not* the legal equivalent of a proceeding under the Federal Bankruptcy Laws. Any discussion of reorganisation under the Federal Bankruptcy Laws is beyond the scope of this chapter.

COMPONENTS OF A PLAN

To be successful, the Plan should address the following components.

Full disclosure

As the debtor company slips into a defensive mode in the negotiation of problem debt, the company will tend to limit the information provided to its creditors and to entrench for a defence or attack. It is essential to a successful consensual reorganisation that the debtor make disclosure of its financial condition on a full and fair basis to all of its creditors. It is only through this process that the creditors can be convinced that their better interests will be served by co-operating in a consensual reorganisation, rather than by pressing the debtor to the wall with the hope of achieving preferential treatment. Many companies consider the information typically demanded by creditors to represent a ceding of power or control to the creditors and, therefore, choose to retain power or control by resisting full disclosure. If the facts support the necessity for a consensual reorganisation or, failing that, relief under the Federal Bankruptcy Laws, full disclosure is unavoidable and is indispensable to a successful reorganisation. Until the creditor's frame of reference is expanded through effective communication and disclosure, the creditor will focus only on its credit and problems, discounting competing claims and the implications of its actions on the debtor, the other creditors and, finally, the consequences of its own actions.

41. See 11 USC §§1101–74 (1990).

Fair treatment of each creditor and each class of creditor

The cornerstone of a consensual reorganisation is fair and equitable treatment of each creditor and each class of creditor, recognising the strengths and weaknesses of their respective positions, but without preferring or favouring one creditor or class of creditor over another, except in recognition of the legal or economic facts. To prefer any creditor or treat any creditor on an inequitable basis will serve as an example to motivate other creditors to seek individual preferential treatment. Many creditors will respond to the debtor company's initial overtures with respect to a consensual reorganisation with "We don't do plans" or "We don't believe your projections" or "The squeaky wheel gets the grease". Only when convinced that the creditor will be treated fairly and equitably and that no other creditor will be preferred to its detriment will a creditor consider reorganisation on a consensual basis.

Maximum return to creditors

It is essential that the information provided in connection with a consensual reorganisation establish conclusively that the creditor's interests would be maximised under such a reorganisation, as opposed to pursuit by the creditor of individual action or precipitating judicial reorganisation or liquidation.

Long-term survival of the company as a going concern

Consensual reorganisation requires some prospect for the long-term survival of the debtor company as a going concern, certainly for a long-enough term of survival to cross the market and achieve higher values as assets are liquidated through the ordinary course of business in response to market demand, rather than through forced liquidation. Before considering any contribution to the long-term survival of the company, the creditors must be convinced of the dedicated concentration of the company upon maintenance of asset quality, operational efficiency and the management credibility and expertise which can be applied, on an economically efficient basis, to the maximisation of values, stabilisation of cash flow and liquidity and return to the creditors. To convince creditors of the prospects for long-term survival of the debtor company, the company may be required to reorganise its management and operations in response to market demands, economic pressure and creditor objectives. Company overhead and all related party fees or other payments, and related party transactions, will be closely scrutinised as a part of such a reorganisation. For a consensual reorganisation Plan effectively to protect the debtor and the creditors, it must be based on a term which will permit the company and its creditors to benefit from market improvement and competitive action, free from ongoing debt renegotiation deadlines.

Going concern v. forced liquidation

A Plan must differentiate clearly the consequences of the long-term survival of the company as a going concern and maximisation of the return to the creditors through disposition or refinancing of its assets on an ongoing basis from the consequences of judicial reorganisation or forced liquidation. The economic information illustrating the consequences of going concern operations, as opposed to forced liquidation, must be credible, accurate and legitimate and, most importantly, the debtor must fully understand the consequences of, and be prepared to resort to, judicial reorganisation and, if necessary, forced liquidation as an alternative to failure of the consensual reorganisation Plan. If the creditors do not believe that forced liquidation is the ultimate and most distasteful alternative, they will not agree upon a consensual reorganisation Plan.

Provision for federal income taxes

A primary concern often overlooked by debtors and creditors and which is dealt with differently in bankruptcy, but which *must* be dealt with by the debtor and the Plan, is provision for the payment of federal income taxes. The Internal Revenue Service will be the debtor's most unforgiving creditor. A general discussion of certain pertinent federal income tax planning issues for a debtor in connection with reorganisation and potential bankruptcy is beyond the scope of this chapter.

Exculpation

The pay-off to the debtor company for facing the unpleasant economic facts, making full disclosure of those facts to its creditors and taking the time, making the effort and going to the expense of formulating, negotiating and implementing a consensual reorganisation Plan is exculpation. Exculpation in this case means generally the release of the debtor company, its affiliates and all individual principals from all liability for repayment of the debts covered by the Plan. Typically, most creditors firmly resist exculpation. Only when convinced that (a) the debtor has made full disclosure of its financial condition, (b) the prospects for return to the creditor under the Plan will exceed the prospects for return under the available alternatives, including forced liquidation, and (c) that if the debtor is not exculpated consensually, it will seek exculpation judicially under the Federal Bankruptcy Laws,[42] might the creditors grant exculpation. Achievement of exculpation judicially under the Federal Bankruptcy Laws would require, in most instances, a separate filing for each entity seeking such an exculpation, independent counsel for each such entity and significant attendant time and expense. As a practical matter, many creditors will attempt to tie exculpation to some performance standard or trigger date, and

42. *Ibid.*

some creditors may grant partial exculpation on the same basis. The debtor company must measure these demands or conditions against the threat they present to Plan acceptance and implementation.

ANALYSIS OF DEBTOR ORGANISATIONAL STRUCTURE

Debtor organisational structures which are more complex provide leverage to the debtor in separating certain assets from creditor claims, giving the debtor flexibility in the creation of a Plan and presenting a disincentive to precipitous creditor action when faced with complex, expensive and time-consuming judicial action as the distasteful alternative. To accommodate and maximise benefits afforded by tax laws and to deal effectively with questions of liability and marketability with respect to fixed assets, ownership must often be traced through layers of affiliated corporations, partnerships, joint ventures and other entities. Often, groups of assets are formed to facilitate administration. These groupings may be based upon project or asset type or administrative responsibility. Where a number of operating units are involved, you will often find additional administrative tiers formed for purposes of centralising and controlling management, cash requirements, accounting, legal administration and similar functions. Where the debtor organisation is closely held, the relationships between the principals, who are generally principals of the overall administrative organisation and possibly significant individual owners when ownership is traced to the affiliate entity, project or asset level, must be organised and communicated to the creditors in a comprehensible fashion to permit understanding of the credit and liability position of each individual principal, each ownership entity, each operating unit and for the entire organisation as consolidated. Computerised schedules and charts can be very useful in the communication process. It is important to validate the explanation against documentation, which can be done internally by the debtor, with review by accountants, lawyers and other professionals.

DATA ACCUMULATION: DOCUMENT EXAMINATION AND LEGAL ANALYSIS—MATERIAL TRANSACTIONS

At the same time as the debtor's financial condition is being measured, organised and detailed by the debtor's certified public accounting firm, legal counsel and other professionals must begin to deal with critical debtor/creditor problems, including pending repossessions and foreclosures, termination of credit lines and vendor accounts, litigation, pending bankruptcies and the like. All material transactions must receive an immediate legal analysis to facilitate a timely response, protect the debtor's equity for the benefit of the Plan and reduce exposure for unsecured claims which would otherwise dilute the Plan asset base. A form of document examination and legal analysis checklist is attached as Annex B, and examples of certain workout strategies for specific creditors or credit relationships is attached as Annex C. Pending sales, transfers or refinancings must be carefully analysed within the context of Plan development, and their progress monitored and success assured if consistent with the Plan. All material transactions which might be subject to challenge by the creditors in bankruptcy should be examined carefully, including possible fraudulent (or otherwise voidable) transfers and preference transactions.[43] Special attention must be given to matters which must be resolved in support of the continued conduct by the debtor of the business as a going concern. All possibilities for deeds in lieu of foreclosure or other transactions which mitigate ultimate exposure and which relieve the debtor of carrying cost responsibility for an asset which will not contribute to the overall success of the Plan should be isolated, and deeds in lieu of foreclosure or agreed foreclosures implemented. Pending litigation must be analysed immediately, and defences, counterclaims and potential claims must be evaluated. Strategic or tactical litigation may be necessary or advisable in furtherance of the Plan. The debtor and its counsel must establish a close system for the management and periodic monitoring of pending litigation, bankruptcies and potential foreclosures.

Special attention must be paid to securities laws disclosure requirements, rights of the holders of equity securities in the debtor or its affiliates, "outside partners" and broker dealers in public or private syndications, and to the fiduciary duties owed by the debtor or its affiliates as a general partner or partners or as a director or controlling shareholder to all parties in connection with the formulation of the Plan.

The debtor and its counsel and other professionals must maintain a regular reporting format so that all pending matters in negotiation, litigation, bankruptcy or under threat of repossession or foreclosure can be properly monitored and timely and effective decisions made and implemented. An individual with overall management responsibility in the debtor organisation must be designated to update the status report, disseminate it and force the decision-making process. Regular status report communication and decision-making and implementation are the keys to the debtor's holding ground and continuing its business while the Plan is formulated, and is the key to implementation of the Plan after its presentation.

STATUS OF DEBTOR'S LIQUIDITY—WORKING CAPITAL LOANS

By the time the debtor has resolved to investigate bankruptcy alternatives and

43. 11 USC §§547, 548 (1990).

the possibility of a consensual reorganisation, the debtor's liquidity position generally is precarious. The expense of formulating a non-judicial Plan or formulating a judicial Plan for reorganisation or liquidation for a complex organisation can be formidable. These expenses arise at a time when the debtor is least able to satisfy them. Inevitably, the debtor has overestimated his diminishing cash flow and underestimated the costs attendant to working out problems, as opposed to closing new and productive deals. A realistic assessment of the debtor's liquidity is imperative.

Often in the process of formulating a Plan, certainly prior to its implementation, the debtor will require a cash infusion. The financing arrangements for such a cash infusion, a working capital loan, will provide emergency financing to sustain the debtor through the formulation of a non-judicial reorganisation Plan. The most likely external source of funding of a working capital loan will be equity holders who perceive value in the debtor as a reorganised going-concern business to be protected by the Plan and unsecured or under-secured creditors, all of whom have the most to gain from a successful reorganisation. The working capital loan must be large enough to satisfy the foreseeable cash requirements through the period when a successful Plan can be implemented and fund operating costs or through a judicial reorganisation, failing the success of a consensual Plan.

Generally, the debtor has a limited amount of collateral with which to secure a new working capital loan. In order to obtain the working capital loan, the debtor should not be stingy with the collateral. The working capital loan ultimately will be retired through liquidation of the collateral or through a priority charge on cash flow after satisfaction of existing secured debt and federal income taxes, but prior to any other claims on the debtor's equity.

NEGOTIATORS—IDENTITY AND TRAINING

Simultaneous negotiations with numerous creditors can place serious time and experience-level demands on the debtor's operations. To the maximum degree possible, experienced members of senior management should undertake the role of workout negotiators with specific creditors or groups of creditors with whom each management officer has credibility and background. Senior level management or principals will be required to negotiate with many creditors, who will insist that the obligated parties deal with them face to face. This will place significant time demands upon the principals and senior officers, who should not shrink from these contracts inasmuch as the most progress can be made most quickly by dealing through the principals.

Other officers of the debtor, members of the certified public accountants, legal counsel or other professionals may be utilised in connection with negotiations. The approach should be non-confrontational. Each negotiator should be trained on the logic of the Plan and be prepared to stay with that logic in the face of the countless responses, qualifications and deviations expected to be presented by the creditors.

CREDITOR MEETINGS

Where the debtor's problems are broad-based among a large number of creditors, a group meeting may be required to present and explain the Plan. The necessity for a group meeting will vary, depending upon composition of the creditor group. It is preferable for the debtor and appropriate where a relatively small number of creditors or a single creditor are the dominant force in negotiation and implementation of the Plan to conduct separate individual meetings between the principals and the affected creditors, and to update the creditor group with correspondence.

CREDITOR COMMITTEE

Particularly where the debtor has a number of friendly creditors who perceive that the Plan will be in their best interests, it is wise to establish a creditor committee. This will enable the debtor to maintain indirect contact with the creditors and to keep "a finger on the pulse" of their attitude.

If the sense of the creditors is mainly hostile, utilisation of a creditor committee may not be in the debtor's interest inasmuch as it may have a tendency to focus and consolidate hostile action and may in fact spawn a "rump" plan proposal or an involuntary bankruptcy filing. On the other hand, creating a creditor committee may have the effect of dissipating hostility and concentrating it in the hands of a meaningful few which can be dealt with more successfully than hit and run hostility from an unco-ordinated creditor body. These concerns must be weighed up in each case.

DOCUMENTATION

Once the Plan is presented, every debtor will wish to tie creditors down to acceptance of the Plan. Utilisation of a form of letter of intent as a summary of negotiation terms is usually suggested. Letters of intent may be proposed and circulated; however, it has been our experience that most of the creditors do not wish to become committed until they see that a substantial majority of the creditors, either in number or amount, will become committed to the Plan. Generally, agreement with the debtor's dominant creditors will turn the decision-making corner for the balance of the creditors. The exchange of drafts of the letter of intent or other written forms of negotiation summaries is a useful device to facilitate negotiation. Executed letters of intent should not be viewed as an end in themselves, however.

A specimen loan modification agreement may be provided to each creditor, consistent with the Plan terms; however, in most instances where agreement to the terms of the loan modification is reached, the creditor will insist upon utilising its own form of loan modification agreement, and great time and expense should not be spent in argument over the form.

The collateral pool agreement will be the determinative agreement for the creditors. Great care, time and expense should be taken in its preparation and finalisation. A specimen collateral pool agreement utilised in connection with a recent non-judicial reorganisation of a complex real property debtor organisation is attached as Appendix 2. Utilisation of a creditor committee which furthers the process of resolution of the form of collateral pool agreement can be beneficial.

The transfer or security documents to be executed pursuant to the collateral pool agreement and the appropriate authority and organisational documents to be assembled will be driven by the requirements of the collateral pool agreement and the specific agreements with creditors.

It should be the debtor's position that the debtor will not provide legal opinions with respect to the loan modification agreements or the collateral pool agreement. In this circumstance, all of the creditors should be adequately represented and in the position to make their own determination with respect to the authorisation of action and the validity and binding effect of the documentation.

ADMINISTRATION OF PLAN AND DEBT NEGOTIATION, MODIFICATION AND ACCEPTANCE

Negotiation theory

The negotiation theory espoused by the representatives of the debtor in negotiations with the creditors should follow very closely the basis for the Plan. This basis must be constantly and calmly reiterated to the creditors, who will not wish to hear the inherent logic in the Plan. Each creditor, whether it admits or not, will wish to force some preferential treatment, to the disadvantage of the other creditors. This must be resisted.

Creditor committee meetings

The creditor committee meetings are a useful device to dissipate individual creditor desires and preferences which would result in disadvantages to the other creditors. The creditor committee meetings can act as a forum in which the debtor has some control and can contribute to the educational process through which the creditors may come to understand what is in their best interest and carefully evaluate the alternatives to the Plan.

Periodic reporting—administrative control

In the process of negotiation and implementation of the Plan, it is difficult to keep a handle on the progress of all the negotiations. Each negotiation impacts the others, and all impact the ultimate success of the Plan.

The wealth of information generated and accumulated by various administrative participants in the debtor's senior management, by legal counsel, by the independent certified public accountants and by other professionals can be mind-numbing. It is essential that the debtor's manager of this process distill the significant items to be monitored and the hot items which require immediate decision and action. We suggest that principal decision-makers meet weekly, if possible, but at least bi-weekly, at a set date, place and time. The manager should establish a formal written agenda, which can be kept on a word processor and updated from meeting to meeting. It should be the responsibility of the manager to update the agenda based upon decisions made at each meeting and synthesise developments during the period prior to the next meeting, updating the agenda just prior to each meeting, for circulation at the meeting. Following the same format and adapting it from meeting to meeting facilitates a quick understanding of changes and enables decision makers to move quickly through the material.

Suggested topics for the agenda include:

(a) critical path progress in completion of the Plan;
(b) status of, and requirements in connection with, negotiations for a working capital loan;
(c) status of engagement of special counsel in connection with particular legal matters;
(d) discussion by major lender relationship and by project, asset or asset group within that relationship of major problem loans;
(e) discussion of negotiations with problem partners, operating units, subsidiaries, affiliates or other interest constituents, such as vendors or suppliers, classes of equity holders or regulatory agencies;
(f) discussion of cash position, including requirements for current company operating expenses and legal, accounting and other professional fees.

Although these items may be discussed within the context of creditor relationships and problem loans, separate supplemental schedules should be prepared detailing litigation status, including answer requirements, discovery dates, hearing dates and other procedural deadlines, demand letters, postings for non-judicial foreclosures, pending bankruptcy cases, and bankruptcy and litigation strategy. It is of the highest importance that reporting at this level should not seek to preserve the technical accuracy of information, as is the case with many reports prepared in connection with the Plan formulation process, but rather, to expedite the decision-making process. To this end, descriptions should be brief and not technical, except where directly pertinent to the decision-making process. The formality of these agendas and reports should expand only to the extent required to serve the decision-making function. Similarly, attendance at the weekly or bi-weekly decision-making sessions may fluctuate, depending upon the necessity of the parties who must attend in light of the matters under consideration.

The debtor must also implement special polices for limitation on distribution of the agenda and limitation on attendees in light of the protection of attorney/client privilege and protection of attorney work product privilege.[44]

GERALD NELS OLSON*

44. The attorney/client privilege generally refers to the client's privilege to refuse to disclose and to prevent other parties from disclosing confidential communications, which are made to facilitate the rendition of professional legal services. Communications between the client or the client's representative and the lawyer or the lawyer's representative which are confidential are protected. See *United States* v. *Kovel* 296 F.2d 918 (2d Cir. 1961) (if it is necessary that the communication be confidential). Confidentiality requires an intention that the communication not be communicated to third parties. See *Dorothy K. Winston & Co.* v. *Town Heights Development, Inc.*, 376 F.Supp. 1214 (DC Dist. 1974) (the communication must be intended to be confidential). In some states the attorney/client privilege is given a strict construction because of its tendency to suppress the truth, see e.g. *San Francisco* v. *Superior Court of San Francisco* 37 Cal. 2d 227, 231 P.2d 26 (1951) (because of its tendency to suppress the truth, attorney/client privilege receives a strict construction), while in other states a more liberal construction is adopted on the theory that a client should be free to discuss all circumstances of a matter with his attorney without fear that his statements will later be used against him. See e.g. *People* v. *Shapiro* 308 NY 453, 126 N.E. 2d 559 (1955) (court favoured a liberal construction on the theory that one consulting a lawyer should be encouraged to communicate all the facts without fear that his statements may possibly be used against him in the future). The privilege belongs to the client, see *Radian Burners, Inc.* v. *American Gas Assoc.*, 320 F.2d 314, cert. denied, 375 US 929 (1963), and only the client may waive its right to the privilege, see *Baird* v. *Koerner* 279 F.2d 623 (9th Cir. 1960) (attorney cannot divulge information that was communicated to him in confidence until the protection afforded by the privilege has been properly waived by the client). In order to ensure protection of the confidentiality of the relationship between the attorney and client, policies should be adopted which limit the scope of the parties, to whom information is disseminated and who are in attendance at meetings. The attorney work product protects, from the discovery process, the work produced and developed by an attorney, for his client, in anticipation of litigation. The "work product" of an attorney in preparing for litigation includes the mental impressions, conclusions, opinions and legal theories of the attorney or other representative of a party to the litigation, see Fed R Civ P 26(b)(3), and is reflected in such things as memoranda, statements, correspondence, interviews and briefs. See *Hickman* v. *Taylor* 329 US 495 (1947). The work product doctrine encourages effective preparation for litigation consistent with the adversarial system, based on the theory that each side should prepare its case independently without unnecessary interference. *Ibid.* Particular litigation need not have actually been commenced in order for the doctrine to apply, but there must be some probability that particular litigation will occur. See *Diversified Industries, Inc.* v. *Meredith* 572 F.2d 596 (8th Cir. 1977) *en banc* (1978). The degree to which specific litigation must be contemplated, and the question of whether the work product doctrine protects documents which were generated other than in the case in which discovery is sought, varies from state to state.

* The author gratefully acknowledges the contribution of Michael N. Maberry, William B. Sechrest, John M. Walker, Jr and Michael R. Corey, all of Winstead Sechrest & Minick, P.C., Dallas, Texas, to the development of the materials presented in this chapter, and additionally, the contribution of Thomas R. Helfand and Scot W. O'Brien, also of Winstead Sechrest & Minick, P.C., in the preparation of the Federal Income Tax analysis attached to this chapter as Annex B and Collateral Pool Agreement attached as Annex C.

ANNEX A. FUNCTIONAL ORGANISATION CHARTS AND AREAS OF PRIMARY RISK, FOCUS AND ALTERNATIVE COURSES OF ACTION

Consensual reorganisation of troubled debtors—functional organisation chart and services available

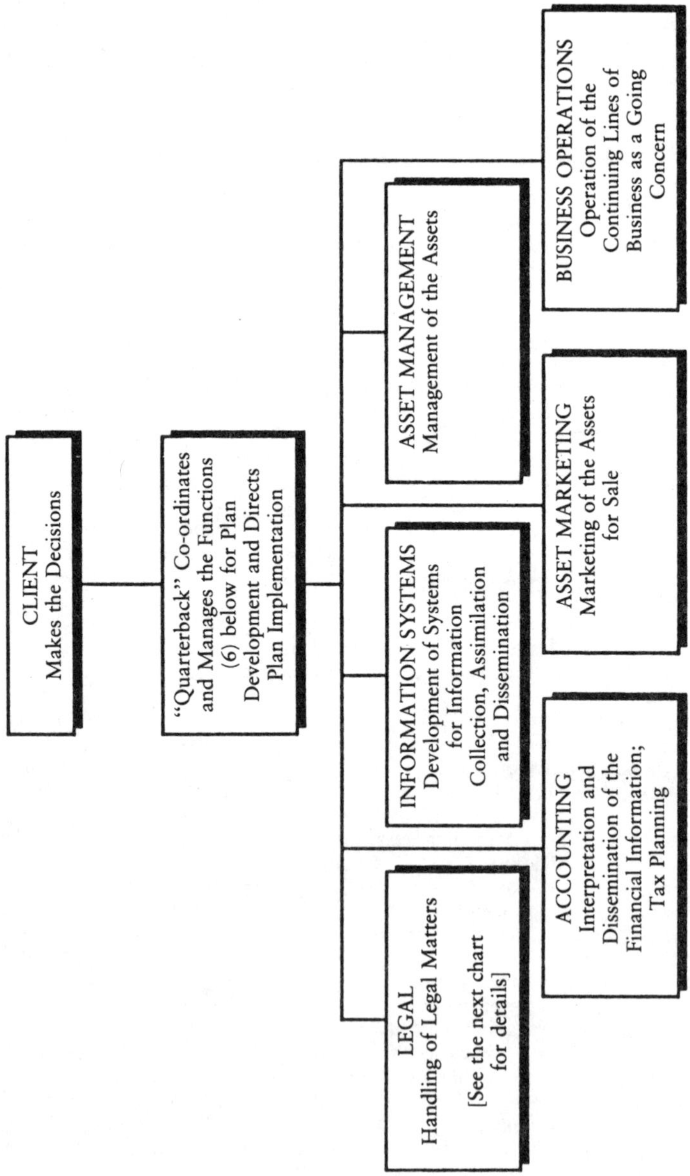

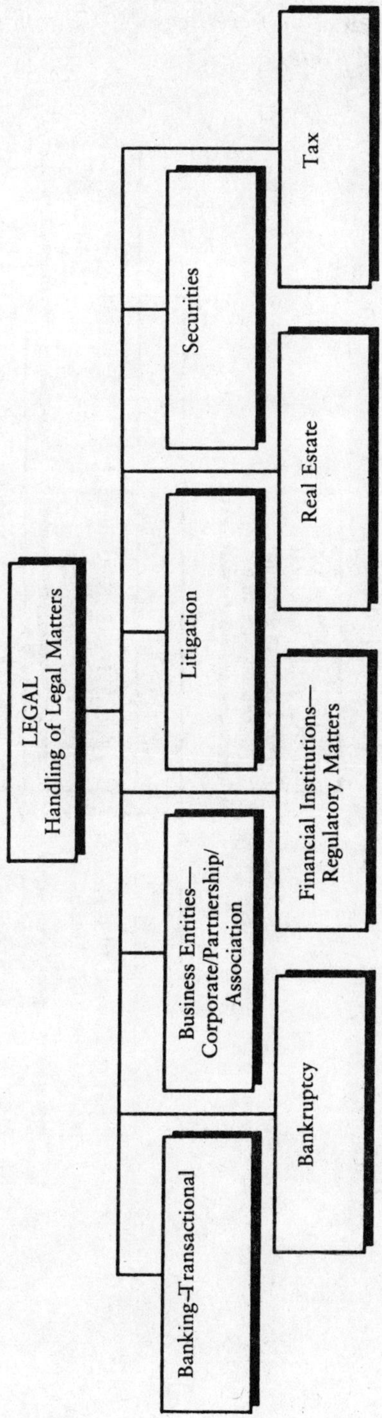
LEGAL
Handling of Legal Matters
Banking–Transactional
Bankruptcy
Business Entities—Corporate/Partnership/Association
Financial Institutions—Regulatory Matters
Litigation
Real Estate
Securities
Tax

Consensual reorganisation of troubled debtors: areas of primary risk, focus and alternative courses of action

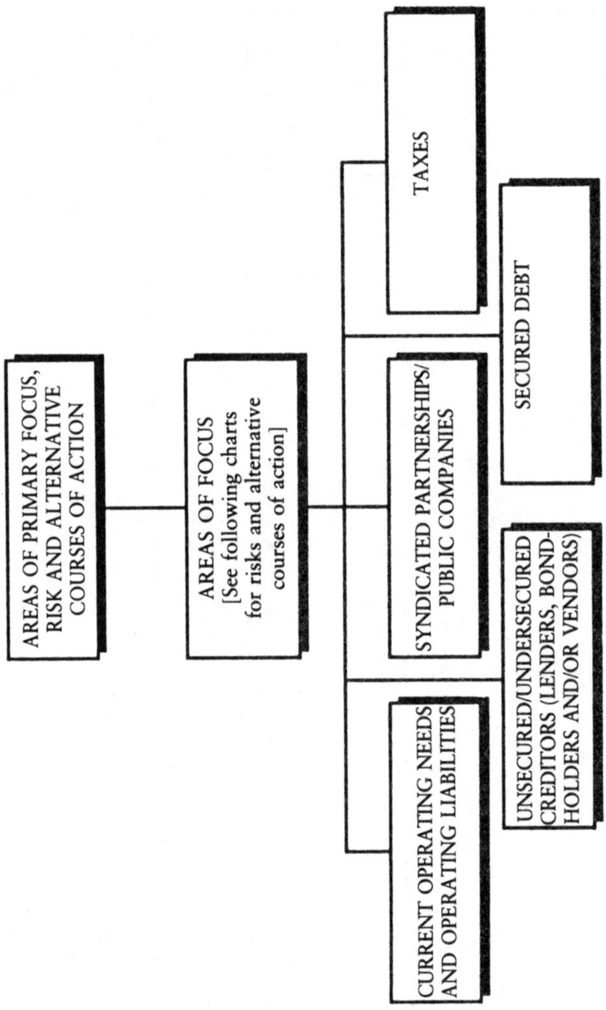

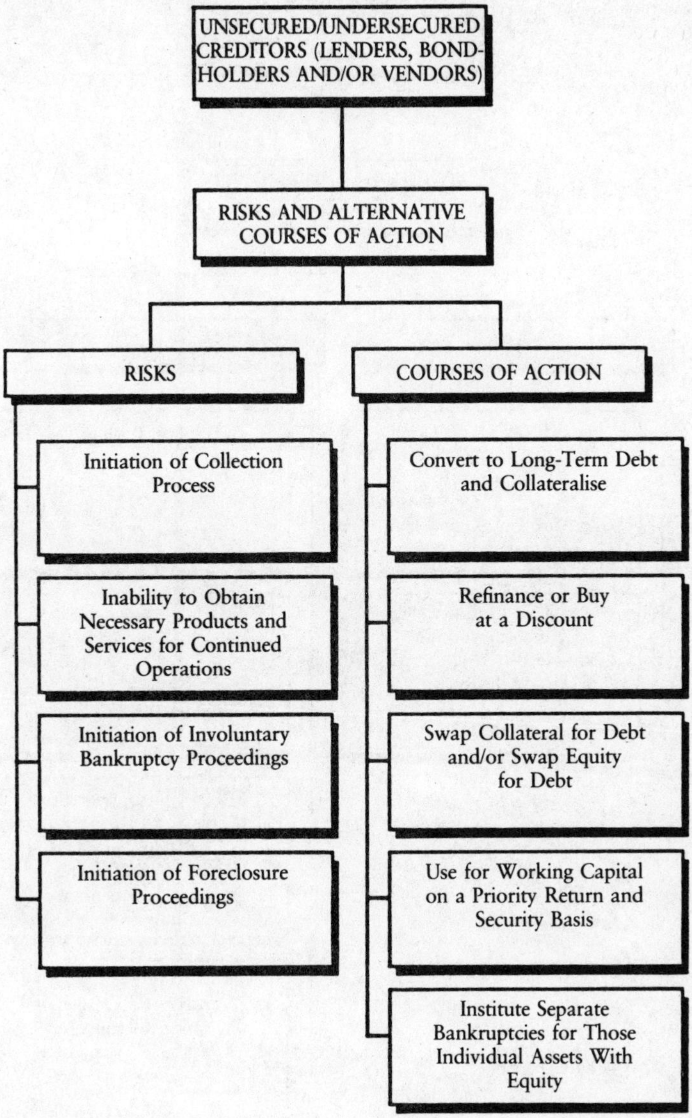
UNSECURED/UNDERSECURED CREDITORS (LENDERS, BOND-HOLDERS AND/OR VENDORS)
RISKS AND ALTERNATIVE COURSES OF ACTION
RISKS
COURSES OF ACTION
Initiation of Collection Process
Inability to Obtain Necessary Products and Services for Continued Operations
Initiation of Involuntary Bankruptcy Proceedings
Initiation of Foreclosure Proceedings
Convert to Long-Term Debt and Collateralise
Refinance or Buy at a Discount
Swap Collateral for Debt and/or Swap Equity for Debt
Use for Working Capital on a Priority Return and Security Basis
Institute Separate Bankruptcies for Those Individual Assets With Equity

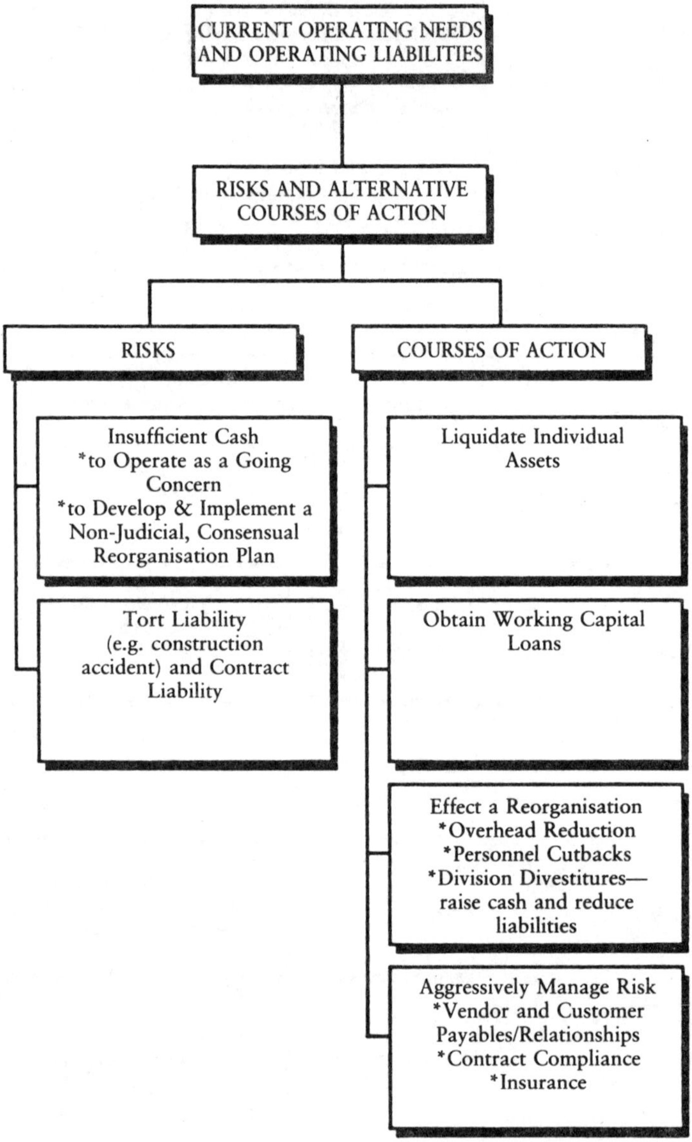
CURRENT OPERATING NEEDS AND OPERATING LIABILITIES
RISKS AND ALTERNATIVE COURSES OF ACTION
RISKS
COURSES OF ACTION
Insufficient Cash
*to Operate as a Going Concern
*to Develop & Implement a Non-Judicial, Consensual Reorganisation Plan
Tort Liability (e.g. construction accident) and Contract Liability
Liquidate Individual Assets
Obtain Working Capital Loans
Effect a Reorganisation
*Overhead Reduction
*Personnel Cutbacks
*Division Divestitures— raise cash and reduce liabilities
Aggressively Manage Risk
*Vendor and Customer Payables/Relationships
*Contract Compliance
*Insurance

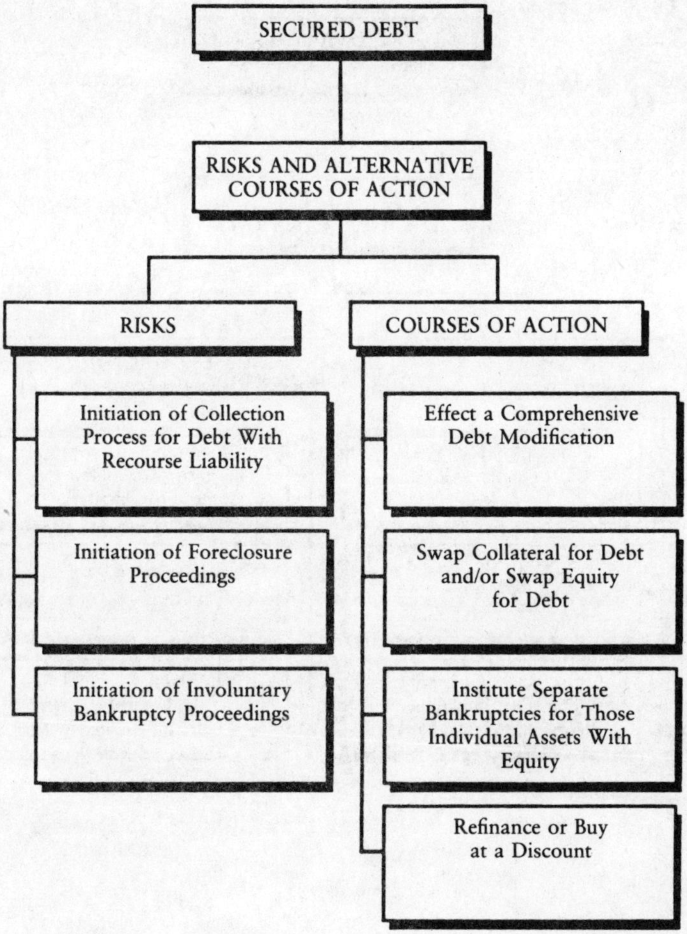
SECURED DEBT
RISKS AND ALTERNATIVE COURSES OF ACTION
RISKS
COURSES OF ACTION
Initiation of Collection Process for Debt With Recourse Liability
Initiation of Foreclosure Proceedings
Initiation of Involuntary Bankruptcy Proceedings
Effect a Comprehensive Debt Modification
Swap Collateral for Debt and/or Swap Equity for Debt
Institute Separate Bankruptcies for Those Individual Assets With Equity
Refinance or Buy at a Discount

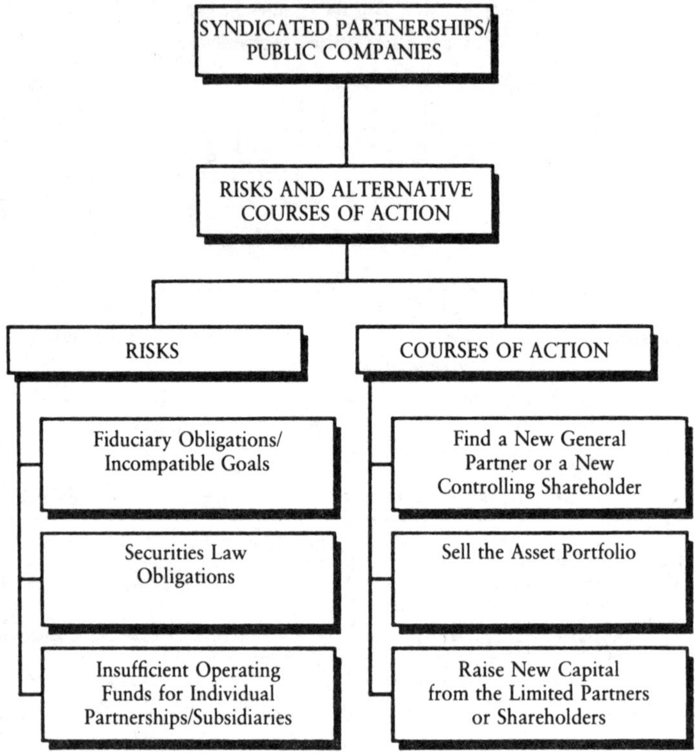
SYNDICATED PARTNERSHIPS/
PUBLIC COMPANIES
RISKS AND ALTERNATIVE
COURSES OF ACTION
RISKS
COURSES OF ACTION
Fiduciary Obligations/
Incompatible Goals
Securities Law
Obligations
Insufficient Operating
Funds for Individual
Partnerships/Subsidiaries
Find a New General
Partner or a New
Controlling Shareholder
Sell the Asset Portfolio
Raise New Capital
from the Limited Partners
or Shareholders

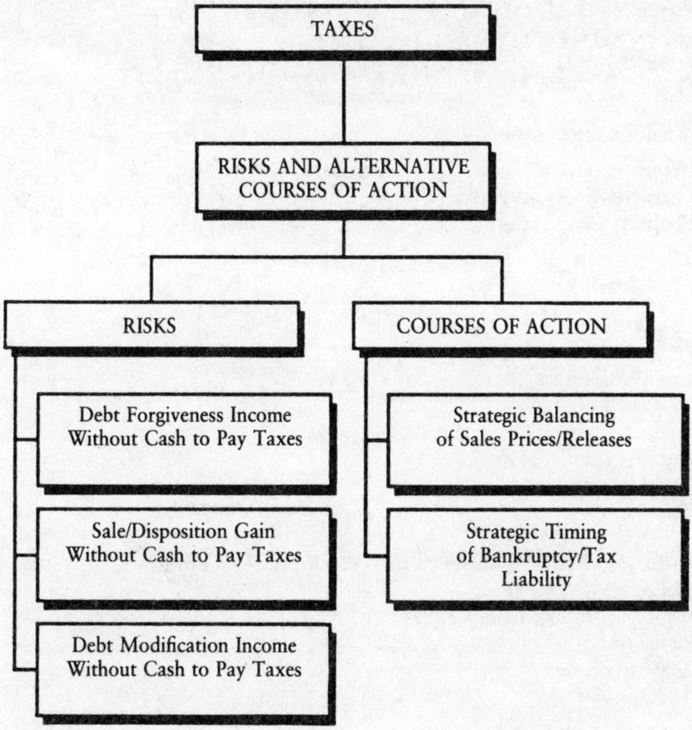
TAXES
RISKS AND ALTERNATIVE COURSES OF ACTION
RISKS
COURSES OF ACTION
Debt Forgiveness Income Without Cash to Pay Taxes
Sale/Disposition Gain Without Cash to Pay Taxes
Debt Modification Income Without Cash to Pay Taxes
Strategic Balancing of Sales Prices/Releases
Strategic Timing of Bankruptcy/Tax Liability

ANNEX B. CONSENSUAL, NON-JUDICIAL DEBTOR REORGANISATIONS. DOCUMENT EXAMINATION AND LEGAL ANALYSIS CHECKLIST

I. Ownership Information

A. Name of partnership, joint venture, etc.
B. Partners (profit interests) and percentage of ownership.
C. Property description (acreage, square feet; net, gross).

II. Loan Information

A. Lender.
B. Commitment amount.
C. Current loan balance:
 1. Principal.
 2. Interest at .... per cent
D. Interest rate:
 1. Floor.
 2. Ceiling.
 3. Terms.
E. Unfunded balance—interest reserve amount—runout.
F. Other fees.
G. Equity (profit) participations.
H. Prepayment penalties.
I. Maturity date:
 1. Original.
 2. Extended.
J. Primary liability.
K. Guarantors:
 1. Several liability—joint and several liability (%).
 2. Limitations on liability.
 3. Possibility of decreasing, or eliminating, liability.
L. Lien priority.
M. Other collateral or security.
N. Permanent or other take-outs.
O. Known participants.

III. Investments Information

A. Partner investments:
 1. Capital contributions.
 2. Loans.
B. Obligations to make contributions or loans, by partner.
C. Known partner defaults.
D. Remedies on partner default.

IV. General Project Information

A. Recent appraisal figures (acres, square feet; net, gross).
B. Aggregate project debt:
 1. Total.
 2. Per acre.

3. Per square foot.

C. Current or foreseeable problems with the property.

V. *Loan Status*

A. Recent refinancing attempts—status of negotiations.

B. Special circumstances (including known defences to loan payment, if any):
1. Usury.
2. Anti-tying (12 USC § 1972, *et seq.*).
3. Duress.
4. Fraud.
5. Tortious interference and control.
6. Good faith and fair dealing.
7. Equitable subordination.
8. Technical drafting errors.
9. Defects in enforcement procedures.

ANNEX C. CONSENSUAL, NON-JUDICIAL DEBTOR REORGANISATIONS WORKOUT ANALYSIS PAPER—ASSESSMENT OF DEBTOR POSITION

As a part of the process of assessing a debtor's financial condition, a determination must be made of the legal position of the debtor *vis-à-vis* his various creditors. Any weaknesses or potentially damaging issues which can be ascertained, either from the loan documents themselves or from discussions between the debtor and his counsel, can be extremely helpful in pursuing negotiations toward a favourably restructured loan. The loan documents must be read with constant consideration to ascertaining the presence of any "Achilles heel" on the part of the creditor. At least the following issues should be considered:

1. *Nature of Recourse Liability.* If the debtor is fully non-recourse, then it is obviously in a stronger position to negotiate with the creditor without fear of exposure, other than loss of the real property, its prior investments therein and potential tax concerns. Conversely, if the debtor (or a guarantor) is fully liable to a creditor, then the creditor has the extra weapon of potential recourse liability against the individuals or entities involved, which it will undoubtedly utilise in its negotiation of a restructure. In addition to the two ends of the spectrum described above for the debtor/guarantor liability (i.e. fully recourse or fully non-recourse), the following "hybrid" types of recourse liability are sometimes utilised:

(a) debtor/guarantor fully non-recourse, with exceptions for taxes, insurance proceeds, rents received after default, etc.;
(b) debtor/guarantor liable for "top x per cent" of indebtedness;
(c) debtor/guarantor liable until "break even" or other performance objective achieved, whereupon liability is negated or diminished;
(d) recourse liability is staggered in amounts throughout term of loan; and
(e) a maximum dollar cap on recourse liability.

Due to the inherent complications with these hybrid structures of liability, close scrutiny should be given to these provisions in the loan documents so as to maximise the debtor's non-recourse position. Potential arguments which might be asserted are as follows.

(i) Where liability is tied to the lack of achievement of a breakeven or other performance standard, consideration should be given as to a method to cause this standard to be achieved.

(ii) Hybrid liability provisions which reference a "top 25 per cent" of the indebtedness or similar provision are also ripe for argument. The creditor will obviously take the position that "top 25 per cent" of indebtedness means the absolute last portion of the indebtedness to be repaid, while a debtor might take the position that "top 25 per cent" means the first 25 per cent of the indebtedness to be repaid. It might also be considered as to how this percentage liability feature works in the setting of a foreclosure sale (i.e. does the bid price at a foreclosure sale apply first to the recourse portion of the indebtedness or the non-recourse portion of the indebtedness?). If any ambiguity is present in these provisions, the client should be made aware of this fact to utilise in its negotiations.

Aside from a review of the promissory note, a review of any guaranty should also be undertaken to determine any potential flaws. One potential flaw which has been asserted is that a guaranty which purports to guarantee debtor's obligation under a non-recourse indebtedness in fact guarantees nothing at all.

2. *Collateral.* A review should be undertaken of all deeds of trust and other collateral documents to determine exactly what type of collateral each creditor claims a lien or security interest against and the validity and priority of such liens. Particular attention might be paid to the following areas:

(a) *Legal Description.* Any flaw in the legal description; this can be as broad as a simple but serious mistake in the metes and bounds description to an omission of an entire tract which the creditor may consider pledged.

(b) *Problems with Adjoining Property.* Determine if the collateral in which the creditor has a lien is dependent in any way on adjoining property owned by the debtor or over which the debtor has control. Obviously, any inconvenience in an adverse debtor and creditor being neighbours might be used as a weapon by the debtor in dissuading the creditor from a foreclosure. This factor might be present where the creditor has a lien on one phase of a two-phase project, where the collateral in which creditor has a lien is dependent on access through adjoining property or in a situation where common areas or a management office is shared with adjoining properties.

(c) *Peculiar Properties.* Ascertain whether the collateral is of a peculiar nature that the creditor would prefer not to own. Properties falling within this category generally are those of a management intensive nature such as very specialised or single-use facilities or slums. The more adept the debtor is in managing such peculiar property, the more persuasive is the debtor's argument that the creditor should allow ownership to remain vested in the debtor via some form of restructured loan.

(d) *Cross-Collateralisation.* Check for "Mother Hubbard"or cross-collateralisation provisions.

(e) *Non-Real Property Collateral.* Examine existence of non-real property collateral (e.g. letters of credit, investor notes, certificates of deposit etc.). The debtor should be appraised of the magnitude of his downside. Often, debtors do not focus on the fact that a draw-down on a letter of credit creates new liability, usually to a totally unrelated institution. Creditors have also been known to be somewhat negligent in monitoring letters of credit, and the debtor should verify that a letter of credit is still in place in favour of the creditor in question. Finally, with respect to investor notes, certificates of deposit and other non-real property collateral, attention should be paid to determine the validity of the creditor's lien and perfection of same. Particularly in the case of investor notes, perfection is sometimes attempted through the utilisation of a somewhat convoluted trust arrangement which might have inherent flaws.

3. *Notice/Acceleration Flaws.* A determination should be made as to whether the creditor has strictly complied with (a) statutory requirements on posting and pursuing a foreclosure, and (b) contractual requirements with respect to notice, acceleration and posting. While these issues do not generally create a fatal problem with respect to the creditor's assertions, it can provide the debtor a much needed 30 or 60- day extension in which to pursue a resolution with the creditor. Obviously this review and considerations at issue will vary from state to state. Particular attention might be paid to the following general areas:

(a) *Notice Methods.* Required method of giving notice pursuant to the loan documents—most loan documents state that notice shall be given by certified mail, return receipt requested, or other specific method. Often, these notice provisions also specify a date whereupon such notice will be effective. Common examples of these effective dates are (i) upon deposit in the US mail, (ii) upon actual receipt, and (iii) upon the expiration of a certain number of days after deposit in the US mail. The determination of any required notice methodology and effective date is the threshold concern in determining whether a creditor has complied with the other requirements described below.

(b) *Notice of Default and Right to Cure.* Very often, loan documents will not entitle the creditor to pursue a default until the expiration of a certain number of days after written notice to the debtor of such default. Compliance by the creditor with this provision should be verified.

(c) *Flawed Acceleration.* This potential flaw might simply be the result of inadequate notice or failure to comply with specific requirements in the loan documents. Where a creditor is attempting to accelerate a wraparound promissory note, it should be ascertained whether the underlying note(s) has also been accelerated. If not, an accelerating creditor should probably only accelerate the "equity portion" of the wraparound promissory note. The most recent case law in the applicable state should be compared to the method of acceleration utilised.

(d) *Flawed Posting for Foreclosure.* In particular, the following verifications might be undertaken:
   (i) Is the county of recordation and posting correct?
   (ii) Was posting done in a timely way within the statutory and contractual requirements (e.g. 21 days in Texas)?
   (iii) Does notice of substitute trustee sale state a permissible time and place for foreclosure (e.g. compliance with three-hour window in Texas)?
   (iv) Is the legal description correct?
   (v) Does the notice of posting comply with the requirements of the deed of trust, as well as with current statutory law? For example, certain prior form deeds of trust in Texas required posting at three different sites within the county. If foreclosure is undertaken pursuant to one of these old forms of deed of trust, this requirement must be complied with, despite no longer being a statutory requirement in Texas.
   (vi) In the event a substitute trustee is being used, was substitution properly effectuated?

4. *Documentation Errors.* Simple errors, mistakes or omissions in the preparation of

loan documents can sometimes provide additional points of leverage for a debtor seeking restructure. Some common examples are as follows:

(a) *Faulty Signature Block.* Is the debtor properly identified in the promissory note and other loan documents? Was the deed of trust actually executed by the entity which holds title to the property?
(b) *Errors and Other Slips.* Missing words or lines in certain key provisions (e.g. the granting paragraph in the deed of trust, the operative sentence of the guaranty etc.) can also prove helpful.
(c) *Errors in Definition of Terms.* For example, if collateral consists of an undivided interest in a piece of property, the deed of trust should be reviewed to be certain that the undivided interest percentage was not cited both in the body of the deed of trust and Exhibit "A" thereto.
(d) *Exhibits.* Exhibits have been known to be referenced but not attached.

5. *Usury Issues.* These issues should be evaluated both from the review of the documents themselves, as well as from the standpoint of actual demands made. Generally, the debtor should evaluate every item which could be characterised as interest in order to determine if a usury issue is present. In particular, the following items should be reviewed:

(a) As a threshold issue, the promissory note should be reviewed to determine the stated interest rate and presence of any "usury savings clause".
(b) Has the creditor been granted a net profits participation or limited partnership interest? If so, the debtor may be in a better position to assert a usury argument. The creditor will argue that any such interest is "speculative and contingent". Helpful evidence from the standpoint of the debtor is any appraisal obtained at the time the transaction was effectuated, as well as any loan-to-value requirements maintained by the creditor.
(c) Did the debtor ever have to assume another's obligations as a requirement for loan renewal or extension? The *Alamo Lumber* case in Texas has been used offensively by many debtors.
(d) Check for clumsily worded demands, pleadings or even pay-off quotes. "Charging" for usurious interest is an easy trap to fall into.

6. *Recharacterisation of Loan.* If a loan can be recharacterised as an investment, and hence the creditor as a "partner" with the debtor, the debtor may be able to assert (a) creditor's co-liability with the debtor on the loan, and (b) a breach of fiduciary duty among partners. In this setting, a debtor might be successful in converting a non-judicial foreclosure action into a judicial partnership dissolution action. Factors which should be considered in determining whether such a recharacterisation is feasible are as follows:

(a) Utilisation of net profits interest or limited partnership interest—generally, the more a creditor "acts" like a partner, the more viability a claim along these lines has.
(b) Heavy utilisation of interest reserve, creating a potential implication that the debtor is not intended to fund out-of-pocket for a lengthy period.
(c) Creditor's heavy-handed use of control features.

7. *Bad Faith/Course of Conduct Claims.* Both creditor and debtor clients should be quizzed at the inception of workout representation as to a full history of the loan transaction, oral communications or commitments, and general conduct of the applicable parties. This area presents the most creative challenge to the debtor's counsel to determine the presence of issues. Similarly, due to the lack of black and white rules in this area, it can be great source of potential leverage.

(a) Situations where the creditor's conduct may exceed the bounds of "good faith and fair dealing":
  (i) Creditor "convinces" the debtor to take on a credit, and then pulls the plug.
  (ii) The loan transaction is just one aspect of the overall relationship between the debtor and the creditor and, when viewed in this light, the creditor's actions are violative. Along these lines, an examination might be made of the transaction to determine any illegal tying arrangements whereas, as an additional inducement for the creditor to undertake this transaction, the debtor may have been required to purchase other assets, participate in other loans or undertake other obligations.
  (iii) Any evidence of creditor bad faith insofar as incentive for being the owner of the property, rather than being a creditor.
  (iv) Any sudden calling of a loan or termination of a line of credit without an objective good reason for doing so.

(b) Course of conduct between parties/oral commitment:
  (i) Did any officer of creditor orally imply or commit to a renewal or extension?
  (ii) Did a course of conduct between the parties supersede understandings evidenced by the loan documents?

While each restructure of a troubled loan is different in nature, many resolutions of these loans are often settled pursuant to the following basic formats:

Format No. 1. Collateral is conveyed to the creditor (or foreclosed upon by the creditor), coupled either with either (i) the debtor's execution and delivery of a deficiency note, or (ii) the full and complete release of the debtor.

Format No. 2. Debtor retains ownership of collateral and the loan is restructured so as to give the debtor relief, at least for a period of time. Typical varieties of restructure arrangements include (a) payments on a cash-flow basis, or (b) payments on a cash-flow basis against a minimum pay rate.

Format No. 3. Lender grants a period of forbearance during which time debtor attempts to facilitate a sale of the collateral property. Upon effectuation of the sale a more permanent solution will be entered with lender similar to that used in Format No. 1 (i.e. a release or deficiency note). Note the potential use of performance standards described below.

In applying these general formats to a particular debtor–creditor relationship, consideration must be given to not only the opportunities and points of leverage described above, but also the following concerns and issues:

1. *Accrual Rates*. Often, a workout is propose that includes the utilisation of a significantly higher "accrual rate" than the current servicing of the loan at the "pay rate". The obvious result of this arrangement is to create an ever-increasing amount of indebtedness against the property. The debtor should be wary of these sorts of arrangements and undertake calculations to determine what the debtor's loan balance is likely to be upon the expiration of the workout period. This concern is particularly significant in the event debtor is recourse on the loan. Even in a non-recourse situation, the concern is still paramount inasmuch as the debtor may have no practical avenue of maintaining ownership of the property at the expiration of the workout period and may prefer to have title conveyed currently.

2. *Tax Concerns*. Irrespective of the format utilised competent tax counsel should be involved in reviewing the workout structure for the tax effect. If a proposed restructure results in a deemed release from indebtedness for tax purposes, the debtor may be solv-

ing its immediate problem only to face a worse liability with the Internal Revenue Service.

3. *Definition of Net Cash Flow.* Most restructures pursuant to Format 2 above would entail some form of definition of "net cash flow" from the subject property. The definition of this term should be carefully reviewed by counsel, particularly as to the following issues.

(a) *Fees Paid to Affiliates.* Many real property owners typically pay brokerage and/or management fees to affiliate companies. Often, the creditors' formal net cash-flow definitions prohibit such fees being considered as expenses. One possible compromise is to allow such fees to be considered as expenses so long as they are "industry standard" or at specified levels.

(b) *Reserves.* Like most business, real property ownership has fluctuations throughout the year in terms of required expenses and available revenues. The debtor should be given the opportunity to maintain reserves to service irregular expenses (e.g. annual *ad valorem* taxes and annual insurance premiums).

(c) *Capital Improvements.* The debtor should evaluate the project in terms of likely capital improvements required in the future (e.g. tenant finish costs, a roof or other major component item in its twilight years etc.) and include these costs as authorised expenses in the net cash-flow formula.

(d) *Budget.* When a creditor requires the expense side of the net cash-flow formula be pursuant to an approved budget, a mechanism should be provided insuring the creditor's timely response to a proposed budget. For example, a proposed budget by the debtor might be deemed approved unless specific objections were received from the creditor within 10 days of proposal.

(e) *Professional Fees.* Legal and accounting fees should be included as allowable expenses in the net cash-flow calculation.

4. *Term of Restructure.* The tendency of many debtors is often toward the quick and easy, but temporary resolution of troubled loans. This natural tendency is enhanced by a creditor's preference to structure short-term arrangements. Particularly when the indebtedness is of a recourse nature, the debtor should consider where these sorts of restructures leave debtor in the next few years. If the debtor is setting itself up for an almost certain bankruptcy in three years' time, then he is wasting the next three years of income earnings against such a certain bankruptcy. Also, in the event a bankruptcy is a very likely alternative, many debtors would prefer examining this alternative in the present economic climate where a certain amount of the stigma has been diminished due to the vast number of bankruptcies currently being pursued.

5. *Performance Standards/Hurdles.* It is not unusual for a creditor to provide incentive to a debtor in a workout scenario whereby debtor's superior performance in some aspect of the transaction can result in a financial benefit to that debtor. These performance standards or "hurdles" can take many forms. In the context of Format No. 1, the debtor might be provided a pre-approved discount number in the event debtor should prepay the indebtedness evidenced by the deficiency note in a more rapid time frame than anticipated. In the context of Format No. 2, the debtor might be provided with a reduction in principal balance in the event net cash-flow production from the subject property is greater than anticipated. Likewise, in the context of Format No. 3, the debtor might be provided with a more aggressive release arrangement in the event a better price is obtained for the eventual benefit of the lender. These provisions obviously require a great deal of analysis. Consideration should also be given to the effect of such an arrangement on debtor's affiliates (e.g. real property brokerage companies) which might otherwise be reasonably expected to obtain a commission on a resale.

6. *Marketing Arrangement.* In the event that Format No. 3 should be utilised, the

lender and debtor should enter into a marketing arrangement to specify each such party's expectations and obligations during the period of forbearance. This marketing arrangement might describe certain of the performance standards or hurdles referenced above. Additionally, the lender's willingness to provide equity enhancement by way of aggressive "third party" financing should be explored. It should also be noted that, in today's environment, a delicate balance exists between the lienholder on the project and potential purchasers. The lender should be asked to enter into a non-disclosure arrangement to prevent interference in borrower's efforts to effectuate a sale transaction. Likewise, the lender may very well have its own concerns relative to non-disclosure and this would also be an appropriate document in which to address those.

7. *Ongoing Debtor Liability*. In each of the basic formats described, the potential for ongoing recourse liability of the debtor or its affiliates exists even after the workout is completed. Obviously, the debtor should carefully weigh this ongoing exposure in light of its financial expectations over the term repayment is required. The lender should also be pressed to consider creative alternatives in dealing with debtor's ongoing liability. Debtor may be able to bring in a new investor to the project and essentially provide a substitute credit. The lender will have to consider this proposed substitute credit in light of whatever debt subordination issues may also be required by the new investor. Another method to limit recourse exposure and provide appropriate incentives to the debtor is to limit debtor's ongoing recourse liability to a more modest specified sum but provide that such sum may magnify significantly in the event of debtor bankruptcy. While these arrangements are not uncommon, certain lenders will have concerns with respect to the legality and/or enforceability of this arrangement.

CHAPTER 10

REHABILITATION AND INSOLVENCY: THE GERMAN APPROACH

A LAW IN TRANSITION

The "bankruptcy of bankruptcy"

Bankruptcy procedure: the battle of the secured creditors

For over a century now, the German law of insolvency has been governed by a time-honoured statute, the Bankruptcy Code of 1877 (Konkursordnung, henceforth "KO"). Still regarded as a piece of legislation of technical excellence, the KO is not only showing signs of age, but increasingly works the opposite way to its very purpose of supplying a fair and effective liquidation procedure for debtors who have become insolvent. A recent study covering the years from 1985 to 1988 found[1] that over 75 per cent of all bankruptcy petitions filed had to be dismissed in the event because the realisable assets of the debtor—the "bankrupt's estate"[2]—did not cover the expenses of the liquidation procedure.[3] In 1950, the same figure had amounted to only 25 per cent.[4] In the few cases where courts do issue a bankruptcy or winding-up order,[5] insolvency proceedings are conspicuous for their failure to achieve anything short of a fair distribution of assets among the creditors. Secured and priority creditors will take the lion's share, whereas ordinary unsecured creditors come out with an average 3–5 per cent of their total claims.[6]

To make sense of these puzzling statistics some brief remarks on the German

1. All statistics are taken from: Regierungsentwurf Insolvenzordnung (InsO) (government-proposed Insolvency Bill) of 21 November 1991, *Official Comment* (Begründung), p. 1, *Bundesratsdrucksache 1/92*, p. 72.

2. "*Konkursmasse*". It is one of the peculiarities of German insolvency law to conceive of the debtor's assets available for distribution as a separate estate, excluding on the one hand property in the debtor's possession but belonging to others, or the debtor's post-insolvency income, but including any third-party property that has been gained through preferential treatment and may therefore be retrieved by the trustee in bankruptcy. See Baur/Stürner, *Insolvenzrecht* (3rd edn, 1991), § 12.

3. See s. 107(1) KO.

4. *Ibid.* (note 1).

5. Contrary to English law, the German insolvency law has never made any systematic distinction between insolvencies of private individuals and company winding-ups. Accordingly, throughout this chapter the term "bankruptcy" will be used indiscriminately for both personal and corporate insolvency.

6. See *supra*, note 1.

law of secured transactions are in order.[7] Due to their high debt–equity ratio, most companies in Germany hold the bulk of their assets not in real estate but in moveables, i.e. inventory of all sorts and accounts receivable. It is this part of their property which is utilised foremost to secure the company's short and middle-term credit financing.[8] To be more specific, the dominant type of security today is non-possessory security over goods and debts.

Suppliers of goods—to begin with the first eminent group of secured creditors—selling on a hire-purchase basis will secure such transactions by way of reserving their ownership of the goods delivered. In the purchaser's bankruptcy, goods delivered under such conditional sales may be recouped by the supplier as personal property.[9] Not in any respect is the supplier a participant in the bankruptcy proceeding: at most he may have to refund the purchaser's instalments to the bankrupt estate.

The matter becomes more complex if the purchaser is a manufacturer compounding or assembling materials which have been supplied by various sellers. For those cases the security instrument usually provides for an "extended" conditional sale,[10] according each supplier, as a substitute for the lost property, a *pro-rata* co-ownership in the end-product—again resulting in a separate realisation of the security in the manufacturer's bankruptcy. With the manufacturer selling the product in the usual course of business the supplier's security again ceases to exist, but, according to standard practice, is substituted by an anticipated (*pro-rata*) assignment of the sales proceeds.[11]

It is at this point that the suppliers' needs for adequate security clash with the competing interests of lenders. As the taking of security in real property hardly ever covers a borrower's overall financing needs and most of the personal property will be encumbered in favour of supplier-creditors,[12] lenders most often seek security by way of an assignment of all accounts receivable, present and future (*Globalzession*).[13] By necessity, such assignments conflict with prior or later assignments in favour of suppliers. Both groups of creditors prefer to carry out transfers "undisclosed", i.e. not communicating them to the debtor's customers until the debtor's financial condition becomes perilous. Therefore, it does not come as a surprise that double or even multiple assignments of the same accounts receivable have come to be common practice. Normally, this perennial conflict situation would be governed by the principle of "first come first serve", putting lenders at an advantage over suppliers. How-

7. The reader will find further useful hints on that topic in Chapter 1 of this volume by Philip Wood.

8. For long-term financing real property mortgages remain the preferred security device.

9. See KO, ss. 1, 43 *et seq.*

10. *Verlängerter Eigentumsvorbehalt.*

11. Creating a lien in money claims is possible but impractical under German law.

12. Banks' taking security in form of chattel mortgages (*Sicherungsübereignung*) is a viable option only to the extent that the claims of suppliers have been satisfied. For details, see Jährig/Schuck, *Handbuch des Kreditgeschäfts* (5th edn, 1989) pp. 667–688.

13. *Ibid.*, pp. 700–704. See also Scholz/Lwowski, *Das Recht der Kreditsicherung* (6th edn, 1986), pp. 536–550.

ever, when asked to address the legal conflict, the Federal Court in a succession of cases took side with the suppliers, invalidating global assignments to lenders as *contra bonos mores*,[14] even if the secured loan transaction had been executed prior to a supplier's "extended" conditional sale.[15]

Assigning sales proceeds or accounts receivable for security is—for reasons not to be explained in this chapter—by and large equivalent to granting a lien. Contrary to a reservation of ownership, this technique does not segregate assignees from a later bankruptcy proceeding against the borrower/purchaser, but ensures them preferential satisfaction in priority to all other debts.[16] It is important to understand that the law grants the holder of such security the privilege to realise his interest on his own, and at the risk and the expense of the bankrupt's estate; the trustee in bankruptcy[17] may take action only if the secured creditor is in default.[18] Only in so far as the proceeds from realisation of the security interest do not match the unpaid balance of the debt will the lender or supplier have to take the role of an ordinary creditor.[19]

All this places secured creditors in a position pre-eminent not only by their substantive but also by their procedural rights. Small wonder then that today's insolvencies are mostly little more than a battle between lenders and suppliers to grasp a larger piece of the pie.[20] Taken by itself, however, the position of secured creditors is far from being satisfactory.[21] Leaving the debtor in possession of the security facilitates his trading freely with the encumbered assets. Granting concurrent or double security in the same asset causes sizeable costs for creditors of identifying and sorting out their relative security interests. Empirical surveys show that both lenders and suppliers suffer considerable losses in the realisation of their security.[22]

Arrangement procedure

Insufficiency of realisable assets and unequal distribution are but two serious shortcomings of the present law of bankruptcy. As early as the First World War an awareness arose that the inevitable and forced liquidation of an insolvent debtor's property, particularly by dismantling a debtor's business as a going concern, was indeed a lamentable waste of economic resources and

14. Civil Code (Bürgerliches Gesetzbuch of 1900), s. 138(1).

15. See Bundesgerichtshof, BGHZ 55, 35; 98, 315. Lenders have reacted to this ruling by explicitly releasing in their instruments such claims that are likely to become subject to a supplier's conditional sale; see Jährig/Schuck, *supra* note 12, at pp. 701–704.

16. Absonderungsrecht; see KO, ss. 4, 47 *et seq*.

17. The term "trustee in bankruptcy" includes the function of an "official receiver" in company winding-ups under UK law.

18. KO, s. 127(2).

19. KO, s. 64.

20. See also following text, accompanying note 54.

21. See J. Drukarczyk, "Insolvenzrecht als Versuch marktkonformer Gestaltung von Verwertungsentscheidungen und Verteilungsregeln", *Zeitschrift für Wirtschaftsrecht (ZIP) 1989*, 341, 345.

22. *Ibid.*

should no longer be the law's sole response to the complex issues of insolvency. The automatic machinery of liquidation had to be supplemented by an alternative collective remedy allowing for a survival of ailing, yet still viable businesses. Thus, after some interim measures, in 1927 new legislation was enacted instituting a supplementary insolvency proceeding ostensively designed to avoid bankruptcy under appropriate circumstances and to protect the "honest but unfortunate" debtor. To implement this policy goal an insolvent debtor was permitted to seek a collective arrangement with his creditors under close supervision by a court.

Although the basic approach of this Arrangement Act (Vergleichsordnung, as amended 26 February 1935, henceforth: "VglO")[23] was remarkable at the time and may be considered an early precursor of modern rehabilitation schemes, the Act has proved to be all but a spectacular success. Its practical relevance has come to be almost negligible, with less than 1 per cent court-approved arrangements in the years subsequent to 1983, compared with 30 per cent in 1950 and 8 per cent in 1970.[24] Whatever could be said in favour of the rehabilitative philosophy of the Act was outweighed by numerous and serious congenital defects, which never let the arrangement procedure perform its intended function as a viable alternative to bankruptcy. Here are just a few of those pitfalls.[25]

1. The debtor has to make his choice whether to file bankruptcy or to go for an arrangement at a moment when the prospects for rehabilitation cannot be sized up with reasonable certainty. Once a bankruptcy order has been made, any petition for arrangement is precluded (cf. VglO, s. 2(2)).
2. It is the debtor who must take the opening move submitting a proposal as to a revision and/or rescheduling of his indebtedness (VglO, ss. 2(1), 3(1)). The creditors are constrained to a largely inactive role, deciding on the debtor's proposal on a take-it-or-leave-it basis.
3. Secured creditors do not by operation of law participate in the collective bargaining being the basis of any arrangement proceeding (VglO,

23. For details of the legislative history see Baur/Stürmer (*supra* note 2) p. 10; see also Bundesministerium der Justiz (ed.), *Erster Bericht der Kommission für Insolvenzrecht* (1985), p. 4.

24. See *Official Comment* (*supra* note 1), p. 72. In recent times, to the knowledge of this writer, there has been just one single large-volume arrangement considered a success; the insolvency of the electronics and engineering concern Allgemeine Elektrizitätsgesellschaft (AEG) in the early 1980s. The success was based upon a set of favourable preconditions.
— The principal creditor banks waived substantial parts of the unpaid balance of their loans.
— Subsequent to the commencement of the arrangement procedure, the company's equity capital was, by resolution of the general assembly, first reduced and then reincreased, with most of the issued stock acquired by the creditor banks.
— A comprehensive asset disposal programme was effected.
— After the remainder of AEG's business units had regained profitability, the banks sold out to Daimler-Benz for a handsome profit.

25. For a brief summary of the shortcomings of the arrangement procedure cf. M. Balz, *Sanierung von Unternehmen oder von Unternehmensträgern*? (1986), p. 14 *et seq.*

ss. 27, 28) because they are supposed to lack an adequate incentive to compromise. As they are not only dominant in value but also have security interests in most of the assets the debtor needs to carry on his business, this provision frustrates if not defeats any meaningful effort at rehabilitation.

4. The debtor is required to offer the creditors a non-negotiable minimum dividend of 35 per cent of their total claims (VglO, s. 7(1)). Given the fact that, almost by tradition, German businesses operate with a comparatively high debt–equity ratio,[26] this lower limit seems unrealistic.
5. In corporate insolvencies there is no way of having the company's members participate in the formal arrangement procedure. This may hamper attempts to make the rehabilitation of the debtor's business contingent upon a corporate restructuring—which is frequently the royal road to success.

As a matter of principle, the availability of two concurrent collective remedies each with different and, to a certain extent, conflicting ends poses some difficulties of its own. The arrangement procedure generally leaves the debtor in possession of his property,[27] at the same time keeping the creditors in an inferior position. From the debtor's filing an arrangement petition until the court order closing the procedure no bankruptcy petition may be presented nor execution be commenced or continued (ss. 13, 46–48 of the VglO). All this is a strong incentive for dishonest debtors to gamble on the point of time where bankruptcy becomes inevitable,[28] thus obstructing the creditors' timely taking charge of the debtor's business activities.

It was a fair view of the current state of the German law of insolvency when, in 1975, one of Germany's most prominent insolvency practitioners proclaimed the "bankruptcy of bankruptcy".[29] Reading such grim diagnoses a foreign observer may wonder how the Germans, beyond merely muddling through, still manage to handle insolvency matters in an orderly and effective fashion. In brief, we stick to the widely held belief that, where a body of law fails to generate efficient results, the market will find ways and means of "contracting around". Creditors, debtors and insolvency practitioners alike have, indeed, long worked their escape routes out of the pitfalls of the black letter law.

26. See Karsten Schmidt, "Die Eigenkapitalausstattung der Unternehmen als rechtspolitisches Problem", *Juristenzeitung 1984*, 771.

27. Appointment of a trustee is mandatory (cf. VglO, ss. 20(1), 38) but the trustee's role is, other than a trustee's in bankruptcy, only supervisory (ss. 39, 40, VglO). The insolvency court can, however, put some constraints on the debtor's capacity to sell or otherwise dispose of his property (VglO, ss. 57–59).

28. The court then has, *ex officio*, to order a "consequential bankruptcy procedure" (*Anschlußkonkurs*, cf. ss. 102 *et seq.* VglO).

29. Joachim Kilger, "Konkurs des Konkurses", *Konkurs-, Treuhands- und Schiedsgerichtswesen (KTS) 1975*, 142.

Escape routes

Voluntary arrangements: "reorganisation through liquidation"

Voluntary and consensual (i.e. out of court) collective arrangements may function as a "silent" liquidation or reorganisation of a corporate debtor who is actually insolvent.[30] Silent liquidations to a certain extent include insolvencies where the debtor's assets would not cover the expenses for a formal proceeding.[31] Furthermore, voluntary agreements have come to be the most common mode of rehabilitating a corporate debtor running into financial difficulties.[32] Paradoxically, even in bankruptcy proceedings, with liquidation of the debtor's property as their ostensible goal, loopholes have been found to prevent precipitous and inefficient liquidations failing to realise the property's value as a going concern.

Occasional practice, particularly in insolvencies of larger firms, are bulk sales by a trustee in bankruptcy of a corporate debtor's entire business, or of single operating units, to another company, which sometimes has been formed by a group of dominant creditors or long-term customers for the very purpose of serving as a buyer in the rescue action.[33] The debtor retains the liabilities of the business entity, but in turn realises a higher liquidation value. It is then the debtor's business rather than the debtor's company which is the target of reorganisation. As total liquidation invariably not only diminishes market value of the assets that are put on sale, but is also a first-rank job killer, this "rehabilitation by way of liquidation"[34] promotes the goals of both economic efficiency and social policy.

German law presents, however, some obstacles to the separation of assets and liabilities being the effect of a bulk sale. Civil Code (BGB), s. 419 provides that any wholesale takeover of a property (or a substantial part thereof[35]) will make the acquiring party jointly liable for the whole of the transferring party's obligations.[36] It has long been recognised, to be sure, that this rule is not to be applied to bulk sales in the course of a bankruptcy proceeding, because its pur-

30. Estimates are that such "silent liquidations" amount to more than 40 per cent of corporate insolvency cases where a bankruptcy petition is filed. Cf. Gessner/Rhode/Strate/Ziegert, *Die Praxis der Konkursabwicklung in der Bundesrepublik Deutschland—eine rechtssoziologische Untersuchung* (1978), p. 539.

31. *Supra*, text accompanying note 1.

32. Cf. Gessner/Rhode/Strate/Ziegert, *supra* note 30, *passim*.

33. For more details see P. J. Groß, *Sanierung durch Fortführungsgesellschaften* (2nd edn, 1988).

34. To quote from the leading insolvency text book; cf. Baur/Stürner, *supra* note 2, at p. 17.

35. The critical margin for such a wholesale takeover lies between 85 and 90 per cent of total assets. The acquiring party needs, however, to be aware of the fact that it is taking over approximately the whole property. Cf. Münchner Kommentar BGB/Möschel § 419, margin number 13.

36. The same is true for taking over a business unit (not necessarily being the vendor's entire property), with the purchaser carrying on the unit's firm name. Here, however, the acquiring party is permitted to disclaim its liability in the sales contract; the disclaimer will be binding on creditors if made public through the medium of the official firm register. See Commercial Code (Handelsgesetzbuch), s. 25.

pose of preventing debtors from putting their property beyond their creditor's reach will not be affected by such transactions.[37] Still, by involving substantial risks for potential buyers s. 419 remains a stumbling stone on the way to successful voluntary rescue operations. Therefore, it stands a good chance of being explicitly repealed by the new insolvency law.[38]

Even more adversely affected are attempts at "reorganisation by way of liquidation" by Civil Code, s. 613a. Implementing an EEC Directive of 1977,[39] s. 613a(1) makes the buyer of a business or a business unit a party to any existing employment contract, succeeding the vendor in rights and obligations arising from such contracts. And subs. 4 bars the purchaser from terminating any employment contract on the sole ground of his becoming the new employer. Again, the courts took great pains to curb the adverse effects of this rule in insolvency cases. Restoring an ailing business to a profitable enterprise will seldom be achieved without some effort at rationalisation and, therefore, cutting back on the work force. Facing the uneasy alternative of either disregarding the unambiguous wording of s. 613a or making an insolvent debtor's business an unmerchantable commodity with, in the event, all of the employees deprived of their jobs, the Bundesarbeitsgericht (the highest German labour court) has chosen to stick to the black letter rule, thus placing a higher value on job security. However, the court tried to ease the new employer's burden by limiting his liability to payments falling due subsequent to the transfer of the business unit; claims with prior maturities[40] have to be asserted and enforced within the regular insolvency proceeding.[41] This ruling may be perceived as an attempt to reconcile the goal of job security underlying s. 613a with the conflicting principle of *par conditio creditorum*, which goes to the root of the law of bankruptcy. According to a recent empirical survey, an overwhelming majority of insolvency practitioners and other persons and agencies handling insolvency matters none the less identify s. 613a as a principal cause for failures, or obstructions, in selling a debtor's business.[42]

There are still other, if less conspicuous, barriers to a bulk sale of a business

37. Cf. Möschel, *supra*, note 35. The same is true for the related provision in Commercial Code, s. 25 (see note 36).

38. Article 8 of the Insolvency Bill 1991. See *infra*, text following note 65. This view of the Insolvency Bill has been challenged for good reasons by Karsten Schmidt, "Was wird aus der Haftung nach § 419 BGB?", *Zeitschrift für Wirtschaftsrecht (ZIP) 1989*, 1025. Professor Schmidt argues that a decision on the separation of assets and liabilities cannot legitimately be made without consent of the creditors.

39. Council Directive of 14 February 1977, 77/187/EEC.

40. Which comprise not only arrears of pay but also expectancies as to future payments from pension funds contingent on the employee's retirement or disablement.

41. See Bundesarbeitsgericht of 17 January 1980, *Official Reporter* vol. 32, 326 (relating to bankruptcy procedure); Bundesarbeitsgericht of 4 April 1989, *Zeitschrift für Wirtschaftsrecht (ZIP) 1989*, 1422 (arrangement procedure). See also K.G. Loritz, "Aktuelle Probleme des Betriebsübergangs nach § 613a BGB", *Recht der Arbeit 1987*, 65.

42. See E. Keller-Stoltenhoff, *Die rechtstatsächlichen Auswirkungen des § 613a BGB im Konkurs* (1986).

unit.[43] One crucial point is that secured creditors go along. They own, or hold charges, liens, or other security on, substantial parts of the firm's productive assets as, e.g. real property, technical equipment or supplies. Among all creditors they have the least to gain from any kind of rescue operation. This disincentive to co-operate is aggravated by the fact that the German law of bankruptcy grants secured creditors—as has been said before[44]—a largely unassailable procedural position by permitting them to pursue their interests individually and more or less apart from the formal bankruptcy proceeding. It is then for the trustee in bankruptcy (or the administrator in arrangement procedures, respectively) to persuade the secured creditors that their interests too will be best served by effecting a standstill agreement rather than breaking away with individual repossessions or foreclosures.

Further difficulties arise because the (provisional[45]) trustee usually has to maintain business operations for a considerable time before a bulk sale can be executed. Subject to creditor approval[46] the trustee is explicitly permitted to act in an entrepreneurial function, as, and as long as, he thinks fit.[47] He will then seek interim financing enabling him to pay the firm's work force[48] and, if he is trustee of an industrial operation, to continue current, and take up new, production. Interim trustees call on the principal creditor bank to provide a short-term loan, taking for collateral the employees' undisbursed social security claims.[49] Financing of other working capital requirements is frequently made available by creditor groups organised as a security pool[50]; new security may be granted from the proportion of future sale proceeds not yet assigned to other creditors.[51] Taking new security, albeit the debtor's predicament has become manifest, does not constitute a voidable preferential treatment of such creditors, as the secured loan is a "cash transaction,"[52] which will not normally impair the position of other creditors.

43. For practical details see B. M. Kübler, "Unternehmenskauf und Konkurs", *Zeitschrift für Unternehmens- und Gesellschaftsrecht (ZGR) 1982*, 498.

44. *Supra*, text accompanying note 16.

45. So-called *Sequester*, appointed by virtue of KO, s. 106(1).

46. Preliminary approval may be granted by the creditors' committee (KO, s. 129(2)), definite approval is reserved for the creditors' meeting (KO, s. 132(1)).

47. Given that any bankruptcy proceeding is to end up in liquidation, the trustee's running the debtor's business has to be a transient matter. It is, however, a matter of controversy how long this state of transiency may last. In a liability suit brought against a trustee in bankruptcy the German Federal Court (Bundesgerichtshof [BGH]) found that carrying on the debtor's business for eight (!) years did not in itself amount to an abuse of the trustee's powers; see BGH in *Zeitschrift für Wirtschaftsrecht 1980*, 851.

48. Arrears of pay which have summed up in the last three months prior to the bankruptcy order are compensated by social security payments (*Konkursausfallgeld*); see Arbeitsförderungsgesetz, ss. 141a *et seq.*

49. See note 48.

50. More on security pools in the following paragraph.

51. B.M. Kübler, *supra* note 43, at 505/6.

52. See Baur/Stürner, *supra* note 2, § 19 lll 2 b aa. The new law will be more explicit on "cash transactions" (*Bargeschäfte*); see Insolvency Bill of 1991, s. 161.

Security pool agreements

Security pool agreements have originated from the practical difficulties arising when, mostly in large-scale insolvencies, a multitude of secured creditors concurs in seeking to realise their respective security interests in the same kind of assets or any portions thereof. As has been said before,[53] it is common practice of both lenders and suppliers to take floating charges as security, generating discrete and highly fragmented rights and interests mainly in inventory and accounts receivable. Since most creditors, when recouping their security from the trustee in bankruptcy, would not assume the burden to prove whether, e.g. the semi-finished products in warehouse X or Y are subject to lender A's or supplier B's charge, groups of secured lenders and suppliers selling on the basis of hire-purchase transactions joined in making security pool agreements,[54] at the outset primarily for the purpose of relieving the burden of proof and none the less ensuring an orderly and fair realisation of the encumbered assets. Normally, the creditors participating in a pool would not co-ordinate their interests by creating a lien in favour of a pool agent,[55] but lump together their relative rights and interests, enabling them to recoup all of the security jointly and to leave distribution according to each participant's share to negotiation among the partners.[56] A related technique to cope with such practical difficulties has bank creditors and suppliers and/or their credit insurance carriers agreeing on fixed quotas of distribution of the moneys available from realisation of the whole of encumbered assets. There is an ongoing debate as to which proportion of the pie might constitute a fair share for each of the two creditor groups.[57]

When pool agreements became popular in the 1970s, they were challenged for their interfering with third-party rights, namely of creditors choosing not to participate. Today, the Federal Court (Bundesgerichtshof) and majority opinion reject this argument since the partners of a pool agreement do not intend to transfer more rights than each partner actually has,[58] and their co-operating for a joint enforcement of their individual rights is a legally valid option.[59] However, for a joint enforcement to work effectively, the organisers of a "mixed" pool[60] need to make every effort in order to have as many

53. See *supra*, text accompanying note 11.

54. The interests of suppliers are frequently represented by credit insurance carriers.

55. As seems to be common practice in the US.

56. Some standard form arrangements are reprinted in E. Bohlen, *Der Sicherheiten-Pool* (1984), pp. 135–155.

57. Cf. Jährig/Schuck, *supra* note 12 at 712/3.

58. It may, however, constitute a voidable preferential treatment if, in a pre-insolvency agreement, the debtor himself grants new security.

59. See Bundesgerichtshof in *Zeitschrift für Wirtschaftsrecht (ZIP) 1982*, 543, 545; *Betriebsberater 1988*, 2340. For the legal literature, see Kuhn/Uhlenbruck, *Kommentar zur Konkursordnung* (10th edn, 1986), § 4, margin number 13.

60. Meaning pools with both lenders and suppliers participating.

suppliers (i.e. co-owners of raw materials, semi-finished products etc.) participate as possible.

As pool agreements came to be more or less unchallenged they have evolved as a powerful and multi-purpose instrument, particularly in the hand of lenders. When dealing with large-scale borrowers involving a larger number of lenders but a limited supply of potential security, banks will effect a pool agreement as early as they are making their respective loan commitments with the debtor.[61] Whereas in the case of post-insolvency security pools the agreement is based on an inter-creditor accord, the debtor now has to be a party to the agreement because the latter is an integral component of the secured transaction. For practical convenience, to secure payment of the claims of all participating lenders an all-inclusive security interest will be created in favour of one agent bank—mostly the principal lender—acting as a trustee for the other partners for all purposes of administration and realisation. The distribution measure will be *pro rata* and tied to a fixed trigger date. If, and to the extent that, the individual lines of credit have not been disbursed in full, netting-out operations will straighten out the undisbursed balances. Advances in excess of an agreed line of credit may, if not made with the others' consent, be compensated if there is a remaining balance after the claims initially agreed upon have been satisfied.[62]

Security pools have become, and will remain under the new law,[63] a major player in rehabilitation schemes.[64] By virtue of their large number, as well as of their holding security interests in most of the inventory, pool creditors have a powerful voice in the collective bargaining preceding any reorganisation. At the least, the participants in a pool agreement will be inclined to allow payments falling due to be deferred, enabling the trustee in bankruptcy to maintain business operations for a limited period of time, such as to realise the fair market value of the encumbered assets instead of a lower break-up value availing in a forced liquidation. Where the assets combined in the pool are vital for a business unit to operate, the pool creditors are likely to gain, and wield, substantial influence on the management of the debtor company. Especially when it comes to asset disposals, any decision-making by the trustee in bankruptcy will be subject to the pool agent's approval. On the other hand, the pool creditors may actively further a rescue operation, e.g. advancing working capital for paying the workforce and maintaining production. Those working capital loans will then enjoy first priority in the order of distribution of the pool cash. Where several security pools are concurring, the trustee will seek to organise a "pool

61. For details the reader is referred to Scholz/Lwowski, *supra* note 13, at pp. 218–223.
62. Scholz/Lwowski, *ibid*. at pp. 220/1.
63. See Insolvency Bill (*supra* note 1), official comment A 3 b; comments on § 30 and § 266.
64. An illustrative example is the form pool agreement reprinted in E. Bohlen (*supra* note 56), at p. 149 *et seq*.

of pools" with *pro-rata* quotas for the distribution of the proceeds expected from a contemplated bulk sale.[65]

Summing up, it may be said that the functioning of some security pools is a parallel private bankruptcy procedure of its own.

A concise chronology of law reform[66]

The "bankruptcy of bankruptcy", heralded in 1975,[67] soon proliferated as a watchword for the first serious movement for law reform in about hundred years. The Federal Minister of Justice set the agenda for reform when, in 1978, he appointed a "Committee for Insolvency Law" made up of experienced insolvency practitioners, academic lawyers and representatives from business organisations, trade unions and the banking industry.

The report of the Committee for Insolvency Law

The assignment of the Committee was defined in broad terms including a thorough review of the entire body of law relating to insolvency and, more specifically, a thorough re-examination of the functioning of non-possessory security over goods and debts. In 1985 the Committee submitted a voluminous report, making a powerful case for fundamental reform and spelling out comprehensive recommendations for a new and integrated law of insolvency.[68] Since a great deal of this has been incorporated into the official Insolvency Bill, I need not go into details here.[69] Some proposals for a more radical change, e.g. the paramountcy of rehabilitation in corporate insolvencies and the discharge by court order to be granted in personal bankruptcies—were in fact imports from the new American Bankruptcy Code of 1976. Remarkable was the new approach of the Committee with respect to non-possessory security interests over moveables. To replenish the "impoverished" insolvent's estate, such security should be made part of the estate. Holders of non-possessory security would not be permitted to recoup or realise the encumbered assets as a rehabilitation procedure was pending. Moreover, under a rehabilitation scheme, their security was at risk of being "devalued" by up to 50 per cent, putting them for the remaining balance in the position of ordinary creditors. In a liquidation procedure, only the trustee in bankruptcy should be entitled to realise the security, discounting a 25 per cent "contribution" from the proceeds. Even mortgagees were to be charged a 10 per cent contribution. Finally,

65. See B. M. Kübler, *supra* note 43, at pp. 504/5.
66. For a more comprehensive historical account see Baur/Stürner, *supra* note 2, § 4.
67. See *supra*, note 28.
68. *Erster Bericht der Kommission für Insolvenzrecht* (Federal Ministry of Justice ed. 1985); *Zweiter Bericht* (1986).
69. See *infra*, p. 207 *et seq*.

the report did away with any kind of preferential debt (namely: remuneration of employees, social security contributions, debts due to Inland Revenue).

The Insolvency Bill of 21 November 1991

In late 1982—just before the Committee put forward its report—a new conservative–liberal federal government had stepped in. The conversion of the political climate in the wake of this change of government could not leave the work of the Committee unaffected. When the incoming administration in 1988 submitted a first Draft Bill authored by the Ministry of Justice,[70] the Bill bore the hallmarks of a more liberal, market-oriented philosophy, its theoretical approach drawing heavily on the American-based economic analysis of law with its emphasis on economic efficiency, its substantive goals aiming at greater procedural autonomy for the creditors and less committed to job preservation and employee (or union) participation.

The movement for law reform seemed to have suffered a perilous blow when German unification came in late 1990. The Unification Treaty of 31 August 1990, while as a rule effecting legal unification plainly by way of adoption of the former West German law, provided that the states on the territory of the former German Democratic Republic (GDR) retain, subject only to a comprehensive reform of insolvency law in all of Germany, their existing insolvency law, the Gesamtvollstreckungsordnung (GesO) of 6 June 1990.

The GesO[71] had been passed by the first (and last) freely elected GDR Parliament when German unification had already become a political necessity. Its substance compounds elements of the old Konkursordnung of 1877 with bits taken from the West German law reform project.[72] The GesO is a statute of a scanty 22 sections; it abounds with unsettled questions and lacunas, by default calling for analogous application of the relevant provisions of the old KO.[73] It should be emphasised that the GesO is *not* inter-temporal law such as being applicable solely to companies residing on GDR territory before unification took effect.

Subsequent to German unification the tenet prevailed that the Federal Government would stay the law-making process for some time to allow the courts and the Treuhandanstalt—the latter appointed a trustee over all the formerly socialist state enterprises—to follow through with the GesO. Therefore,

70. A semi-official "*Diskussionsentwurf*" of August 1988 was soon followed by a *Referentenentwurf Gesetz zur Reform des Insolvenzrechts* of 1 November 1989 (Federal Ministry of Justice ed. 1989).

71. Reprinted in *Zeitschrift für Wirtschaftsrecht (ZIP) 1990*, 1231–1237.

72. Cf. GesO ss. 8(2), 17(1) (bulk sales by administrator); also s. 18(2) (limited discharge by exempting post-bankruptcy income of the debtor, which is "appropriate" to his life style, from execution). By virtue of a complementary statute (Gesetz über die Unterbrechung von Gesamtvollstreckungsverfahren, also reprinted in *Zeitschrift für Wirtschaftsrecht 1990* 1234–1236), the procedure may be stayed to prevent precipitous liquidations, if a guarantor (basically the Treuhandanstalt or banks) files a petition to this effect.

73. For any details see S. Smid (ed.), *Gesamtvollstreckungsordnung Kommentar* (1991).

it took most experts by surprise when the government in November 1991 came forward with an official Insolvency Bill (Regierungsentwurf Insolvenzordnung of 21 November 1991[74]; for convenience henceforth: "Insolvency Bill"). The Bill is a slightly revised follow-up of the Draft Bill of 1988/89.[75] Of monumental dimensions, it is accompanied by comprehensive and detailed official comments which will continue to provide a point of reference for some time to come. The odds are—if we may speculate about the timetable for enactment—that the Bill will be presented to the legislative bodies in the course of 1992, and that the new Insolvency Act may take effect by 1993/94.[76]

THE LEGAL POSITION OF BANK CREDITORS UNDER THE INSOLVENCY BILL

Principles and policy considerations of the Insolvency Bill

In its Official Comment, the Insolvency Bill is remarkably explicit about the principles and policy goals it seeks to implement.[77] It almost emphatically embraces a philosophy of "let the market take care of itself".[78] Whatever may survive of this philosophy in after-enactment day-to-day court practice, it has been pivotal for quite a number of both substantive and procedural principles forming the framework of the new law.[79] In this chapter, I will focus on aspects of particular relevancy to banks.[80]

The paramountcy of creditor governance

The Bill shifts emphasis from the goal of fair distribution of the debtor's assets to the goal of providing an economically efficient realisation procedure with a minimum of transaction costs. Efficiency is best served if decision-making is committed to an unhampered collective bargaining among creditors, owners (company members, shareholders), and employees who, acting as mobile financiers, pursue and balance their respective interests. The principle of

74. See *supra*, note 1.

75. See text *supra*, accompanying note 68. A survey of the revised provisions is given by H. G. Landfermann, " Regierungsentwurf einer neuen Insolvenzordnung vom 21.11.1991", *Zeitschrift für Wirtschaftsrecht (ZIP) 1991*, 1660.

76. The law-making process will no doubt gain momentum from adverse experience made in practising the GesO in the former GDR.

77. See *Official Comment*, Part A. See also the authentic interpretation of the reformers' policy goals by the former legal counsel to the Minister of Justice, Manfred Balz; M. Balz, "Die Ziele des Reformentwurfs", in B. Kübler (ed.), *Neuordnung des Insolvenzrechts* (1989), pp. 1–19.

78. Unmindful of the golden rule that legislators should make good law rather than embark on theoretical adventures.

79. For an economic analysis of the Draft Bill see J. Drukarczyk, "Insolvenzrecht als Versuch marktkonformer Gestaltung von Verwertungsentscheidungen und Verteilungsregeln", *Zeitschrift für Wirtschaftsrecht (ZIP) 1989*, 341.

80. Skipping such interesting details as the provisions relating to discharge or to the position of employees in their employer's insolvency.

creditor governance is paramount; both the administrator (Insolvenzverwalter)—who will replace the trustee in bankruptcy of present law—and the insolvency court[81] are kept to a subordinate position.

The insolvency court is not, in the first instance, a defender of the public interest and an advocate of social policy, but a guardian over procedural propriety and fairness, and an intermediary dealing with conflicting demands. Only if invoked for the protection of a minority of creditors is the court permitted to exercise overriding powers by setting aside a resolution of the creditor meeting which discriminates against individual or groups of creditors.[82] Similarly, the administrator shall not conceive of his office as a controlling person, but as a trustee for the creditors. Therefore, in all matters of importance, he has to seek approval of his decisions by the creditor meeting.

At the core of autonomous decision-making by creditors and owners lies the choice between an insolvent liquidation and rehabilitation, be it of the debtor company or of the company's business. While the Committee Report had considered rehabilitation of the corporate debtor the remedy of first order, whereas liquidation should avail as a remedy of last resort,[83] the Insolvency Bill does not attempt to impose either remedy, but facilitates an autonomous choice by granting groups of priority creditors, or major company members, the privilege to propose an insolvency plan of their own making.[84] Furthermore, as to the substance of insolvency plans, the Bill allows considerable leeway to depart from the legal order of distribution.[85]

Facilitating rehabilitation in an integrated procedure

It is not only the option to submit an insolvency plan which is designed to facilitate rehabilitation. The "classical" grounds on which the court may order the commencement of insolvency proceedings[86]—namely the debtor's inability to pay his debts as they fall due; for corporate debtors in addition, the deficiency of the assets as compared with liabilities (balance sheet insolvency)—have been supplemented by a novel ground of "imminent insolvency",[87] enabling debtors *and* creditors—especially employees—to enjoy the advantages of the formal procedure before the debtor's financial condition becomes hopeless. Another "barrier to entry" has been removed by allowing a bankruptcy order to be

81. A specialised division of the court of first instance, the Amtsgericht; see Insolvency Bill, s. 2.

82. See Insolvency Bill, s. 89 (general provision), s. 298 (resolutions approving insolvency plan). The protection of minorities in resolutions over insolvency plans has widely been criticised as too far-reaching by giving rise to blackmail actions by minority creditors; see B. M. Kübler, "Die Stellung der Verfahrensorgane im Lichte der Gläubigerautonomie", in B. M. Kübler (ed.), *supra* note 77, at p. 74 *et seq.*

83. See *Erster Bericht* (*supra* note 68), Leitsatz 1.3.4.4 (at p. 149 *et seq.*).

84. Insolvency Bill, ss. 254–255.

85. Insolvency Bill, ss. 253, 264–269.

86. See KO, ss. 102, 207, 209.

87. Insolvency Bill, s. 22. Insolvency is defined as being "imminent" if the debtor will presumably be unable to pay his existing debts by the time they fall due; *ibid.*, s. 22(2).

issued even if the realisable assets will cover only the expenses of the initial stage of the procedure—leaving the rest to the imagination of the participants.

The need for more flexibility and adaptability to changing circumstances made a compelling case for an integrated insolvency procedure. Not only does the Bill put an end to the compartmentalisation of insolvent liquidation (bankruptcy) and rehabilitation (arrangement), providing a unified procedural frame for either purpose; it lets the participants throughout make their choices short of forced liquidation as they think fit.

Secured creditors

As has been observed at the outset of this chapter, the fatal flaw of present bankruptcy law is that it does not ensure the bankrupt's estate will retain adequate assets such as to allow the commencement of a formal procedure in the first place; and it is the holders of non-possessory security who take the blame for "plundering" what is left of the insolvent debtor's property. To remedy this shortcoming the Insolvency Bill does not adopt the proposal, advocated by radical opponents of the present law, to substantially curtail, if not do away with, privileges growing out of non-possessory security in the debtor's insolvency.[88] Following through with its market-oriented philosophy, the Bill takes for granted the privilege of creditors-financiers to safeguard themselves against the hazards of insolvency by means of pre-insolvency contractual arrangement. At the same time it rejects any attempts to make insolvency law an instrument of redistribution among different classes of creditors.[89]

To a certain extent, however, this "pure theory" fell victim to the political trade-offs to be made in the course of every legislative procedure.[90] As employees and the state were divested of their status as priority creditors,[91] the Bill charged holders of non-possessory security with a lump sum contribution to "liquidation expenses" in the amount of 11 per cent of the moneys availing from the realisation of their security.[92] Again, it must not be overlooked that the market will "contract around" this provision, with creditors exacting security such as to compensate them for any liquidation costs. Since holders of reserved title under a conditional sale of goods are not in this comfortable position, they have been exempted from paying any contributions.

While the Insolvency Bill imposes hardly any restrictions on the substantive claims of secured creditors, it is all the more eager to involve them in the

88. To a certain extent, this had been the approach of the Committee Report; see *supra*, text accompanying note 68.

89. More on the order of distribution in the following paragraph.

90. See Landfermann, *supra* note 75, at 1661.

91. See *infra*, text accompanying note 98.

92. Six per cent thereof for "identification expenses", 5 per cent for "realisation expenses"; see Insolvency Bill, s. 196. It is subject to proof that the real expenses exceed, or fall short of, the lump sum. For the realisation of chattel mortgages an additional discount for VAT has to be made; *ibid.*, s. 195(2).

collective bargaining and decision-making being the essence of the new insolvency procedure. The KO let them pursue their interests outside the bankruptcy proceeding with its specific pressure to compromise. Indeed, the KO vested them, by virtue of their holding claims on all assets essential to carry on the debtor's business, with some kind of veto power over any efforts at rehabilitation. The Insolvency Bill provides for an automatic stay of individual remedies in the hand of secured creditors such as repossession of mortgaged chattels or collection of accounts receivable assigned for security.[93] Utilisation, administration and realisation of all non-possessory[94] security *other than reserved ownership*[95] are assigned to the administrator who is authorised to postpone realisation of moveables while they are needed to carry on the debtor's business.[96] To be sure, imposing a co-responsibility for optimal realisation of the insolvent's estate may amount to a partial expropriation of secured creditors. Accordingly, they are entitled to some compensation for this forced contribution. After a waiting period of up to three months they are permitted to claim post-insolvency interest on their debt; if the administrator utilises an encumbered asset for the estate, he has to compensate holders of such security through periodic payments for the wear and tear.[97]

Order of distribution

For purposes of what it thinks to be a fair distribution, the KO has established—beyond segregating secured creditors—13 different classes of preferential debt,[98] most prominent among them the claims of employees, pension funds, social security and Inland Revenue. "Class societies" are almost inherently unjust; moreover, they are ill-suited to engage in co-operative problem-solving. Accordingly, the Insolvency Bill abolishes all preferential debts other than the costs and expenses of the proceeding and the liabilities incurred by the

93. Insolvency Bill, ss. 58, 191. Note that the creditor may collect accounts receivable by himself, if the assignment has been disclosed to the third-party debtor (*ibid.* s. 191(2)); however, such "disclosed" assignments seldom occur in practice.

94. Assets charged with possessive security are not part of the debtor's "operative" assets; hence, realisation of such security by creditors will not impede the administrator carrying on the debtor's business. This is of practical importance for banks, which, by virtue of No. 19 of their standard form contract, hold charges in all of their customer's moveables being in their possession (e.g. negotiable instruments, stock certificates, bonds etc.).

95. By a last-minute amendment, reservation of title by conditional sale of goods remains the only type of non-possessory security to be realised outside the insolvency procedure; *ibid.* s. 54. Only by electing to perform the sales contract fully (i.e. paying the agreed price instead of a mere insolvency dividend), can the administrator impede retrieval of the delivered goods by the seller; see Insolvency Bill, ss. 117, 121(2). By contrast, vendors' security rights on an *extended* conditional sale (*supra*, note 10) are treated like other non-possessory security. It remains to be seen if, and to what extent, this exemption will impair efforts at rehabilitation.

96. Insolvency Bill, ss. 191–194.

97. Insolvency Bill, ss. 194(3), 197(1).

98. KO, ss. 60, 61.

administrator while carrying on the debtor's business.[99] To hold or not hold security is what makes all the difference. As a novelty in German insolvency law, the Bill creates a class of "subordinated debt", i.e. claims which were not even admitted to proof in a bankruptcy procedure under the KO, such as post-insolvency interest on debts, claims based on gratuitous promises or shareholders' claims for repayment of a loan substituting equity.[100]

Some selected problems

Leasing, factoring

Section 55(2) of the Draft Bill 1989[101] had stated that any transaction intended to achieve effects similar to those of non-possessory security instruments—notably capital good leases or sale-and-leaseback transactions, both of them frequently financed by banks[102]—be treated equally with such security devices. The provision was designed to prevent transactions *in fraudem legis*, i.e. intended to keep secured creditors from becoming involved in the insolvency procedure. Without achieving substantive change, the Insolvency Bill skipped this general clause. The Draft Bill had raised some controversy as to whether leasing agreements over moveables may be equivalent to a taking of non-possessory security, if the agreement makes the lessee a *de facto* owner of the leased goods.[103] In practice, this will hardly ever be the case, since the effectiveness of the lease as a tax-saving device is contingent upon the lessor's retaining his ownership.[104] That aside, it is open to question—and subject to the concrete design of the lease agreement—whether capital goods leasing is a secured credit transaction in the first place.[105]

Factoring is a financial service carried out in two different ways. In a "factoring proper" relationship the purchase of accounts receivable is immune against cancellation by the factor, burdening the latter with the full risk arising from a customer's default or insolvency. Thus, factoring proper is a pure cash transaction. If, however, the factor may cancel the purchase once the payment becomes delinquent, the essence of the transaction is financing, with the factor advancing cash subject to the collectibility of the purchased claim. Hence, the factor receives the same treatment as a lender who has been assigned accounts receivable for security. Yet, in his client's insolvency, the factor may realise his

99. e.g. debts from working capital loans or purchases of goods. See Insolvency Bill, s. 64.
100. Insolvency Bill, s. 46.
101. *Supra* note 70.
102. Even if the lease is not financed, leasing is considered a financial service, because the larger leasing companies often are subsidiaries or joint ventures of banks.
103. See D. Rümker, "Die kreditwirtschaftlichen Aspekte der neuen Insolvenzordnung", in B. M. Kübler (ed.), *supra* note 77, at p. 138.
104. The preconditions on which the Revenue recognises the lessor's ownership are spelled out in Jährig/Schuck, *supra* note 12, at p. 289.
105. D. Rümker, *supra* note 103, *ibid*.

claims against the client's customers by himself, as generally the purchase (and the assignment, for that matter) will have been disclosed to the customers.[106]

Security pool agreements

As the Official Comment accompanying the Bill repeatedly emphasises, security pools will remain a major player in the new insolvency procedure.[107] It is quite clear, however, that the security pools under the new law will operate as post-insolvency pools in the first instance. Since holders of non-possessory security have been largely deprived of their privileged segregated status,[108] pools designed to function as a device for a separate and self-determined realisation of security have had their day. Pre-insolvency pools will retain some importance so as to allow for a fair *ex ante* distribution of a limited supply of security among competing creditors.[109] Even then they are discriminated against through voting rules according but one vote to creditors who are jointly entitled to a given asset.[110] By contrast, post-insolvency pools will come to be a prime tool to aggregate split votes and concentrate bargaining power, especially when it comes to making insolvency plans aiming at rehabilitation.

Voting rights

Voting rights were one of the most controversial subject matters in the course of the law reform. While the Draft Bill required votes on a creditor meeting to be calculated according to the amount of the creditor's debt[111] the Insolvency Bill, seeking to curb the dominance of principal creditors, mandates that the majority vote be counted by heads.[112] For the purpose of voting on insolvency plans, the Bill establishes classes of creditors—basically secured, ordinary, and subordinated creditors[113]—each casting a separate vote by majority.[114]

Representatives of the banking industry[115] had challenged the "head count" method, arguing that it is the principal creditors who assume the burdens and liabilities concomitant with a rehabilitation effort, and apprehensive of the prospect, lest minor creditors should be given a potential for "blackmail". To mitigate these potentially adverse effects the Bill indeed generally requires that,

106. Insolvency Bill, s. 191(2); see also *supra*, text accompanying note 93.
107. See *Official Comment*, Part A 3b; comments on ss. 30, 266.
108. *Supra*, text following note 92.
109. *Supra*, text following note 60.
110. Insolvency Bill, ss. 87(3), 289(2).
111. *Referentenentwurf* (*supra* note 70), s. 83(3).
112. Insolvency Bill, s. 289.
113. Insolvency Bill, s. 265.
114. Insolvency Bill, ss. 288, 289(1). Secured creditors, however, have voting rights only to the extent that either they waive their security or the proceeds from realisation do not cover their debt. As a matter of course, they are not entitled to vote if the insolvency plan does not affect their rights; see Insolvency Bill, ss. 281–282.
115. See D. Rümker, *supra* note 103, at pp. 145/6.

beyond a *per capita* majority, the amount of the approving creditors' debt exceeds 50 per cent of the debt of the vote (majority in value).[116]

Working capital loans made to the insolvent's estate

It is a matter of course that working capital loans made in the course of an insolvency procedure enjoy first priority in the order of distribution.[117] The Insolvency Bill extends this privilege both to middle-term loans (or other credit) extended beyond the date when the insolvency procedure is closed and to those made during a "review period", subsequent to the approval of a rehabilitation plan.[118]

LEGAL ISSUES TO BE ADDRESSED IN A VOLUNTARY SUPPORT OPERATION

It remains to be seen if and to what extent the rehabilitative philosophy of the Insolvency Bill will work out in practice.[119] Voluntary support operations, from the very outset, have been a subject matter consciously left out of insolvency law reform. As a saying goes in Germany, pre-emptive rehabilitation to be successful has to be "timely, expeditious, and quiet".[120] None the less, there remains a host of legal issues to be addressed by banks participating in a voluntary support operation, lest the failure of such operation should end up with a heavy burden of liability. The relevant body of law has been left largely unaffected by the insolvency law reform; only the rules relating to fraudulent conveyances and preferences will be revised to a small degree.

Preferential treatment of bank creditors

The adjustment of pre-insolvency transactions of a debtor—the *actio Pauliana* of Roman law—seems to be part of the common core of different national insolvency laws. Among the various types of transactions which a debtor heading for insolvency may be tempted to perform in order to give single creditors preferential treatment to the prejudice of the general body of creditors,[121] only

116. Insolvency Bill, s. 289(1).
117. *Supra*, text accompanying note 98.
118. Insolvency Bill, ss. 311–312. The review period has to be mandated through the insolvency plan and may cover three years at most; *ibid.*, s. 315(1). For further details see D. Rümker, *supra* note 103, at p. 148 *et seq.*
119. Remember *supra*, note 95.
120. Karsten Schmidt, *Möglichkeiten der Sanierung von Unternehmen durch Maßnahmen im Unternehmens-, Arbeits-, Sozial- und Insolvenzrecht* (1982), p. D 97.
121. Cf. KO, ss. 30–32a; Insolvency Bill, ss. 145–155.

a few are likely to involve banks. Thus, a secured loan transaction may constitute an unfair preference[122] in favour of the lender in a workout situation, if neither borrower nor lender acted in good faith as to the auspicious prospects of the rescue operation and the loan was designed solely to refinance and reduce the lender's commitment.[123] While such a situation appears to be rather exceptional, a lender's taking of new security for pre-existing debt may be a more frequent practice. The latter is regarded as an unfair preference, even if pursuant to a previous *general* agreement to grant security,[124] because such agreement did not entitle the lender to take security in a specific kind of assets.[125] Even if pursuant to an agreement to grant security in a *specified* asset the transaction may be set aside in the event that it was executed during the last three months prior to the filing of an insolvency petition, and the lender had actual or constructive knowledge that the debtor was insolvent.[126] Since under present law only actual knowledge of the signals presaging the commencement of an insolvency procedure triggers the adjustment of a secured transaction, the new law may present a disincentive for lenders generously to make loans in a workout situation.[127]

Lender liability

The concept of lender liability is largely unknown to German lawyers.[128] I shall discuss under this label some miscellaneous causes of action supporting the liability of banks for improperly exercising certain rights and remedies in the course of a rescue operation.

Conflict of interest situations

When asked by a debtor company who has run into financial difficulties to make further advances, a bank faces the uncomfortable choice either to accel-

122. *Absichtsanfechtung*; see KO s. 31 No. 1; Insolvency Bill s. 148(1). Under the new law, the relevant time for adjustment of such transactions may extend up to 10 years prior to the filing of an insolvency petition.

123. See Bundesgerichtshof (Federal Court) in *Neue Juristische Wochenschrift 1984*, 1893, 1898/9.

124. Usually based upon No. 19 of the Standard Form Contract.

125. KO, s. 30, No. 2; Insolvency Bill, s. 146. Under the Bill the relevant time is the month preceding the filing of an insolvency petition; the period covers up to three months if the debtor was already insolvent at the time the security was granted, regardless of the lender's—actual or constructive—knowledge of this fact.

126. Insolvency Bill, s. 145(1). Insolvency has to be cash-flow insolvency, as opposed to balance-sheet insolvency. Alternatively, the granting of security may be invalidated if it was effected subsequent to the filing of an insolvency petition, and the creditor had actual or constructive knowledge thereof. However, this case is unlikely to occur in a voluntary rescue operation.

127. See D. Rümker, *supra*, note 103, at p. 151.

128. See, however, J. Köndgen, "Die Haftung der Kreditbank in den USA—Vorbild oder Alptraum?", *Die Bank 1991*, 283.

erate its loan if the debtor's condition seems hopeless[129]—at the risk of misjudging the debtor's potential for recovery, thus breaching its duty to act in good faith arising from the loan contract,[130] *or* to make further advances—at the risk of recklessly ignoring the alarm bells, thereby becoming liable to the general body of creditors in tort for impeding the timely commencement of an insolvency procedure.[131] Banks cannot expect the requisite guidance on how to resolve what is basically a conflict of interest situation from recent case-law, nor can they rely on a majority opinion in the legal literature.[132] In a rare, clear-cut case, the Federal Court has held a major German bank liable in tort for recklessly pursuing its own interest at the prejudice of the general body of creditors and the investing public. The defendant bank—which was also a shareholder to the debtor company—had, by a tricky manoeuvre, covertly reduced both its line of credit and its equity, at the same time taking an active part in raising new equity financing by underwriting an issue of stock to the general public.[133]

Interfering with corporate governance

When banks take the lead in a rescue operation they should be aware of the risks of overreaching. If they enter into a secured transaction granting them security in most of the debtor's property and, at the same time, control over the debtor's business and financial affairs to the point that the debtor is a mere instrument in the hand of the lender, such a transaction may be invalidated by a court as being unconscionable.[134] Whether lenders when interfering with the debtor company's legitimate corporate governance may be held responsible for breach of their fiduciary duties as *shadow directors* is open to question. The doctrine of shadow directors has not gained strong foothold in the jurisprudence,[135] and there has been no case-law applying it to lenders.

129. If the debtor is indeed headed for an insolvent liquidation, the bank may accelerate its loan even if adequate security is still available; see Oberlandesgericht Celle in *Zeitschrift für Wirtschaftsrecht (ZIP) 1982*, 942.

130. The legal literature under appropriate circumstances advocates a contractual duty to refrain from "untimely" acceleration; cf. C.W. Canaris, *Bankvertragsrecht* (2nd edn 1981), margin Nos. 1341, 1262.

131. So-called "*Konkursverschleppung*"; the cause of action would be Civil Code (BGB), s. 826—tort of "wilful or reckless infliction of harm". Recent case-law increasingly construes "recklessness" as an equivalent to gross negligence.

132. The reader will find a comprehensive analysis of both the relevant case-law and the literature in T. Möllers, *Die Haftung der Bank bei der Kreditkündigung* (1991).

133. See Bundesgerichtshof in *Zeitschrift für Wirtschaftsrecht (ZIP) 1986*, 14 = *Wertpapiermitteilungen 1986*, 2. To the subscribers of new stock, liability was also grounded on the bank's underwriting a misleading prospectus; see Bundesgerichtshof in *Zeitschrift für Wirtschaftsrecht 1982*, 923.

134. Oberlandesgericht Celle, *supra* note 129, at 950 came close to such a ruling, but in the event found that the lender had indeed closely monitored the debtor's conducting his business but had not assumed operative control.

135. See, however, Bundesgerichtshof, BGHZ 104, 44 (1988), holding a shadow director of a GmbH liable for failure to present a bankruptcy petition (a statutory duty imposed on corporate directors).

Lenders as shareholders

Finally, I will refer briefly to the special responsibility of banks acting in a dual role as both lender and company member. Even if the lender is not in the position of a controlling shareholder,[136] its claim for repayment of a loan granted to the company which is lacking adequate capital is excluded in the event of bankruptcy.[137] Under the Insolvency Bill, the claim will be subject to equitable subordination,[138] the rationale of these rules being that a company member, once it elects to remedy its company's need for capital, must not do so other than through equity financing. Since much of the law relating to loans substituting equity is covered in Chapter 1,[139] I shall focus here on some recent developments.

In a landmark case of 1988,[140] the principal lender to the debtor company had become a trustee over company shares by virtue of taking a major shareholder's shares as security for a syndicated loan extended to the company, with the assigning shareholder reserving his right to vote on company meetings. In addition, the bank had been appointed managing agent and trustee for the loan syndicate for all purposes of doing business with the borrower. The formidable question the Federal Court had to address was whether, first, the bank holding its share in the company only for transient financing purposes was subject to the same responsibility as an ordinary shareholder, and, in the affirmative, (b) the bank was excluded with its repayment claim to the full amount of the syndicated loan or only with its own, relatively small contribution.

1. With regard to the first part of the question, the majority opinion in Germany had long argued against a bank raising the defence that it became a shareholder only for the purpose of financing a support operation (so-called bank privilege).[141] Should this also be true if the lender holds the shares as a quasi-lien, even allowing the transferring shareholder to exercise the voting right? The Federal Court ruled in the affirmative arguing for a formal analysis, irrespective of the bank's motives for becoming a shareholder.[142]
2. The Federal Court avoided addressing the second question. The bank's defence was indeed not without its merits. The law does not, as a rule, require a shareholder to furnish additional equity

136. This may trigger the special duties imposed by the law relating to groups of companies which I cannot deal with in this place; for details, cf. H. P. Westermann, "Banken als Kreditgeber und Gesellschafter", *Zeitschrift für Wirtschaftsrecht 1982*, 379, 382 *et seq.*

137. A fair representation of the present law is given in Chapter 1 of this volume.

138. Insolvency Bill, s. 46(1), No. 5.

139. *Ibid.*

140. Bundesgerichtshof in BGHZ 105, 168 (1988)—"Hamburger Stahlwerke".

141. See most recently M. Lutter, "Neues zum Gesellschafterdarlehen?", *Zeitschrift für Wirtschaftsrecht 1989*, 477, 479.

142. The holding was widely acclaimed in the literature; see M. Lutter, *ibid.* at 482/3; H. J. Priester, "Eigenkapitalersetzende Landesbankdarlehen", *Zeitschrift für Bankrecht und Bankwirtschaft 1989*, 30, 33.

whenever the company's capital base becomes insufficient. Only if he does choose to provide financing, will this be treated as the equivalent of equity. Under this rationale, the bank had elected to finance the debtor company only to the extent of its relative quota of the loan,[143] allowing it to retrieve the remainder from the bankrupt's estate.

JOHANNES KÖNDGEN

143. M. Lutter, *ibid.* at 483.

CHAPTER 11

OFFICIAL REMEDIES: INQUIRIES UNDER SECTION 432(2) OF THE COMPANIES ACT 1985

INTRODUCTION

Section 432(2) of the Companies Act 1985 gives the Secretary of State for Trade and Industry the power to appoint one or more competent inspectors to investigate the affairs of a company[1] and to report to him on them in such manner as he directs if it appears to him that there are circumstances suggesting:

(a) that the company's affairs are being or have been conducted with intent to defraud its creditors or the creditors of any other person, or otherwise for a fraudulent or unlawful purpose, or in a manner which is unfairly prejudicial to some part of its members, or
(b) that any actual proposed act or omission of the company (including an act or omission on its behalf) is or would be so prejudicial, or that the company was formed for any fraudulent or unlawful purpose, or
(c) that persons concerned with the company's formation or the management of its affairs have in connection therewith been guilty of fraud, misfeasance or other misconduct towards it or towards its members, or
(d) that the company's members have not been given all the information with respect to its affairs which they might reasonably expect.

The Secretary of State may publish the report he receives from the inspectors,[2] although he is not obliged to do so. Inspectors can be appointed on the basis that their report is not for publication.[3]

In recent years there has been an increasing number of high-profile inquiries under s. 432(2). Those inquiries often lead to criminal prosecutions, to the disqualification of directors, to disciplinary action by regulators or to the making

1. Company means a company formed and registered under the Companies Act ("CA") 1985 or various earlier Companies or Joint Stock Companies Acts: s. 735, CA 1985. The Secretary of State's powers, however, extend to bodies corporate incorporated in and having a principal place of business in Great Britian (s. 718 and Sch. 22, CA 1985) and to bodies corporate incorporated outside Great Britain but which carry on (or have at any time carried on) business there (s. 453, CA 1985—but subject to certain limitations set out in s. 453).
2. Section 437(3), CA 1985.
3. Section 432(2A), CA 1985.

of winding-up orders.[4] Adverse criticism by inspectors in published reports has damaged or ended careers. The fairness of the process to the individuals involved in it has increasingly been questioned, although inevitably most vociferously by those most heavily criticised by inspectors. The House of Commons Trade and Industry Committee has recently reviewed and reported on company investigations, but their report will lead to very few changes to the law or practice relating to s. 432(2) inquiries.[5]

The purpose of this chapter is to examine the powers of the inspectors, the manner in which inquiries are carried out and the fairness of the balance between the powers of the inspectors and the rights of the individual.

THE POWERS OF INSPECTORS AND THE CONDUCT OF INQUIRIES

Inspectors are appointed by the Secretary of State. A public announcement is made of any appointment in respect of a public company. The inspectors are given wide terms of reference (e.g. "to investigate and report on the affairs of X plc"). Although the appointment of inspectors can, of itself, cause significant damage to a company, the Secretary of State's decision to appoint inspectors is effectively unchallengeable. The Court of Appeal has held[6] that the Secretary of State's decision to appoint inspectors can only be challenged on the grounds that his decision was made in bad faith or for an improper purpose. The burden of proof is on the applicant. Since the Secretary of State cannot be compelled to give reasons for his decision to appoint inspectors and in practice does not do so, it is an impossible burden to discharge.

The DTI's practice in the case of an investigation into a large public company is to appoint two inspectors. One is usually a senior partner in a firm of accountants and the other a QC or leading solicitor. The accountant's or solicitor's staff provide the administrative support. The Secretary of State is, however, free to appoint anybody who is competent, and in smaller investigations it is usual for DTI officials to be appointed.

Inspectors are free to conduct the inquiry in the way which seems to them to be most appropriate, subject to an overriding, but limited, obligation to observe the rules of natural justice. This is considered in more detail below. Nevertheless, inquiries follow a broadly similar pattern:

(a) request for and review of documents;
(b) questioning of witnesses;
(c) submission of proposed criticisms to witnesses; and
(d) submission of report to the Secretary of State.

4. Memorandum submitted by the DTI to the House of Commons Trade and Industry Committee in October 1989.
5. See the Trade and Industry Committee Report dated 2 May 1990 and the government's response, dated August 1990.
6. *Norwest Holst Limited* v. *Secretary of State for Trade and Others* [1978] 1 Ch 201.

DOCUMENTS

Inspectors are given powers to require production from any person of documents relating to matters which they believe to be relevant to their investigation.[7] Document requests are usually made in wide terms and it is often difficult for the recipient to ascertain from the request itself what lies behind it and in what matters the inspectors are really interested. The inspectors, if asked, will usually decline to say.

In addition to the power to request wide classes of documents, inspectors are given powers of entry and search. If the inspectors can satisfy a Justice of the Peace on information given on oath that there are reasonable grounds for believing that documents requested have not been produced, the inspectors can obtain a warrant to enter and search premises to find and remove the documents.[8] The inspectors can also obtain such a warrant[9] if they satisfy a Justice of the Peace on information given on oath:

(a) that there are reasonable grounds for believing an offence has been committed for which the penalty on conviction on indictment is imprisonment for a term of not less than two years and that there are on any premises documents relating to whether the offence has been committed,
(b) that the Secretary of State, or the person so appointed or authorised, has power to require the production of the documents under this Part, and
(c) that there are reasonable grounds for believing that if production was so required the document would not be produced but would be removed from the premises, hidden, tampered with or destroyed.

In this latter case the warrant can also authorise the removal of any other documents relevant to the investigation.[10] A police officer has to be present while the warrant is executed.[11] Any person named in the warrant can be required to provide an explanation of the documents or to state where they may be found.[12]

In addition to their powers of entry and search, the inspectors have the power to certify a refusal to produce documents to the court. The court may enquire into the refusal and, after hearing evidence and any statement which may be offered in defence, may punish the person refusing to produce documents as though he were guilty of contempt of court.[13] This can involve heavy fines and imprisonment.

7. Section 434(2)(a), CA 1985.
8. Section 448(1), CA 1985.
9. Section 448(2), CA 1985.
10. Section 448(4), CA 1985.
11. Section 448(3), CA 1985.
12. Section 448(3)(d), CA 1985.
13. Section 436, CA 1985.

QUESTIONING OF WITNESSES

The inspectors have the power to compel individuals who may be in possession of information relating to a matter believed to be relevant to the investigation to testify before them on oath.[14] A refusal to answer questions can be certified to the court in the same way as a refusal to supply documents. An answer given to a question from the inspectors may be used in evidence against the person giving it.[15] The inspectors' practice as to the manner of conducting oral interviews varies. Some indicate to witnesses in advance those documents which they intend to put to the witnesses. Some indicate the areas, sometimes even the questions, which they intend to cover. Others do none of these things. Evidence is usually taken on oath and is recorded verbatim by a shorthand writer. The questions are primarily asked by the lawyer inspector. The witness is allowed to have his lawyer present, although the degree to which the lawyer is invited or permitted to intervene, or to address the inspectors or question the witness varies. The witness is usually provided with a copy of his transcript of evidence and invited to correct it or to add to it. The practice varies as to whether the witness will be allowed to keep the transcripts. In some inquiries concern over confidentiality leads the inspectors to request the return of the transcripts. On occasions, the inspectors will ask witnesses to undertake not to discuss their evidence with other witnesses. (It is, in any event, good practice for the lawyer advising witnesses to ensure that they do not discuss their evidence with each other. If they do, the value of their evidence will be reduced and there is an increased risk of adverse comment by the inspectors.) No witness has the right to see other witnesses' evidence or to cross-examine other witnesses.

The inspectors are not entitled to call for documents or information covered by legal professional privilege,[16] although it has been known for inspectors to exert considerable pressure on witnesses to waive that privilege. Nor can inspectors compel a person to produce documents or information in respect of which he owes an obligation of confidence by virtue of carrying on the business of banking unless:

(a) the person to whom the obligation of confidence is owed is the company or other body corporate under investigation,
(b) the person to whom the obligation of confidence is owed consents to the disclosure or production, or
(c) the making of the requirement is authorised by the Secretary of State.[17]

This exception does not apply where the bank owing the obligation of confidence is itself the company under investigation.[18]

14. Section 434(2) and (3), CA 1985.
15. Section 434(5), CA 1985.
16. Section 452, CA 1985.
17. Section 452(1A), CA 1985.
18. Section 452(1B), CA 1985.

SUBMISSION OF PROPOSED CRITICISM TO WITNESSES

The obligation of the inspectors to give a person whom they are minded to condemn or criticise an opportunity to meet the case against him is dealt with in more detail below. Although the inspectors are not, strictly speaking, obliged to do so, they often do give a witness a draft of their proposed criticism of him and invite the witness to make representations on it. Some even provide the relevant passages from their draft report.

THE MAKING OF THE REPORT

The inspectors may, and if directed to do so by the Secretary of State must, make interim reports to the Secretary of State. On the conclusion of their investigation they must make a final written report to him.[19] The inspectors may, and if directed to do so by the Secretary of State must, inform the Secretary of State of any matters coming to their knowledge as a result of their investigations.[20] Information which the inspectors pass to the Secretary of State can be used, or can be passed to others for them to use, for a number of defined purposes, including the institution or furtherance of criminal proceedings, disciplinary proceedings by regulators, proceedings for disqualification of directors and petitions by the secretary of state to wind up companies.[21] Such information often is used for these purposes.

If the Secretary of State considers that matters have come to light in the course of the inspectors' investigation which suggest that a criminal offence has been committed, and those matters have been referred to the appropriate prosecuting authority, he may direct the inspectors to take no further steps in the investigation or to take only such further steps as he may specify.[22] If the Secretary of State makes such a direction, the inspectors only make a final report if and when the Secretary of State directs them to do so.[23]

The Secretary of State can publish the inspectors' report, but does not have to do so.[24] Reports on the affairs of a public company are usually published. Reports on the affairs of private companies are not, unless they raise some point of general public interest. If criminal proceedings are contemplated, the Secretary of State will only publish if he is satisfied that publication would not prejudice the criminal proceedings. There has been much recent criticism of apparent inconsistency in the manner in which the Secretary of State has exercised this discretion. The County NatWest Report was published immediately, despite the fact that criminal proceedings followed. The House of Fraser

19. Section 437(1), CA 1985.
20. Section 437(1A), CA 1985.
21. Section 451A, CA 1985.
22. Section 437 (1B), CA 1985.
23. Section 437(1C), CA 1985.
24. Section 437(3)(c), CA 1985.

Report, on the other hand, was held back from publication for a considerable time while the Serious Fraud Office and the police considered whether to bring charges.

Inspectors can be appointed on the basis that their reports are not for publication.[25] In these cases, the inspectors can, in theory, complete their work more speedily since they will not be obliged (see below) to put the substance of any adverse evidence to persons they are minded to criticise and give them the opportunity to deal with it. The DTI are particularly likely to appoint inspectors on this basis, where the purpose of the investigation is to ascertain as speedily as possible whether there are grounds for prosecution or regulatory action[26] and where there is no wider public interest which might be served by the publication of a report.

The length of time inquiries take varies. The County NatWest Report was published within seven months of the appointment. The Alexander Howden Group plc Report was only completed five years after the appointment. The average is about two and a half years.

THE INSPECTORS' DUTY TO ACT IN ACCORDANCE WITH THE RULES OF NATURAL JUSTICE

The inspectors have very wide powers. Obviously, they cannot exceed those powers or exercise them for improper or collateral purposes. But are there any legal constraints on inspectors who remain within their statutory powers? Does the individual have any guarantee that the procedure adopted by the inspectors will be fair?

The law on procedural fairness in s. 432(2) investigations is to be found in two Court of Appeal decisions.[27] The combined effect of those decisions is as follows.

1. An inquiry under s. 432(2) of the Companies Act 1985 is *sui generis*. It is more than just an investigation (to which the rules of natural justice and procedural fairness would not apply), because the inspectors have a duty, having investigated, to produce a report which may be made public and may cause severe injury to an individual by its findings. On the other hand, the inquiry is something less than a judicial proceeding. There is no issue or question before the inspectors which they are called on to determine:

   > the inspectors' function is in essence to conduct an investigation designed to discover whether there are facts which may result in others taking action. It is

25. Section 432(2A), CA 1985.
26. Memorandum submitted by the DTI to the House of Commons Trade and Industry Committee in October 1989.
27. *Re Pergamon Press Ltd* [1971] Ch 388 and *Maxwell* v. *Department of Trade and Industry & Ors* [1974] QB 523.

no part of their function to take a decision whether action be taken, and *a fortiori*, it is not for them finally to determine such issues as may emerge if some action eventuates.[28]

2. Given the nature of s. 432(2) inquiries, and in particular the fact that they may lead to the publication of a report which may be highly damaging to those criticised in it, the inspectors are under a duty to act fairly. That duty, however, means only that the inspectors must offer anybody they are minded to condemn or criticise in their report "a fair opportunity for correcting or contradicting what is said against him"[29] before the report is published.
3. The person whom the inspectors are minded to criticise must therefore be told sufficient of the case against him to enable him to have a fair opportunity of correcting or contradicting that case. Precisely what he needs to be told, and how, depends on the particular circumstances of each case and no detailed rules should be laid down.
4. An individual has no automatic right to see the inspectors' proposed criticisms or conclusions in draft to comment on them (although inspectors in practice often permit this). Nor does he have the right to see the transcripts of evidence of other witnesses or to see documents adverse to him.
5. An individual has no right to cross-examine other witnesses.
6. Save for this, the inspectors are, and should be, masters of their own procedure.

The lack of information available to those involved in DTI inquiries means that there is, in practice, no real remedy against inspectors who infringe the limited controls on their wide powers. There is no right of appeal. It will be rare in practice that an individual is so confident that the inspectors are exceeding their powers, or exercising them for an improper purpose, that he will decline to answer questions or provide documents and challenge the inspectors' demands in court. Equally, especially if he is not given a draft of the relevant section in the inspectors' report, an individual will not usually know that the inspectors have failed to comply with the rules of natural justice or have reached "irrational" conclusions as far as he is concerned until he sees the published report. At that stage, he cannot seek an injunction to restrain publication. Publication has already taken place and in any event no injunction lies against the Crown. Nor can he seek a declaration that the report is null and void.[30] Nor, save in the most exceptional circumstances, will he be granted a declaration that natural justice has not been observed:

In my judgment a man who has been unfairly criticised in a report . . . is in the same position as one who has been unfairly criticised in a speech made in Parliament. He has

28. *Per* Sachs LJ in *Re Pergamon Press Ltd.*
29. *Per* Lord Denning MR in *Re Pergamon Press Ltd.*
30. *Maxwell* v. *DTI.*

suffered "*damnum*" but not "*injuria*". Cases may occur (although they are unlikely to do so as long as the Minister appoints competent and experienced professional men as inspectors) in which the inspectors had behaved so unfairly that the public interest requires a court to say so.[31]

Nor can the inspectors be sued for making defamatory statements in their report unless the statements are irrelevant to their investigation or motivated by malice.[32]

PRIVILEGE AGAINST SELF-INCRIMINATION

The inspectors' report, or information passed by the inspectors to the DTI, often leads to criminal prosecutions. Indeed, one of the reasons for appointing inspectors under s. 432(2) is to obtain evidence for use in possible future criminal proceedings:

> The effectiveness of the investigation process needs to be considered against the objectives it is designed to serve. An investigation may be said to be effective if it contributes to the reduction of commercial malpractice. It may achieve that if it leads to prosecution, winding-up or disqualification (of directors); or to regulatory or disciplinary action; or where the mere fact of the investigation acts as a deterrent.[33]

Can an individual refuse to answer the inspectors' questions on the grounds that his answers may incriminate him? It is clear that it is the courts, and not the inspectors, who must determine that question,[34] but how will the courts determine it?

The right to decline to answer incriminating questions (a common law right now contained in s. 14(1) of the Civil Evidence Act 1968) can be excluded by statute. Such an exclusion may be express.[35] It is not, however, necessary that the exclusion should be express[36]:

> Some statutes expressly provide that incriminating answers may be used against the person who gives them and some statutes expressly provide that they may not. Where . . . there is no such express provision the question whether such answers are admissible evidence must depend on the proper construction of the particular statute.[37]

31. *Per* Lawton LJ in *Maxwell* v. *DTI*.
32. Although there is no authority directly in point, the inspectors' report must, as a matter of principle, be protected by qualified privilege. Lord Denning MR's *obiter* remark in *Re Pergamon Press Ltd* that the inspectors' report is protected by absolute privilege is unsupported by authority and seems contrary to principle.
33. Memorandum submitted by the DTI to the House of Commons Trade and Industry Committee in October 1989.
34. Section 436, CA 1985; *McLelland, Pope & Langley Limited* v. *Howard* [1968] 1 All ER 569 (HL) and *Selangor United Rubber Estates, Ltd* v. *Cradock* [1968] 1 All ER 567.
35. See s. 31, Theft Act 1968; s. 72, Supreme Court Act 1981.
36. *Reg* v. *Harz* [1967] 1 AC 760 (HL); see too *Reg* v. *Scott* (1856) 169 ER 909; *Reg* v. *Erdheim* [1896] 2 QB 260; *In re Atherton* [1912] 2 KB 251; *In re Paget* [1927] 2 Ch 85 (CA); *DPP* v. *Ellis* [1973] 1 WLR 722; *EMI Records Ltd* v. *Spillane* [1986] 1 WLR 967.
37. *Reg* v. *Harz* [1967] 1 AC 760, *per* Lord Reid at p. 876.

It is a matter of construction of the individual statute whether the exclusion of the right to refuse to answer incriminating questions applies after the individual has been charged as well as before.[38]

In the case of s. 432(2) inquiries the privilege against self-incrimination is not expressly excluded. On the proper construction of Part XIV of the Companies Act 1985, parliament has, however, shown a clear intention that an individual should not have the right to refuse to answer incriminating questions, at any rate before he is charged[39]:

1. Inspectors are appointed in the circumstances set out in s. 432(2). These circumstances include fraud and unlawful conduct. Section 432(2) therefore envisages in terms that the inspectors will investigate conduct which is criminal.
2. Various provisions of Part XIV of the Companies Act envisage that information obtained in the course of a DTI inquiry will lead to criminal proceedings.[40]
3. Individuals must answer questions put to them by the inspectors and must answer on oath.[41]
4. The answers can be passed to the prosecuting authorities "with a view to the institution of or otherwise for the purpose of criminal proceedings".[42]
5. The answers may be used in evidence against the individual.[43] Nothing in the wording of Part XIV of the Act suggests that the answers may only be used in evidence against the individual in *civil* proceedings. Nor is it at all likely that this is what parliament intended. It is clear that a least one purpose of a s. 432(2) inquiry is to facilitate the detection and punishment of commercial crime and of fraud in particular. To regard s. 434(5) as limited to civil proceedings would be more likely to defeat than to further parliament's intention.
6. Section 452 expressly preserves legal professional privilege and, to a limited degree, the banker's duty of confidentiality. Neither s. 452 nor any other section of Part XIV, however, makes any mention of privilege against self-incrimination. If parliament had intended that privilege to apply, it would have been logical for it to have been expressly mentioned in s. 452.

38. *EMI Records Ltd* v. *Spillane* [1986] 1 WLR 967 (right excluded before and after charge); cf. *A* v. *HM Treasury* [1979] 1 WLR 1056 (right excluded only before charge).

39. *Re London United Investments plc* (CA, 19 December 1991, unreported); *Reg* v. *Seelig and Spens* [1992] 1 WLR 148; *Reg* v. *Harris* [1970] 1 WLR 1252; see too *London and County Securities Ltd* v. *Nicholson* [1980] 3 All ER 861 and *Sociedade Nacional de Combustiveis de Angola UEE* v. *Lunqvist* [1990] 3 All ER 283, 302.

40. Section 437(1B) and (1C), CA 1985; s. 451A, CA 1985.

41. Section 434(2) and (3), CA 1985.

42. Section 451A, CA 1985.

43. Section 434(5), CA 1985.

There is no authority on the question of whether the exclusion of the privilege should be restricted to the period before an individual is charged.

An individual has, therefore, no right to refuse to provide self-incriminating answers to an inspector's questions, at any rate before he has been charged, even after it has become apparent to the inspectors that there is sufficient evidence for a prosecution against that individual to succeed. He may, indeed, have no such right even after he has been charged. In at least one case (the Guinness Inquiry) the inspectors refrained from asking questions in the latter situation, and the courts suggested that they might, in the exercise of their discretion under the Police and Criminal Evidence Act 1984, exclude evidence obtained in the latter situation. It is, however, hard to see why an individual should be compelled to rely on the inspectors' self-restraint or the court's discretion, rather than on a legal right.

Although the individual has no *right* to refuse to answer incriminating questions, the inspectors cannot themselves insist on an answer to an incriminating question, but must refer a refusal to answer to the court. The court has a discretion not to take action against an individual who refuses to answer on grounds that his answer may incriminate him. Since the individual has no right to refuse to answer incriminating questions, the court cannot regard the fact that the answer may be incriminating as decisive. It can only regard it as one factor, to be considered with others, in deciding, as a matter of discretion, what action to take. If the answer would be of real assistance in the investigation, the individual will very probably be compelled to answer. If the question, or line of questioning, has such a remote or doubtful bearing upon the investigation that the harm which may be done to the individual will outweigh any benefit to be obtained, the court might take no action against somebody who refused to answer. The stage a criminal investigation has reached (e.g. whether the individual has been charged) might well also be relevant.[44]

The position of inspectors in s. 432(2) inquiries in this respect may be contrasted with the powers of the Serious Fraud Office ("SFO") under the Criminal Justice Act 1987. The SFO was set up to investigate and to prosecute serious or complex fraud.[45] To that end, it has been given powers to compel individuals and companies to answer questions and to produce documents similar to the powers enjoyed by DTI inspectors.[46]

Unlike the Companies Act, however, the Criminal Justice Act 1987[47] provides that a statement made to the SFO pursuant to their statutory powers can only be used in evidence against a person if he is prosecuted for knowingly making a false statement or is prosecuted for another offence and, in giving evidence, makes a statement inconsistent with his previous statement.

44. Cf. *Mortimer* v. *Brown* (1970) 122 CLR 493; and see *Re London United Investments plc* (CA, 19 December 1991, unreported).
45. Section 1, Criminal Justice Act 1987.
46. Section 2, Criminal Justice Act 1987.
47. Section 2(8) and 2(14), Criminal Justice Act 1987.

Moreover the SFO cannot compel an individual to answer questions after charges have been brought against him in relation to the offences with which he has been charged (although he can be compelled under s. 2 of the Criminal Justice Act 1987 to answer questions about other suspected offences).[48]

As a matter of principle, the position under the Criminal Justice Act is surely more satisfactory than the position under the Companies Act. It is, moreover, hard to see any justification for the difference between the individual's rights before DTI inspectors and his rights before the SFO.

Moreover, although DTI inspectors are, in practice, used to investigate possible criminal offences, they are not, unlike the SFO,[49] subject to the controls imposed by the Police and Criminal Evidence Act 1984 and the Codes of Practice made thereunder as to the manner in which they conduct their investigation. The Police and Criminal Evidence Act 1984 provides[50] that:

> Persons other than police officers who are charged with the duty of investigating offences or charging offenders shall in the discharge of that duty have regard to any relevant provision of [the Code of Practice].

It appears that DTI inspectors are not normally "charged with the duty of investigating offences", but merely with the duty to investigate the affairs of a company at large and then to report.[51] They do not therefore fall within s. 67(9). While this may be correct as a matter of law, it seems unfortunate that an individual does not, for example, have a right to legal representation during questioning, a right to have the interview with the inspectors transcribed and a right to have an opportunity of correcting the transcript. Obviously, in practice, inspectors normally permit all of these things, but it is hard to see why the individual does not have a right to them. The contrast between the restraints on the SFO in questioning both individuals who have been charged and individuals against whom there is sufficient evidence for a prosecution to succeed and the absence of restraints on DTI inspectors in questioning the same people is equally hard to justify.

THE HYBRID NATURE OF S. 432(2) INQUIRIES: BALANCING THE POWERS OF THE INVESTIGATORS AGAINST THE RIGHTS OF THE INDIVIDUAL

Section 432(2) inquiries are hybrid. They are more than an investigation, since they may involve the publication of a report which will have damaging consequences to individuals criticised in it. They are less than a judicial hearing,

48. *Reg* v. *The Director of the Serious Fraud Office, ex parte Smith* (Div Ct) [1992] 1 All ER 730; *Reg* v. *The Director of the Serious Fraud Office, ex parte Ernest Saunders* (Div Ct) [1988] Crim LR 837.

49. *Ibid.*

50. Section 67(9), Police and Criminal Evidence Act 1984.

51. *Reg* v. *Seelig and Spens* [1992] 1 WLR 148.

since no charge is being tried and no issue being determined: but damaging conclusions are, nevertheless, reached and published. Such a hybrid system has inherent flaws:

1. The inspectors, however eminent, are investigators who have been given extremely wide powers. They are subject to the same temptations (e.g. to form theories and to gather, or be more receptive to, information which fits in with those theories) and the same risks of excess of zeal as all investigators. The evidence put before them is not reviewed or tested by those against whom the evidence is given and who may be condemned by it.
2. There is no corrective balance. Individuals are reluctant to challenge the inspectors, even with good cause, for fear of antagonising them. There is no right of appeal. The right to judicial review is of little practical help and the tendency of the courts (see *Pergamon* and *Maxwell*) is to trust the inspectors to police themselves.
3. A report is published with little restraint on what may be said, save for the self-control of the inspectors and the DTI. Not surprisingly, that self-control is not always exercised. The media, given the eminence of the inspectors and the official nature of their appointment, tend to treat the inspectors' conclusions more as a result of a trial than a preliminary investigation. The effect of an adverse report on somebody's career can be devastating.

Is such a hybrid system, with its inherent flaws, necessary? Wide powers to investigate the affairs of companies are no doubt needed. Companies are economically powerful and the law gives them great privileges. The ownership and the management of the business are usually divorced and the controls on an entrenched secretive management are often lacking. To be effective, investigations must be thorough and fast. But must the report of the investigation be published? If so, must it contain criticisms or is it sufficient that it merely ascertain the facts, leaving others to draw conclusions and take any necessary action?

It is suggested that it is highly desirable, probably even necessary, that the Secretary of State be able to publish the report. First, such a power operates as a deterrent. Secondly, inspectors are often appointed in cases where the authorities or the public are concerned at the manner in which the affairs of public companies appear to have been conducted. In such a case the public have a legitimate interest in knowing what has happened, not least because they are actual or potential shareholders in the company. The publication of a report dispels rumours. It enables others to learn from it and it may provoke debate about legal or regulatory reform or changes in practice.

Moreover, it is inevitable—and desirable—that any report of an investigation contain some criticisms. At the most basic level, it is impossible to give any understandable account of complex factual situations without reaching conclusions which may, expressly or implicitly, be critical of certain individuals. If, for example, one witness's version of events is at complete variance with another's, the inspectors will have to decide which they prefer, even if it is quite apparent to the reader that that decision must have involved a conclusion on the part of the inspectors that one of the witnesses was deliberately not telling the truth. If criticisms or conclusions are not drawn, it will be hard for the outsider to understand the report, to determine how some of the acts described could have happened or sensibly to determine responsibility for those acts. He may wrongly ascribe blame in situations where the inspectors, with their greater knowledge of the facts and with the benefit of seeing the witnesses testify, would not have done so. Questions will be left unanswered and the value of the report in the public's eyes will be adversely affected, even to the point where its value and credibility is seriously damaged.

On the other hand, it is not necessary or desirable for the inspectors to make criticisms or reach conclusions which are not needed to enable the reader of the report properly to understand and appreciate what has taken place. The DTI indeed encourage inspectors only to make criticisms "to the extent necessary for a proper appreciation of their report".[52]

If wide powers of investigation must exist, and if it is appropriate that reports be published and contain criticisms, the hybrid and the flaws described earlier are inevitable. Complete protection for the interests of the individual could probably only be obtained in some kind of judicial inquiry, with all interested parties having a right to be heard, to call evidence and to cross-examine. Such a lengthy and cumbersome process would frustrate the aim of a speedy investigation.

The search for a perfect balance between the needs of the investigator and the interests of the individual under investigation will, no doubt, always prove elusive. It is, nevertheless, noteworthy that although recent inquiries have provoked substantial criticism of the present system, the government proposes to make no real change.[53] The question for the future is whether it is sufficient, as the government would wish, to rely on the professional standards and common sense of the inspectors to ensure an appropriate balance or whether it is necessary to impose more clearly defined legal restrictions on the manner in which s. 432(2) inquiries are conducted.

IAN TAYLOR

52. DTI Investigation Handbook (p. 44), published October 1990.

53. See the Trade and Industry Committee Report dated 2 May 1990 and the government's response dated August 1990.

APPENDIX 1*

STRUCTURE AND PRINCIPAL TERMS OF INTER-BANK AND SUPPORT AGREEMENTS

INTER-BANK AGREEMENT—STRUCTURE AND PRINCIPAL TERMS

1. Recitals.
2. Definitions.
3. Appointment of the Agent Bank as agent for the banks (for defined purposes).
4. Protection for the agent—a statement of the agent's duties and immunities.
5. Covenants and representations between the banks—these provisions create mutual obligations between the banks confirming and underpinning the support agreement between the Agent Bank and the borrower. For example, there will usually be a provision which stipulates that each bank will not, during the support period, make demand against the borrower.
6. Obligations on the Agent in relation to distribution of funds on repayment and cancellation of facilities.
7. Apportionment of payments to the agent in respect of costs—this provision will enable the agent to discharge its own costs first when receiving a reimbursement payment from the borrower.
8. Loss sharing: equalisation payments and credits. This provision will establish the obligation to make, and the mechanics for determining the amount of, equalisation payments and credits between the banks to equalise the exposure of the banks.
9. Dealing with realisations under security—the agent will hold security realisations on trust for itself and the banks to be distributed in accordance with the provisions of this clause.
10. Treatment of sums recovered under rights of set-off and as preferential payments. The object of these provisions is to ensure that any amounts recovered by banks either by way of set-off or by way of preferential payments are to be shared amongst all the banks in accordance with the sharing arrangements in the inter-bank agreement. They will be paid over to the agent for distribution to the other banks.
11. Termination of the agent's agency.

SUPPORT AGREEMENT—STRUCTURE AND PRINCIPAL TERMS

1. Recitals.
2. Definitions.
3. Conditions Precedent.

* Kindly supplied by Nick Segal.

4. Certificate of the Agent Bank confirming that the conditions precedent have been fulfilled to its satisfaction.
5. Restatement of bank facilities, putting all bank facilities on an equal footing and converting the facilities to term facilities. This provision will indicate that these facilities are available from the commencement of the support period (which will be defined in the Support Agreement) until the expiry date (which will also be defined).
6. Position under existing facility agreements. This provision will ensure that the terms of the support agreement govern the relationship between the banks and the borrower in substitution for and to the exclusion of the provisions of existing facility agreements (until the end of the support period).
7. Commitment of the banks to make facilities available until the expiry of the support period.
8. Dealing with sale proceeds or other pre-payments made by the borrower. This provision will usually require proceeds of sale and other sums to be paid into a specific designated account. The agent will be authorised to permit withdrawals from the account to enable the borrower to meet its working capital commitments. The balance above, the amounts needed for working capital purposes, will be held until a specific distribution date at which point they will be paid, on an agreed basis, to the banks.
9. Representation and warranties by the borrower.
10. Covenants, including negative pledge by the borrower.
11. The provision of information by the borrower. This is a crucial provision.
12. Events of default. These need to be tailor-made to the conditions applying during the support period.
13. Illegality.
14. Indemnities by the borrower to the banks, including the payment of expenses and fees.
15. The role of investigating accountants. This provision gives the agent the right to appoint, or require the borrower to instruct, reporting accountants to report to the agent and the banks on the financial position of the borrower and any other matters which may arise. This provision will establish the basis on which the appointment is to be made and who is to be liable for the actions, and the fees, of the investigating accountant.
16. Governing law.
17. Schedules. There will be a variety of schedules listing the borrowers and their subsidiaries, the banks; the basic facilities; the standard terms applicable to the basic facilities during the support period and details of the expenditure programme and permitted expenditure.

APPENDIX 2*

COLLATERAL POOL AGREEMENT

THIS COLLATERAL POOL AGREEMENT ("Agreement") is entered into as of the Effective Date by and among ...., ..., ... and each individual listed on Schedule One and executing this Agreement as a participating partner (collectively, the "Participating Partners"), ..., a .... corporation, as the plan agent (the "Plan Agent"), and each party listed on Schedule One and executing this Agreement as a creditor (collectively, the "Creditors").

RECITALS:

A. Each of the Creditors has made one or more loans to, or is the holder of one or more other obligations of, a member of .... and/or one or more of the Participating Partners (collectively, the "Loans").

B. Some of the Loans have been guaranteed, in whole or in part, by one or more of the Participating Partners.

C. In consideration for the rights and benefits provided by the Participating Partners to the Creditors under this Agreement, each of the Creditors has agreed to modify its Loans pursuant to the terms of separate documents executed in connection with this Agreement (the "Modification Documents") and to exculpate and release all of the Participating Partners who are obligated on such Loans from personal liability for the repayment of the Loans (regardless of whether such obligations are direct, indirect, liquidated, unliquidated or contingent).

D. Each of the Participating Partners acknowledges that he has become a party to this Agreement for his own benefit, and jointly with the other Participating Partners for the mutual benefit of all of the Participating Partners and all of the Creditors, and that each Participating Partner has entered into this Agreement with the expectation that all of such Participating Partner's business creditors will become a party to this Agreement, but the effectiveness of this Agreement is not contingent upon all such business creditors becoming a party hereto.

E. This Agreement, prepared pursuant to the Loan Modification Plan, represents the "Settlement Trust", as such term is used in the Loan Modification Plan, but this Agreement is not intended to be a trust agreement, and it does not establish a trust under either federal or state law.

F. The definitions of all capitalised words used in this Agreement are set forth in Section 16.

* Kindly supplied by Gerald Nels Olson.

AGREEMENT:

NOW, THEREFORE, in consideration of the premises and mutual covenants contained herein, and other good and valuable consideration, the receipt and sufficiency of which are hereby acknowledged, the Participating Partners, the Plan Agent and the Creditors agree as follows:

SECTION 1: TERM OF AGREEMENT

1.1 Initial term of agreement

This Agreement shall be binding upon and inure to the benefit of the parties hereto for the period from the Effective Date to December 31, 19.. , at which time all obligations hereunder shall terminate and be of no further force and effect (except the obligations of the Plan Agent under Sections 13.5 and 5.4, the rights of the Plan Agent under Section 13.4, the mutual release contained in Section 15.13 and the non-recourse provisions of Section 12.3) if (a) each Creditor's Deficiency has been determined, and all Deficiencies and Deficiency Certificates have been satisfied in full, or (b) all of the Collateral Pool Assets have been converted to cash and all of the Collateral Pool Cash has been disbursed in accordance with this Agreement.

1.2 Extended term of agreement

If on December 31, 19.. , (a) each Creditor's Deficiency has not been determined or all of the Deficiencies and Deficiency Certificates have not been satisfied in full, and (b) there remain Collateral Pool Assets which have not been converted to cash, then this Agreement shall continue in full force and effect until the earlier of (i) December 31, 19.. , (ii) the date on which the last remaining Collateral Pool Asset is converted to cash and all Collateral Pool Cash is disbursed in accordance with the Agreement, or (iii) the date on which all Deficiencies have been determined and all Deficiencies and Deficiency Certificates have been paid in full, at which time this Agreement shall terminate and be of no further force or effect (except the obligations of the Plan Agent under Section 13.5, the rights of the Plan Agent under Section 13.4, the mutual release contained in Section 15.13, and the non-recourse provisions of Section 12.3 shall survive).

1.3 Early termination of agreement

Notwithstanding Sections 1.1 and 1.2, this Agreement and all Liens granted herein shall terminate if a Participating Partner commences or has commenced against it any proceedings under Debtor Relief Laws (and any involuntary proceeding thereunder is not dismissed, stayed or vacated within thirty (30) days of its commencement) prior to ninety (90) days after the Effective Date, and Determining Creditors elect to terminate this Agreement by written notice to the Plan Agent given within thirty (30) days following either (a) the filing of the voluntary petition, or (b) the earlier of (i) the expiration of the thirty (30) day period after an involuntary petition is filed without same being dismissed, stayed or vacated, or (ii) the filing of an answer to such involuntary petition admitting the material allegations of such involuntary petition. If this Agreement terminates pursuant to this Section 1.3, then all Rights and obligations under this Agreement (other than the obligations of the Plan Agent under Section 13.5) shall terminate and be of no further force and effect, including specifically the releases granted in Section 15.13 and the non-recourse provisions of Section 12.3.

SECTION 2: DEFICIENCIES AND DEFICIENCY CERTIFICATES

2.1 Determination of deficiency; issuance of deficiency certificates

(a) Within thirty (30) days after the earlier to occur of (i) the sale of a particular Creditor's Existing Collateral, (ii) .... and such Creditor agreeing upon the amount of such Creditor's Deficiency with respect to unsecured Creditors, or (iii) the Current Balance of such Creditor's Modified Loan being reduced through the application of proceeds available from a refinancing or otherwise and such Creditor releases its Existing Lien, the Plan Agent shall issue to such Creditor a Deficiency Certificate in a face amount equal to such Creditor's Deficiency, if any.

(b) If a Creditor's Existing Collateral has not been sold as of December 31, 19.. , and if such Creditor agrees, or has agreed, to extend the maturity date of its Modified Loan to correspond to the Extended Term of this Agreement, then as of such date, the Plan Agent shall determine the Deficiency with respect to such Existing Collateral and disburse Collateral Pool Cash to such Creditors and other Deficiency Certificate Holders pursuant to Section 5.3. If a Creditor's Existing Collateral has not been sold as of December 31, 19.. , and if such Creditor does not agree to extend the maturity date of its Modified Loan to correspond to the Extended Term of this Agreement, then such Creditor shall not be entitled to any disbursements pursuant to either Section 5.3 or Section 5.4.

(c) If on December 31, 19.. , all of the Collateral Pool Assets have not been converted to cash, then the Plan Agent shall determine the Deficiency of each Creditor who has not previously received a Deficiency Certificate and disburse the Collateral Pool Cash and the Collateral to the Creditors pursuant to Section 5.4.

2.2 Creditor withdrawal from plan

At any time during the term of this Agreement, a Creditor may elect to foreclose its Existing Lien against its Existing Collateral. If a Creditor elects to exercise its rights under an Existing Lien through foreclosure, then the Participating Partners will not contest, and will use their best efforts to cause a Collateral Pool Entity which owns the Existing Collateral not to contest, the Creditor in such foreclosure proceedings; provided, however, that if the Fair Market Value of the Existing Collateral exceeds the Current Balance of the Modified Loan, or if a Participating Partner could be in breach of his fiduciary obligation to another Person if he fails to contest, then the Participating Partners may contest, and may cause a Collateral Pool Entity owning the Existing Collateral to contest, such foreclosure. If a Creditor exercises its rights pursuant to an Existing Lien and forecloses its security interest in the Existing Collateral, or accepts the Existing Collateral as payment of its Modified Loan in lieu of foreclosure, then such Creditor shall not be entitled to receive a Deficiency Certificate even if such Creditor's Modified Loan with respect to such Existing Collateral is not satisfied in full.

2.3 Reduction of modified loan balance

(a) If a Creditor agrees to extend the maturity date of a Modified Loan pursuant to Section 2.1(b) and Collateral Pool Cash is disbursed to a Creditor pursuant to Section 5.3, then such Creditor shall reduce the Current Balance of its Modified Loan by the amount of the distribution made to such Creditor pursuant to Section 5.3.

(b) To the extent a Creditor receives a disbursement of Collateral Pool Cash or Collateral pursuant to Section 5.4, then such Creditor shall reduce the Current Balance of its Modified Loan or Deficiency Certificate by an amount equal to the sum of the cash and the Appraised Value of the Collateral disbursed to such Creditor.

2.4 Interest on certificates

If a Creditor executes this Agreement before March 31, 19.., such Creditor shall earn interest at the rate of ten per cent (10%) per annum on the unpaid balance of each Deficiency Certificate which such Creditor holds. If, however, a Creditor executes this Agreement after March 31, 19.., then, at the election of ...., such Creditor shall earn interest on the unpaid balance of each Deficiency Certificate which such Creditor holds as follows: Five per cent (5%) if the Agreement is executed after March 31, 19.., and on or before April 30, 19.. ; four per cent (4%) if the Agreement is executed after April 30, 19.., and on or before May 31, 19.. ; three per cent (3%) if the Agreement is executed after May 31, 19.., and on or before June 30, 19.. ; two per cent (2%) if the Agreement is executed after June 30, 19.., and on or before July 31, 19.. ; and one per cent (1%) if the Agreement is executed after July 31, 19.., and on or before August 31, 19... If a Creditor executes this Agreement after August 31, 19.., such Creditor's Deficiency Certificate shall not bear interest.

SECTION 3: SECURITY AGREEMENT

3.1 Collateral

(a) To secure full and complete payment and performance of the obligations and covenants of the Participating Partners under this Agreement, but subject to the Permitted Liens and the claims of the IRS (which IRS claims, if any, shall in all circumstances be prior to the claims of Creditors, other than Creditors whose Lien claims constitute Existing Lien claims, but only to the extent of such Existing Lien claims), the Participating Partners hereby severally (and not jointly) grant and convey to, and create in favour of, the Plan Agent, on behalf of the Creditors, a Lien in, to and on their respective Rights and interests in the following items and types of property (collectively, the "Collateral"):

(i) Subject to Sections 3.1(b), (c) and (d), all Distributions made by or with respect to, or cash proceeds received from, the ownership, operation, condemnation, refinancing of (net of proceeds used for the exclusive benefit of the subject Collateral Pool Asset) and/or sale of, any Collateral Pool Asset.

(ii) The Collateral Pool Cash Account and all Collateral Pool Cash (including the Tax Escrow Account and the cash therein, subject as set forth below) and all checks, drafts and other cash items ever received by the Plan Agent for deposit in the Collateral Pool Cash Account in accordance with Section 4.2.

Notwithstanding anything contained herein to the contrary, although the Tax Escrow Account shall at all times be subject to the Lien established pursuant to the terms of this Agreement generally for the benefit of the Creditors, it is understood and agreed that the Tax Escrow Account is established and maintained for the purpose of paying the Taxes of the Participating Partners.

(b) Except for Distributions made with respect to the Collateral Pool Assets listed on Schedule Two, all Distributions shall be deposited in the Collateral Pool Cash Account pursuant to Section 4.2, and accounted for among the Participating Partners pursuant to Section 4.3, prior to the application of, or adjustment under, the Netting-Out Agreements. However, the Collateral Pool Assets listed on Schedule Two are attributable to Collateral Entity Projects (each as defined in the Loan Modification Plan), and the lien granted pursuant to Section 3.1(a) hereof with respect to the Collateral Pool Assets listed on Schedule Two shall be a lien in any and all monies that the Participating Partners receive after the application of, and adjustment under, the Netting-Out Agreements, and not a lien on the Distributions from the Collateral Pool Assets listed on Schedule Two. Further, the lien granted pursuant to Section 3.1(a) hereof with respect to the Collateral Pool Assets listed on Schedule Two shall be expressly subject to the Netting-Out Agreement and the Cash Calls (as defined in the Netting-Out Agreements) that may have been previously granted by the Participating Partners to .... or ...., as appropriate, pursuant to those certain Security Agreements Regarding Partnership Interests dated variously and executed by the Participating Partners, as pledgor, and .... or ...., as appropriate, as secured party, for the benefit of the Benefited Parties (as defined in the Security Agreements), which prior liens, whether perfected or not, granted to .... or ...., as appropriate, shall remain a prior lien over any conveyances and/or subordinated liens made pursuant to this Collateral Pool Agreement.

(c) Notwithstanding anything contained herein to the contrary, the Creditors acknowledge and agree that the stock in the various property management companies of ...., the non-exempt personal assets described in the Loan Modification Plan, and the stock or partnership interests of the Persons owning the leases, tenant improvements, goodwill, personal property and similar assets of the various offices of members of .... will not be included as a Collateral Pool Asset.

(d) The Participating Partners hereby severally (and not jointly) grant and convey to, and create in favour of the Plan Agent on behalf of, the Creditors a Lien in, to and on such Participating Partner's respective Rights and interests in the Collateral Pool Assets in which the Participating Partner has an ownership interest which Lien becomes effective, subject to Section 1.3, immediately prior to the commencement of any proceeding under Debtor Relief Laws by, or against, ..., ... or ....; provided, however, (i) this Section 3.1(d) shall have no force and effect, and no Lien shall arise, if a Creditor or an Affiliate of a Creditor commences, or causes the commencement of, any proceeding under the Debtor Relief Laws against ...., ... or ...., and (ii) the Lien granted under this Section 3.1(d) shall be fully released and extinguished if and when such proceeding is discharged or dismissed.

3.2 Termination of security interest

The Plan Agent and the Creditors shall co-operate with the Participating Partners to cause the Lien granted under this Agreement to be released when the Participating Partners are entitled to have such Lien released under the terms of this Agreement. When a Lien terminates under this Agreement, the Plan Agent and each Creditor shall co-operate with the Participating Partners in causing such terminated Lien to be released of record.

3.3 Working capital loans

(a) To secure full and complete payment and performance of the obligations and covenants of the Participating Partners under any Working Capital Loan, but subject to the Permitted Liens and the claims of the IRS (which IRS claims, if any, shall in all circumstances be prior to the claims of Creditors other than Creditors whose Lien Claims constitute Existing Lien claims but only to the extent of such Existing Lien claims and other than Working Capital Lenders to the extent otherwise provided in Sections 5.1 and 5.2, but only to the extent of such Working Capital Loans), the Participating Partners hereby severally (and not jointly) grant and convey to, and create in favour of, any Person now or at any time hereafter advancing proceeds of a Working Capital Loan (a "Working Capital Lender") to one or more of the Participating Partners, Liens (the "Working Capital Liens") in, to and on their respective Rights and interests in the Collateral or any portion thereof, which Liens shall, regardless of when granted, conveyed or created, be superior to the Liens granted by Section 3.1 and shall exist for the equal and ratable benefit of all the Working Capital Lenders. Each Creditor hereby agrees that the Lien granted to the Plan Agent on behalf of the Creditors in Section 3.1 is and shall be inferior and subordinate to the Working Capital Liens granted by this Section 3.3, and further agrees that the Plan Agent shall not be authorised to act in respect of the Liens granted in Section 3.1 without giving fifteen (15) days' prior written notice of such proposed action to the Working Capital Lenders.

(b) In addition to or in lieu of the Working Capital Liens granted in the Collateral, a Participating Partner may, at its option and with the prior written consent of .... during the Preference Period, grant to a Working Capital Lender a Lien in, to and on specific Collateral Pool Assets to secure a Working Capital Loan. The consent of .... shall not be unreasonably withheld and shall be deemed to have been given if no response is received by the Plan Agent within twenty-one (21) days after written notice of the potential Lien is provided to ....

(c) If a Creditor provides a Working Capital Loan, the Participating Partners will co-operate in granting such Creditor cross-collateralisation of its Modified Loans; provided, however, that during the Preference Period, cross-collateralisation will be granted only if such Working Capital Loan is on substantially the same terms, conditions and provisions as ....'s Working Capital Loan.

(d) At the direction of ...., the Plan Agent shall withdraw money from the Tax Escrow Account and loan it to the Participating Partners through its deposit in the Collateral Pool Cash Account. Such loan shall constitute a Working Capital Loan and shall have such terms and conditions as are generally applicable to other Working Capital Loans; provided, however, no payments of interest or principal shall be made during the Preference Period with respect to a Working Capital Loan made by the Participating Partners through the Tax Escrow Account, and the Liens securing such Working Capital Loans shall be subordinate and inferior to all other Liens in favour of the other Working Capital Lenders during the Preference Period.

(e) Payment of interest and principal required under the terms of a Working Capital Loan shall be made from the available Collateral Pool Cash as provided in Sections 5.1 and 5.2.

(f) The Participating Partners hereby agree not to borrow, in the aggregate, more than .... and No/100 Dollars ($.........) as Working Capital Loans.

(g) Each Plan Participant acknowledges that .... has made or may make a $......... loan to ...., and .... has made or may make a $......... loan to .... Both of these loans shall be characterised as Working Capital Loans for purposes of this Agreement.

3.4 Future advances against existing collateral

If a Creditor advances additional funds pursuant to the terms of a Modified Loan, and such Modified Loan is secured by an Existing Lien against Existing Collateral, then all such further advances under such Modified Loan shall also automatically be evidenced and secured by the Existing Lien and shall be superior to Liens granted in Sections 3.1 and 3.3. All proceeds from loans made pursuant to this Section 3.4 must be retained by the owner of the Existing Collateral with respect to which such loan was made and utilised for the exclusive benefit of such Existing Collateral. Further advances made pursuant to this Section 3.4 will not be classified as Working Capital Loans.

SECTION 4: COLLATERAL POOL CASH ACCOUNT

4.1 Establishment of collateral pool cash account

Within seven (7) days after the Effective Date, the Plan Agent shall establish the Collateral Pool Cash Account with one or more Eligible Institutions.

4.2 Deposits into the collateral pool cash account

Each Participating Partner shall deposit into the Collateral Pool Cash Account during the term of this Agreement (a) subject to Section 3.1(b), all Distributions received by such Participating Partner on and after the Effective Date, (b) all money received by such Participating Partner in settlement or satisfaction of judgments relating to Litigation concerning the Collateral Pool Assets, (c) all money arising out of the ownership, operation, condemnation, refinancing of (net of proceeds used for the exclusive benefit of the subject Collateral Pool Project) and/or sale of each Collateral Pool Project after payment of debt service of any Modified Loan secured by such Collateral Pool Project and other Collateral Cash Requirements expenses, (d) all money arising from the sale or refinancing of a Collateral Pool Asset, or any portion thereof, and (e) all proceeds from Working Capital Loans, except that proceeds from the Working Capital Loans shall be disbursed as required or permitted under the terms of such loans, which will include an initial disbursement to the Tax Escrow Account of the Participating Partners' Estimated Taxes in an amount not less than $......... the acquisition of, or investment in, an interest in Newco in an amount approximately equal to $......... (the "Newco Investment") and the establishment, for the benefit of ...., of an interest and *ad valorem* tax reserve in an amount approximately equal to $......... pursuant to the ....Working Capital Loan. In addition, subject to Section 6.2(d), ... shall be required to deposit, and shall deposit into the Collateral Pool Cash Account, all distributions of cash made to .... with respect to the Newco Investment.

4.3 Account among participating partners and collateral pool entities

(a) As provided in Section 5, the Creditors are distributed Collateral Pool Cash in satisfaction of their Deficiencies and Deficiency Certificates without regard to the source of such Collateral Pool Cash. As a result, and because of the varying Rights and interests which the participating Partners have in the Collateral Pool Assets and the varying obligations of the Participating Partners under the Debt, the Plan Agent shall identify the source of the Collateral Pool Cash and credit the Participating Partner who would have received such amounts were it not for this Agreement (and, subject to Section 3.1(b), before application of the Netting-out Agreements). To the extent a Participating Partner's interest in the Collateral Pool Cash is utilised to satisfy all or a portion of another Participating Partner's Several Share of a Debt (including, without limitation, the payment of Taxes), such amounts shall be treated as a loan as between such Participating Partners, bearing interest at the same rate as provided in the Netting-Out Agreements. This loan shall be satisfied from distributions made to the Participating Partners pursuant to Sections 5.4(a)(iii) and 5.4(b) and under the Netting-Out Agreements.

(b) The disbursement of the Collateral Pool Cash and the Collateral to the Creditors in satisfaction, in whole or in part, of such Creditor's Deficiency or Deficiency Certificate is made directly from the Participating Partners to the Creditors even though the Deficiency or Deficiency Certificate may be an obligation of, or attributable to an obligation of, a Collateral Pool Entity. As a result, as between the Participating Partners and the Collateral Pool Entity whose obligation is paid with Collateral Pool Cash or Collateral, such payment shall be characterised as a loan or capital contribution by the Participating Partners to such Collateral Pool Entity, as may be determined by the Parties.

SECTION 5: DISBURSEMENTS OF COLLATERAL POOL CASH

5.1 Preferential payments of working capital lenders

(a) Notwithstanding anything to the contrary contained in this Section 5.1, in no event shall the Plan Agent be required to make any distributions of Collateral Pool Cash under Section 5.1(b) until such time as deposits totalling $......... have been made to the Collateral Pool Cash Account from sources other than Working Capital Loan proceeds.

(b) On the twentieth day of each calendar month during the Preference Period, all of the monies in the Collateral Pool Cash Account, other than monies representing Working Capital Loan proceeds and the $.......... deposited pursuant to Section 5.1(a), shall be distributed as follows:

(i) First, subject to Section 5.1(c), to the Plan Agent in an amount equal to its Overhead Expenses for the previous calendar month;

(ii) Next, to replenish the .... *ad valorem* tax reserve to the extent required by the terms of ....'s Working Capital Loan;

(iii) Next, to replenish the interest reserve established for the benefit of .... to the extent required by the terms of ....'s Working Capital Loan;

(iv) Next, except as otherwise provided by Section 3.3(d), to the Working Capital Lenders, pro rata in accordance with the Current Balance of the Working Capital Loans, in such amount and until such time as $......... has been disbursed to .... pursuant to this Section 5.1(b)(iv);

(v) Next, as designated by ...., to the Tax Escrow Account, unless prohibited by Section 3.3(d) and/or the Participating Partners in full or partial satisfaction of their Collateral Cash Requirements, until such time as $......... has been disbursed pursuant to this Section 5.1(b)(v);

(vi) Next, except as otherwise provided by Section 3.3(d), to the Working Capital Lenders, pro rata in accordance with the Current Balance of the Working Capital Loans, in such amount and until such time as $......... has been disbursed to .... pursuant to this Section 5.1(b)(vi); and

(vii) Finally, except as otherwise provided by Section 3.3(d), fifty per cent (50%) to the Working Capital Lenders pro rata in accordance with the the Current Balances of the Working Capital Loans and fifty per cent (50%) to the Tax Escrow Account and/or to the Participating Partners (as designated by ....) in full or partial satisfaction of their Collateral Cash Requirements, in such amounts and until such time as $......... has been disbursed to .... pursuant to this Section 5.1(b)(vii).

(c) Amounts distributable to the Plan Agent for Overhead Expenses pursuant to Section 5.1(b)(i) shall not exceed $......... for Overhead Expenses attributable to the period commencing upon the Effective Date and continuing until December 31, 19.. . Thereafter, Overhead Expenses distributable to the Plan Agent pursuant to Section 5.1(b)(i) shall not exceed, in any Plan Year, $......... in the Plan Year ending December 31, 19.. , $.......... in the Plan Year ending December 31, 19.. , or $......... in each Plan Year thereafter.

5.2 Other distributions

(a) On the twentieth day of each calendar month during the term of this Agreement, the Participating Partners shall submit to the Plan Agent a certificate setting forth (1) the Participating Partners' Collateral Cash Requirements for the next following calendar month, (2) the Participating Partners' Estimated Taxes for the preceding calendar month, and (3) the amounts due and owing on Working Capital Loans. The Plan Agent shall make monthly disbursements of Collateral Pool Cash requested in such certificates, but only in accordance with the following:

(i) Except as otherwise permitted by Section 4.2(e), during the Preference Period, the Collateral Pool Cash attributable to Working Capital Loan proceeds and the $......... deposited pursuant to Section 5.1(a) shall be distributed:

(A) First, to the Plan Agent in an amount equal to its Overhead Expenses for the previous calendar month which were not otherwise satisfied from disbursements under Section 5.1(b)(i);

(B) Next, if and to the extent determined appropriate by ...., to pay amounts then due and owing on Working Capital Loans, to the extent such amounts are not paid from Distributions to .... from .... and .... or from the interest reserve referenced in Section 5.1(b)(iii) (Advances made from the Collateral Pool Account pursuant to this Subsection 5.2(a)(i)(B) arising from timing differences will be reimbursed from Distributions to .... from .... and .... in accordance with the terms of ....'s Working Capital Loan); and

(C) Finally, to each Participating Partner in the amount shown on the certificate establishing the Collateral Cash Requirements of such Participating Partner for the next calendar month or in such lesser amount as determined appropriate by ....; provided, however, in no event shall proceeds from Working Capital Loans made after the Working Capital Loans of .... and .... be disbursed to Participating Partners to satisfy Collateral Cash Requirements which are not Preference Period Collateral Cash Requirements.

(ii) After the Preference Period, the Collateral Pool Cash shall be distributed:

(A) First, to the Plan Agent in an amount equal to its Overhead Expenses for the previous calendar month;

(B) Next, if and to the extent determined appropriate by .... to pay amounts then due and owing on Working Capital Loans;

(C) Next, to the Tax Escrow Account, in the aggregate amount of the Participating Partners' Estimated Taxes attributable to the prior calendar month and those Estimated Taxes attributable to prior calendar months which have not yet been disbursed to the Tax Escrow Account; and

(D) Finally, to each Participating Partner in the amount shown on the certificate establishing Collateral Cash Requirements of such Participating Partner for the next calendar month or such lesser amount as determined appropriate by ....

(b) Any remaining Collateral Pool Cash not distributed pursuant to Section 5.2(a) shall be retained in the Collateral Pool Cash Account to be subsequently used or disbursed as provided in this Agreement.

5.3 Disbursement as of December 31, 19.., if plan term extended

If on December 31, 19.., the term of this Agreement is extended pursuant to Section 1.2, then after the Plan Agent has made the disbursements required by Sections 5.1 (if applicable) and 5.2 and after the Deficiency, if any, of each Creditor has been determined as of December 31, 19.. (other than Deficiencies for which a Deficiency Certificate has previously been issued), a disbursement of Collateral Pool Cash shall be made by the Plan Agent to the Creditors with a Deficiency and to the Deficiency Certificate Holders (except as provided in Section 2.1(b)), pro rata in accordance with the amount of the Deficiency of the Creditors and the Current Balance of the Deficiency Certificates, in an amount equal to the lesser of (a) the aggregate balance of the Deficiencies plus the aggregate Current Balance of the Deficiency Certificates, or (b) the Collateral Pool Cash less such amount determined by .... to be held in reserve to meet the subsequent estimated Overhead Expenses, Collateral Cash Requirements, Estimated Taxes and debt service on Working Capital Loans.

5.4 Disbursements at conclusion of plan term

When the term of this Agreement has ended, then, after the disbursements required by Sections 5.1 (if applicable) and 5.2 have been made, after the Plan Agent has received the Final Tax Liability Notice for each Participating Partner and after the Deficiency, if any, for each Creditor has been determined, a final disbursement of all funds in the Collateral Pool Cash Account and the Collateral, if necessary, shall be made by the Plan Agent on the later to occur of the May 31 following the calendar year in which the term of this Agreement ended, or ten (10) days after the Plan Agent has received a Final Tax Liability Notice from each Participating Partner. Such disbursements shall be made in the manner set forth below.

(a) If all Collateral Pool Assets have been converted to cash, the Collateral Pool Cash shall be disbursed as follows:

- (i) First, to the Tax Escrow Account in an amount equal to the sum of the amounts set forth on the Participating Partners' Final Tax Liability Notices;
- (ii) Next, to the Creditors with a Deficiency and to the Deficiency Certificate Holders pro rata in accordance with the amount of the Deficiency of the Creditors and the Current Balance of the Deficiency Certificates, in an amount equal to the lesser of (A) the aggregate balance of the Deficiencies plus the aggregate Currency Balance of the outstanding Deficiency Certificates, or (B) the amount determined by taking seventy per cent (70%) of the sum of the Collateral Pool Cash plus the amount of Collateral Pool Cash distributed to the Creditors pursuant to Section 5.3, and subtracting from such amount the Collateral Pool Cash distributed pursuant to Section 5.3*; and
- (iii) Thereafter, to the Participating Partners, all of the remaining Collateral Pool Cash.

(b) If all of the Collateral Pool Assets have not been converted to cash and there is insufficient Collateral Pool Cash to satisfy the disbursements required by Sections 5.4(a)(i) and (ii), then, after the application of all Collateral Pool Cash distributed pursuant to Section 5.4(a), the Plan Agent shall disburse the Collateral in-kind to the Plan Participants, in satisfaction of their remaining claims. The procedure for this disbursement shall be as follows:

- (i) The Plan Participants may unanimously agree as to which Collateral each Plan Participant shall receive in complete satisfaction of such Plan Participants interest in the Collateral;
- (ii) If the Plan Participants cannot agree upon which Plan Participant shall receive which Collateral within ninety (90) days after the distributions are made pursuant to Section 5.4(a), then (A) the Participating Partner with the largest claim may choose, and shall be distributed, thirty per cent (30%) of one piece of Collateral in full or partial satisfaction of his claim; (B) next, the Plan Agent shall divide the remaining Collateral into the number of groups determined below, with each group of Collateral being equal in value; (C) next, on the basis of the unsatisfied claims of the Creditors and Deficiency Certificate Holders, beginning with the Creditor or Deficiency Certificate Holder holding the largest unsatisfied claim and followed by each Creditor and Deficiency Certificate Holder in the order based upon the high-

* For example, if \$......... of Collateral Pool Cash is available for distribution at the conclusion of the plan term, and \$......... was previously distributed to the Creditors pursuant to Section 5.3, then the amount distributable to the Creditors under this Section 5.4(a)(ii) is \$......... (seventy per cent [70%] [\$......... + \$........] − \$.........). If the figure determined under this calculation is \$0 or a negative number, then no disbursement shall be made to the Creditors under Section 5.4(a)(ii).

est to the lowest unsatisfied claims, each Creditor and Deficiency Certificate Holder shall select one or more groups of Collateral until such time as a Creditor's or Deficiency Certificate Holder's claim is reduced to zero; (D) and finally, the remaining Collateral shall be distributed to the Participating Partners. After taking into account distributions of Collateral in amounts equal to the Participating Partners' Final Tax Liability, if there are insufficient assets to satisfy each Plan Participant's remaining claim in full, then only a percentage of each claim shall be distributed to a Plan Participant, which percentage shall be determined by dividing the value of the Collateral available for distribution by the total amount of Plan Participant remaining claims. The Collateral shall be divided into a number of groups which is evenly divisible by the highest common denominator of the unpaid claims of the Plan Participants after the distributions provided for in Section 5.4(a)(ii) have been made, rounded to the nearest $.......... For example, if there are four Plan Participants with unpaid claims of $........., $........., $........ (rounded to $........) and $........., then the Collateral should be divided into groups, each with a value of $..........

Before the Plan Agent disburses the Collateral pursuant to this Section 5.4(b) and before the Plan Agent forecloses upon the Collateral pursuant to Section 12.1(e), the Plan Agent shall determine which Participating Partner will received which Collateral. Thereafter, the Plan Agent shall foreclose upon only the Collateral or portion of the Collateral which is to be distributed to Plan Participants, other than the Participating Partner who owns and will receive such Collateral. Thus, if a Participating Partner is to receive Collateral pursuant to Section 5.4(b) which he already owns, no foreclosure shall be carried out with respect to such Collateral.

5.5 Disbursements for taxes

(a) During the term of this Agreement, the Plan Agent shall distribute from the Tax Escrow Account to the respective Participating Partner, as payments of federal and state income Taxes are required to be paid, the actual amount of federal and state income Taxes owing by the respective Participating Partner as a result of transactions entered into in conjunction with, or as contemplated under, the Loan Modification Plan as determined or approved by .... When the term of this Agreement has ended, the Plan Agent shall distribute to each Participating Partner an amount equal to such Participating Partner's Final Tax Liability.

(b) If additional funds remain in the Tax Escrow Account after the distribution to each Participating Partner of an amount equal to the Final Tax Liability, then the Plan Agent shall transfer all of such remaining Tax Escrow Account funds to the Collateral Pool Cash Account.

(c) In all events, ... shall have the absolute right to reduce the amount distributable from the Tax Escrow Account to an amount which, in ....'s discretion, accurately reflects federal and state income Taxes payable by a Participating Partner solely as a result of the transactions entered into in conjunction with, or as contemplated under, the Loan Modification Plan.

5.6 Limitation on disbursements

Notwithstanding anything to the contrary contained herein, no Creditor shall ever be entitled to receive any disbursement under this Agreement in excess of such Creditor's Deficiency or the Current Balance of such Creditor's Deficiency Certificate, as the case may be.

5.7 Excess collateral pool assets or collateral pool cash

Upon payment in full of the amounts due to the Creditors under Section 5.4, each of the Creditors shall release its Lien on the Collateral. Thereafter, the Plan Agent shall disburse to the Participating Partners one hundred per cent (100%) of any remaining Collateral Pool Cash.

5.8 Disbursements free of lien

Each disbursement of Collateral Pool Cash properly made pursuant to the provision of this Section 5 shall be made to the distributee free of any Liens created pursuant to Sections 3.1, 3.3 or 3.4.

5.9 Disbursement to participating partners

All disbursements from the Plan Agent to the Participating Partners (except for Taxes and Collateral Cash Requirements) shall be made to .... as agent for each of the Participating Partners pursuant to the provisions of the Netting-Out Agreements. The Participating Partners agree that disbursements (except for Taxes and Collateral Cash Requirements) are subject to set-offs under such agreements and that no Participating Partner is entitled to any disbursement hereunder except to the extent the same is netted against all such set-offs.

5.10 Order of disbursements

After the Preference Period and except as provided in Section 4.2(e), disbursements of Collateral Pool Cash will be made first from all sources of Collateral Pool Cash other than proceeds from Working Capital Loans, and then from the proceeds of Working Capital Loans.

5.11 Application of payments of working capital loan preference

Disbursements of Collateral Pool Cash to .... and .... pursuant to Sections 5.1(b)(iv), (vi) and (vii) shall be applied so as to reduce the next scheduled principal payments to .... and .... pursuant to their Working Capital Loan, If disbursements of Collateral Pool Cash to .... and .... pursuant to Section 5.2(a)(i)(B) are applied to reduce the unpaid principal balance on ....'s and/or ....'s Working Capital Loan, such disbursements shall also act to reduce the next amount distributable to .... and/or ...., as the case may be, under Sections 5.1(b)(iv), (vi) and (vii) by an equivalent amount.

SECTION 6: DISPOSITION OF COLLATERAL POOL ASSETS

6.1 Contol of collateral entity project sales

Decisions as to whether to sell any Collateral Entity Project and the terms of such sale shall be governed by the Organisational Documents of such Collateral Pool Entity and the Modification Documents for any Modified Loan secured with a Lien on such Collateral Entity Project.

6.2 Control of collateral pool asset sales

Decisions as to whether to sell any particular Collateral Pool Asset, and the terms of any such sale, shall be governed as follows:

(a) If the Collateral Pool Asset in question does not secure any Modified Loan, all decisions relating to the sale of the Collateral Pool Asset shall rest solely with the Participating Partner who owns such Collateral Pool Asset, subject to any restrictions or limitations contained in the Organisational Documents governing such Collateral Pool Asset, in which case the terms of such Organisational Documents will control.

(b) If the Collateral Pool Asset in question does secure a Modified Loan, the decision relating to the sale of such Collateral Pool Asset shall rest with the Participating Partner who owns such Collateral Pool Asset, subject to any restrictions or limitations contained in the Organisational Documents governing such Collateral Pool Asset, and in the Modification Documents for any Modified Loan secured with a Lien, other than the Lien granted by Section 3.1, on such Collateral Pool Asset.

(c) If any sale of a Collateral Pool Asset or Collateral Entity Project is to be made to a member of ...., a Participating Partner or an Affiliate of either, such sale shall be permissible only if (i) the consideration received therefor is not less than the Fair Market Value of such Collateral Pool Asset or Collateral Entity Project, and (ii) the terms and conditions of such sale are, in the opinion of ...., fair and reasonable terms and conditions no less favourable than could be obtained in an arm's-length transaction with a Person of comparable professional skills, knowledge, ability and performance record which is not an Affiliate of the proposed purchaser. The approval of .... shall not be unreasonably withheld, and .... shall be deemed to have consented to such sale if no response is received by the Plan Agent within twenty-one (21) days after written notice of such sale is provided to .... Notwithstanding anything to the contrary contained in this Section 6.2(c), ... has no right of approval with respect to the redemption of the interest in Newco if made pursuant to the terms of Section 6.2(d).

(d) Notwithstanding anything to the contrary contained in this Agreement, ... has the absolute right to acquire the Newco Investment (excluding any residual interest in Newco attributable to the Newco Investment as more fully described in the Memorandum of Issuance of Units in the Minimum Core Capital Account Unit Class, Unit Class No. 1) by depositing an amount equal to the amount originally paid by .... for the Newco Investment into the Collateral Pool Cash Account. Upon such payment, the Lien granted under this Agreement in the Newco Investment shall terminate. In addition, ... may, at his option, purchase any residual interest which the Newco Investment has in Newco, for an amount equal to the Fair Market Value of such residual interest.

SECTION 7: RELEASES UPON SALE OF COLLATERAL

Upon sale by the owner of any Collateral Pool Asset in accordance with Section 6 and the application of the proceeds from such sale to a Modified Loan, if any, which is secured by such Collateral Pool Asset (which the purchaser does not assume or acquire the asset subject to), the Plan Agent shall promptly execute and deliver to such owner a release of the Lien created by this Agreement, in a form reasonably satisfactory to such owner and the purchaser of such Collateral Pool Asset.

SECTION 8: PARTICIPATING PARTNER REPRESENTATIONS AND WARRANTIES

The Participating Partners severally represent and warrant, to the best of their actual knowledge, as follows:

8.1 Litigation

As of the Effective Date, except for the Litigation and judgments described on Schedule Five, no Participating Partner is aware that any member of .... is involved in any material Litigation, nor is he aware of any material outstanding or unpaid judgments against any member of ....

8.2 Properties; liens

(a) Except for the Permitted Liens, each Participating Partner has good and indefeasible title to their respective Collateral Pool Assets, and such assets are not subject to any Liens.

(b) Except for the Permitted Liens, the Collateral Pool Entities which are members of .... have good and indefeasible title to all their respective Collateral Entity Projects, and such assets are not subject to any Liens.

(c) To the best knowledge of the Participating Partner, Schedule Three itemises each and every material asset, property, right, claim or other property right which would be classified as an asset on a balance sheet of a Participating Partner dated as of the Effective Date if prepared in accordance with modified tax basis accounting principles, other than the Participating Partner's interest in the assets described in Section 3.1(c) and in the Loan Modification Plan.

8.3 General

There are no material facts or conditions known to the Participating Partners as of the Effective Date relating to any of the Collateral which would cause a Material Adverse Effect and which have not been related to the Creditors; and all writings exhibited or delivered to the Creditors by or on behalf of (but only to the extent specifically authorised by ....) any member of .... were and, to the extent hereafter exhibited or delivered, will be genuine and in all material respects what they purport and appear to be.

8.4 Conflict

To the best knowledge of the Participating Partners, without inquiry, the execution and delivery of this Agreement does not conflict with any contract or law to which the Participating Partner is subject, and the Participating Partner has obtained all necessary consents to effectuate the transactions contemplated by this Agreement.

8.5 Binding obligation

This Agreement has been duly executed and delivered and is a legal and binding obligation of each Participating Partner enforceable in accordance with its terms.

8.6 Financial information

The financial information previously delivered to each Creditor represents the good faith estimate of .... of the financial condition of the projects contain therein.

SECTION 9: CERTAIN COVENANTS

So long as this Agreement is in effect, unless a Participating Partner receives a prior notice from the Plan Agent that Determining Creditors do not object to a deviation (provided, however, that no deviation from the provisions of Sections 9.1, 9.14, 9.15 9.16, 9.17, 9.18, 9.19, 9.20 and 9.21 shall be permitted without approval of all Creditors), and subject to Section 9.22, the Participating Partners severally covenant and agree with the Creditors as follows:

9.1 Use of funds

Each Participating Partner will use any disbursements made to such Participating Partner from the Collateral Pool Cash Account pursuant to Section 5.2 only as represented in the certificates submitted pursuant to Section 5.2. Other than the Working Capital Loan proceeds supplied by .... and .... , all Working Capital Loan proceeds shall be used to enhance or preserve the value of the Collateral Pool Assets.

9.2 Transfer of funds

Subject to Section 3.1(b), immediately upon receipt, each Participating Partner will deposit all Distributions and other money described in Section 4.2 (except as provided in Section 4.2(e)) into the Collateral Pool Cash Account. Except as provided in Section 3.1(b), during the Preference Period, all Collateral Pool Entities shall be directed by each Participating Partner to deposit amounts distributable to the Participating Partners directly into the Collateral Pool Cash Account.

9.3 Books and records

Each Participating Partner will, and will use reasonable efforts to cause the Collateral Pool Entities to, keep proper and complete books, records and accounts with respect to its assets and operations and permit the Plan Agent or any Creditor to inspect the same and make and take away copies thereof.

9.4 Items to be furnished

.... will cause the following to be furnished to the Plan Agent:

(a) On the twentieth of each calendar month, a summary of cash activity for the immediately preceding calendar month for each Collateral Pool Project and for each Collateral Pool Entity which is a member of .... ;

(b) Within one hundred twenty (120) days of the end of each Plan Year, a cumulative general ledger setting forth all deposits and disbursements made to and from the Collateral Pool Cash Account;

(c) Copies, promptly after a Participating Partner receives one, of all reports, statements, documents, plans and other written communications furnished by or on behalf of the Collateral Pool Entities to their respective equity interest holders or to any Tribunal, including, but not limited to, the Securities and Exchange Commission (to the extent that a Participating Partner is not prohibited from disbursing such reports, statements, documents, plans and other written communications by the terms of such Collateral Pool Entity's Organisational Documents or otherwise);

(d) Notice, promptly after a Participating Partners knows or has reason to know of, (i) the existence and status of any material Litigation with respect to any Collateral Pool Entity which would, in the event of an unfavourable outcome, have a Material Adverse Effect, (ii) any material change in any material fact or circumstance represented or warranted in this Agreement, or (iii) a Default or Potential Default, specifying the nature thereof and what action such Participating Partner has taken, is taking, or proposes to take with respect thereto; and

(e) Promptly upon request by the Plan Agent, such information (not otherwise required to be furnished under this Agreement) which is available to and prepared or maintained in the ordinary course of business by a Collateral Pool Entity, as the case may be, respecting the business affairs, assets and liabilities of any Collateral Pool Entity, and such opinions certifications and documents otherwise in respect of any Collateral Pool Entity to which a Participating Partner, as the case may be, has access, in addition to those mentioned in this Agreement, as the Plan Agent may reasonably request (to the extent that a Participating Partner is not prohibited from disbursing such information by the terms of any Organisational Documents or otherwise).

Copies of all of the foregoing will be delivered to any Creditor upon request.

9.5 Inspection

Each Participating Partner shall allow, and will use reasonable efforts to cause each Collateral Pool Entity to allow, the Plan Agent and/or any Creditor to inspect any Collateral Pool Project or Collateral Entity Project and to discuss any of the affairs, conditions and finances of the Collateral Pool Entity with any director, officer or employee thereof, from time to time, during reasonable business hours.

9.6 Maintenance of priority of creditor liens

Each Participating Partner will perform such acts and duly authorise, execute, acknowledge, deliver, file and record such additional assignments, security agreements, deeds of trust, mortgages and other agreements, documents, instruments and certificates (including, without limitation, any amendments, modifications or supplements to any of the foregoing in order to accommodate any successor Plan Agent) as the Determining Creditors may reasonably deem necessary or appropriate in order to perfect and maintain the Liens granted by Section 3 in favour of the Plan Agent on behalf of the Creditors and preserve and protect the Rights of the Plan Agent and the Creditors.

9.7 Liens

Except as provided in Section 3.3, each Participating Partner shall refrain from, and will use reasonable efforts to cause each Collateral Pool Entity to refrain from, directly or indirectly, creating, incurring or suffering, or permitting to be created or incurred or to exist any Lien upon any of its Collateral Pool Assets or Collateral Entity Projects, as the case may be, (other than the Rights of and benefits to each Participating Partner under this Agreement) except Permitted Liens.

9.8 Distributions

Each Participating Partner will use his best efforts to cause each Collateral Pool Entity to declare, make and pay Distributions as frequently as is permitted by the Organisational Document of such Collateral Pool Entity and as is warranted in the ordinary course of business by sound business judgement.

9.9 Issuance of securities

Except to the extent the proceeds thereof are deposited into the Collateral Pool Cash Account, the Participating Partners will use reasonable efforts to cause each Collateral Pool Entity to refrain from, directly or indirectly, issuing, selling or otherwise disposing of (a) any of its shares of capital stock or other investment securities of any class or partnership interests therein, (b) any securities convertible into or exchangeable for any such shares, or (c) any carrying Rights, warrants, options or other Rights to subscribe for or purchase any such shares or partnership interests.

9.10 Transactions with affiliates

Except as provided in Sections 6.2(c) and (d), no Participating Partner will approve a Collateral Pool Entity, directly or indirectly, entering into any transaction (including, but not limited to, the sale or exchange of property or the rendering of service) with any of its Affiliates, *other than* (a) upon fair and reasonable terms no less favourable than such Collateral Pool Entity could obtain or could become entitled to in an arm's-length transaction with a Person of comparable professional skills, knowledge, ability and performance record which was not an affiliate of such Collateral Pool Entity, and (b) as permitted under this Agreement.

9.11 Sale of assets

No Participating Partner will approve a Collateral Pool Entity, directly or indirectly, selling, leasing or otherwise disposing of all or any substantial part of its assets, *other than* (a) sales of inventory in the ordinary course of business, (b) sales of equipment for a fair and adequate consideration, provided that if any such equipment is sold, and a replacement is necessary for the proper operation of the business of such Collateral Pool Entity, such Collateral Pool Entity will replace such equipment with adequate equipment, and (c) sales of the Collateral Entity Projects in accordance with the provisions of Section 6.

9.12 Compliance with laws and documents

Each Participating Partner will use reasonable efforts to cause each Collateral Pool Entity to refrain from, directly or indirectly, violating the provision of any Laws, its Organisational Documents or any material agreement of any Collateral Pool Entity if such violation alone, or when aggregated with all other such violations, would cause a Material Adverse Effect.

9.13 Joinder of creditors

Each Participating Partner will use his best efforts to cause every business creditor of the Participating Partners associated with or attributable to members of .... existing on the Effective Date to become a Creditor under this Agreement.

9.14 Conduct of business

Each Participating Partner will use reasonable efforts to cause each Collateral Pool Entity to preserve and maintain its legal existence and all of its leases, privileges, franchises, qualifications and rights that are necessary or desirable in the ordinary conduct of its business. Additionally, each Participating Partner will use his reasonable efforts to cause each Collateral Pool Entity to conduct its business as presently conducted in an orderly and efficient manner in accordance with good practices.

9.15 Maintenance of collateral entity projects

Each Participating Partner will use reasonable efforts to cause each Collateral Pool Entity to maintain its respective Collateral Pool Project in good condition and repair.

9.16 Mergers, acquisitions and dissolutions

Each Participating Partner will use reasonable efforts to prevent any Collateral Pool Entity from becoming a party to a merger or consolidation, or from purchasing or otherwise acquiring all or a substantial part of the assets of any Person or any shares or other evidence of beneficial ownership of any Person, or dissolving or liquidating until such time as a Collateral Pool Project owned by the respective Collateral Pool Entity has been sold and all Partnership business wound up.

9.17 Maximisation of return

Each Participating Partner will use reasonable efforts to maximise the amount of cash distributable to the Creditors pursuant to the terms of this Agreement; provided, however, that the foregoing shall not be construed to prohibit a Participating Partner or an Affiliate from entering into transactions with the Collateral Pool Entities or owners of Collateral Pool Projects so long as the terms of such transactions do not violate the other terms of this Agreement.

9.18 Performance of duties

Each Participating Partner will use his best efforts to perform his duties and obligations under this Agreement, and to cause the other Participating Partners to perform their duties and obligations under this Agreement, in a timely and expeditious manner. Thus, for example, the Participating Partners will use their best efforts to deliver to the Plan Agent the Final Tax Liability Notice as expeditiously as reasonably possible.

9.19 Capital expenditures

During the Preference Period, each Participating Partner will not permit, and will use his best efforts to prevent each Collateral Pool Entity from permitting, expenditures with respect to Collateral Pool Projects and Collateral Entity Projects for extraordinary renovations, additions or developments unless approved by ....; provided, however, this Section 9.19 shall not apply to tenant improvements which are amortised over the term of the lease nor to expenditures for ordinary (consistent with historical standards) maintenance, upkeep and improvements.

9.20 Good faith dealings

Each Participating Partner shall act in good faith in its dealings with the Collateral Pool Entities, Affiliates, Creditors and the other Participating Partners and will not enter into contracts or other arrangements which may be technically permissible under this Agreement but which are to circumvent its provisions in a manner which adversely affects the Creditors.

9.21 Loans to affiliates

Except as provided in Section 4.3(b) and 6.2(c), and except as determined by a Participating Partner to be the appropriate manner to satisfy Collateral Cash Requirements, no Participating Partner shall make, and each Participating Partner shall use its best efforts to prevent a Collateral Pool Entity from making, loans to Affiliates.

9.22 Application to Newco

Notwithstanding anything contained in this Section 9 to the contrary, the representations and warranties made by each Participating Partner and contained in Sections 9.5 through 9.21 do not, and shall not, apply to Newco, its assets or operations.

9.23 Notice of default

Each Participating Partner with knowledge thereof shall promptly notify the Plan Agent and each Creditor of any Material Adverse Change, any Potential Default, any Default and the commencement of, and any material determination in, any proceeding before any governmental authority affecting any Participating Partner.

SECTION 10: CREDITOR REPRESENTATIONS AND COVENANTS

10.1 Representations and warranties

Each Creditor hereby represents and warrants that:

(a) It has credited against the outstanding indebtedness owed to it by an Obligated Party any and all payments or property received by it in partial or full satisfaction of any Modified Loan, Debt or judgment, and that, as of the date such Creditor executes this Agreement, taking all such payments and property into account, the amount outstanding on its Modified Loan, Debt or judgment is as set forth opposite its name on Schedule One hereto.

(b) Such Creditor is entering into this Agreement for itself and not for any other person or entity and will acquire any Deficiency Certificate delivered to it pursuant to this Agreement for itself and not for any other person or entity.

(c) Such Creditor is an "accredited investor" as defined in Rule 501(a) under the Securities Act of 1933, as amended.

(d) Such Creditor has been furnished with all information that it has requested from the Participating Partners regarding its decision to enter into this Agreement and regarding the Deficiency Certificates.

(e) Such Creditor has not offered or sold its interests in this Agreement or any Deficiency Certificates to, or solicited offers to buy any such interest or Deficiency Certificates from, or otherwise approached or negotiated with respect to such interest or Deficiency Certificates with, any prospective purchaser, or taken any other action which would result in a violation of Section 5 of the Securities Act of 1933, as amended, or any applicable state securities laws.

(f) Such Creditor is not entering into this Agreement with a view to resale of its interest in this Agreement.

(g) Such Creditor will not acquire any Deficiency Certificate with a view to resale.

(h) Such Creditor will not transfer, sell, pledge, encumber or otherwise dispose of its interest in this Agreement or any Deficiency Certificate in any manner which would result in a violation of Section 5 of the Securities Act of 1933, as amended, or any applicable state securities laws.

10.2 Covenants

Each Creditor hereby covenants and agrees with each Participating Partner and the Plan Agent that:

(a) Such Creditor will promptly deliver to the Plan Agent and the Participating

Partners, when reasonably requested, a certificate in the form attached hereto as Exhibit "B" setting forth the Current Balance owed to it by an Obligated Party on its Modified Loan. The failure of a Creditor to deliver its certificate as aforesaid on a timely basis shall entitle the Participating Partners to estimate on a reasonable basis (and in accordance with their best knowledge and belief) the Current Balance on such Creditor's Modified Loan as of the time in question. Such estimate by the Participating Partners shall be relied upon by the Plan Agent as the certificate required to be delivered by the Creditor pursuant hereto and shall be binding upon such Creditor for all purposes hereof unless otherwise required by the Participating Partners or until such Creditor issues the certificate.

(b) Upon the execution of this Agreement, each Creditor shall execute and deliver to the Plan Agent and to each Participating Partner a certificate in the form attached hereto as Exhibit "C".

SECTION 11: DEFAULT

The term "Default" as used in this Agreement, means the occurrence of any one or more of the following events; *provided that*, if any such event occurs and the Plan Agent, upon discovering such event, calls a Meeting of Creditors, and Determining Creditors agree at such meeting that they will not instruct the Plan Agent to exercise any Rights hereunder as a result thereof, the occurrence of such event shall no longer be deemed a "Default" hereunder insofar as the state of facts giving rise to such event is concerned, but the same shall not operate as or be deemed to be a waiver with respect to any identical or similar state of facts in existence or occurring theretofore or thereafter:

11.1 Actions by ....

(a) The failure or refusal of ...., ... or .... to punctually and properly perform, observe and comply with any covenant, agreement or condition contained in this Agreement and such failure or refusal continues for a period of ten (10) days after such Participating Partner has been sent written notice thereof from the Plan Agent, provided that if the breach of any covenant, agreement or condition contained in this Agreement is not susceptible of cure within ten (10) days after notice from the Plan Agent is sent, then no Default shall exist so long as such Participating Partner (i) notifies the Plan Agent and each Creditor within ten (10) days that such Participating Partner intends to cure such failure, breach or compliance, (ii) such Participating Partner commences action to cure such failure, breach or compliance within ten (10) days of such notice and diligently prosecutes such cure to completion, and (iii) such Participating Partner completes the cure of such failure, breach or compliance with sixty (60) days of such notice.

(b) ...., ... or .... challenge the validity of this Agreement, or the Liens granted herein, in a Tribunal and do not prevail.

(c) ...., ... or .... commence, or have commenced against them, any proceeding under Debtor Relief Laws and such proceeding is not discharged or dismissed within ninety (90) days; provided, however, no Default shall arise pursuant to this Section 11.1(c) if a Creditor, or an Affiliate of a Creditor commences, or causes the commencement of, any proceeding under the Debtor Relief Laws against ...., ..., or ....

(d) A Default occurs under Section 11.2 and, prior to such Default, the Creditors have on three (3) occasions foreclosed the Liens granted in Section 3.1 by the Participating Partners on three (3) Participating Partners pursuant to Section 12.1(c).

(e) The discovery that any statement, representation or warranty in this Agreement or in any writing ever delivered to any Creditor pursuant to this Agreement, made by ...., ... or ...., was, at the time made, false or erroneous in any material respect.

11.2 Action by other participating partner

(a) The failure or refusal of a Participating Partner other than ...., ... or .... to punctually and properly perform, observe and comply with any covenant, agreement or condition contained in this Agreement and such failure or refusal continues for a period of ten (10) days after such Participating Partner has been sent written notice thereof from the Plan Agent, provided that if the breach of any covenant, agreement or condition contained in this Agreement is not susceptible of cure within ten (10) days after notice from the Plan Agent is sent, then no Default shall exist so long as such Participating Partner (i) notifies the Plan Agent and each Creditor within ten (10) days that such Participating Partner intends to cure such failure, breach or compliance, (ii) such Participating Partner commences action to cure such failure, breach or compliance within ten (10) days of such notice and diligently prosecute such cure to completion, and (iii) such Participating Partner completes the cure of such failure, breach or compliance within sixty (60) days of such notice.

(b) A Participating Partner other than ...., ... or .... challenges the validity of this Agreement, or the Liens granted herein, in a Tribunal and does not prevail.

(c) A Participating Partner other than ...., ... or .... commences, or has commenced against it, any proceeding under Debtor Relief Laws and such proceeding is not discharged or dismissed within ninety (90) days; provided, however, no Default shall arise pursuant to this Section 11.2(c) if a Creditor or an Affiliate of a Creditor commences, or causes the commencement of, any proceeding under the Debtor Relief Laws against a Participating Partner.

(d) The discovery that any statement, representation or warranty in this Agreement or in any writing ever delivered to any Creditor pursuant to this Agreement, made by a Participating Partner other than ...., ... or ...., was, at the time made, false or erroneous in any material respect.

11.3 Termination on December 31, 19...

The termination of this Agreement pursuant to the provisions of Section 1.2(i) on December 31, 19.. , without satisfaction in full of amounts distributable to the Creditors pursuant to Section 5.4(a)(ii).

SECTION 12: CERTAIN RIGHTS AND REMEDIES

12.1 Remedies upon default

(a) Should any Potential Default occur and be continuing, the Plan Agent shall call a Meeting of Creditors. If Determining Creditors so direct at such meeting, the Plan Agent shall promptly notify the Participating Partners of the existence of a Potential Default. At such meeting the Determining Creditors may also direct the Plan Agent to take any of the applicable actions set forth in Sections 12.1(b), 12.1(c) and 12.2 if, after applicable grace and cure periods, the Potential Default becomes an actual Default; provided, however, that regardless of how many Creditors are present and voting at such meeting, the Plan Agent shall only be authorised to act upon the direction of Creditors sufficient to constitute Determining Creditors.

(b) Should any Default occur and be continuing under Section 11.1, the Plan Agent shall, upon the request of Determining Creditors, (i) foreclose, in accordance with the provisions of the UCC or other applicable Laws, any or all Liens granted in Section 3.1

by the Participating Partners, or otherwise realise upon any and all of the Rights Creditors may have in and to the Collateral, or any part thereof (in the amount directed by Determining Creditors), in which event the Plan Agent shall hold such Collateral or the proceeds thereof for the benefit of all of the Creditors; and (ii) exercise any and all other legal or equitable Rights afforded by this Agreement, the Laws of the State of Texas or any other jurisdiction as Determining Creditors shall deem appropriate, or otherwise, including, but not limited to, the Right to bring suit or other proceedings before any Tribunal either for specific performance of any covenant or condition contained in this Agreement or in aid of the exercise of any Right granted to Creditors in this Agreement.

(c) Should any Default occur and be continuing under Section 11.2, the Plan Agent shall, upon the request of Determining Creditors, (i) foreclose in accordance with the provisions of the UCC or other applicable Laws, any or all Liens granted in Section 3.1 by the Participating Partner who is in default, or otherwise realise upon any and all of the Rights Creditors may have in and to the Collateral owned by the Participating Partner who is in default, or any part thereof (in the amount directed by Determining Creditors), in which event the Plan Agent shall hold such Collateral or the proceeds thereof for the benefit of all of the Creditors; and (ii) exercise any and all other legal or equitable Rights against the Participating Partner who is in default afforded by this Agreement, the Laws of the State of Texas or any other jurisdiction as Determining Creditors shall deem appropriate, or otherwise, including, but not limited to, the Right to bring suit or other proceedings before any Tribunal either for specific performance or any covenant or condition contained in this Agreement or in aid of the exercise of any Right granted to Creditors in this Agreement.

(d) Notwithstanding anything contained in Sections 12.1(b) or (c) to the contrary, upon the occurrence of a Default under Sections 11.1 or 11.2, the Plan Agent shall under no circumstances whatsoever be entitled to foreclose upon the Tax Escrow Account or make any distributions therefrom whatsoever to Creditors, but shall continue to make deposits into and disbursements from the Tax Escrow Account to or for the benefit of the Participating Partner who is in default in accordance with the provisions of Sections 5.1, 5.2, 5.4 and 5.5, as appropriate; provided, however, that upon foreclosure pursuant to Section 12.1(e), ... shall be replaced by a nationally recognised accounting firm designated by the Plan Agent to determine how much is to be distributed to the Tax Escrow Account.

(e) Should any Default occur under Section 11.3, the Plan Agent shall first immediately distribute the Collateral Pool Cash in accordance with the distribution priorities of Section 5.4(a) (after determination of the Final Tax Liability); next, determine which Plan Participants are to receive which Collateral; and thereafter, except as limited by Section 5.4(b), foreclose any or all Liens granted in Section 3.1 or otherwise realise upon any and all of the Rights Creditors may have in and to the Collateral, or any part thereof (in the manner directed by Determining Creditors and in accordance with the provisions of the UCC or other applicable Laws), in which event the Plan Agent shall hold such Collateral for final distribution in accordance with the distribution priorities of Section 5.4(b) (after determination of the Final Tax Liability). Notwithstanding anything contained herein to the contrary, upon the occurrence of a Default under Section 11.3, the Plan Agent shall under no circumstances whatsoever be entitled to foreclose upon the Tax Escrow Account or make any distributions therefrom whatsoever to Creditors, but shall continue to make deposits into and disbursements from the Tax Escrow Account to or for the benefit of a Participating Partner in accordance with the provisions of Sections 5.4 and 5.5. Further, prior to the making of any disbursements to Creditors pursuant to Section 5.4 and this Section 12.1(c), the Final Tax Liability of each Participating Partner shall be determined and the Tax Escrow Account shall be adjusted so that it contains sufficient cash and Collateral to pay such amount.

12.2 Performance by the plan agent

If any covenant, duty or agreement of a Participating Partner is not performed in accordance with this Agreement, the Plan Agent shall, at the direction of Determining Creditors, perform, or attempt to perform, such covenant, duty or agreement on behalf of such Participating Partner. In such event, any amount expended by the Plan Agent in such performance or attempted performance shall be payable from the Collateral Pool Cash Account. Notwithstanding the foregoing, it is expressly understood that the Plan Agent does not assume and shall never have, except by express written consent of the Plan Agent, any liability or responsibility for the performance of any covenant, duty or agreement of a Participating Partner hereunder.

12.3 Limitation of liability for defaults—non-recourse provisions

Nothwithstanding anything contained in this Agreement, any Organisational Documents, any Modification Documents or any other documents, instruments or agreements evidencing, governing or relating to this Agreement, the Modified Loans or the Loans which could be interpreted to the contrary, no recourse (including, without limitation, recourse under any deficiency judgment) shall be had for payment or performance of any Participating Partners' or any other Obligated Parties' obligations under the Loans, the Modified Loans, this Agreement, any Modification Documents or any other documents, instruments or agreements evidencing, governing or relating to this Agreement, the Modified Loans or the Loans against any Participating Partner (in whatever capacity, including as a guarantor or as a partner), against any successors, assigns, representatives, employee, officer, director, principal, agents, consultants, attorneys, spouse and accountants of a Participating Partner (collectively, with the Participating Partners, the "Non-Recourse Parties") or any of their respective assets; provided, however, that the foregoing shall not prevent recourse to any Collateral for payment or performance of any obligations hereunder, under the Modified Loans, the Modification Documents or any other documents, instruments or agreements evidencing, governing or relating to this Agreement or the Modified Loans. In furtherance of the foregoing and notwithstanding anything contained in this Agreement, any Organisational Documents, any Modification Documents or any other documents, instruments or agreements evidencing, governing or relating to this Agreement or the Modified Loans which could be interpreted to the contrary, neither the Plan Agent, any Creditor nor any Participant shall be entitled to seek, and the Plan Agent, each Creditor and each Creditor on behalf of its Participants hereby waive the right to seek or assert, with respect to any liability, indebtedness or obligations arising under this Agreement, any Modification Documents, the Modified Loans or any documents, instruments or agreements evidencing, governing or relating to this Agreement, and Modified Loans or the Loans, (i) any liability against any Non-Recourse Parties, (ii) a judgment against any Non-Recourse Parties, (iii) any other legal action against any Non-Recourse Parties, or (iv) any other right or remedy against any Non-Recourse Parties available except for the rights and remedies arising under this Agreement and under the Modification Documents in connection with the Collateral.

12.4 Waivers by creditors

No delay or omission by Creditors in exercising any Right under this Agreement shall impair such Right or be construed as a waiver thereof or any acquiescence therein, nor shall any single or partial exercise of any such Right preclude other or further exercise thereof, or the exercise of any other Right under this Agreement or otherwise.

12.5 Cumulative rights

All Rights available to Creditors under this Agreement are cumulative of and in addition to all other Rights granted to Creditors at law or in equity subject to the limitations imposed by Section 12.3.

12.6 Expenditures by creditors

Each of the Creditors shall be responsible for the payment of all court costs, attorneys' fees, other costs of collection and other sums spent by Creditors pursuant to the exercise of any right hereunder, and no Participating Partner nor any members of .... shall have any liability therefor; provided, however, if ...., ... or .... challenge the validity and enforceability of this Agreement and the Creditors prevail in such contest, then ...., ... and .... shall be personally liable for all reasonable attorneys' fees and other reasonable costs spent by the Creditors in the prosecution of such contest, notwithstanding anything to the contrary herein contained.

SECTION 13: THE PLAN AGENT

13.1 Appointment of plan agent by participating partners

Each Participating Partner hereby appoints the Plan Agent its agent and nominee, on its behalf, (a) to hold and account for the Collateral Pool Cash, and (b) to disburse the Collateral Pool Cash in accordance with the terms hereof.

13.2 Appointment of plan agent by creditors

Each Creditor hereby appoints the Plan Agent its agent and nominee, on its behalf, (a) to take such action as may be requested by the Determining Creditors (when the Determining Creditors are entitled to make such request), (b) to be the secured party, mortgagee, beneficiary and similar party in respect of, and to receive, as the case may be, the collateral assignment of the Collateral for the benefit of the Creditors, and (c) to promptly distribute to each Creditor such Creditor's Pro Rata Part of the Collateral Pool Cash in accordance with the terms hereof.

13.3 Delegation of duties; reliance

(a) The Plan Agent may exercise any of its duties hereunder by or through its officers, directors, employees, attorneys, independent contractors and agents (collectively, "Representatives"). The Plan Agent may employ ...., a member of .... or an Affiliate of either to perform ministerial functions of the Plan Agent so long as the fees and expenses paid therefor do not exceed those which would be charged by non-Affiliated Persons for the performance of similar functions. An Affiliate of .... will be employed to monitor and administer, under the Plan Agent's supervision, the cash flow from the Collateral Pool Entities and the Collateral Cash Requirements of Participating Partners owning an interest in the Collateral Pool Entities, utilising the cash management systems and employees currently used by .... for such purpose. The Plan Participants hereby acknowledge and consent to the employment of such Affiliate for these purposes if, and only so long as, such purposes are performed in a manner acceptable to the Plan Agent.

(b) The Plan Agent and its Representatives shall (i) be entitled to rely upon any writing, resolution, notice, consent, certificate, affidavit, letter, cablegram, telegram, telex or teletype message, statement, order or other document or conversation believed by it or them to be genuine and correct and to have been signed or made by the proper Person and, with respect to legal matters, upon opinion of counsel selected by the Plan Agent, (ii) be entitled to treat each Person reflected in the records of the Plan Agent to be the holder of a Deficiency Certificate as the owner and holder thereof until the Plan Agent has modified its records to reflect an assignment or transfer pursuant to Section 14 (and, any request, authorisation, consent or approval of any Person who, at the time, is the holder of any Deficiency Certificate according to the records of the Plan Agent shall be conclusive and binding on each subsequent holder, assignee or transferee thereof or Participant therein or of or in any certificate or certificates issued in exchange therefor), and (iii) not be deemed to have notice of the occurrence of a Default unless notified thereof by a Creditor, a Participating Partner or a member of ....

13.4 Limitation of plan agent's liability

(a) Neither the Plan Agent nor any of its Representatives shall be liable for any action taken or omitted to be taken by it or them in good faith and believed by it or them to be within the discretion or power conferred upon it or them by this Agreement or be responsible for the consequences of any error of judgment, except for gross negligence or wilful misconduct, and neither the Plan Agent nor any of its Representatives has a fiduciary relationship with any party to this Agreement by virtue of this Agreement.

(b) Unless indemnified to its satisfaction against liability and expense, the Plan Agent shall not be compelled to do any act or to take any action toward the execution or enforcement of the powers created under this Agreement or to prosecute or defend any suit in respect hereof. If the Plan Agent requests instructions from Creditors or from Determining Creditors, as the case may be, with respect to any act or action in connection with this Agreement, the Plan Agent shall be entitled (but shall not be required) to refrain (without incurring any liability to any Person by so refraining) from such act or action unless and until it has received such instructions. In no event, however, shall the Plan Agent or any of its Representatives be required to take any action which it or they reasonably determine could incur for it or them criminal or civil liability.

(c) The Plan Agent shall not be responsible in any manner to any Creditor or any Participant for, and each Creditor represents and warrants that it has not relied upon the Plan Agent in respect of, (i) the creditworthiness of any Obligated Party and the risks involved to such Creditor in the agreements contained herein and in the Modification Documents, (ii) the effectiveness, enforceability, genuineness, validity or the due execution of this Agreement or the Modification Documents, (iii) any representation, warranty, document, certificate, report or statement made herein or furnished hereunder or in connection with this Agreement, (iv) the adequacy of the Collateral as security for the performance of any of the duties and covenants of the Participating Partners hereunder, (v) the existence, priority or perfection of any Lien granted or purported to be granted hereunder, (vi) the existence, priority or perfection of an Existing Lien, or (vii) observation of or compliance with any of the terms, covenants or conditions of the Modification Documents or hereof on the part of any member of .... The Plan Participants hereby jointly and severally agree not to sue or otherwise pursue or seek damages from the Plan Agent for an action taken or omitted by the Plan Agent under or pursuant to this Agreement except for actions or omissions which constitute gross negligence, wilful misconduct or fraud. In addition, the Plan Participants hereby grant the Plan Agent the absolute right to use Collateral Pool Cash which would otherwise be available for distribution under Sections 5.1 and 5.2, to the Participating Partners or to the Tax Escrow Account, to pay any and all liabilities, obligations, losses, damages, penalties, actions, judgments, suits, costs, reasonable expenses and reasonable disbursements of any kind or nature whatsoever which may be imposed on, asserted against or incurred by the Plan Agent in any way relating to or arising out of this Agreement or any action taken or omitted by the Plan Agent under this Agreement, except to the extent the same result solely from gross negligence, wilful misconduct or fraud by the Plan Agent.

13.5 Agreement of the plan agent

The Plan Agent shall (a) deal with the account for the Collateral Pool Cash in accordance with this Agreement, (b) disburse the Collateral Pool Cash in accordance with this Agreement, (c) subject to the provisions of Section 13.4, taken only such action as may be requested by the Determining Creditors in accordance with this Agreement, or as may be otherwise authorised hereby, (d) act as secured party, mortgagee, beneficiary and similar party in respect of, and receive, as the case may be, the collateral assignment of the Collateral for the benefit of the Creditors, (e) distribute to each Creditor such Creditor's *Pro Rata* Part of the Collateral Pool Cash and the Collateral in accordance with this Agreement, and (f) promptly disburse to the Participating Partners the balance of the Collateral Pool Cash Account and the Tax Escrow Account as provided for herein upon termination of this Agreement.

13.6 Resignation of plan agent

The Plan Agent may resign and be discharged of its duties hereunder by written notice of resignation sent to the Participating Partners and the Creditors not less than one hundred twenty (120) days before the date such resignation is to take effect.

13.7 Removal of plan agent

Either .... or the Determining Creditors may, with the written approval of the other and not less than thirty (30) days' written notice to the Plan Agent, remove the Plan Agent at any time, with or without cause. Any such removal shall not take effect, however, until the appointment of a successor Plan Agent.

13.8 Appointment of successor plan agent

(a) If the Plan Agent or any successor Plan Agent resigns or is removed, ... and the Determining Creditors shall agree upon a successor. Upon its appointment, the successor Plan Agent shall mail notice of the appointment of such successor to all Creditors. If no agreement is reached concerning appointment of a successor Plan Agent within ninety (90) days after the Plan Agent has given notice of its resignation or has been removed, the Plan Agent, ... or the Determining Creditors shall have the right to petition a court of competent jurisdiction to appoint a successor Plan Agent.

(b) If the Plant Agent dissolves, if its property or business is taken under the control of any Tribunal or if the Plan Agent dies or becomes mentally incapacitated, then .... shall select one of the six largest United States based accounting firms to act as temporary Plan Agent and such accounting firm shall immediately become the temporary Plan Agent, until such time as a permanent Plan Agent is appointed pursuant to the provisions of Section 13.8(a). The temporary Plan Agent shall immediately send notice to each Participating Partner and Creditor of its appointment as the temporary Plan Agent.

(c) Upon its appointment in accordance with the terms of Section 13.8(a) or (b) and the mailing of notice of such appointment to each Plan Participant, the successor Plan

Agent shall become fully vested with all of the estates, properties, rights, powers, trusts, duties and obligations or its predecessor Plan Agent with like effect as if originally named Plan Agent. Upon request of the successor Plan Agent, the predecessor Plan Agent shall deliver all records, Collateral Pool Assets, securities and moneys held by it as Plan Agent to its successor and provide an accounting for all receipts and expenditures which it made.

13.9 Specific duties of the plan agent

In addition to the various obligations and duties of the Plan Agent described elsewhere in this Agreement, the Plan Agent shall have the following specific duties:

(a) To maintain accurate and complete records with respect to the transactions occurring pursuant to this Agreement;

(b) To issue the Deficiency Certificates in accordance with this Agreement;

(c) To invest the cash in the Collateral Pool Cash Account and in the Tax Escrow Account, as directed by ...., in (i) obligations of the United States of America and its agencies or obligations guaranteed by the United States of America, or (ii) accounts at or certificates of deposit issued by an Eligible Institution (up to the maximum insured amount), or (iii) accounts at or certificates of deposit issued by commercial banks organised under the Laws of the United States of America or any state thereof and having a combined capital, surplus and undivided profits of not less than $.........;

(d) To receive and keep available for inspection by any Plan Participant (upon reasonable notice to the Plan Agent) all reports, documents, financial statements, notices and certificates required or permitted to be delivered to the Plan Agent by the terms of this Agreement, and to deliver copies thereof to the Plan Participants at the time in question, and if such documents are not delivered as required by the provisions hereof, to request and take all reasonable action necessary to obtain;

(e) To call a Meeting of Creditors upon its determination that such meeting is necessary or desirable, or upon written request from Creditors holding the percentage of Debt required by Section 15.18, and to preside at such meetings;

(f) To act as the secured party, mortgagee, beneficiary and similar party on behalf of the Creditors in respect of, and to receive, as the case may be, the collateral assignment of the Collateral under Section 3 of this Agreement, and to take such actions to declare Defaults and to enforce the Liens granted under this Agreement as may be directed by Determining Creditors;

(g) To inspect any of the properties of any Collateral Pool Entity and to discuss any of the affairs, conditions and finances of the Collateral Pool Entities with any director, officer or employee thereof, to the extent requested to do so by Determining Creditors;

(h) To notify the Creditors promptly after becoming aware of the occurrence of any Potential Default or Default (other than through receipt of a written notice thereof from a Participating Partner, which the Plan Agent shall promptly deliver to Creditors pursuant to Section 9.4(d));

(i) To meet and correspond with individual Creditors and to provide such information as may be reasonably requested by such Creditors and which is available to the Plan Agent;

(j) To amend from time to time the list of Participating Partners and Creditors set forth on Schedule One as additional Persons elect to participate under this Agreement;

(k) To disburse the Collateral Pool Cash in accordance with this Agreement;

(l) To select and appoint an appraiser when and as necessary under this Agreement;

(m) To take such action on behalf of a Participating Partner as is required by such Participating Partner under the terms of this Agreement when such action is, in the Plan Agent's discretion, necessary or appropriate and such Participating Partner refuses to act; and

(n) To prepare and deliver the monthly and annual reports contemplated in Sections 9.4(a) and (b).

13.10 Fees and expenses of plan agent

The Plan Agent shall be paid a fee, as agreed between the Plan Agent and ...., payable out of Collateral Pool Cash pursuant to Sections 5.1 and 5.2, for the performance of its duties. In addition, the Plan Agent shall reimburse itself out of Collateral Pool Cash for all reasonable costs and expenses incurred in the performance of any of its duties, including the costs, expenses and fees of any Person employed by the Plan Agent pursuant to Section 13.3 to perform duties delegated to such Person by the Plan Agent. The Plan Agent shall not be entitled to reimbursement for any expense as may be attributable to its wilful misconduct or gross negligence.

13.11 Accounting and asset management fee

.... will utilise its employees and other resources in the preparation of financial reports and tax returns for each Collateral Pool Entity and for the management, marketing and sale of the Collateral Pool Projects and Collateral Entity Projects. These services, and the expenses associated therewith, are not provided for in the property management contracts governing the respective Collateral Pool Project and Collateral Entity Project. Accordingly, each Collateral Pool Entity, and the owner of each Collateral Pool Project, will be charged a reasonable fee for the services described above. This fee will be limited to an amount necessary to meet the expenses of .... incurred in providing such services.

13.12 Bonding of plan agent

Prior to performing any of its duties, the Plan Agent shall procure, for the benefit of the Plan Participants, a fidelity bond issued by a reputable surety company acceptable to .... and the Determining Creditors, initially in the amount of $......... conditioned upon (a) a proper accounting of any and all money deposited with or invested by the Plan Agent pursuant to this Agreement and for any return on such money, (b) prompt repayment or distribution pursuant to this Agreement of such money and return, and (c) faithful performance of the Plan Agent's duties under this Agreement. The cost for such bond shall be paid from the Collateral Pool Cash.

SECTION 14: TRANSFER OF DEFICIENCY CERTIFICATES

14.1 Participations

Each Creditor shall be entitled to sell its Modified Loan in whole only, and not in part, prior to the date such Creditor is granted a Deficiency Certificate. In addition, each Creditor shall be entitled to hold its Deficiency Certificate for the benefit of any Person who is a Participant in a Modified Loan. The foregoing provisions of this Section 14.1 are in all respects subject to the following (a) in each case, all applicable Laws must be complied with by both the grantor Creditor and its Participant (and such Creditor and such Participant shall have all responsibility and liability in respect of such compliance), and the Plan Agent, and Participating Partners do not, by virtue of this Agreement, assume any duty with respect to, or assure, any such compliance; (b) neither the Plan Agent nor any Participating Partner shall have any obligation or liability to, or any obligation to negotiate or confer with, any such Participant; and (c) the Plan Agent shall be entitled to treat each Creditor as the sole owner of all of its Deficiency Certificate without regard to notice or actual knowledge of any such participation.

14.2 Record ownership

The records of the Plan Agent shall be conclusive as to what Persons are Deficiency Certificate Holders for any particular purpose at any give time. With respect to Deficiency Certificates or portions thereof transferred pursuant to this Section 14, the Plan Agent shall make all distributions in respect of a Deficiency Certificate to the holders of such Deficiency Certificate as their interests are reflected in the records of the Plan Agent.

14.3 Transfer of deficiency certificates

A Deficiency Certificate Holder may sell or transfer all or any portion of a Deficiency Certificate without the consent of any Person. Written notice of such sale or transfer shall be given to the Plan Agent by the transferor following such sale or transfer. If a Deficiency Certificate, or portion thereof, is sold or transferred, then the Plan Agent shall thereafter cancel the Deficiency Certificate then held by the transferor and issue a new Deficiency Certificate to the transferee, and to the transferor, if necessary, evidencing the correct ownership interests. Each Deficiency Certificate Holder shall be bound by the terms of this Agreement.

SECTION 15: MISCELLANEOUS

15.1 Headings

The headings, captions and arrangements used in the Agreement are for convenience only and shall not be deemed to limit, amplify or modify the terms of this Agreement, nor affect its meaning.

15.2 Communications

Whenever this Agreement requires or permits any consent, approval, notice, request or demand from one party to another, such communication must be in writing to be effective and shall be deemed to have been given on the day actually delivered or, if mailed, on the third day after it is enclosed in an envelope, addressed to the party to be notified at the address stated below, properly stamped, sealed and deposited in the appropriate official postal service. Until changed by notice pursuant hereto, the address for each party for purposes hereof is set forth below the signature line of such party.

15.3 Form and number of documents

Each agreement, document, instrument or other writing to be furnished to Creditors under the Agreement must be in form and substance and in such number of counterparts as may be satisfactory to the Plan Agent and its counsel.

15.4 Survival

All covenants, agreements, undertakings, representations and warranties made herein shall survive execution of this Agreement by each party executing this Agreement and, except as otherwise indicated, shall not be affected by any investigation made by any party.

15.5 Governing law

This Agreement is being executed and delivered, and is intended to be performed, in the State of Texas, and the Laws (other than conflict of laws provisions thereof) of the State of Texas shall govern the Rights and duties of the parties hereto and the validity, construction, enforcement and interpretation of this Agreement.

15.6 Venue; service of process

Each party hereto hereby (a) irrevocably submits to the jurisdiction of the state and federal courts of the State of Texas and agrees and consents that service of process may be made upon it in any legal proceeding arising out of or in connection herewith by service of process as provided by Texas Law, (b) irrevocably waives, to the fullest extent permitted by law, any objection which it may now or hereafter have to the laying of venue of any Litigation arising out of or in connection with this Agreement brought in district courts of .... County, Texas, or in the United States District Court for the .... District of Texas, ... Division, (c) irrevocably waives any claims that any Litigation brought in any such court has been brought in an inconvenient forum, (d) agrees to designate and maintain an agent for service of process in ...., Texas, in accordance with any such Litigation and to deliver to the Plan Agent evidence thereof, (e) irrevocably consents to the service of process out of any of the aforementioned courts in any such Litigation by the mailing of copies thereof by certified mail, return receipt requested, postage prepaid, to such party at its address set forth herein, and (f) irrevocably agrees that any legal proceeding against any party hereto arising out of or in connection with this Agreement shall be brought in the District Courts of .... County, Texas, or in the United States District Court for the .... District of Texas, ... Division. Nothing herein shall affect the Right of the Plan Agent to commence legal proceedings or otherwise proceed against any Creditor in any jurisdiction or to serve process in any manner permitted by applicable law.

15.7 Invalid provisions

If any provision of this Agreement is held to be illegal, invalid or unenforceable, such provision shall be fully severable, and in lieu of such illegal, invalid or unenforceable provision, there shall be added automatically as a part of this Agreement a provision as similar in terms to such illegal, invalid or unenforceable provision as may be possible and be legal, valid and enforceable. This Agreement shall then be construed and enforced in view of the illegal, invalid or unenforceable provision as modified.

15.8 Entirety and amendments

(a) This Agreement embodies the entire agreement among the parties and supersedes all prior agreements and understandings (other than the Modification Documents), if any, relating to the subject matter hereof, including, without limitation, the Loan Modification Plan.

(b) Except as provided in Section 13.9(j), this Agreement may be amended only by an instrument in writing executed jointly by ...., the Plan Agent and Determining Creditors and supplemented only by documents delivered or to be delivered in accordance with the express terms hereof. Notwithstanding the foregoing, any amendment to this Agreement which purports to accomplish any of the following must be by an instrument in writing executed by .... and the Plan Agent, and executed or approved by each Creditor (i) extends the date of any distribution to be made hereunder; (ii) changes the definition of "Pro Rata Part", or "Determining Creditors"; or (iii) changes this Section.

15.9 Multiple counterparts

This Agreement has been executed in a number of identical counterparts, each of which shall be deemed an original for all purposes and all of which constitute, collectively, one agreement; but, in making proof of this Agreement, it shall not be necessary to produce or account for more than one such counterpart. It is not necessary that the Participating Partners, the Plan Agent and each Creditor execute the same counterpart so long as identical counterparts are executed by each party. It is contemplated that Creditors and additional Participating Partners may from time to time after the date this Agreement becomes effective pursuant to Section 15.14 elect to become parties to this Agreement by executing identical counterparts of this Agreement, and all of such counterparts shall constitute part of this Agreement even though not executed at substantially the same time. The Plan Agent is authorised to insert from time to time each of the executed signature pages into one or more counterparts of this Agreement containing signatures of all parties hereto, each of which counterparts shall be deemed an original of this Agreement for all purposes.

15.10 Creditors; parties bound; successors and assigns

This Agreement shall be binding upon and inure to the benefit of each Participating Partner, the Plan Agent and each of the Creditors, and their respective permitted successors and assigns. No Participating Partner may, without the prior written consent of all Creditors or as otherwise permitted herein, assign any duties or obligations hereunder, provided, that each Participating Partner shall (without the necessity of consent from, or notification to, Creditors) have the absolute right to transfer, sell, assign, hypothecate, pledge, encumber and otherwise deal with their respective Rights hereunder.

15.11 Money

Unless stipulated otherwise, all references in this Agreement to "dollars", "money", "payments" or other similar financial or monetary terms are references to currency of the United States of America.

15.12 Number and gender of words

Whenever in this Agreement the singular number is used, the same shall include the plural where appropriate, and vice versa; and words of any gender in this Agreement shall include each other gender where appropriate.

15.13 Mutual release

By their execution of this Agreement, each of the parties hereto hereby releases, remises, acquits and for ever discharges each of the other parties hereto, their successors, assigns, representatives, employees, officers, directors, principals, agents, consultants, attorneys and accountants, past and present, from any and all claims, rights, demands, liabilities, damages, losses, expenses, detriments, injuries, controversies, contributions, indemnities and causes of action, past or present, of any nature or of whatever kind or character, whether or not now known, arising from the beginning of time to the Effective Date of this Agreement out of or relating to, growing out of, resulting from or connected in anywise with any and all claims asserted or assertable that such party may now have in connection with the Loans or the Modified Loans, or any transaction or occurrence related in any way thereto, except for the obligations and indebtedness relating to the Modified Loans continued or created herein or in any Modification Documents.

15.14 Effective date of agreement

This Agreement shall become effective when counterparts hereof have been executed by ...., ... and ...., the Plan Agent and at least one Creditor, and ....'s Working Capital Loan is initially funded. A certificate from .... will be presumptive evidence of the funding date.

15.15 Delegation of duties and rights

Upon providing adequate notice to the Plan Agent of such officer's, director's, employee's, attorney's, agent's or other representative's authority, a Participating Partner, the Plan Agent or any Creditor may exercise any of its duties or Rights under this Agreement by or through its officers, directors, employees, attorneys, agents or other representatives.

15.16 Construction of provisions

No inference in favour of, or against, any party shall be drawn from the fact that such party has drafted any portion of this Agreement.

15.17 Creditors committee

At the election of Determining Creditors, Determining Creditors may form a committee of Creditors (the "Creditors Committee"). The Determining Creditors shall have the right to delegate all of the rights, duties and obligations of the Determining Creditors under this Agreement to the Creditors Committee, provided that the Plan Agent and .... are advised of same, in writing. Upon such delegation, all decisions of the Creditors Committee may be relied upon by the Plan Agent, the Participating Partners and other members of .... as being the decisions of the Determining Creditors. Further, the Plan Agent and .... will cooperate with and recognise any Creditors Committee so formed. The Determining Creditors shall be responsible for establishing the byelaws pursuant to which the establishment and operation of the Creditors Committee will be governed.

15.18 Meetings of creditors

Meetings of the Creditors, for any purpose or purposes, may be called by Creditors holding at least fifteen per cent (15%) of the aggregate amount of Debt. Written or printed notice, stating the place, date and hour of the meeting and the purpose or purposes for which the meeting is called, shall be delivered by the Plan Agent not less than fifteen (15) days before the date of the meeting, either personally or by mail, to each Creditor. Creditors may participate in and hold a meeting by means of conference telephone or similar communications equipment by means of which all persons participating in the meeting can hear each other, and participation in such meeting shall constitute presence in person at such meeting.

15.19 References to ....

References in this Agreement to ...., except for references in Section 11, shall be understood to mean ...., his administrators, his executor, his designee or such other

Person authorised by .... to act on his behalf with respect to the subject determination.

15.20 Limitation of participating partner rights

Notwithstanding anything contained in this Agreement to the contrary, if a Participating Partner's Rights or duties are limited under any Organisational Documents, such limitations shall apply to this Agreement.

SECTION 16: CERTAIN DEFINITIONS

As used in this Agreement, the following terms have the meanings indicated:

Affiliate means, with respect to any Person, a Person (a) controlling, controlled by or under common control with the Person in question, whether direct or through one or more intermediaries, or (b) who is a director, officer or general partner of any member of ...., or is a family member of any of the Persons described in this clause (b). The term "control", as used in the immediately preceding sentence, means, with respect to a Person that is a corporation, the right exercise, directly or indirectly, more than fifty per cent (50%) of the voting rights attributable to the shares of the controlled corporation and, with respect to a Person that is not a corporation, the possession, directly or indirectly, of the power to direct or cause the direction of the management or policies of the controlled Person. The term "family member", as used in this definition of Affiliate, means, with respect to any individual, the spouse of such individual, or any parent or sibling of such individual, or any lineal descendant (whether by adoption or consanguinity) of such individual or of any of the foregoing at the time in question. For purposes of this Agreement, each Participating Partner shall be deemed as Affiliate of each other Participating Partner and each member of..........

Agreement means this Collateral Pool Agreement.

Appraised Value means as to each item of Existing Collateral (a) the gross fair market value of the subject Existing Collateral as agreed to by the owner of such Existing Collateral, the Creditor holding a Lien thereon and the Plan Agent, (b) if no agreement can be reached pursuant to (a) above, and if the higher of the following two appraised values does not exceed by more than ten per cent (10%) the lower appraised value, the average of (i) the fair market value of the Existing Collateral as appraised for the current use by an appraiser selected by (and at the expense of) the owner of the Existing Collateral in question (the "Owner Appraised Value"), and (ii) and fair market value of the Existing Collateral in question as appraised for the current use by an appraiser selected by (and at the expense of) the Creditor holding a Lien thereon (the "Creditor Appraised Value"), or (c) if the difference between the Owner Appraised Value and the Creditor Appraised Value is more than ten per cent (10%) of the lower appraised value, the average of (i) the Owner Appraised Value, (ii) the Creditor Appraised Value, and (iii) the fair market value of the Existing Collateral in question as appraised for the current use by an appraiser appointed by agreement of the appraisers selected by the owner of the Existing Collateral in question and the Creditor holding a Lien thereon. The owner of the Existing Collateral and the Creditor holding a Lien thereon shall each be responsible for fifty per cent (50%) of the cost of the third appraisal. If (i) either party fails to appoint an appraiser as set forth above, (ii) a third appraiser is not appointed as provided above, or (iii) any person appointed as an appraiser by or on behalf of either party dies, fails to act, resigns or become disqualified and the party by or on behalf of whom such appraiser was appointed shall fail to appoint a substitute appraiser within ten (10) days after being requested to do so by the other party, the appraiser in question shall be appointed by the Chief Judge of the United States District Court, ... District of Texas, ... Division (acting in his non-judicial capacity or, to the extent he refuses to act in that capacity, in his judicial capacity), upon application of either party.

Collateral has the meaning given in Section 3.1.

Collateral Cash Requirements means (i) capital contributions, loans, advances, principal, interest and other payments with respect to Collateral Pool Assets and Collateral Entity Projects which a Participating Partner should make (including, without limitation, costs and expenses directly related to the ownership, operation, maintenance and disposition of the Collateral Pool Assets and Collateral Entity Projects, *ad valorem* property taxes, assessments [whether governmental or private], legal and accounting fees [and any retainers required with respect thereto], appraisal costs and other charges related to, or secured by, the Collateral Pool Assets and Collateral Entity Projects, prevailing market rate leasing and property management fees due under property management agreements, based on gross rental income from such Collateral Pool Projects and Collateral Entity Projects, and any other project cost related thereto and not otherwise paid from the net operating income, if any, from the Collateral Pool Projects and Collateral Entity Projects in question or from the Creditor holding an Existing Lien thereon, if any), (ii) amounts necessary to fund any settlements entered into by a Participating Partner with a bona fide third Person who is not an Affiliate of such Participating Partner or a judgment against a Participating Partner held by a bona fide third Person who is not an Affiliate of such Participating Partner, (iii) expenses estimated by a Participating Partner to be incurred for legal representation of such Participating Partner in connection with any Collateral Pool Asset or any disputed Debts or Taxes related to any Collateral Pool Entity, Collateral Entity Project or Collateral Pool Asset, or this Agreement (including any retainers required with respect to any such representation), (iv) principal, interest and other charges attributable to the guaranteed portion of the loan made by .... in the original principal amount of $......... which are not otherwise paid from the collateral which secures such loan, (v) amounts owed by a Participating Partner to other partners in members of .... for payment of Taxes attributable to periods prior to the Effective Date, and (vi) another partner's respective share of expenses for each of the Collateral Pool Entities and Collateral Pool Projects which, under the relevant partnership or joint venture agreement or otherwise, should be paid by other partners, venturers or owners, but which have not been paid.

Collateral Entity Projects means the real property owned by the Collateral Pool Entities, or a subsidiary of a Collateral Pool Entity, and listed on Schedule Three under the heading "Collateral Entity Projects", together with any improvements thereon.

Collateral Pool Assets means all of the interests of the Participating Partners in the Collateral Pool Entities, Collateral Pool Projects and the other assets shown on Schedule Three, plus all distributions of property other than cash made by a Collateral Pool Entity to the Participating Partners who are owners thereof.

Collateral Pool Cash means all money deposited into the Collateral Pool Cash Account in accordance with Section 4, together with any earnings thereon.

Collateral Pool Cash Account means one or more bank accounts established by the Plan Agent at Eligible Institutions and into which Collateral Pool Cash is deposited in accordance with Section 4, as may thereafter be invested.

Collateral Pool Entity means any corporation, partnership, joint venture or other legal entity in which a Participating Partner owns an interest of any kind directly or through one or more legal entities and which is listed on Schedule Three under the heading "Collateral Pool Entities".

Collateral Pool Projects means the real property and the personal property (excluding the interests of a Participating Partner in a Collateral Pool Entity) listed on Schedule Three under the heading "Collateral Pool Projects".

Creditor means (a) a Person named on Schedule One as a creditor who has executed this Agreement as a creditor, (b) a Person receiving a Deficiency Certificate in satisfaction of obligations of one or more Partners to such Person, or (c) any Person who becomes a party to this Agreement as a creditor in accordance with the terms hereof. Creditors with more than one Modified Loan (or other Debt) shall be accounted for separately for each Modified Loan (or Debt). Thus, for example, a Creditor with more than one Modified Loan shall be treated as a separate Creditor with respect to each Modified Loan.

Current Balance means, as of any date, the outstanding principal balance of and accrued but unpaid interest on a Deficiency Certificate, Debt, Modified Loan or Working Capital Loan, as the case may be.

Debt means the aggregate outstanding principal balance, and accrued but unpaid interest thereon, of all obligations of the applicable Person which should be classified upon such Person's balance sheet as liabilities.

Debtor Relief Laws means the Bankruptcy Code of the United States of America and all other applicable liquidation, conservatorship, bankruptcy, moratorium, rearrangement, receivership, insolvency, reorganisation, suspension of payments or similar debtor relief Laws affecting the Rights of creditors generally.

Default has the meaning set forth in Section 11.

Deficiency means, as of any date:

(a) With respect to any Creditor which is or was the payee under a Modified Loan and such Modified Loan is or was secured by an Existing Lien on Existing Collateral, (i) the amount by which the then Current Balance of such Creditor's Modified Loan exceeds the amount of net proceeds derived by such Creditor from the sale of the Existing Collateral, (ii) the amount of the Current Balance of such Creditor's Modified Loan after the application of proceeds received through refinancing or otherwise, if such Creditor's Existing Lien is released, and (iii) if the Existing Collateral has not been sold prior to December 31, 19.. , or December 31, 19.. , as the case may be, the amount by which the then Current Balance of such Creditor's Modified Loan exceeds the Appraised Value of such Existing Collateral on such date, plus such amount theretofore recovered from Persons, other than Participating Partners, as payment on the Modified Loan (or any guarantee or similar obligation with respect thereto); or

(b) With respect to any judgment Creditor of a Participating Partner, the lesser of (i) the amount of the judgment which remains unsatisfied on the date such judgment Creditor elects to become a Deficiency Certificate Holder, or (ii) the amount which such judgment Creditor has agreed to accept in satisfaction of such judgment; or

(c) With respect to any Creditor to whom any member of .... is obligated as a result of any Person drawing upon a letter of credit under which such member of .... is the account party, the amount by which the outstanding amount of such indebtedness exceeds the amount of any net proceeds derived from the sale of the Existing Collateral against which such Creditor has a Lien on the date such sale occurs; or

(d) With respect to any Creditor who is a party to a lawsuit involving any member of ...., or any Creditor who is otherwise involved in a dispute with any member of .... or is otherwise owed a general unsecured Debt, and with whom such member of .... has reached an agreement as to the settlement of such lawsuit or other dispute or as to the amount of such Debt, the amount of any sum which such member of .... has agreed to pay to such Creditor which remains outstanding and unpaid on the date such Creditor elects to become a Deficiency Certificate Holder.

Deficiency Certificate means a certificate substantially in the form attached hereto as Exhibit "A", issued by the Plan Agent to a Creditor, its transferee and any certificate subsequently issued by the Plan Agent in substitution therefor or replacement thereof.

Deficiency Certificate Holder means the lawful owner and holder of a Deficiency Certificate as registered in the records of the Plan Agent at the time in question.

Determining Creditors means, as of any date, Creditors who are owed more than fifty per cent (50%) in amount of the Debt the Participating Partners and Collateral Pool Entities owe to the Creditors at the time in question (whether such Debt is evidenced by a Modified Loan or a Deficiency Certificate).

Distribution means (i) with respect to any shares of any capital stock or other equity securities issued by a Collateral Pool Entity, (a) the retirement, redemption, purchase or other acquisition for cash of any such securities, (b) any dividend paid on or with respect to any such securities, (c) any loan or advance by a Collateral Pool Entity to, or other investment by a Collateral Pool Entity in, the holder of any such securities, and (d) any other payment made by a Collateral Pool Entity with respect to such securities; (ii) with respect to any partnership interest, joint venture interest or trust interest in a Collateral Pool Entity, (a) any distribution by a Collateral Pool Entity to a Participating Partner with respect to his interest therein, (b) any loan or advance by a Collateral Pool Entity to, or other investment by a Collateral Pool Entity in, the holder of such partnership, joint venture or trust interest, and (c) and other payments made to a Participating Partner with respect to such partnership, joint venture or trust interest; and (iii) with respect to any Collateral Pool Asset which is a promissory note, all payments made to the holder of such note with respect thereto.

Effective Date means the date on which this Agreement has been executed by ...., ... and ...., the Plan Agent and at least one Creditor, and the .... Working Capital Loan is initially funded.

Eligible Institution means a federal or state chartered banking association or corporation or savings and loan association, the deposits of which are insured by the Federal Deposit Insurance Corporation.

Estimated Taxes means an amount equal to the sum of (a) the deemed state and federal income Taxes (as estimated by such Participating Partner) attributable to (i) the management, ownership, maintenance, operation, disposition and foreclosure of the Collateral Pool Assets and the Collateral Entity Projects, (ii) the payment, cancellation, disposition and IRC Section 752 deemed distribution of the Debts of such Participating Partner or Collateral Pool Entities which affected a Participating Partner, (iii) depreciation recapture and investment tax credit recapture, (iv) transactions entered into in conjunction with, or as contemplated in, the Loan Modification Plan, plus (b) the estimated state and federal income Taxes of the Participating Partner, the payment of which is anticipated to arise but has been deferred to subsequent taxable years (e.g. a Participating Partner's state and federal income Taxes attributable to realised, but not yet recognised, gain in an instalment sale note, depreciation recapture, investment tax credit recapture, discharge of indebtedness and minimum gain allocations under IRC Section 704). Such state and federal income Taxes shall be determined in accordance with the provisions of the IRC and other applicable laws in effect at the time of determination and without regard to other items affecting the determination of taxable income or loss (i.e. net operating loss carryovers).

Estimated Value shall be determined at the end of each Plan Year and means an amount estimated by .... and reviewed by .... and based upon ten (10) year cash flow projections of such Collateral Pool Project or Collateral Entity Project. If the Collateral Pool Project or Collateral Entity Project is unimproved property, the Estimated Value shall mean its Fair Market Value.

Exhibit means an exhibit attached to this Agreement unless otherwise specified.

Existing Collateral means, with respect to a Creditor, the Collateral Pool Assets or the Collateral Entity Projects which secured a Loan of such Creditor prior to such Creditor's execution of this Agreement, which Loan was secured by an Existing Lien.

Existing Liens means those Liens encumbering the Existing Collateral immediately prior to the establishment of the Liens contemplated by this Agreement, as such Existing Liens may be increased as a result of further advances made pursuant to Section 3.4.

Extended Term means the period of time from January 1, 19.... , until the termination of this Agreement pursuant to the provisions of Section 1.2 hereof.

Fair Market Value means the gross fair market value of the subject Collateral Pool Asset or Collateral Entity Project determined (i) by agreement between the owner of such Collateral Pool Asset or Collateral Entity Project, the Creditor holding a Lien thereon and the Plan Agent, or (ii) if no agreement is reached, as appraised for the current use by a qualified appraiser appointed by the Plan Agent.

Final Tax Liability means, with respect to each Participating Partner, the amount of Taxes set forth on the Final Tax Liability Notice shown to be payable by such Participating Partner.

Final Tax Liability Notice means a notice prepared by a certified public accountant on or before April 15 of the calendar year following the conclusion of the term of this Agreement, as may be extended if required by such certified public accountant, setting forth a final cumulative calculation of state and federal income Taxes equal to the sum of (a) the state and federal income Taxes of such Participating Partner attributable to (i) the management, ownership, maintenance, operation, disposition and foreclosure of the Collateral Pool Assets and Collateral Entity Projects, (ii) the payment, cancellation, disposition and IRC Section 752 deemed distributions of the Debts of such Participating Partner or Collateral Pool Entities which affect a Participating Partner (including gains or losses resulting from the final payment, satisfaction or cancellation of Deficiency Certificates), (iii) depreciation recapture and investment tax credit recapture, (iv) transactions entered into in conjunction with, or as contemplated in, the Loan Modification Plan, (b) the estimated state and federal income Taxes of the Participating Partner, the payment of which is anticipated to arise but has been deferred to subsequent taxable years (e.g. a Participating Parter's state and federal income Taxes attributable to realised but not yet recognised gain in an instalment sale note, depreciation recapture, investment tax credit recapture, discharge of indebtedness and minimum gain allocations under IRC Section 704), plus (c) the estimated federal and state income Taxes payable when the remaining Collateral Pool Assets and/or Collateral Entity Projects are sold or otherwise disposed of. Such state and federal income Taxes shall be determined in accordance with the provisions of the IRC and other applicable Laws in effect on the immediately preceding December 31 and shall be prepared conservatively, without regard to other items affecting income and loss (i.e. net operating loss carryovers) and assuming tax return reporting positions which are most likely to be asserted by the IRS.

IRC means the Internal Revenue Code of 1986, as amended.

IRS means the Internal Revenue Service.

Laws means all applicable statues, laws, ordinances, rules, regulations, orders, writs, injunctions or decrees of any state, commonwealth, nation, territory, possession, county, parish, municipality or Tribunal.

Lien means any lien, mortgage, security interest, pledge, charge or encumbrance of any kind, including, without limitation, the Rights of a vendor, lessor or similar party under any conditional sales agreement or other title retention agreement or lease substantially equivalent thereto, and any other right of or arrangement with any Creditor to have its claim satisfied out of any property or assets, or the proceeds therefrom, prior to the general creditors of the owner thereof.

Litigation means any proceeding, claim, lawsuit or investigation conducted or threatened by or before any Tribunal.

Loan Modification Plan means that certain Restructure and Loan Modification Plan dated ...., 19.... .

Material Adverse Effect means any set of circumstances or events which (a) will have a material adverse effect upon the validity, performance or enforceability of this Agreement, or (b) will preclude a Participating Partner from fulfilling his material obligations under the terms and conditions of this Agreement, or (c) will cause a Default or a Potential Default.

Meeting of Creditors has the meaning given in Section 15.18.

Modification Documents has the meaning given in the Recitals of this Agreement.

Modified Loan means a Loan, as amended and modified by the Modification Documents and this Agreement. The term Modified Loan shall be understood to include a Loan of a Creditor, whether or not Modification Documents are executed with respect to such Loan.

Netting-Out Agreements means those certain netting-out agreements executed by the Participating Partners with respect to their ownership interest in a member of ...., which agreements require that all distribution made with respect to such ownership interest be delivered to .... , or such other designated entity, to be held, distributed, set off or otherwise conveyed in accordance with the terms of such agreements. Any references in this Agreement to Netting-Out Agreements governing the Collateral Pool Assets listed on Schedule Two shall mean the Netting-Out Agreements as defined in the Security Agreements referred to in Section 3.1(b).

Newco means ....

Newco Investment means ....

Obligated Party means the maker, obligor or guarantor of a Debt.

Organisational Documents means the articles of incorporation, byelaws, certificate of incorporation or partnership, joint venture or trust agreement, as the case may be, of any Person.

Overhead Expenses means the expenses incurred by the Plan Agent, or by Person's performing duties delegated to such Person by the Plan Agent, in the administration of the Plan, including, without limitation, legal fees, accounting fees, office expenses, travel expenses, expenses attributable to overseeing the administration and sale of the Collateral Pool Assets, Collateral Pool Entities and Collateral Pool Projects and the fee payable to the Plan Agent. Overhead Expenses shall not include any expense, cost or compensation paid to a Participating Partner for efforts expended in the management of such Participating Partner's Collateral Pool Assets, or Collateral Pool Projects held by Collateral Pool Entities in which such Participating Partner owns an interest.

Participant means any Person which at any time owns any participation interest in any Modified Loan or Deficiency Certificate.

Participating Partners has the meaning set forth in the Recitals.

Permitted Liens means (a) the Liens on the Collateral granted in Section 3, (b) any Lien for Taxes not yet due and payable, (c) any mechanic's Lien and materialmen's Lien for services or materials for which payment is not yet due or which is being contested in good faith by appropriate proceedings, (d) any landlord's Lien for rental not yet due and payable, (e) Liens securing any purchase money obligation, (f) Liens related to any capitalised lease (g) Existing Liens, (h) pledges or deposits made to secure payment of workmen's compensation, or to participate in any fund in connection with workmen's compensation, unemployment insurance, pensions or other social security programs, (i) good faith pledges or deposits made to secure contracts or leases or statutory obligations, surety or appeal bonds, or indemnity, performance or other similar bonds in the ordinary course of business, (j) encumbrances consisting or zoning restrictions, easements or other restrictions on the use of real property, (k) Liens related to any financing or refinancing, and (l) if the validity or amount thereof is being contested in good faith and by appropriate and lawful proceedings diligently conducted and so long as levy and execution thereon have been stayed and continue to be stayed, and they do not in the aggregate materially detract from the value of the property of the Person in question, or materially impair the use thereof in the operation of its business: claims and Liens for Taxes due and payable; claims and Liens upon, and defects of title to, real or personal property (other than any of the Collateral), including any attachment of personal or real property or other legal process prior to adjudication of a dispute on the merits; claims and Liens of mechanics, materialmen, warehousemen, carriers, landlords or other like Liens; and adverse judgments on appeal.

Person means any individual, firm, corporation, association, partnership, joint venture, trust, Tribunal or other entity.

Plan Agent means .... , a .... corporation, and all successors to the initial Plan Agent appointed in accordance with this Agreement.

Plan Participant means each of the Creditors and each of the Participating Partners.

Plan Year means the period of time from the Effective Date to and including December 31, 19.... , and any calendar year thereafter during the term of this Agreement.

Potential Default means the occurrence of any event which, with notice or lapse of time or both, would become a Default.

Preference Period means the period of time commencing upon the Effective Date and ending on the day when all disbursements required by Section 5.1(b) have been made.

Preference Period Collateral Cash Requirements means Collateral Cash Requirements except that, unless approved by ...., (i) capital contributions, loans, advances, principal, interest and other payments which a Participating Partner should make with respect to a Collateral Pool Project and/or Collateral Entity Project shall not be made if such payment would cause the amount paid by all of the Participating Partners holding an interest in such Collateral Pool Project or Collateral Pool Entity with respect to such Collateral Pool Project or Collateral Entity Project to exceed $.......... during the respective Plan Year and if the Estimated Value of such Collateral Pool Project or Collateral Entity Project is less than the Current Balance of Debt secured by such Collateral Pool Project or Collateral Entity Project, (ii) amounts necessary to satisfy any settlement entered into by a Participating Partner with a bona fide third Person who is not an Affiliate of such Participating Partner or judgment against a Participating Partner held by a bona fide third Person who is not an Affiliate of such Participating Partner shall not exceed $......... per settlement or judgment, or in the aggregate, $......... per Plan Year, and (iii) the payments made by the Participating Partners to satisfy another partner's share of expenses with respect to a Collateral Entity Project which, under the relevant partnership or joint venture agreement or otherwise, should be paid by other partners, venturers or owners, but which have not been paid, will comply with the provisions with (i) above.

Pro Rata Part means, for each Creditor with a Deficiency and for each Deficiency Certificate Holder, the proportion that aggregate amount of the Deficiency of such Creditor or the Current Balance of such Creditor's Deficiency Certificates bears to the aggregate of the Deficiencies of all Creditors and the Current Balance of all Deficiency Certificates at the time in question.

Representatives has the meaning given in Section 13.3.

Rights means rights, remedies, powers, privileges and benefits.

Schedule means a schedule attached to this Agreement.

Section means a section or subsection of this Agreement.

Several Share means with respect to any Person, the portion of any Debt for which such Person could not seek reimbursement from any other Person also obligated on such obligation under applicable Laws or Organisational Documents.

Tax Escrow Account means a separate escrow account established to hold the amounts distributed to it pursuant to Section 5.

Taxes means all federal, state and local income, franchise, sales, *ad valorem*, payroll and other taxes, assessments, fees, levies, imposts, duties, deductions, withholdings or other charges of any nature whatsoever from time to time or at any time imposed by any Law or Tribunal, including those items in the nature of a penalty or fine.

Tribunal means any court or governmental department, commission, board, bureau, agency or instrumentality of the United States or of any state, commonwealth, nation, territory, possession, county, parish or municipality, whether now or hereafter constituted or existing.

UCC means the Uniform Commercial Code as enacted in the State of Texas or other applicable jurisdiction, as amended.

Working Capital Lender means a Person who has made a Working Capital Loan, which Working Capital Loan had not, at the time of determination, been fully satisfied.

Working Capital Liens has the meaning given in Section 3.3.

Working Capital Loan means (i) a loan made to one or more of the Participating Partners, at the request of the Participating Partner, with respect to a Collateral Pool Asset after the Effective Date of this Agreement not constituting a future advance made pursuant to Section 3.3 and which is secured with a Working Capital Lien, and (ii) the loans contemplated in Section 3.3(g) from .... and ....

EXECUTED effective as of the Effective Date.

PARTICIPATING PARTNERS:

...., 19....

....
Address: ....
....
....

...., 19....

....
Address: ....
....
....

...., 19....

....
Address: ....
....
....

PLAN AGENT:

...., 19....

....
By: ....
Address: ....
....
....

CREDITOR SIGNATURE PAGE

Attached to and made a part of the Collateral Pool Agreement of .... By execution below, the undersigned Creditor does hereby accept and agree to be bound by all of the terms, provisions, covenants, conditions and agreements of the Collateral Pool Agreement.

CREDITOR: ....

Date: ...., 19.... By: ....
Title: ....

Address for Notice:

....

....

PARTICIPATING PARTNER SIGNATURE PAGE

Attached to and made a part of the Collateral Pool Agreement of .... By execution below, the undersigned Participating Partner does hereby accept and agree to be bound by all of the terms, provisions, covenants, conditions and agreements of the Collateral Pool Agreement.

PARTICIPATING PARTNER: ....

Date: ...., 19.... By: ....
Title: ....

Address for Notice:

....

....

EXHIBIT "A". DEFICIENCY CERTIFICATE

DATE ISSUED: ....
REGISTERED HOLDER: ....
PLACE FOR PAYMENT: ....
DEFICIENCY AMOUNT: $ ....

FOR VALUE RECEIVED, this certifies that the Registered Holder is entitled to receive at the Place For Payment distributions in an aggregate amount not to exceed the sum of the Deficiency Amount, plus interest on the outstanding balance thereof equal to ten per cent (10%) (or a lesser percentage provided in Section 2.4 if Creditor executes Agreement after December 31, 19....) per annum pursuant to, and in accordance with, that certain Collateral Pool Agreement (the "Collateral Pool Agreement") by and among ...., ... and ...., as participating partners ("Participating Partners"), ... , a ....corporation, as the plan agent (the "Plan Agent") and, among others, the Registered Holder, as its Deficiency (as defined in the Collateral Pool Agreement) evidenced by this Deficiency Certificate.

THIS DEFICIENCY CERTIFICATE IS NON-TRANSFERABLE EXCEPT AS PERMITTED BY THE TERMS OF THE COLLATERAL POOL AGREEMENT AND, IN ANY EVENT, SHALL NOT BE DEEMED TRANSFERRED UNTIL AFTER THE PLAN AGENT HAS REGISTERED THE TRANSFEREE ON ITS BOOKS AND RECORDS AS A REGISTERED HOLDER AND ONLY AFTER THE SURRENDER OF THIS DEFICIENCY CERTIFICATE TO THE PLAN AGENT BY THE REGISTERED HOLDER IN PERSON OR BY ATTORNEY, PROPERLY ENDORSED TO THE TRANSFEREE.

Distributions due to the Registered Holder under this Deficiency Certificate are subject, in all respects, to the terms, provisions and conditions of the Collateral Pool Agreement. By its acceptance hereof, the Registered Holder acknowledges that it has received, carefully reviewed and fully understands the Collateral Pool Agreement and that it is bound by all the terms, provisions and conditions thereof.

This Deficiency Certificate is valid only if executed by the Plan Agent below.

PLAN AGENT:
....
By: ....
Title: ....

EXHIBIT "B". CREDITOR DEBT BALANCE CERTIFICATE

The undersigned, being a Creditor pursuant to the provisions of that certain Collateral Pool Agreement, by and among ....("........."), ... (".........") and .... ("........."), as participating partners, ... , a .... corporation as the plan agent (the "Plan Agent"), and, among others, the undersigned, hereby certifies, represents and warrants to ...., ..., ... and the Plan Agent that, after crediting any and all payments or property received by it in partial or full satisfaction of the indebtedness described below, such indebtedness, as of December 31, 19.. , has an outstanding principal balance of $......... and accrued and unpaid interest of $........., said indebtedness being described as follows:

Original/Current Maker:	____________________
Original/Current Payee:	____________________
Date of Instrument:	____________________
Original or Stated Principal Balance:	$ ____________________
Security (if applicable):	____________________
Deed of Trust or Security Agreement Reference (if applicable):	____________________

The undersigned hereby acknowledges that ...., ..., ... and all other Participating Partners and the Plan Agent are relying on the certifications, representations and warranties contained herein.

....
By: ....
Title: ....

EXHIBIT "C". CREDITOR NON-RECOURSE CERTIFICATE

The undersigned, being a Creditor under the provisions of that certain Collateral Pool Agreement (the "Collateral Pool Agreement"), by and among .... ("........"), ... (".........") and .... ("........."), among others as participating partners, ... , a .... corporation, as the plan agent (the "Plan Agent"), and the undersigned, hereby acknowledges that it is bound by the terms and provisions of the Collateral Pool Agreement with respect to all indebtedness owing to the undersigned Creditor from any Participating Partner as more fully described, below, including, without limitation, the provisions of Sections 12.3 and 15.13 thereof, said Creditor's indebtedness being described as follows:

Original/Current Maker:	______________________
Original/Current Payee:	______________________
Date of Instrument:	______________________
Original or Stated Principal Amount:	$ ____________________

All terms used herein with their initial letters capitalised shall have the same meanings as in the Collateral Pool Agreement. The undersigned Creditor hereby acknowledges that ...., ... and ...., the Plan Agent and all other Participating Partners are relying on the acknowledgments contained herein.

....
By: ....
Title: ....

SCHEDULE ONE. PARTICIPATING PARTNERS/CREDITORS

Participating Partners

Name	*Address*
....	....
	....
	....
....	....
	....
	....
....	....
	....
	....

Creditors

		Creditor Debt Amounts as of Execution Date	
Date of Execution	*Creditor Name and Address*	*Principal*	*Accrued Interest*

SCHEDULE TWO. REGION ASSETS

[TO BE PROVIDED UPON REQUEST]

SCHEDULE THREE. COLLATERAL POOL ASSETS

COLLATERAL POOL ENTITY	COLLATERAL ENTITY PROJECTS
Mixed-Use Projects	
Multi-Family Projects	
Office Projects	
Residential Projects	
Retail Projects	
Land Syndications	
Equities Syndications	

COLLATERAL POOL PROJECTS

Investments In Stock of Financial Institutions

Investments In Closely Held Companies

Miscellaneous Assets And Investments

Separate Property Contributed By

SCHEDULE FOUR. MEMBERS OF

(i) ....
....
....

(ii) ....
....
....

(iii) ....
....
....

(iv) ....
....
....

(v) ....
....
....

(vi) ....
....
....

(vii) ....
....
....

(viii) ....
....
....

(ix) ....
....
....

(x) ....
....
....

SCHEDULE FIVE. SCHEDULE OF EXISTING LITIGATION AND JUDGMENTS

Name and Location of Court	*Title of Case*	*Nature of Case*
District Court of	....	....
.... County, Texas,	....	....
..... th Judicial District	....	....

INDEX

Administration
United Kingdom, 121–122
Administration order, 26–29
conditions for, 27
effect, 27
floating charge, and, 29
United Kingdom, 122–123
effect, 123–124
Administrative receiver, 108–109
agent of company, as, 109
functions, 109
good faith, 112–113
powers, 109
status, 109
Administrator, 28–29
duties, 28–29
United Kingdom, 124–125
powers, 28
United Kingdom, 124
role, 28
statement of proposals, 29
Affidavit
summary judgment, and, 32–33

Bank
shadow director, as, 142–144
Bank of England
support operations, and, 149–150
Bankruptcy, 35–36
Germany. *See* Germany
Belgium
security, 6
Big pocket liability, 11–12

Cherry-picking, 9–11
Closure of account, 22
Collateral pool agreement, 243–287
agreement, 243
collateral pool assets, 286
collateral pool cash account, 248–249
covenants, 256–261
creditor debt balance certificate, 284
creditor non-recourse certificate, 284–285
Collateral pool agreement—*cont.*
creditor representations and covenants, 261–262
creditor signature page, 282
default, 262–263
deficiencies, 245–246
deficiency certificates, 245–246, 283–284
definitions, 275–282
disbursements of collateral pool cash, 249–254
disposition of collateral pool assets, 254
document examination checklist, 194–195
existing litigation, 287
judgments, 287
legal analysis checklist, 194–195
non-judicial debtor reorganisations workout analysis, 195 *et seq.*
participating partners/creditors, 285
participating partner representations and warranties, 255–256
participating partner signature page, 283
plan agent, 266–270
recitals, 243
region assets, 286
releases upon sale of collateral, 255
rights and remedies, 263–266
security agreement, 246–248
term of agreement, 244
transfer of deficiency certificates, 270–271
Combination of accounts, 18–21
accounting situation, as, 19–20
current account set-off, as, 20
exclusion of right, 18
single debt, whether, 20
theoretical analysis, 19
Commercial actions, 29–30
Company doctor, 160
Computer database
document, whether, 38–39
Confidentiality
cross-border court orders, and, 91–100
Constructive trust, 145, 146

Court orders
cross-border. *See* Cross-border court orders
Cross-border court orders, 91–100
attachment of assets, 94–96
attachment of English bank accounts in support of foreign proceedings, 96–97
confidentiality, and, 91–94
"civil or commercial" matters, 92–93
public interest, and, 92–94
context, 91
disclosure orders relating to foreign assets, 96
evidence, 98–100
Mareva injunctions, 94–96. *See also Mareva* injunctions
recognition of judgments, 97
subpoenas, 98–100
tracing of assets, 98
witnesses, 98–100

Debenture holders
liabilities in receivership or liquidation, 115–117
Default judgment, 30–31
Directors' duties, 134–141
bona fides, 139–140
disqualification, and, 140–141
fraudulent trading, 137–139. *See also* Fraudulent trading
general fiduciary duties, 139–140
wrongful trading. *See* Wrongful trading
Discovery, 37–52
automatic, 41
checklist, 42, 49–50
documents held at branch, 49
documents held at regional office, 50
continuing obligation, 48
description of document, 51–52
documents "relating to matter in question", 38
embarrassment at trial, 41
further and better, application for, 47
further lines of enquiry, and, 42
gauging opponent's case, and, 40–41
grouping of documents, 42
importance of, 40–41
inspection, 46
meaning, 37–40
method, 41–48
notice to inspect, 52
plaintiff's/defendant's list of documents, 50–52
privilege, and, 43–45. *See also* Privilege
proper means to acquire document, and, 40
refusal to order, 37
solicitor, and, 41
use of documents produced on, 46–48
Discovery—*cont.*
"without prejudice" negotiations, and, 46–47
Disqualification of directors, 140–141
Distress, 101
Documents
discovery. *See* Discovery
meaning, 38–39

Enforcement of security, 23–25
conclusive evidence clauses, and, 23–24
removal of pre-conditions, 24–25
English bank accounts
attachment in support of foreign proceedings, 96–97
English law
remedies. *See* Remedies: English law
Execution, 35
Extrajudicial remedies, 101–119. *See also* Receivership
civil law systems, 118–119
German law, 118
lien, 102, 103

Floating charge
administration order, and, 29
receivership, and, 104–105, 106
France
insolvency, 4–5
security, 6–7
Fraudulent trading, 137–139
bank, liability of, 138–139
civil remedy, 138
dishonesty, 137

Germany
arrangement procedure, 205–207
bankruptcy
discharge, 128
Eastern Germany, 128–129
fresh start, 128
protection of employees, 128
Restschuldbefreiung, 128
bankruptcy code, 126–129
"bankruptcy of bankruptcy", 203–207
bankruptcy procedure
battle of secured creditors, 203–205
bankruptcy reform, 127–128
chronology of law reform, 213–215
escape routes, 208–213
Insolvency Bill 21 November 1991, 214–215
law in transition, 203–215
legal issues to be addressed in voluntary support operation, 221–225
conflict of interest situations, 222–223
interfering with corporate governance, 223
lenders as shareholders, 224–225

Germany—*cont.*
legal issues to be addressed in voluntary support operation—*cont.*
lender liability, 222–225
preferential treatment of bank creditors, 221–222
legal position of bank creditors under Insolvency Bill, 215–221
facilitating rehabilitation in integrated procedure, 216–217
factoring, 219
leasing, 219
order of distribution, 218–219
paramountcy of creditor governance, 215–216
principles and policy considerations, 215–216
secured creditors, 217–218
security pool agreements, 220
voting rights, 220
working capital loans made to insolvent's estate, 221
rehabilitation, 203–225
reorganisation/insolvency plan, 127–128
"reorganisation through liquidation", 208–210
report of committee for insolvency law, 213–214
restriction of privileges of preferred creditors, 127
security, 6
security pool agreements, 211–213
transfer of debts by way of security, 118
voluntary arrangements, 208–210

In-house lawyer
privileged document, and, 45
Inquiries under Companies Act 1985, 227–239
balancing powers of investigators against rights of individual, 237–239
conduct of, 228
documents, 229
hybrid nature of, 237–239
inspectors' duty to act in accordance with rules of natural justice, 232–234
making of report, 231–232
powers of inspectors, 228
privilege against self-incrimination, 234–237
questioning of witnesses, 230
submission of proposed criticism to witnesses, 231
Insolvency
approaches other than formal procedures, 131–162
change of control of company, 159–160
company doctor, and, 160
directors' duties, 134–141. *See also* Directors' duties
Insolvency—*cont.*
documentation, 151–158
formal, avoidance of, 131–162
French example, 4–5
lender liability. *See* Lender liability
negotiation, and, 133
practicalities of support operation, 147–151. *See also* Support operation
risk of fiduciary relationship arising, 147
security. *See* Security
set-off, 9–11
suggested scale, 1–2
comments on, 3–4
key determinants, 2–3
Yellow Book obligations, and, 159
Inspection of documents, 46
Inter-bank agreement, 154–155
principal terms, 241
structure, 241
Interrogatories, 48

Japan
security, 6
Judgment, 35
execution, 35
recognition, 97

Lender liability, 144–146
bank receiving benefit from transaction, 145–146
intermeddling in trust, 144–145
power of directors, and, 146
Lien, 21–22, 102, 103
extent of, 21–22
Liquidation, 35–36
liabilities of lenders and debenture holders, 115–117
Luxembourg
security, 6

Mareva injunctions, 34–35
conditions for grant, 34–35
cross-border court orders, and, 94–96
foreign assets, and, 94–95
scope, 94
third parties, and, 95
Mortgagee
accounting for rents, 162
Multi-opinion facilities, 151

Netherlands
security, 6
Non-judicial debtor reorganisations in United States, 163–201
administration of plan, 183–185
alternative courses of action, 186–193
analysis of debtor organisational structure, 179

Non-judicial debtor reorganisations in United States—*cont.*
areas of primary risk, 186–193
basis for action by debtors, 174
causes, 165–170
components of plan, 176–179
exculpation, 178
fair treatment of each creditor and class of creditor, 177
full disclosure, 176
going concern v. forced liquidation, 178
long-term survival of company as going concern, 177
maximum return to creditors, 177
provision for federal income taxes, 178
creditor committee, 182
creditor committee meetings, 183
creditor meetings, 182
data accumulation, 179–180
debt negotiation, modification and acceptance, 183–185
delays in dealing with non-performing loans caused by, 171–172
document examination, 179–180
documentation, 182
financial institutions, and, 172–174
foundation for plan, 174–176
functional organisation charts, 186–193
historical background, 164–165
increase in operating expenses, 171
legal analysis, 179–180
loss of operating income, and, 170–171
material transactions, 179–180
negotiation theory, 183
negotiators
identity, 181–182
training, 181–182
periodic reporting: administrative control, 184–185
re-regulation of thrifts, and, 168–169
status of debtor's liquidity, 180–181
systemic problem of capital deterioration, 163–164
tax incentives, and, 169–170
working capital loans, 180–181

Pre-trial proceedings in US courts, 53–90
admissions, 78
answer, 57–58
complaint, 57
counterclaims, 58–59
cross-claims, 58–59
discovery, 75–88
Aerospatiale decision, 84–85
bank secrecy laws, impact of, 86–87
"blocking", impact of, 86–87
compelled from third parties not subject to US jurisdiction, 83–84

Pre-trial proceedings in US courts—*cont.*
discovery—*cont.*
depositions, 77–78
depositions of corporate personnel located abroad, 82–83
document requests, 77
extraterritorial, 80–88
interrogatories, 76–77
jurisdictional, 87–88
mechanisms, 75–76
non-party, 78–79
outside US, 81–82
post *Aerospatiale* decisions, 85–86
relationship between Hague Evidence Convention and Federal rules, 84–86
resisting, 79–80
scope, 75
forum non conveniens, 72–74
forum selection, 71–75
Hague Service Convention, 69–71
background, 69
circumventing, 71
exclusivity, 70
Schlunk case, 71
service by mail under Art. 10(a), 70–71
motion to dismiss, 58
personal jurisdiction, 59–67
"arising from", 64
citizenship, 62
consent to jurisdiction, 67
continuous and systematic business contracts, 61–62
domicile, 62
due process clause, 60–61
general jurisdiction, 61
incorporation, 62
jurisdiction based upon corporate affiliation, 67
long-arm statutes, 59–60
national contacts, 65–67
purposeful availment, 63–64
reasonableness, 64–65
specific jurisdiction, 61, 62–65
"tag service", 62
pre-trial conferences, 88–89
raising and proving issues of foreign law, 74–75
scheduling orders, 88–89
service of process, 68–71
federal rules, under, 68
Hague Service Convention, 69–71
third-party complaints, 58–59
venue, 71–74
Privilege, 43–45
client, of, 45
confidentiality, and, 45
document addressed to in-house lawyer, 45

Privilege—*cont.*
  documents prepared for obtaining legal advice, 43
  "litigation", 44

Quasi-security, 8–9

Receivership, 101–119
  administrative receivers, 108–109. *See also* Administrative receiver
  agent of company, 108
  appointment, 103
  appointment by court, 107
  appointment out of court, 106–107
  Chancery Court jurisdiction, 104
  character, 104–109
  common law jurisdiction, 117–118
  conduct of, 110–117
  debenture holders, liability of, 115–117
  disposal of assets, 110
  duties in realising company's assets, 114–115
  executory contracts of company, 113–114
  explicit power of appointment, 107
  floating charge, and, 104–105, 106
  harm to company's goodwill, 114–115
  lenders, liability of, 115–117
  origin, 104–109
  powers, 111–113
  present and future book debts, 111–112
  procuring breach of contract, 113–114
  purpose, 110–111
  realisation of assets, 110
  shadow directors, and, 116–117
  title to goods, and, 112
Recognition of judgments, 97
Registration of security, 7–8
Rehabilitation, 131–162
  Germany. *See* Germany
Remedies: English law, 13–36
Remedies and risk
  international comparisons, 1–12
Re-payment, right to demand, 13–18
  demand, 14–15
  events of default, 15–16
  minor error in statement of amount due, 17–18
  service of default notice, 16
  terms of contract of loan, 15
  valid demand, requirements of, 17
Rescue, assistance in, 25–29

Schemes of arrangement, 161–162
Security, 5–7
  Belgium, 6
  France, 6–7
  Germany, 6
Security—*cont.*
  hostility to, 5
  Japan, 6
  Luxembourg, 6
  Netherlands, 6
  quasi, 8–9
  registration, 7–8
  right to enforce. *See* Enforcement of security
  Switzerland, 6
Security agreements, 155–158
  existing security, where, 156
  floating charge, and, 158
  new security, and, 156–157
  preference, and, 157–158
Self-help remedies, 101–119
Set-off, 9–11
Shadow directors, 141–144
  bank as, 142–144
  meaning, 141
  receivership, and, 116–117
Solicitor
  discovery, and, 41
Subpoena *duces tecum*, 48–49
Subpoenas
  cross-border court orders, and, 98–100
Sue, right to, 29–31
Summary judgment, 31–33
  affidavit, 32–33
  application by summons, 31–32
  triable, whether, 32–33
Support agreement, 152–154
  disposal programme, 153
  principal terms, 241–242
  structure, 241–242
  "support period", 152
  terms, 153
Support operation
  alternatives to, 158–162
  Bank of England, views of, 149–150
  basis for proceeding, 149
  context, 147–151
  co-ordination of action, 148
  documentation, 151–158
  initial standstill agreement, 152
  inter-bank agreement, 154–155
  investigating accountants, and, 149
  multi-option facilities, 151
  practicalities, 147–151
  preservation of status quo, 148
  principles, 147–151
  review of borrower's affairs, 148–149
  security agreements, 155–158. *See* also Security agreements
  support agreement, 152–154. *See also* Support agreement
Switzerland
  security, 6

Tracing of assets, 98
Trust
  intermeddling in, 144–145

United Kingdom
  administration, 121–122
  administration orders, 122–123
  effect, 123–124
  administrator
    duties, 124–125
    powers, 124
  voluntary arrangements, 125
United States
  Depositary Institutions Deregulation and Monetary Control Act (DIDIMCA), 165–166
  Economic Recovery Tax 1981, 166–167
  non-judicial debtor reorganisations, 163–201. *See also* Non-judicial debtor reorganisations in the United States
US Courts
  pre-trial proceedings in. *See* Pre-trial proceedings in US Courts
US federalism, 53–56
  divided legislative authority, 53–54
  dual judicial system, 54
  "Erie" problem, 55–56
  limited federal subject-matter jurisdiction, 54–55
  removal, 56

Voluntary arrangements, 25–26, 161–162
  United Kingdom, 125

Witnesses
  cross-border court orders, and, 98–100
Writ of summons, 30
Wrongful trading, 134–137
  cautious approach, need for, 137
  knowledge or conclusion, and, 134–135
  lenders, and, 141–144
  prospect of avoiding insolvency, and, 135
  refinancing, and, 136
  shadow directors, and, 141–144. *See also* Shadow directors
  support operation, and, 135–136